中国田野考古报告集

考古学专刊

丁种第九号

庙底沟与三里桥

(黄河水库考古报告之二)

中国社会科学院考古研究所　编著

文物出版社

北京·2011

封面设计　张希广
责任印制　陈　杰
责任编辑　谷艳雪

图书在版编目(CIP)数据

庙底沟与三里桥:汉英对照／中国社会科学院考古研究所编著.
—北京:文物出版社,2011. 10
ISBN 978 – 7 – 5010 – 3269 – 3

Ⅰ.①庙… Ⅱ.①中… Ⅲ.①水利工程－文化遗址－中国－汉、
英 Ⅳ.①K878

中国版本图书馆 CIP 数据核字(2011)第 188586 号

庙 底 沟 与 三 里 桥
Miaodigou and Sanliqiao
（中英文双语版）

中国社会科学院考古研究所　编著

*

文 物 出 版 社 出 版 发 行
（北京东直门内北小街 2 号楼）

http://www. wenwu. com

E-mail:web@ wenwu. com

北京盛天行健印刷有限公司印刷
新 华 书 店 经 销
787×1092　1/16　印张:25　插页:1
2011 年 10 月第 1 版　2011 年 10 月第 1 次印刷
ISBN 978 – 7 – 5010 – 3269 – 3　定价:290. 00 元

Miaodigou and Sanliqiao

Archaeological Excavations at the Yellow River Reservoirs Report No. 2

Edited by

The Institute of Archaeology
Chinese Academy of Social Sciences

Cultural Relics Press
Beijing · 2011

1(H46:128)

2(H338:36)

庙底沟仰韶文化彩陶盆、罐

Painted pottery basin and jar of the Yangshao culture from Miaodigou

1. A10g 彩陶盆(Painted basin)　2. A16h 彩陶罐(Painted jar)

出版说明

《庙底沟与三里桥》初版于1959年，全面报告了庙底沟与三里桥两个遗址的仰韶和龙山文化的堆积，发现并首次提出了"庙底沟二期文化"，从而确立了仰韶—庙底沟二期—龙山文化的连续发展序列。这一序列的确立，对20世纪三四十年代构建的所谓仰韶文化在西、龙山文化在东的二元对立学说提出了极大挑战。该书被张光直先生誉为"中国新石器时代考古学的一个重要的里程碑"（见本书张光直《序》）。1959年出版之后，即引起国际学术界的关注，更在上世纪80年代由美国宾夕法尼亚大学人类学系教授波西尔和纽约美国自然博物馆的瓦特·费尔赛维思博士组织翻译了英文，还邀请张光直先生为英译本写了序，只是最终未能出版。事情的缘起和其中的曲折，详见陈星灿先生《后记》。

《庙底沟与三里桥》是中华人民共和国成立以来中国科学院考古研究所（1977年改属中国社会科学院）最早的几本考古报告之一，至今还经常被人引用。其确立的发展序列直到今天在豫西地区依然有效，在中国考古学史上的价值毋庸置疑。该书初版早已售罄，英译本又有成稿。在出版52年后的今天，在考古学研究日益国际化的大背景下，出版中英文双语版，有着积极的现实意义。诚如陈星灿先生《后记》所言："中文与英文对照出版，使国内外读者一册在手，都能使用，又使更多的青年学子知道如何用另外一种语言表述某种考古现象或考古遗物，则幸何如也！"

本书中文文本部分以科学出版社1959年出版的《庙底沟与三里桥》为底本排印，线图和图版则由中国社会科学院考古研究所提供的底图和照片重新制版。

张光直先生为英译本写的序作为本双语版《序》。为兼顾中英文读者，将原插在正文中的线图单列，放在正文之后、图版之前。因为已有英译全文，本书删去原书英文和俄文提要。

文物出版社编辑部

2011年10月

目　　次

庙底沟与三里桥

序

张光直

　　摆在大家面前的这部被译成英文出版的考古报告——《庙底沟与三里桥》，是中国新石器时代考古学的一个重要的里程碑。简单回顾原报告产生的历史背景，对读者或许不无裨益。

　　直到中华人民共和国成立之前的 40 年代后期，中国新石器时代考古学其实可以用两个概念加以总结：仰韶和龙山。仰韶是河南西部渑池县的一个村庄，1921 年安特生在这里发现了中国第一个新石器时代遗址。作为"新石器时代晚期"文化的代表，它的年代被推定为公元前三千纪，以彩陶和截面呈椭圆形的磨光石斧为特征。仰韶文化主要分布在华北西部的黄土地带，集中于河南西部、山西、陕西和甘肃。龙山是山东中部的一个小镇，地处华北东部，1928 年在这里发现了一个新石器时代遗址，因此就用它命名中国的第二个"新石器时代晚期"文化，它以发亮的蛋壳黑陶和方形的磨光石锛著称。

　　考古学上所谓的仰韶文化和龙山文化，通过一系列遗址的发现和很少几个遗址的发掘，确实在 40 年代后期得以确立，但是它们各自的年代和地理分布范围，它们之间的关系，却远非清楚。对仰韶文化遗址调查最为深入的安特生，相信该文化也许是公元前三千纪中叶从西亚进入华北西部地区的。龙山城子崖遗址考古发掘队的领导人李济和梁思永，却认为龙山文化的居民是土著的中国人，分布在东部沿海地区。这两个文化，一个由西向东发展，一个由东向西发展，似乎在河南相遇。河南的考古遗址，出土遗物兼有上述两种文化的特征，既出彩陶也有黑陶片。这些所谓"混合遗址"很自然地被视为两种文化相接触的产物。

　　如果庙底沟的发现是在 40 年代，那它很可能也会贴上"混合遗址"的标签。但是，50 年代的考古发生了很大变化，新发现带来了新认识，导致重新估价中国新石器时代考古学。庙底沟和三里桥这两个遗址就对新认识的提出做出了自己的贡献。

　　随着中华人民共和国的成立，有两件事情对考古学的发展产生了深远影响。第一件是众多大型基本建设项目的实施，使从史前到历史时代的数不尽的考古遗址意外发现。第二件是文物保护法规在全国范围内得以实施。今天，考古学家必须与基建工程的工作人员协同作战，意外的发现也必须妥善处理。

　　50 年代最重要的基建项目，是基于电力和灌溉需要而进行的华北地区多处黄河水库的建设。其中就包括河南西北部三门峡附近的三门峡水库。中国科学院考古研究所(1977 年改属中国社会科学院)因此组成了三门峡水库考古队,在 1955 – 1959 年间做了大量工作。庙底沟和三里桥就是在此期间因为水库建设而发现和发掘的两个遗址。

庙底沟和三里桥遗址出土各类文化遗物的特征,以及它们出土的文化层,本报告均予描述。简要概括如下:三里桥是河南西北部陕县境内的一个小村庄,在这里发现了仰韶文化和典型的龙山文化(即习见的河南类型)遗存。在同属陕县的另外一个村庄,三里桥村南仅 1400 米的庙底沟村,也发现有叠压关系的两种文化遗存。早期的庙底沟一期文化属于仰韶,晚期的庙底沟二期文化,兼有仰韶和龙山两种文化的特征,与 40 年代晚期所谓的混合文化遗址相类似。两个遗址三种文化的年代关系略如下述:

仰韶文化(庙底沟一期和三里桥一期)
“混合文化”(庙底沟二期)
龙山文化(三里桥二期)

这说明所谓“混合文化”遗址实在只是“过渡期”文化的遗存,也就是说它代表了连续发展的新石器时代文化的一个新的阶段,始于仰韶,终于龙山。这个看似微不足道的结论,却动摇了华北中国的新石器时代考古学。黄河流域的河南,因此不再被不认为是一个起源于东、一个起源于西的两个同时代史前文化的相遇之地,相反,它担当起史前文明发源地的角色,这个史前文明显然是经历了自身内在发展和变化的历史时期中国文明的前身。无怪乎就在《庙底沟和三里桥》这部专刊出版的 1959 年,有几篇文章差不多同时提出中国史前文化的连续发展说,这其中就包括安志敏的《试论黄河流域新石器时代文化》(《考古》1959 年 10 期,第 559 – 565 页),石兴邦的《黄河流域原始社会考古研究上的若干问题》(《考古》1959 年 10 期,第 566 – 570 页);许顺湛的《关于中原新石器时代文化的几个问题》(《文物》1960 年 5 期,第 36 – 39 页);和我本人的《中国新石器时代文化断代》(《史语所集刊》(1959)30,第 259 – 309 页)。

庙底沟和三里桥并不是建立仰韶—庙底沟二期和龙山文化连续发展序列的孤例,50 年代后期调查的河南西部的其他一些遗址,特别是洛阳的王湾,也具有同样的性质。但是,本专刊报告的两个遗址,是经过最全面发掘的,它们依然是仰韶文化(庙底沟类型)和庙底沟二期文化的典型遗址,其上述发展序列直到今天在豫西地区依然有效。

但是,在 1959 年以后的二十多年间,我们从中国考古学的研究中获益良多,我们有关中国新石器时代考古学的某些观点,与本专刊出版时候的看法大相径庭。指出下面这些新进展对读者也许不无补益,因为它们仍跟庙底沟和三里桥的发现有关。

1. 中国科学家从60年代开始测定考古标本的碳素年代,并在1972年发表了第一批数据,因此对我们有关史前中国年代学的认识带来革命。在他最近发表的综合性研究论文《碳–14测定年代和中国史前考古学》(《考古》1977年4期,第217–232页)中,中国社会科学院考古研究所的夏鼐所长,把仰韶文化放在公元前5000–前3000年,龙山文化放在公元前2800–前2300年。后者在夏鼐的概念里包括龙山早期(庙底沟二期)和晚期(河南龙山文化)。庙底沟和附近一个遗址的年代与这个年代框架恰相符合。

    1. 庙底沟一期(仰韶)

ZK110　5030±100BP(半衰期5568)或3910±125BC(树轮校正)

ZK112　4905±170 BP(半衰期5568)或3545±190BC(树轮校正)

    2. 庙底沟二期(庙底沟二期)

ZK111　4140±95BP(半衰期5568)或2780±145BC(树轮校正)

    3. 王湾二期(河南龙山文化)

ZK126　3838±95BP(半衰期5568)或2390±145BC(树轮校正)

最后一个年代数据来自洛阳王湾遗址的龙山文化层,王湾位于陕县之东,其龙山文化同三里桥刚好平行。(以上数据均取自夏鼐1977年的论文,只有ZK112采自《考古》1978年4期)。随着华北特别是豫西地区年代数据的增长,庙底沟和三里桥遗址的新石器时代年代学将会更加完善和准确,但是上述数据仍能给我们一个清晰的概念。

2. 如果说庙底沟和三里桥在史前中国文化连续发展序列的建设初期发挥了至关重要的作用,那么这本专刊发表之后华北地区的考古工作则进一步强化了对文化连续性的认识。尽管庙底沟一期仅仅代表仰韶文化一个地方类型的晚期阶段,但是仰韶文化作为一个整体,在河南北部和陕西至少可以上溯到公元前5000年却早为人知。现在,从70年代后期开始,一系列早期遗址在河北南部、河南中部、陕西和甘肃最东部的渭水流域被发现,这些遗址,以河北南部的磁山和河南中部的裴李岗遗址为代表,经碳十四年代测定在公元前六千纪,其文化遗存在许多方面早于仰韶文化。我们目前在考古上非常接近黄河流域中国农业生活方式的起始阶段了。

3. 现在很清楚正是由于庙底沟和三里桥的发掘开始解决河南龙山文化的

起源问题。但是,山东和沿海地区龙山文化又当如何呢? 在 1959 年讨论仰韶—龙山文化连续发展的文章中,安志敏和石兴邦都十分慎重地申明,庙底沟的证据只适用于河南龙山文化,山东龙山文化的起源仍然不明。

为了试图解释山东龙山文化的起源,及庙底沟二期文化和同时期几个文化的相似性,我在 1959 年提出了"龙山形成期"的概念。所谓"龙山形成期"是指一个跨地区的文化层,即很大范围内的中国史前文化均具有类似的文化形貌,这主要包括河南的庙底沟二期文化、江苏的青莲岗文化、湖北的屈家岭文化、浙江的早期良渚文化等。因为当时河南之外的任何一个地区都没有发现早于这些文化的史前文化,我推测整个龙山形成期文化都是从河南向周围地区的迅速扩张中造成的,这个扩张既包括文化扩张也包括人的移动,起因则是华北核心地区农业革命带来的内部动力。

关于龙山形成期文化起源的假说现在看来是不太可能的。首先,碳素测年不支持庙底沟二期文化是龙山形成期最早期的文化。更重要的是,比龙山形成期更早的很可能是其沿海地区先导文化的史前文化,也相继发现。

另一方面,上述以及一些其他新发现的大致同时的许多龙山形成期文化形貌上的相似性这一重要事实,仍需要加以解释。这个文化层似乎表示一个很大范围的交互作用圈的存在,这是我从已故的约瑟夫·考德威尔借用的概念,交互作用圈由发源于中国不同地区的几个更早的先导文化所构成。这篇新作最近发表在《美洲科学家》(第 69 卷 2 期,1981 年 3 - 4 月号,第 148 - 160 页)上。

4. 以三里桥二期文化为代表的河南龙山文化的走向,是中国考古学界讨论的一个重要话题。实际上河南龙山文化遗址众多,至少可以细分为三种地方类型,即豫中和豫西类型、豫北类型和豫东类型。豫西和豫中地区的河南龙山文化,又被称为王湾类型,一般认为是二里头文化的源头,二里头文化的碳素测年集中在公元前 2000 年前后的几个世纪,二里头文化被许多学者视为是首先从庙底沟和三里桥建立起来的文化发展程序中的夏文明,因此河南龙山文化现在也被纳入中国文明的连续发展的历史长河之中。

这些新进展充分说明华北地区的新石器时代考古学已经迈入一个复杂而多彩的时代,这是 1959 年这本专刊出版时我们无法预见的。但是,这本专刊对这些新进展的发生发挥了至关重要的作用,其中的考古发现依然有效和重要。本书的英文版无疑将有助于把它置于世界考古经典之列。

(陈星灿 译)

目　录

插图目录

图版目录

叁拾　庙底沟仰韶文化细泥红陶甑、杯、盂、罐

叁壹　庙底沟仰韶文化细泥红陶罐

叁贰　庙底沟仰韶文化细泥红陶罐、瓶

叁叁　庙底沟仰韶文化细泥红陶瓶、器盖、器座

叁肆　庙底沟仰韶文化细泥红陶器座,泥质灰陶盘、碗、盆

叁伍　庙底沟仰韶文化泥质灰陶盆

叁陆　庙底沟仰韶文化泥质灰陶盆、罐

叁柒　庙底沟仰韶文化泥质灰陶器盖,细泥黑陶罐,夹砂粗红陶罐、釜

叁捌　庙底沟仰韶文化壁虎塑像残陶片

叁玖　庙底沟仰韶文化夹砂粗红陶釜、灶、鼎、盘

肆拾　庙底沟仰韶文化夹砂粗红陶碗、盆

肆壹　庙底沟仰韶文化夹砂粗红陶盆、杯、盂

肆贰　庙底沟仰韶文化夹砂粗红陶罐

肆叁　庙底沟仰韶文化夹砂粗红陶罐

肆肆　庙底沟仰韶文化夹砂粗红陶罐

肆伍　庙底沟仰韶文化夹砂粗红陶器盖及陶刀

肆陆　庙底沟仰韶文化陶制工具及装饰品

肆柒　庙底沟仰韶文化陶、石器

肆捌　庙底沟仰韶文化石器

肆玖　庙底沟仰韶文化石器

伍拾　庙底沟仰韶文化石铲

伍壹　庙底沟仰韶文化石锤等

伍贰　庙底沟仰韶文化石、骨器

伍叁　庙底沟仰韶文化骨镞等

伍肆　庙底沟仰韶文化骨笄

伍伍　庙底沟仰韶文化骨、角、蚌、牙器

伍陆　庙底沟龙山文化夹砂粗灰陶罐、盆

伍柒　庙底沟龙山文化夹砂粗灰陶罐

伍捌　庙底沟龙山文化夹砂粗灰陶罐

伍玖　庙底沟龙山文化夹砂粗灰陶罐、鼎

陆拾　庙底沟龙山文化夹砂粗灰陶鼎

陆壹　庙底沟龙山文化夹砂粗灰陶鼎

陆贰　庙底沟龙山文化夹砂粗灰陶斝

陆叁　庙底沟龙山文化夹砂粗灰陶灶、器盖

壹 序 言

根治黄河水害与开发黄河水利的综合工程是中国人民与自然作斗争的伟大工程之一,它将彻底改变黄河流域的自然面貌,使滚滚数千里、为害数千年的浊浪转化为造福人民的清流。这是党所领导的伟大的社会主义建设事业之一。三门峡水库是这个综合规划中第一期计划的主要工程,是一座规模巨大的防洪、发电、灌溉的综合工程。这座水库已于1957年4月13日开始施工,这表示着根治黄河水害与开发黄河水利的伟大计划已在逐步实现,中国人民数千年来"黄河清"的美丽愿望变成事实已指日可待。

黄河流域是我国古代文化的摇篮。三门峡水库正处在中原地区黄河转弯的三角地带,自古以来这里就是交通的枢纽,在政治、经济以及文化上都占有重要的地位。为了了解三门峡水库区内的古代文化遗存,以便在蓄水以前采取保护措施和进行考古发掘,1955年10月中华人民共和国文化部和中国科学院联合组成了黄河水库考古工作队,由中国科学院考古研究所夏鼐副所长担任队长,有领导有组织地进行了调查。调查中共发现了古代遗址211处,古墓葬73处,古代纪念物13处[1]。这里的古代文化遗存,不仅含量丰富,而且包括了不同的时期,甚至于可以被视为中国历史上一个阶段的缩影。它们对说明中国古代文化的形成及其发展具有极重要的价值。

继调查工作之后,从1956年起,以河南陕县为中心并配合三门峡市区基本建设工程所进行的发掘工作,计有庙底沟和三里桥的新石器时代遗址,上村岭虢国墓地,后川东周、汉、唐墓地,刘家渠汉、唐墓地等,都有了丰富的收获[2-4]。从1959年起,又在水库区内的豫、晋、陕三省进行广泛的试掘或发掘工作,也都获得了很重要的考古资料。以上的工作改变了过去尚为空白地区的我国考古学的面貌,也提出了不少的问题。国家所进行的大规模的社会主义建设事业,给考古工作开辟了宽阔的道路,三门峡水库的建设便是最典型的一个例子。这些工作充分说明了唯有在社会主义的优越制度下,中国考古学才能得到真正的发展,唯有配合伟大的社会主义建设工程,才可能扩大我们的眼界与积累更丰富的资料。

本报告只是我们工作的一部分,它包括庙底沟和三里桥两个新石器时代遗址,为黄河水库考古报告的第二种,其他的发掘工作也将陆续编写报告,作为专刊或单独发表。本报告由安志敏、郑乃武、谢端琚合写。报告的壹、贰之一和肆、伍部分由安志敏执笔,贰二之(二)2、(三)、四、五、六由谢端琚执笔,其余是郑乃武执笔,经安志敏整校一遍,最后由夏鼐先生校阅全文并加以指正。本报告的俄、英文提要由张轶东、王俊铭分别译成;兽骨经中国科学院古脊椎动物研究所贾兰坡先生鉴定。

在历次调查及发掘过程中,得到豫、晋、陕三省的省、市、县人民委员会以及黄河三门峡工程局等有关单位的大力协助,使工作得以顺利开展,并取得了相当大的收获,均此致谢。

贰　庙底沟

一　地理环境及工作概况

庙底沟遗址位于陕县南关的东南,在这一带有着比较丰富的古代遗存。这里首先介绍陕县的地理环境。陕县旧属陕州,在河南西部,北临黄河与山西平陆相对。著名的三门峡在县城东约50华里。随着三门峡水库及水电站的兴建,在县城东的会兴镇附近的原野上出现了一座新兴的三门峡市。

陕县境内河流交错,除黄河外,最主要的有两条河流,一条是青龙涧,即《水经注》上所谓的橐水:"橐水出橐山西北流,……其水又西北经陕县城西,西北入于河"。这条河横贯在陕县境内,将县城与南关截开,目前的城区繁荣中心及车站均在青龙涧南岸,而北岸的城区则较为冷落。另外一条是苍龙涧,即《水经注》上所谓的谯水:"谯水导源于常丞之山,俗谓之干山,盖先后之异名也。山在陕县城南八十里,其川流也,二源双导,同注一壑,西北流注于河"。这条河也是在县城的附近注入黄河的。此外尚有很多较小的河流,交错流注于上述各水。无论大小河流的沿岸,都有新石器时代及早期文化的遗址。这是因为河流汇集,土地肥沃,适于古代人类生产和栖息。特别是陕县县城附近,北有黄河,汇纳青龙、苍龙两条涧水,从地理形势上来讲,更是重要,因而许多时代复杂范围广大的遗址,皆集中在陕县的县城附近(图一),如庙底沟(仰韶、龙山、东周)、三里桥(仰韶、龙山、东周)、七里堡(仰韶、龙山、殷、东周、汉)等是。而与陕县县城相对的平陆境内则有盘南村(仰韶、龙山、东周)。由于上述的情况,我们就以陕县县城为中心,首先选择了庙底沟和三里桥作为工作地点,其他遗址从1958年起,也陆续开展了发掘工作。

庙底沟位于青龙涧南岸、陕县车站的东边。在一块比较平坦的黄土原上,被两条南北向的深沟所切断。西边的俗称庙底沟,深约40多米。沟旁营造着许多窑洞,为庙底村的中心地区。东边的俗称此龙沟,深亦40多米。沟底有一条小河,它发源于40华里以外的窑头,由窑头至陈栋一段称为火烧阳沟,而陈栋以下则称为此龙沟。溪水由南向北流,经年不绝,注入青龙涧,疑即《水经注》上所说的"南出近溪,北流注橐"的渎谷水。北边濒临青龙涧,因受河水浸蚀,形成高约40米的峭壁,而陇海铁路在涧河岸的附近东西穿过。南边的韩庄却是高出约20余米的黄土台地,边缘部分已辟成梯田。

从上述的地形来看,庙底沟是北临涧河,南傍韩庄,东西为两道深沟所夹住,形成了一个大体上是菱形的平原地带。新石器时代遗址主要分布在这块平原上,另外在此龙沟东岸靠近涧河的一角也有部分的遗址存在(图版玖叁)。这里适是此龙沟溪水汇流注入青龙涧的三角地带,当是新石器时代人类居住与生产活动的良好场所。在东西两条沟旁断崖以及陇海铁路路沟两侧,均曝露着灰层或灰坑的痕迹。遗址的总面积约为 240,000 平方米,比陕县附近的大村落还要大得多。这里隔河与北岸的三里桥新石器时代遗址相对,中间隔着一条较宽的河谷,相距约 1,400 米。

　　遗址上面的绝大部分都是耕地,现在的村落是聚集在遗址的西部及沟旁穿凿窑洞,至于地面上的建筑仅有一座后土祠,现改为庙底沟小学。所谓"庙底"或"庙底沟"是指遗址西部的村落而言,为了便利起见,我们将整个遗址的所在地统称为庙底沟。按庙底名称的来源甚早,且与后土祠有着一定的关系。据后土祠明成化十八年(公元 1482 年)的碑文:"州治南里许有庙曰后土,稽诸郡志,乃大定二年郡人高大建,俗因呼为高家庙。迨我朝洪武二十五年弘农卫指挥周鉴重修。庙之下有数姓,曰高姓者迨三之二。自始至今高族世奉其庙之香火。"另外我们在发掘中曾遇到一块明弘治十六年(公元 1503 年)的朱书买地券:"河南陕州西樊二里人氏,现在庙底居住"。可知庙底的名称,至迟在明代便已经存在了。这个遗址是 1953 年秋季由中国科学院考古研究所河南考古调查队首先发现[5],黄河水库考古工作队在普查及复查时都做了重点的勘查。由于遗址范围广大,文化遗存丰富,我们便选择了这个地点,结合训练干部在三门峡水库区内进行第一次的大规模发掘,以为今后的工作打下基础。在这里共发掘了两次,第一次于 1956 年 9 月 30 日开始,至 12 月 6 日结束,先在遗址东端开了 4×4 米的探方 103 个,编号 T1－100(包括附号 3 个,简称 T1 区,见图版玖肆),继又在稍西的地方开了 53 个探方,编号 T100－150(包括附号 3 个,简称 T100 区)。第二次于 1957 年 3 月 26 日开始,至 7 月 25 日结束,继续向西发展开了 40 个探方,编号 T203－285(编号不相连接,包括 3 个附方,简称 T200 区)。又向西约在遗址的中心部分开了 72 个探方,编号 T301－359(包括附号 11 个,大小不等,简称 T300 区。见图版玖伍)。至于遗址的较西部分仅开了 3 个探方,因附近有窑洞而中止发展,编号 T401－T403(简称 T400 区)。另外在此龙沟东岸的三角地带,发现了一块以龙山文化为主的遗存,当是在这个遗址的东部边缘,开了 27 个探方,编号 T551－566(包括附号 11 个,大小不等,简称 T500 区)。通过两次工作,我们共发掘了 280 个探方,总面积达 4480 平方米。在这里共发现了仰韶灰坑 168 个,房子 2 座,龙山灰坑 26 个,房子 1 座,窑址 1 座,另外还发现了墓葬 156 座,绝大部分是属于龙山文化的。这里以新石器时代的仰韶文化为主,龙山文化次之,并有明确的地层交叠证据,此外也有较薄的东周文化层和少数汉唐墓葬。关于他们的分布及遗存情况,均详见下节。

　　庙底沟遗址的发掘,是三门峡水库区开始发掘工作以来集中干部人数最多与工作规模最大的一次。1956 年度的工作人员达 75 人,除了中国科学院考古研究所的工作人员以外,还包括了中华人民共和国文化部以及各省文管会、博物馆等单位所抽调的干部20人,和西北大学进修教师1人。在考古所的干部中有初次参加工作的41人,因而这次工作也起到训练干部的作用。第二次工作人员共26人,虽然人数减少,但由于积累了经验,在工作质量上皆有所提高。1956年秋季和1957年春季两次都参加的工作人员为安志敏、吴汝祚、洪晴玉、郑乃武、谢端琚、阳吉昌、郑笑梅、叶小燕、刘增堃、王兆燕、王玉福、任玉梅、董希篯、海棣华、宋瑞贞、时桂山、沈淑贞、温孟元、张长庆、武纪元、王兆莹、白荣金、邓文章、支沉洪等同志;参加1956年工作的还有陈作良、王克林、高东陆、赵瑞亭、赵鸿德、钟玲、张子明、王其腾、毕宝启、龚琼英、李进、徐殿魁、郑大成、施楚宝、王秀清、赵自洁、王极庆、蒋忠义、戴复汉、杨斌涛、张国辉、高洪岐、赵荣光、张青侠、邓德宝、关启生、刘永才、庞中威、许觉、唐士和、杜玉生、敖承隆、郭仁、程铭发、徐秉琨、张季、赵岐、云希正、张守中、罗少牧、张才俊、孙维锠、许清泉、包恩黎、黎忠义、祝志成、朱国忱、区泽、赵之祥、梁仁智、贾德耀等同志。参加1957年工作的还有张振邦、丁六龙同志。

二 文化堆积

(一)地层情况

遗址的发掘分为六区进行,探方均为4×4米(附加方例外),方向正南北(T500区因地形关系不作正方向),编号由北到南,自东而西,计前后共发掘了4480平方米。各区的地层情况,虽有所不同,但基本上可以分为仰韶的,仰韶、龙山交迭的,仰韶、战国交迭的三种堆积。现分区说明如下:

1. T1区　发现仰韶文化灰坑36个,龙山文化陶窑1座,墓葬145座,唐墓1座,时代不明者2座;另外在北边与东边各有近代壕沟1条,南边还有几个近代墓(图版玖肆)。这一区的地层堆积,主要是战国层压在仰韶文化层的上面,仅在西边龙山陶窑的附近,有一部分属于龙山文化层。龙山墓葬都打破了仰韶文化层和灰坑,或者压在仰韶灰坑的上面,排列甚整齐,当是一个氏族成员的公共墓地。现以8、18、28、38四个探方的南壁剖面为例,来加以说明:第1层,耕土,厚0.15－0.3米。出有仰韶、战国陶片,也夹有一些汉瓦及近代陶片。第2层,战国层,土呈黄褐色,质较硬,厚0.3－0.5米。包含物除了战国陶片外,还出有仰韶陶片及盘状器等物。在此层的东边被一条近代壕沟所打破,一直到了生黄土。第3层,仰韶文化层,已被五座龙山墓葬所打破。按土色、土质的不同,又可分为两小层:3A层,土呈灰色,质松软,厚0.25－0.3米;3B层,土呈红褐色,质较硬,含有少量姜石,厚0.35－0.56米,出有仰韶陶片、残陶环及盘状器等物(图二,1)。

2. T100区　发现有仰韶文化灰坑42个,龙山文化灰坑2个,南部被一条东西曲折的近代壕沟穿过,另外在此区内也散布有几座近代墓。这一区的地层堆积,除了仰韶文化层外,在东边还发现有两个龙山灰坑(H27、35)打破了仰韶灰坑的现象。

3. T200区 发现有仰韶文化灰坑5个,圆形硬面1处,灰沟1条,路沟1条,龙山文化灰坑1个。仰韶文化灰沟(HG201)原是一条自然沟,自发掘区的东北曲折通往西南,沟口距地表2.35、口宽4.75－7、底宽3.5－5、深4.2米。沟内堆积可分为五大层,包括有灰褐土、黄褐土、红褐土以及淤土等不同的土色,土质一般较松。从出土的遗物看来,系属于同一时期的。路沟(LG201)也是一条自然沟,自发掘区的南半部曲折通往东边,沟口距地表1.3－1.5、口宽3－4.6、底宽2.4－2.9、深2－3.4米。沟内路土多层,间杂有黄褐土、红褐土、黑灰土等不同土色的堆积,所出遗物亦同属于一个时期的。这一区的地层堆积,除了仰韶文化层外,在南边还发现有龙山灰坑(H202)打破了仰韶路沟的现象。

4. T300区 发现有仰韶文化灰坑83个,房子2座,墓葬1座,汉代灰沟1条,瓮棺3座,瓦棺1座,时代不明的墓葬2座,另外还有几座近代墓(图版玖伍)。这一区的地层堆积,除了北边有一小部分很薄的汉代层和一条南北贯穿的汉代灰沟外,都属于仰韶文化的。

5. T400区 发掘面积仅48平方米,地层自耕土以下系属于仰韶文化的堆积。

6. T500区 发现有仰韶文化灰坑2个,灰沟1条,龙山文化灰坑23个,灰沟2条,另外还有几座近代墓。这一区的地层堆积,主要是龙山文化的,但也发现有龙山文化层压在仰韶文化层的上面,以及龙山灰坑打破了仰韶灰坑的现象。现以558、560、562三个探方的东壁剖面为例,来加以说明:第1层,耕土,厚0.08－0.2米,出有近代陶片少许。第2层,龙山文化层,土呈黄褐色,质较松,厚0.24－0.35米,包含物除了龙山陶片外,也出有仰韶陶片少许。在此层的下面尚有两个灰坑相压着,上一个系龙山文化灰坑(H567),分为三层:1层,按土色、土质的不同,又可分为两小层:1A层,土呈黄灰色,质松,厚0.15米;1B层,土呈黑灰色,质较上层更松,厚0.1－0.2米。2层,土呈黄灰色,质松,厚0.2－0.5米。3层,土色与上层同,惟质较硬,厚0.15－0.36米。以上各层均出有龙山陶片,但也夹有少量的仰韶陶片。下一个为仰韶文化灰坑(H571),分为两层:1层,黄色杂土,质松,厚0.51米;2层,土呈黑灰色,质松,厚0.24米,均出土仰韶陶片。第3层,仰韶文化层,土呈红褐色,质松,厚0.45－0.75米,出有仰韶陶片。在此层的下面尚压着一条仰韶文化的灰沟(HG552),内填微呈灰色红土,质较硬,深0.75－1米,出有仰韶陶片少许(图二,2)。

(二)建筑遗存

1. 仰韶文化

(1)房子

仰韶文化的房子共发现了2座,均在T300区内,都被一条南北贯穿的汉代灰沟(HG301)和几个仰韶灰坑所打破。这两座房子的结构,基本上是相同的,从残存的部分尚能看出其大体的轮廓;都是南北向的方形浅竖穴,在南面的正中,有一条窄长斜坡式的门道;屋内距门不远,有一个圆形的火塘,屋基中部有四个带石柱础的柱洞,在浅竖穴四周的坑壁上,敷有一层草泥土,并有排列整齐的柱洞,但两座房子所残存的数量不同,而且都没有石柱础;另外在浅竖穴的底部,敷有一层草泥土的居住面。现将两座房子分别说明如下:

301 号房子,位于 T311A、321、321A、321B、331、331A、331B 七个探方内。该屋倒塌后的上部堆积,在距地表 0.36 - 0.53 米左右开始露出;其范围东西约 6、南北约 7.86 米;经全面揭露后,始现出整个房子的轮廓。除屋内西南部被汉代灰沟穿过(浅竖穴坑壁、堆积以及居住面等均被破坏),南壁西边、东南角以及门道的东半角各被仰韶灰坑 376、305、323 打破外,其余保存尚完整(图三,1;图版贰,1)。

屋的方向 206 度,门道长 2.84、宽 0.6 - 0.72 米,作 11 度的斜坡,两壁残高 0.43 - 0.76 米,与斜坡的路面均敷有一层厚 7 - 14 厘米的草泥土。进门便是居住面,略呈长方形,南边长 7.42、北边长 6.8、东边长 6.18、西边长 6.27 米,系用厚 7 - 14 厘米的草泥土敷成,呈灰白色,质极坚实(图三,3)。

浅竖穴的四壁,均敷有一层厚 6 - 8 厘米的草泥土,残存坑壁最高为 0.68、最低为 0.34 米。柱洞残存共 37 个,屋内中部 4 个,对称作方形,用以支撑屋顶,下面置有石柱础(其中 4 号柱洞已破坏,无柱础),系用两面平整的天然砾石(图三,4)。四壁 33 个,排列甚整齐,有的露出于壁外,有的则隐存在壁内。洞有直立,也有倾斜的(南壁部分全为直立,其他三壁则直、斜都有),斜度最大者为 16.5 度。洞径最大为 24、最小则仅 14 厘米。这些柱洞当木柱埋下时,均于空隙处填塞草泥土以使其稳固。从剖面上看,往往有的柱洞原系直的,而所埋置的木柱痕迹却成为倾斜的形状。在洞内填土中,常发现有少量木灰,当为木柱腐朽后的遗迹。另外在几个洞内还出有仰韶陶片及残兽骨等物,这可能是房子废弃后才填进去的。现将各柱洞的位置、大小及深度等,见仰韶文化 301 号房子柱洞登记表。

仰韶文化 301 号房子柱洞登记表 (单位:米)

位置		编号	口径	底径	洞深		说 明
					居住面上	居住面下	
屋内中部	东南	1	0.23	?	/	0.03 - 0.07	
	东北	2	0.23 - 0.25	?	/	0.035 - 0.065	
	西北	3	0.27	?	/	0.05 - 0.055	
	西南	4	?	?	/	?	已被破坏,无柱础
南壁(东)		5	0.17	0.14	0.26	0.525	
		6	0.18	0.14	0.3	0.47	
		7	0.16	0.12	0.29	0.43	
		8	0.17	0.11	0.25	0.47	
		9	0.19	0.12	0.21	0.36	

续表

位置	编号	口径	底径	洞深 居住面上	洞深 居住面下	说 明
东壁	10	0.18	0.14	0.44	0.35	洞微向内斜,出有残兽骨
	11	0.21	0.18	0.4	0.72	洞向内斜6.5°,出有陶片
	12	0.14	0.12	0.35	0.59	洞向内斜5°
	13	0.16	0.15	0.3	0.49	洞微向内斜,出有陶片
	14	0.17	0.16	0.3	0.62	
	15	0.16	0.13	0.25	0.67	
	16	0.17	0.13	0.31	0.51	洞微向内斜,出有陶片
	17	0.16	0.14	0.28	0.46	洞向内斜14.5°
东北角	18	0.16-0.2	0.1-0.11	0.15	0.68	洞向内斜16°,出有陶片
北壁	19	0.17	0.16	0.12	0.48	洞微向内斜
	20	0.16	0.15	0.2	0.42	出有陶片
	21	0.18	0.12	0.3	0.59	
	22	0.14	0.12	0.25	0.49	洞向内斜8°
	23	0.18	0.105	0.35	0.6	洞微向内斜
	24	0.2	0.15	0.38	0.34	洞向内斜16.5°
	25	0.18	0.15	0.2	0.37	
	26	0.18	0.16	0.29	0.48	
	27	0.17	0.16	0.16	0.55	洞微向内斜
西北角	28	0.18	0.17	0.2	0.48	洞向内斜8°
西壁	29	0.19	?	0.12	0.48	洞微向内斜
	30	?	0.14	0.45	0.46	洞微向内斜
	31	0.18	0.15	0.46	0.5	洞略向外斜
	32	0.19	0.13	0.46	0.3	洞略向外斜,出有陶片
西南角	33	0.17	?	0.49	0.6	洞微向内斜
南壁(西)	34	0.17	0.14	0.49	0.4	洞微向内斜
	35	0.17	0.16	0.3	0.48	
	36	0.19	0.17	0.35	0.46	
	37	0.17	0.12	0.31	0.5	出有陶片

火塘在屋内南部的正中,恰与门道相对。作圆形竖穴,口径1.17、底径0.91、深1.24米。口部留有烟熏痕迹,近处居住面亦呈青黑色。坑的内壁及底部有一层坚硬的红烧土,厚

3—6 厘米,愈近底部则愈硬,当为长期经火烧烤的缘故。坑内堆积分为五层:第 1 层,土微呈红色,质硬,厚 5—15 厘米,未见出土物。第 2 层,黄土,质较松,厚 18—32 厘米,上面有一小层由石头和草泥土排列成的堆积,当为火塘废弃后人们把它填上的,出有 5 件大小不一的盘状器。第 3 层,黄灰土,质较松,厚 0.26—0.51 米,出有仰韶陶片。第 4 层,草灰土,质极松,厚 0.17—0.3 米,出有仰韶陶片少许。第 5 层,黑灰土,质松,厚 0.1—0.28 米,未见出土物(图三,3)。

屋顶及墙壁均已塌陷,堆积于屋内及其周围,距地表约 0.8 米,厚 18—37 厘米,呈黄色,上部较松,下部较硬,内含有多量的草茎。从这些堆积的遗存看来,可以知道当时屋顶及墙壁上敷有草泥土。

房子的堆积可分为七层:除第 1 层耕土,第 2 层红褐土(汉代层)外,以下皆为仰韶文化的堆积。第 3 层,黑灰土,内夹有黄色碎土及红烧土碎块,质松,厚 5—43 厘米,堆积范围大体上与房子的面积相等,唯北部则有一部分跨出屋壁之外。第 4 层,灰色土,质松,厚 5—23 厘米,堆积在屋内。第 5 层,黄色土,质松,厚 5—20 厘米,堆积在屋内。以上三层系屋顶及墙壁倒塌后的堆积,均出有仰韶陶片,其中第 3 层还出有盘状器及骨镞等物。第 6 层,草泥土,系屋顶及墙壁塌下的堆积(见前面屋顶及墙壁部分)。第 7 层,按土色、土质的不同,又可分为三小层:7A 层,厚 8—30 厘米,上部土色微红,质较硬;下部土呈黄色,质较松,堆积在屋内,唯北部东边及门道处较高。7B 层,黑灰土,质松,厚 3—6 厘米,堆积在屋内。7C 层,厚 10—20 厘米,堆积情况与 7A 层大体相同,唯在此层开始露出屋内中部的四个柱洞,出有仰韶陶片及残蚌笄(?)等。以上三小层都是在房子未塌之前形成的,可能是居住时期的堆积(图三,2)。

房子 302,位于 T347、348、349、357、358、359 六个探方内,距 301 号约 25.2 米。该屋倒塌后的上部堆积,在距地表 0.12—0.2 米左右开始露出,其范围南北长约 6.2 米(东西不详)。保存情况与 301 号房子大体相同,唯东边被汉代灰沟(浅竖穴坑壁、堆积以及居住面等均被破坏),西边以及门道的前端各被仰韶灰坑 383、391 所打破,破坏程度较甚(图四,1;图版贰,2)。

屋的方向 205 度。门道残长 2、宽 0.48—0.54 米,原来的路面已破坏(见生黄土),两壁残高 0.63 米,敷有厚约 15 厘米的草泥土。居住面的结构与 301 号略有不同,除了草泥土之外,还羼有红烧土碎末,呈棕红色,厚 2 厘米,表面光滑,质极坚实。从残存的部分看来,居住面的形状与 301 号房子相同,也是略呈长方形的,残长南边 6、北边 3.4、西边 4 米。在门道至火塘间的一段,已被破坏,于近门口处出残石刀 1 件。居住面之下至浅竖穴底部间,尚有一层草泥土堆积。质坚硬,厚 10 厘米,可能是在建屋时所填筑的屋基,也许就是原来的居住面,而上面的棕红色居住面是后来因原有的居住面损坏了,才第二次增筑的(图四,3)。

浅竖穴的坑壁,均敷有一层厚 3—4 厘米的草泥土,残存坑壁最高为 0.63、最低为 0.34 米。柱洞残存共 21 个,屋内中部 3 个(原为 4 个,1 个已被汉代灰沟打破),下面均有扁平的砾石柱础(图四,4)。四壁 18 个,洞皆直立,其中大部分在木柱与洞壁空隙之间,也填有草泥土。在四壁柱洞中,除了 9 号柱洞的下半部为灰土堆积,出一残石斧外,其他洞中均未见灰土及出土物。各柱洞的位置、大小及深度等见仰韶文化 302 号房子柱洞登记表。

火塘的位置、形状与 301 号房子相同,口径 1、底径 0.76、深 0.71 米。坑的内壁及底部,曾用草泥土涂过(与 301 号房子的火塘略有不同),经火烧后变成红烧土,厚 3 - 10 厘米,口部留有烟熏痕迹。坑内堆积分为两层:第 1 层,草泥土,黄色,质较硬,厚 5 - 46 厘米,是屋顶塌下时的堆积,出有仰韶陶片少许。第 2 层,灰烬,质松软,厚 2 - 26 厘米,是原来烧火时的堆积,仅出仰韶陶片 3 片。

屋顶及墙壁下塌后,堆积在居住面上,距地表 0.7 - 0.78 米,厚 25 - 40 厘米;另外在屋外西北角亦有小部分堆积,都是草泥土,呈黄色,出有仰韶陶片少许。

房子的堆积可分为三层:除第 1 层耕土外,以下都是仰韶文化的堆积。第 2 层,按土色、土质的不同,又可分为四小层:2A 层,灰土,质较细,厚 10 - 38 厘米;2B 层,黑灰土,质细,厚 3 - 5 厘米,以上两层堆积在屋内南半部。2C 层,灰褐土,质较粗,厚 12 - 48 厘米;2D 层,含姜石黄土,质较粗,厚 10 - 30 厘米,以上两层堆积在屋内北半部。上述各层均出有仰韶陶片少许。第 3 层,草泥土,系屋顶及墙壁塌下的堆积(见前面屋顶及墙壁部分)。这座房子在草泥土层的下面即为居住面,未见有其他的堆积(图四,2)。

上述两座房子,由于没有保存较好的屋顶堆积,还难以复原他们的结构,不过根据亚洲其他国家所发现的新石器时代房屋遗址或现存较原始的房屋结构,也可以得到若干启示,我们不妨根据这些线索来加以复原。关于 F301 和 F302 的共同特点,是近方形的浅竖穴,屋基中部的四根木柱下面垫有石柱础,门南有斜坡式的门道,相似的房屋遗址在陕西西安半坡也有发现(但半坡不见石柱础),或者可以说它是仰韶文化房屋的一种基本型式。首先,我们在亚洲北部的原始房屋中,也可以找到类似的结构,如苏联库页岛虾夷(Ainu)人房屋,也是一个方形的浅竖穴,屋基中部有四根木柱支撑着用木柱斜铺成圆锥形的屋顶,屋顶外面涂以很厚的草泥土,由外观察成为一个圆锥形的房屋[6]。日本新石器时代房屋遗址也同样是浅竖穴而屋内有四根立柱,至于屋顶结构曾根据铜铎、铜镜上的房屋图像以及埴轮(日本古代立在墓冢周围的陶制明器)中的陶屋复原成有重檐的屋顶[7],是否完全可信还值得考虑。这里仰韶文化的房屋虽有四根立柱,但结构上却不会与上述两类房屋相同,因为 F302 周围墙上的柱洞都是直的,而 F301 柱洞的斜度也不大,不可能由地面上用木柱斜铺成圆锥或四角锥形的屋顶。据我们推测周围墙内柱洞的木柱,除了支撑屋顶以外,还有兼作墙壁骨架的作用,而屋内的四根木柱则主要是支撑屋顶的。这样上面就成为四角锥形的屋顶,而周围墙上的木柱高出浅竖穴,或直立,或微向里倾斜形成围墙(图五、六)。在西伯利亚汉特(Ханты)族的桦皮树房屋中还可以找到类似的外貌[8]。因此,我们相信上述的复原是可能比较接近于真实情况的。当时在屋顶和墙壁上涂有较厚的草泥土,在屋内所发现的草泥土堆积,便可能是它们的遗存。

仰韶文化 302 号房子柱洞登记表 （单位:米）

位置		编号	口径	底径	洞深		说　明
					居住面上	居住面下	
屋内中部	东南	1	0.22 - 0.27	?		0.19	
	西南	2	0.28 - 0.33	?		0.13	
	西北	3	0.23	?		0.12	
南壁（东）		4	0.22 - 0.24	0.07	0.4	0.62	
		5	0.22 - 0.26	0.1	0.4	0.78	
		6	0.28 - 0.3	0.1	0.43	0.58	
北壁		7	0.24	0.1	0.24	1.05	
		8	0.26	0.11	0.2	0.5	
		9	0.22 - 0.26	0.09	0.17	1	深 0.6 米处出残石斧一
		10	0.2 - 0.23	0.1	0.18	0.45	
		11	0.22 - 0.26	0.11	0.19	0.85	
西壁		12	0.22 - 0.26	0.12	0.21	0.5	
		13	?	0.16	?	0.92	上部已被灰坑 383 打破
		14	?	0.14	?	0.97	同上
		15	?	0.11	?	0.7	同上
		16	?	0.1	?	0.41	同上
西南角		17	0.24	0.12	0.5	0.75	
南壁（西）		18	0.23	0.13	0.58	0.76	
		19	0.18 - 0.23	0.08	0.4	0.76	
		20	0.16	0.1	0.4	0.87	
		21	0.19	0.08	0.44	0.74	

　　除了两座房子外,在 T227 探方内,尚发现有圆形硬面一处(F207)。距地表 2.2、直径 1.5 - 1.65 米,厚 6.5 - 13 厘米,面呈黄褐色,中心略偏东南处有一个柱洞,口径 21 - 23、底径 11、深 22 厘米。洞内底部有厚约 8 厘米的草泥堆积,呈浅黄色,内含草成分甚多,上部填土皆为灰褐色。在此硬面的南边略偏西处,尚有残路土一段,自北向南稍作斜坡。面上及其周围均有零散的草泥土堆积,可能是上部塌下的遗迹。从上述的情况看来,这个建筑遗存面积既小,结构也很简单,可能是一个圆锥形的棚子。中央用一根木柱支撑着,当属于储存什物的地方,并不适于住人。此外,在硬面的东边,有一条仰韶文化的路沟(LG201),西北边还有一条仰韶文化的灰沟(HG201),而小棚正坐落于两沟中的一个小土墩上。

　　（2）灰坑

　　仰韶文化灰坑共发现了 168 个,有圆形和椭圆形两种,前者居多,计 103 个,后者较少,计 65 个。灰坑的分布,几乎遍于整个遗址(T400 区因发掘面积仅 48 平方米,未发现灰坑),而以 T300 区的分布较密,如在 F301 仰韶文化房子的西边,约 100 平方米的范围内即发现有 20 多个灰坑,其中打破关系甚为复杂,多者竟有 17 个互相套在一起。灰坑保存得完整者甚少,仅 42 个,占本遗址中已发掘的仰韶文化灰坑总数的四分之一。此外,绝大部分的灰坑都有打破关系,其中少者两个,多者如上述达 17 个。这些灰坑除了相互打破外,有一部分是被仰韶文化的灰沟(HG201)、路沟(LG201)和汉代灰沟(HG301)打破的,另外还有几个是被近代墓或后期扰乱坑打破的。

灰坑的大小不一,一般口径多在 2－3 米间,但个别大者亦有达到 5.7 米,小者仅 0.54 米,深度多在 1－2.5 米左右,最深者 3.9 米,最浅者 0.45 米,但都属于少数。灰坑的内壁多不整齐,按斜度的不同,大体上可以分为口大底小、直壁、口小底大三种类型;其中以口大底小如斗状者占最大多数,直壁如筒状者次之,而口小底大如袋状者最少。其比例如下表:

仰韶文化灰坑类型统计表(一)

形状 ＼ 类别	口大底小	直壁	口小底大	共计
圆形	74	18	11	103
百分比	71.85	17.48	10.68	100%

仰韶文化灰坑类型统计表(二)

形状 ＼ 类别	口大底小	直壁	口小底大	共计
椭圆形	51	11	3	65
百分比	78.47	16.93	4.62	100%

灰坑的底部一般较平坦,但也有少数不甚平整的。在所发现的灰坑中,曾有四个坑壁及底部敷有一层草泥土,厚 10－20 厘米,有的底部还有许多不规则的浅小洞。这种现象因发现得不多,还无法了解其原来的用途。

坑内堆积按土色、土质的不同,多者可以分为十余层,少者则仅一层。出土遗物除少数较小或较浅的灰坑外,一般均甚丰富,其中以陶片为最多,另外还有石器、骨器、角器以及自然遗物等出土。

在上述灰坑中,有 9 个除了一般的文化遗物出土外,还发现有人和家畜的骨架遗存,这可能是利用当时废弃的灰坑来作为埋葬之所;其中有 4 个灰坑出人骨架,3 个灰坑出狗骨架,2 个灰坑出猪骨架(内一个还兼出狗骨架)。骨架的保存情况,绝大部分不完整。现将各灰坑的出土骨架数目,列表如下:

仰韶文化灰坑出土骨架登记表

灰坑号	人骨架	猪骨架	狗骨架	保存情况
12			1	不完整
22		1	3	不完整
25	2			一具完整 一具不完整
40		1		不完整
41			1	不完整
44			4	不完整
49	1			不完整
51	1			不完整
62	1			不完整

从上面的表中可以看出，凡出有人骨架的灰坑，皆未见家畜骨架（是否因发现较少或另有意义，则尚待今后进一步的考察）。现举两例说明如下：

22 号灰坑，位于 T128、133 两个探方内，坑口距地表 1、口径 2.4、底径 3、深 1.75 米，系一圆形口小底大的袋状灰坑。坑的北边被另一仰韶灰坑（H44）打破少许。坑内堆积分为两层：第 1 层，红土，厚 1.5 米，出有仰韶陶片及残兽骨等物。在此层底部（即第 2 层的上面）的东边，距坑口 1.5 米处，发现有不甚完整的狗骨架 1 具。第 2 层，黑灰土，厚 0.25 米，出土物与上层同。在此层的底部中央，发现有不完整的猪骨架 1 具；另外在南边及西南边，也发现有零乱的狗骨架 2 具（图七，1）。

25 号灰坑，位于 T123 探方内，坑口距地表 1.85、口径 1.4、底径 2.2、深 0.75 米，也是圆形口小底大的袋状灰坑。坑的东北部被另外两个仰韶灰坑（H40、43）打破少许。坑内堆积仅一层，土呈黄灰色，厚 0.75－1 米，出有仰韶陶片及残兽骨等物。在距坑口 0.4 米处出人骨架 1 具，位于坑的中央，头向北，俯身，右手向上高举，手心向下，左手侧曲举，两腿向左侧斜，两足跟交叉，左边压在右边上（图七，2）。另外在距坑口 0.8 米处，也发现有人骨架 1 具，位于靠近坑的东北边，头向东，足朝西，仰身，左手向上屈伸，右手不存，两腿交叉，左股骨压在右股骨上（图七，3），身下即到生黄土。

此外，还有三个灰坑中所出的人骨架，姿势亦各不相同，有的仰身伸直，有的侧身屈肢。其中在灰坑 49 出的一具人骨架（已零乱不全），左手的无名指上，还戴有一个完整的蚌制精美的指环（H49：01）。

在所发现的 168 个仰韶文化灰坑中，绝大部分是有打破关系的。值得注意的是，这些灰坑中是否有着早晚不同的差别呢？关于这个问题，我们曾选择了 20 多个打破关系较清楚的圆形和椭圆形的灰坑，以及一条仰韶文化的灰沟（HG201），作了一些初步的比较。所得的结果是：这些相互打破的灰坑，似乎在器形与纹饰上还看不出有什么显著的差别。因此,它们在时间上可能相距不会太久的。

2. 龙山文化

(1)房子

在 T500 区内发现龙山文化房子一座。它打破了仰韶灰坑(H552),本身又被龙山灰层及晚期墓葬打破了一部分,但保存尚完整。它是一个圆形的袋形竖穴,底部有白灰面,东面有阶梯式的门道,竖穴的周围有排列整齐的柱洞(图八;图版叁,1)。

房子的底径 2.7、墙高 1.24 米,口小底大,系在生土中挖成,先就底部铺一层厚 0.4 厘米的草泥土,然后再铺上一层厚 0.3－0.5 厘米的石灰质作为居住面,表面光滑平整。西半部的白灰面已经剥落,露出草泥土。中央偏北处有一直径 0.08、深 0.15 米的柱洞。柱洞的周围填有碎陶片和草泥土,用以加固木柱。墙壁光滑整齐,部分经火烧过呈灰白色的硬烧面。由居住面至墙根高 6 厘米处涂有一层薄厚约 0.1 厘米的白灰面。在西边偏南的墙上高出居住面 8 厘米处有一个半圆形的土龛深入墙中,高 0.45、宽 0.4、深 0.5 米,附近被火烧成红烧土,在它附近的白灰面土也遗有零星的红烧土块,可能这里是当时的灶址。

房子的东面有一个长方形的窄门道,方向为 330°,长 0.74、宽 0.56 米,并有一个高 0.28 米的台阶,在台阶上也铺有草泥土和白灰面。

竖穴周围距坑口约 0.2 米处,环绕着一周柱洞,因被后期破坏仅残存 10 个。柱洞在生土中,深达 0.38 米,呈圆锥形,直径 0.09 米,稍向里倾斜,斜度为 8°,内填灰褐土,不见木质的痕迹。

房屋的内部满填灰土,可以分为三层:第 1 层,灰褐土,质地松,厚 0.41 米。第 2 层,黄灰土,质地较硬,厚 0.27－0.34 米。第 3 层,灰土,质地较松,杂有部分草泥土,厚 0.11－0.14 米。文化层所包含的全系龙山文化的遗物。

从这座房子的结构情况来看,它可以复原成一座尖锥顶状的房屋。由居住面中央的粗木柱支撑着屋顶的中心,周围的木柱除了支撑屋顶以外,还起着墙壁骨架的作用,由于房屋周围柱洞的斜度不大,它们可能还是竖立的。屋顶及墙壁上当时可能均涂有草泥土(图九、一〇)。

(2)窑址

仅在 T94 内发现 1 座,保存还比较完整。窑的构造是由窑室、火口、火膛、火道及窑箅等构成。火口、火膛及火道均就生土挖成轮廓,然后涂一层草泥土,窑箅等部分也是用草泥土所作成,因经火烧烤变为坚硬的红烧土(图一一;图版叁,2)。

窑室呈圆形,距地表深 2 米,南北直径 0.93、东西直径 0.78 米,窑壁已残缺,东壁残高达 0.48 米,可以看出它的弧度,原来当是一个半球状的窑顶。

火口紧靠在窑室的西面,近椭圆形,长 0.4、宽 0.26 米。火膛作长方形竖穴,长 0.94、宽 0.6、深 0.96 米。

火道分作八股,由火膛向上通入窑室的底部。中央部分有三股火道,而左右两股又分成3-4股,火道的长短、宽度不等,长0.1-0.36、宽度一般为0.07、高约0.08米。在左右两股火道的窑箅上还有半圆形的浅穴洞,可能是火道被填塞后所遗留的痕迹。火道的上面用草泥土涂成窑箅,厚0.16-0.3米,上面有25个火眼。火眼的形状,从剖面上看是底大口小,大小不一,最大可达0.23、最小只有0.03米。

在窑的上部填土中以及火膛内,发现有不少陶片和红烧土,其中主要是龙山陶片,也有少量仰韶陶片。根据地层及其出土物,可以断定是属于龙山文化的遗存。

(3)灰坑

龙山灰坑共发现26个,除H27、H35在T100区,H202在T200区外,其余均在T500区。

灰坑有圆形与椭圆形两类。圆形中又可分为口小底大和口大底小两种,前者共17个,后者仅5个。其大小、深度不等,口径1.6-3.39、底径2-4.42、坑深度0.31-2.61米。这种口小底大的袋形灰坑是龙山灰坑的主要形式,坑壁经过修整,一般都比较齐整。

椭圆形灰坑只发现4个,都是口大底小的,口径2.5-2.65、底径2.15-2.32、坑深1.1-2.7米。

龙山灰坑互相打破的有13个,龙山灰沟打破同时代灰坑的有6个,龙山灰坑打破仰韶灰沟的有7个,有的打破仰韶灰沟后又被同时代灰坑打破,最多的,仅在96平方米的范围内就有6个互相套在一起。完整的灰坑只有4个。从出土的遗物来观察,这些互相打破的龙山灰坑的年代相隔不会太久。

灰坑里各层的文化堆积不尽相同,现选取具有代表性的灰坑(H563)作为典型,加以说明:第1层,浅灰土,质地松软,厚0.3米。第2层,深灰土,质松,厚0.12-0.32米。第3层,黄褐土,质硬,含有部分草泥土,厚0.17-0.18米。第4层,灰褐土,质较松,厚0.13-0.6米。第5层,灰黑土,质松,厚0.04-0.24米。第6层,灰黄土,质较硬,厚0.2-0.32米。第7层,棕褐土,质坚硬,杂有部分草泥土,厚0.2-0.6米。第8层,黄褐土,质较松,厚0.1-0.53米。所包含的都是龙山文化的遗物。

在两个袋形灰坑中,各出土一具人骨架。35号灰坑人骨架位于第2层的北边,葬法是仰身直肢,头东脚西,方向120度,面向南,头低脚高,保存尚完好。202号灰坑内的人骨架位于第2层北边,除头部和左指骨残缺外,余保存尚完好,葬法也是仰身伸直,头东脚西,面向上,方向95度。均无随葬品。

这两具人骨的葬法、方向皆相同。可能是利用废弃的窑穴来葬死人,但排列比较整齐,不像仰韶文化的那样杂乱无规律。

此外在HG553的北壁发现了许多当时人们的工具痕迹,大部分是交叉密集的条痕。经我们仔细观察,发现是用双齿形的工具做成的。每齿的直径是4厘米,两齿之间的距离也是4厘米,有的宽达6厘米的。长度不甚清楚,约在20厘米左右。我们选择了五组比较清楚的痕迹画了下来(图一二);此外并用石膏将清楚的痕迹翻成模型(图版玖贰)。它的器形可能和殷周时期的木末近似。

(三)墓葬

共发现墓葬 156 座,其中包括了仰韶墓 1 座(M307),龙山墓 145 座,汉墓 4 座(M301、302、303、305),唐墓 1 座(M100),另外时代不明者有 5 座(M34、136、142、149、304)。

墓地位于庙底沟遗址的东部和中部,也就是分布在 T100 区和 T300 区中。T100 区墓号从 1 号起,有龙山墓 145 座,唐墓 1 座,时代不明的 3 座,共 149 座。这里是龙山文化的葬地,分布密集,排列整齐。T300 区墓号从 301 起,有仰韶墓葬 1 座,汉墓 4 座,时代不明的 2 座,共 7 座。

在 156 座墓葬中,除了汉墓 4 座、仰韶墓 1 座和龙山墓 18 座遭到破坏外,其余 127 座的龙山墓葬中,人架保存大体完好,这对研究龙山文化的人类体质特征提供了丰富的材料。

再按墓葬的时代顺序,分别叙述。

1. 仰韶墓葬

仰韶墓葬仅有 1 座(M307),位于 F301 门道的东侧。为长方形竖穴墓,距地面深 1.24 米。因被仰韶灰坑(H323)及房子(F301)门道所打破,墓圹不甚清楚。

人骨只保存了上半身的头骨、肋骨和右臂骨。人架仰卧,头北,面向东,方向180°[应为 0°——编者],无葬具的痕迹。值得提出的是这一座墓人架较为特别,昂头,曲颈,屈右上肢,其他部分均残缺,骨架的放置稍成倾斜(图一三)。

墓葬中虽没有随葬品,但被仰韶文化的房子及灰坑(H323)所打破,其时代不会晚于仰韶文化。

2. 龙山墓葬

龙山墓葬共发现 145 座。都是长方形竖穴墓。墓圹比较清楚,一般的长度为1.8-1.9、宽度为 0.41-0.51 米,墓的深度距地表一般在 1-2 米左右。由于有的墓葬被近代壕沟打破,也有的破东周时代的路土所踏毁,现存的墓口深度并不足以说明原来的深浅。

人骨大部分保存尚好,计有 127 座可以看出人骨的完整轮廓,其余 18 座经后来扰动,人骨残缺,都没有发现葬具的痕迹。

这里的墓都是单身葬,南北向,头北,脚南,方向都在 175°-190°之间[与图一四方向不一致——编者]。可见在当时的墓葬已有固定制度。在葬法上可分为直身和屈肢葬两种,直身葬的有 138 座,屈肢葬的有 2 座,其余因经扰动葬法不详的有 5 座。

仰卧伸直葬的面向无一定的规律,两臂放置的姿势也有不同。右臂伸直、左臂斜放在盆骨上的有 6 座,两手相叠放在盆骨上的有 2 座,其余两臂都是垂直身旁。

屈肢葬的人架被破坏或腐朽较甚,头向南,面向东或向西,两臂垂直于身旁或肘骨向内折手放在盆骨上。腿骨屈度不同,墓 19 的腿骨向东侧微屈作 110°。墓 143 的腿骨也向东侧微屈,右腿骨屈度为 150°,左腿骨屈度为 160°。

一般的墓葬均无随葬品,仅在两座墓葬中(M72、99)各出土小陶杯 1 件。72 号墓的放置在臂骨与肋骨之间,99 号墓放置在右臂骨旁(图一四)。

这些墓葬全部打破了仰韶文化层而深入生土中(图二,1),有的还压在仰韶灰坑的上面,因而在填土中除了龙山陶片外,也混有不少仰韶陶片。墓口的上面则被东周文化层所压住,甚至有的路土层把龙山墓葬人骨都踏毁,这很清楚地说明了它们时代的上下限。72 和 99 号墓出土的小陶杯,在龙山灰坑中也有出土,根据它们的地层关系和随葬品可以断定这批墓葬是属于龙山文化的遗存。

3. 汉代墓葬

共发现 3 个瓮棺葬和 1 个瓦棺葬(M301)。瓦棺葬是用两块绳纹板瓦对合在一起。人骨已腐朽成粉末,瓮棺葬的墓圹作不规则的长方形竖穴,墓的大小深度不同。302 号墓,长 2.7、宽 0.7 – 1.14、深 1.55 米。303 号墓,方向 268°,长 1.7、宽 0.97、深 2.18 米。瓮棺及瓦棺内均无随葬品,可能是西汉时期用以埋葬儿童的。

三　仰韶文化遗物

(一)陶器

仰韶文化陶器经复原者有 690 多件。按用途的不同,可以分为容器、炊器、工具、装饰品和玩具等几种。

1. 容器、炊器

都是当时的日常用具。陶质可以分为细泥红陶、泥质灰陶、细泥黑陶和夹砂粗红陶四个陶系。纹饰除素面或磨光者外,有彩绘、线纹、篮纹、划纹、弦纹、布纹、席纹、附加堆纹以及镂孔等。这些纹饰除单独使用外,有的还两三种同时并用。器形可识别者,有杯、盘、碗、盆、罐、盂、瓶、甑、鼎、釜、灶、器盖、器座等。现在先以四个出土陶片较多的灰坑作为代表,将其陶质、纹饰和器形加以统计,列表如下:

仰韶文化(灰坑 5、10、363、387)陶系及纹饰统计表

陶系	细泥红陶					泥质灰陶		细泥黑陶	夹砂粗红陶					总计
数量	9169					1663		4	5246					16082
百分比	57.02					10.34		0.03	32.62					100%
纹饰	彩绘	线纹	篮纹加线纹	布纹	素面	附加堆纹	素面	素面	线纹	线纹加划纹	弦纹	附加堆纹	素面	16082
数量	2254	4741	76	3	2095	12	1651	4	3441	168	23	146	1468	16082
百分比	14.02	29.48	0.48	0.02	13.03	0.08	10.27	0.03	21.4	1.05	0.15	0.91	9.13	100%

仰韶文化(灰坑 5、10、363、387)陶器器形统计表(以能看出器形者为限)

陶系	细泥红陶						泥质灰陶			细泥黑陶	夹砂粗红陶								总计
器形	碗	盆	罐	瓶	甑	器盖	碗	盆	罐	器座	罐	杯	碗	盆	罐	釜	灶	器盖	
数量	521	3126	1089	3125	3	11	92	924	119	2	4	12	87	1027	3754	3	3	4	13906
百分比	3.75	22.48	7.84	22.48	0.03	0.08	0.67	6.65	0.86	0.02	0.03	0.09	0.63	7.39	27	0.03	0.03	0.03	100%

A. 细泥红陶系　陶质细腻,可能绝大部分陶土经过淘洗的手续,仅小部分似未经过精细淘洗,间或含有较细的砂粒。

制法全部是手制的,除小陶杯、器盖等用捏塑法以外,其余全部采用泥条筑成法,个别器物的内部尚遗有明显的痕迹,口沿多经慢轮修整,因而器口整齐并遗有轮纹。制成以后,表面予以精细打磨,有的还拍印线纹或篮纹。

陶质坚硬,一般作红色或橙黄色,也有个别的标本在烧制过程中,因未能全部氧化而部分作灰褐色或有灰斑。此外,尚有一小部分近似白陶者,皆施彩绘,现暂收入本陶系内,质料可能是采用高岭土,唯尚有待于化验来证明。

素面陶器多经过精致磨光,有的打磨较粗糙,甚至于遗有压磨的痕迹。在少数的碗、盆上,还施有深红色或白色的陶衣,前者有光泽,多仅施陶衣,加绘彩纹者较少;后者绝少,多在口沿及器腹上仅涂一段白衣,然后在上面绘彩,兼用红、黑两种彩纹的,也多见于这种白衣彩陶。

陶器的纹饰,计有彩绘、线纹、篮纹、划纹、布纹、席纹、附加堆纹、镂孔等。彩绘的颜色主要采用黑色,红色的很少见,兼用两种颜色的更少。彩纹主要绘在器腹上,也有绘在折沿盆的口沿上,但器内绘彩者却绝无存在。图案的组织比较复杂,而且也富于变化,基本上是用条纹、涡纹、三角涡纹、圆点纹、方格纹等所组成(图版肆—捌)。从结构上大体可以分为两组:一组是用对称的几个单元构成整体图案,间或用不同或不对称的单元插在里面。这种情况往往是开始绘画以前没有很好的计划,以致画到最后还缺一小段,因而不得不插入其他的单元来填补。当然也有故意插入其他的单元以增加变化的。另外一组是用流利连续的花纹构成整体图案,每个单元是形态变化互相交叉,常常无从断开(图一五、一六)。前者多见于碗,而少见于盆、罐,后者多见于盆,而少见于罐,但不见于碗。至于动物纹,仅有蛙形纹一种,都见于敛口盆的残片上;一片比较完整,另外两片是头部及前爪和股部及后肢的残片(图版玖,1—3),形态生动,在彩陶图案中尚属少见。此外,还有彩绘与线纹或划纹并用的,见于盆与罐的口部残片上(图版柒,5、6),也有抹平线纹的一段,施以白色陶衣并加绘彩纹的,仅见于小口瓶的腹片上,但很少见(图版柒,9、11)。线纹斜行排列,多见于瓶与罐上。篮纹横行或斜行,常与线纹交互应用,单独使用者较少,多见于瓶与甑上。划纹皆平行排列,多施于盆与罐上。附加堆纹多为凹凸的波浪形泥条,也有作圆饼形的,前者除作装饰外,附在盆腹两旁还起着耳的作用。布纹见于瓶耳及附加堆纹上,系制作陶器时垫布压成的痕迹(图版捌,11)。席纹见于瓶耳上,系制作附件时放在席子上印成的(图版捌,12、13)。镂孔仅见于器盖的纽上。后三种可能无装饰上的作用。至于陶器的附件,除了瓶耳和盖纽以外,尚发现有鸟头形的器耳(图版玖,4—6),但不知属于何种器形。器形经复原者,有杯、盘、碗、盆、罐、盂、瓶、甑、器盖、器座等。

(1)圜底罐(A1;图一七;图版拾,1) 仅1件。敛口,深腹,圜底。周身线纹,腹部附有九个凸纽。

(2)盘(A2;图一七;图版拾,2) 仅发现1件残片。大口,浅腹直壁,平底。腹上有彩绘。

(3)浅腹碗(A3;图一七;图版拾,3-7;图版拾壹,1、2;图版拾贰,2-7) 共22件。大口,浅腹,腹壁弧形向下往里收缩成平底。有素面和彩绘两种。

(4)深腹碗 大口,深腹,平底。都有彩绘,一般仅在口沿上绘简单花纹,个别的在腹部绘有彩纹。可分两式:

A4a(图一七;图版拾壹,3-5) 共4件。腹壁弧形向下往里收缩。H327:06一件系红彩绘。

A4b(图一七;图版拾壹,6) 仅1件。腹壁成反弧形向下往里收缩。

(5)敞口碗 敞口,腹壁向下往里收缩成平底。有素面和彩绘两种。素面者外表多未经精致打磨,甚至在腹壁还遗有明显的压磨痕迹。可分三式:

A5a(图一七;图版拾贰,1) 共6件。腹壁向下略往里收缩,底部较大,约占口径的四分之三。

A5b(图一七;图版拾叁,2) 共5件。腹壁弧形收缩,底部外张。如假圈足。

A5c(图一七;图版拾叁,3、4) 共3件。腹壁微有弧度。

(6)曲腹碗 大口,腹壁曲向往里收缩成平底。有素面和彩绘两种。可分两式:

A6a(图一七;图版拾叁,5-7;图版拾肆,1-7;图版拾伍,1、2) 共29件。器形与前式近似,唯腹壁曲度较为显著。T24:12一件系红黑彩兼用,除腹部中间一道条纹及圆点纹用黑彩绘外,其余两道条纹都是红彩绘。

A6b(图一七;图版拾伍,3-7;图版拾陆,1-7;图版拾柒,1-7;图版拾捌,1、2) 共95件。腹壁成反弧形收缩。

(7)圈足碗 大口,腹壁斜行向下往里收缩成平底或圜底,底部带圈足。从器形上看,这类陶器也可能做器盖使用。有素面和彩绘两种。可分两式:

A7a(图一八;图版拾捌,3) 仅1件。平底,底下圈足有压印纹。

A7b(图一八;图版拾捌,4) 仅1件。圜底,圈足甚矮,圜底凸出,腹上有彩绘。

(8)浅腹盆 大口,浅腹,平底。绝大多数系素面,仅少数在口沿上绘彩,至于在腹部绘彩者,仅属个别。可分四式:

A8a(图一八;图版拾捌,5) 共6件。口沿外折,除素面外,有的也在口沿上绘彩。

A8b(图一八;图版拾叁,1) 共 3 件。与前式相似,唇部外侈。

A8c(图一八;图版拾玖,1) 仅 1 件。口沿外卷,腹壁略成弧形收缩。

A8d(图一八;图版拾玖,2) 仅 1 件。器形与前式近似,唯腹壁收缩较甚。

(9)敛口盆 敛口,腹壁向下往里收缩成平底。除素面和彩绘两种外,有的在近口部或腹部还加饰几道划纹,或在腹部两旁各饰一附加堆纹。可分九式:

A9a(图一八;图版拾玖,3、4) 共 3 件。口部微敛,浅腹。除素面外,有的在腹部绘彩。

A9b(图一八;图版拾玖,5、6;图版贰拾,1) 共 9 件。口略内敛,腹壁斜行收缩。

A9c(图一八;图版贰拾,4) 共 4 件。器形与前式相似,唯口沿外卷。

A9d(图一八;图版贰拾,2、3) 共 2 件。器形与前式近似,唯口沿收敛较甚。

A9e(图一九;图版贰壹,1) 共 4 件。口沿略向外卷,腹部较深。

A9f(图一九;图版贰壹,2) 共 3 件。器形与前式近似,唯底部的收缩程度较小。

A9g(图二〇;图版贰壹,3) 仅 1 件。腹壁成反弧形收缩。

A9h(图二〇;图版贰壹,4) 仅 1 件。器形与前式近似,唯口部收敛较甚。

A9j(图二〇;图版贰贰,1) 仅 1 件。鼓腹,向下往里收缩成小平底。

(10)深腹盆 折沿,深腹,腹壁向下往里收缩成平底。除素面和彩绘两种外,有的在近口部或腹部还加饰几道划纹,或在腹部两旁各饰一附加堆纹,个别的在腹部下折处,还饰有整齐的压印纹。可分九式:

A10a(图二〇;图版贰贰,2) 共 3 件。大口,腹壁斜行收缩。

A10b(图二〇;图版贰贰,3) 共 3 件。器形与前式近似,唯腹壁曲向往里收缩。

A10c(图二〇;图版贰贰,4) 仅 1 件。大口,鼓腹,向下折成棱角往里收缩。

A10d(图二〇;图版拾捌,6;图版贰贰,5;图版贰叁,1-3) 共 30 件。器形与前式近似,唯腹壁成弧形收缩。

A10e(图二一;图版贰叁,4、5) 共 11 件。器形与 A10c 式近似,唯腹壁下折处棱角不显著。

A10f(图二一;图版贰肆,1-4) 共 17 件。器形与前式近似,唯腹部微向外鼓。

A10g(图二一;图版贰肆,5、6;图版贰伍,1-5;图版贰陆,1、2;图版贰柒,1) 共 15 件。器形与前式近似,唯腹部较鼓。

A10h(图二一;图版贰柒,2) 仅 1 件。腹部显著鼓出。

A10j(图二一;图版贰柒,3) 共 2 件。器形与前式近似,唯腹部较深。

(11)椭圆盆 椭圆形,直壁或斜壁,平底。皆为素面。可分两式:

A11a(图二一;图版贰柒,4) 仅 1 件。平沿,直壁。

A11b(图二一;图版贰柒,5) 仅 1 件。口沿外折,腹壁向下略往外扩张成大平底。

（12）筒状盆 筒状，深腹，平底。皆为素面。可分四式：

A12a（图二二；图版贰捌，1） 共 2 件。大口，腹壁斜行收缩。

A12b（图二二；图版贰捌，2） 仅 1 件。厚唇，近直壁。

A12c（图二二；图版贰捌，3） 仅 1 件。口沿外卷，近直壁。

A12d（图二二；图版贰捌，4） 仅 1 件。唇微外侈，腹部微鼓。

（13）甑 盆形，素面或腹部饰有篮纹。可分四式：

A13a（图二三；图版贰捌，5a、b） 仅 1 件。大口，腹壁斜行向下往里收缩成平底。底穿四孔，椭圆形，相对称。

A13b（图二三；图版贰玖，1a、b） 仅 1 件。大口卷沿，腹壁向下往里收缩成平底。底穿四孔，椭圆形，相对称。

A13c（图二三；图版贰玖，2a、b） 仅 1 件。器形与 A13a 式近似，唯口沿外卷，底穿七孔。

A13d（图二三；图版叁拾，1a、b） 仅 1 件。器形与 A13b 式近似，唯底部穿八孔，圆形。

（14）杯 大口，直壁或斜壁，平底。可分两式：

A14a（图二二；图版叁拾，2） 仅 1 件。浅腹，近底部有划纹数道。

A14b（图二二；图版叁拾，3） 共 2 件。深腹，口沿压成锯齿形，口部两旁各有一个耳，周腹线纹。

（15）盂（A15；图二二；图版叁拾，4） 仅 1 件。敛口，凸腹，平底。器内壁两旁各有一个横置的短耳。

（16）敛口罐 敛口，鼓腹，向下往里收缩成平底。除素面和彩绘两种外，有的在腹部还饰有划纹及附加堆纹。可分三式：

A16a（图二二；图版叁拾，5） 仅 1 件。口沿外卷。

A16b（图二二；图版叁壹，1） 仅 1 件。唇微外侈。

A16c（图二四；图版叁壹，2、3） 共 2 件。器形与前式近似，唯短颈，唇不向外侈。

（17）长颈罐 长颈，凸腹，向下往里收缩成平底。有素面和彩绘两种，其中有的彩绘与划纹并用。可分三式：

A17a（图二四；图版叁壹，4） 仅 1 件。侈口，外加深红色陶衣，磨光发亮。

A17b（图二四；图版叁贰，1） 仅 1 件。器形与前式近似，唯颈部更长。

A17c（图二四；图版叁贰，2） 仅 1 件。口略向外侈，腹部成弧形凸出。

（18）瓶 有尖底和平底两种。皆小口。带耳者较少。纹饰多半是先在腹部拍印篮纹，然后通身再压印线纹，有的在近底部将纹饰抹平，单独压印篮纹或线纹者较少。除经复原为完整的器形外，尚有葫芦形、短颈重唇、长颈卷沿等口部残片（图版叁贰，3－6）。但不知属于何种器形。内长颈卷沿一种系彩绘，有的还加有白色陶衣。此外，在一件残底部

的内外壁尚发现有红色染料的粉末(图版叁贰,7),可能是赤铁矿磨成的。可分两式:

A18a(图二四;图版叁贰,8、9)　共5件。尖底。

A18b(图二四;图版叁叁,1、2)　共5件。平底。

(19)器盖　多为破片,能复原者极少,有的仅残存纽部。可分四式:

A19a(图二四;图版叁叁,3)　仅1件。盖背隆起如球面,口沿外卷,竖纽,上宽下窄。

A19b(图二四;图版叁叁,4)　仅1件。残存纽部,圜顶,长颈,颈部穿四孔,圆形,相对称,顶边有整齐的压印纹。

A19c(图二四;图版叁叁,5)　仅1件。残存纽部,尖顶,下端断口有磨痕,可能此纽断后复经加磨作为别的用途,顶部印有线纹。

A19d(图二五;图版叁叁,6)　仅1件。大口,上端收缩成小孔,两旁各有一段附加堆纹。此件器盖若将其倒置过来,即成为漏斗,可能兼作两用。

(20)器座　可能用来放置圜底器物。可分三式:

A20a(图二五;图版叁叁,7)　仅1件。口部两端皆平沿,腰部微束。

A20b(图二五;图版叁肆,1)　仅1件。侈口,束腰,口部一端较小,另一端略大。

A20c(图二五;图版叁肆,2)　共2件。敛口,腹壁向下往外张,无底。腹部饰有线纹,穿四孔,椭圆形,斜行,相对称。

B. 泥质灰陶系　陶土未经精细淘洗,未加羼和料,外表多为素面磨光,加纹饰者甚少;有篮纹、划纹、附加堆纹、镂孔等几种。附加堆纹皆见于盆腹的两旁,除装饰外还兼作器耳,划纹见于长颈罐的颈部,篮纹见于敞口碗,镂孔见于器盖的纽上。色泽有灰色和灰褐色两种。器形有盘、碗、罐、器盖、器座等。

(1)盘(B1;图二五;图版叁肆,3)　仅1件。大口,浅腹,平底。

(2)敞口碗(B2;图二五;图版叁肆,4)　仅1件。敞口,腹壁斜行向下往里收缩成平底。

(3)曲腹豌　大口,腹壁曲向往里收缩成平底。可分两式:

B3a(图二五;图版叁肆,5)　共6件,腹壁曲度不显著。

B3b(图二五;图版叁肆,6)　仅1件。腹壁成反弧形收缩。

(4)浅腹盆　大口折沿,腹壁向下往里收缩成平底。可分三式:

B4a(图二五;图版叁肆,7)　共14件。腹壁略成弧形收缩。

B4b(图二五;图版叁伍,1)　仅1件。腹壁折向往里收缩。

B4c(图二六;图版叁伍,2)　仅1件。器形与前式近似,唯腹部较深。

(5)敛口盆　敛口,腹壁斜行向下往里收缩成平底。可分四式:

B5a(图二六;图版叁伍,3)　共2件。口部成弧形往里收敛。

B5b(图二六;图版叁伍,4)　仅1件。口部略往里收敛。

B5c(图二六;图版叁伍,5) 共6件。口部折成棱角往里收敛,腹部两旁各有一段附加堆纹。

B5d(图二六;图版叁陆,1) 共2件。器形与前式近似,唯器体特大,高49、口径70、底径25、厚1.2厘米。

(6)敛口罐 敛口,鼓腹,平底。可分三式:

B6a(图二七;图版叁陆,2) 仅1件。口沿不向外卷。

B6b(图二七;图版叁陆,3) 仅1件。器形与前式近似,唯口沿略向外卷,腹部更鼓。

B6c(图二七;图版叁陆,4) 仅1件。器形与B6a式近似,唯口沿略向外卷。

(7)长颈罐(B7;图二八;图版叁柒,1) 仅发现残口片1件。器形与A17c式近似,颈部有划纹。

(8)器盖 多为残缺的纽部,能复原者甚少。可分四式:

B8a(图二八;图版叁柒,2) 共4件。残存纽部,圜顶,短颈,顶边有整齐的压印纹一周。

B8b(图二八;图版叁柒,3) 共2件。残存纽部,圜顶,长颈。

B8c(图二八;图版叁柒,4) 共5件。残存纽部,顶如圆锥状,上有整齐的镂孔,下端有压印纹一周。

B8d(图二八;图版叁柒,5) 共5件。盖作覆碗形,纽顶透空,纽盖相接处有显著的接合痕迹。

(9)器座(B9;图二八;图版叁柒,6) 共3件。圆形束腰,如两个半圆锥对合状,口部上端较小,下端略大。

C. 细泥黑陶系 在仰韶文化中发现较少。表里黑色,胎呈灰色或红褐色。器形经复原者仅有圜底罐一种。另外还发现一件残口片,上有浮雕壁虎一只,生动逼真,唯前半身已残(图版叁捌,1)。

(1)圜底罐(C1;图二八;图版叁柒,7) 仅1件。直口,圆肩,鼓腹,圜底。

D. 夹砂粗红陶系 陶质粗糙,含有大量细砂。纹饰以线纹为主,皆斜行,多见于罐、釜;素面者次之,多属盆类;划纹、弦纹、附加堆纹所占的比例较少,其中划纹、附加堆纹常与线纹相配合,弦纹仅见于个别的罐、鼎和釜上。在夹砂粗红陶中还发现有一件外加深红色陶衣的圜底罐,实为过去所罕见的标本。此外,也发现有两片浮雕壁虎的残口片;一只较完整,一只尾部已残(图版叁捌,2,3)。器形有杯、盘、碗、盆、罐、盂、鼎、釜、灶、器盖等。

(1)圜底罐(D1;图二八;图版叁柒,8) 仅1件。口部已残,深腹,圜底。外加深红色陶衣。打磨甚光滑。

(2)釜 小口,平肩或斜肩,圜底。可分四式:

D2a(图二八;图版叁柒,9) 仅1件。斜肩,鼓腹。

D2b(图二八;图版叁玖,1) 仅1件。斜肩,原为圜底,陶坯制成后复经压成小平底。

D2c(图二八;图版叁玖,2) 共4件。肩部斜度较前式小。

D2d(图二九;图版叁玖,3) 仅1件。平肩。

(3)鼎(D3;图二九;图版叁玖,4) 仅1件。系遗址附近采集,由D2c式釜附加三个扁足而成,足下端已残。

(4)灶(D4;图二九;图版叁玖,5、6) 仅1件。器身如匜形,前有火门,下有三个矮足,另外在器内壁近口沿处尚有三个凸瘤。陶釜可置于上面使用。

(5)盘(D5;图二九;图版叁玖,7) 仅1件。大口,浅腹直壁,平底。

(6)敞口碗 敞口,腹壁斜行向下往里收缩成平底。可分四式:

D6a(图二九;图版肆拾,1) 仅1件。浅腹。

D6b(图二九;图版肆拾,2) 共2件。器形与前式近似,唯腹部较深。

D6c(图二九;图版肆拾,3) 共4件。腹壁略往里收缩,底部较大,约占口径的五分之三。

D6d(图二九;图版肆拾,4) 共2件。口微敛,腹壁收缩较甚,底部仅有口径的二分之一左右。

(7)浅腹盆 大口,浅腹,平底。可分三式:

D7a(图二九;图版肆拾,5) 共2件。口沿外折,腹壁斜行向下往里收缩。

D7b(图二九;图版肆拾,6) 仅1件。器形与前式近似,唯腹壁的收缩程度较小。

D7c(图二九;图版肆拾,7) 仅1件。口沿外卷,腹壁略成弧形收缩。

(8)深腹盆 大口,深腹,平底。可分两式:

D8a(图三〇;图版肆拾,8) 仅1件。腹壁斜行向下往里收缩。

D8b(图三〇;图版肆壹,1) 共2件。器形与前式近似,唯腹部微鼓。

(9)杯 皆为小杯,绝大多数饰有线纹,素面者甚少,出土数量较其他复原的陶器都多,其中有的还是完整的。可分四式:

D9a(图三〇;图版肆壹,2) 仅1件。大口,腹壁斜行向下往里收缩成平底。

D9b(图三〇;图版肆壹,3、4) 共124件。侈口,腹壁向下略往里收缩成平底,近底部有圆形或椭圆形的小凹窝一周。

D9c(图三〇;图版肆壹,5、6) 共2件。侈口,直壁,平底。有的在近底部带椭圆形深凹窝一周。

D9d(图三〇;图版肆壹,7) 共4件。筒形,深腹,平底。

(10)盂 敛口,鼓腹,平底。可分两式:

D10a(图三〇;图版肆壹,8) 仅1件。腹部微鼓。

D10b(图三〇;图版肆壹,9) 仅1件。器形与前式近似,唯腹部更鼓,器内壁两旁各有一个横置的短耳。

(11)敛口罐 敛口,鼓腹,平底。可分十式:

D11a(图三〇;图版肆贰,1) 仅1件。口微收敛,腹壁向下略往里收缩。

D11b(图三〇;图版肆贰,2) 共4件。器形与前式近似,唯腹壁收缩较甚。

D11c(图三〇;图版肆贰,3) 共5件。腹部略向外鼓,然后作反弧形向里收缩。

D11d(图三一;图版肆贰,4) 仅1件。口部较敛,腹部显著鼓出。

D11e(图三一;图版肆贰,5) 仅1件。器形与前式近似,唯口沿不向外侈。

D11f(图三一:图版肆贰,6) 仅1件。腹部凸出折成棱角向下往里收缩。

D11g(图三一;图版肆叁,1) 仅1件。口略内敛,腹壁斜行向下往里收缩。

D11h(图三一;图版肆叁,2、3) 共5件。腹部微鼓,向下略往里收缩。

D11j(图三一;图版肆叁,4;图版肆肆,1、2) 共4件。器形与前式近似,唯腹部较鼓。

D11k(图三二;图版肆肆,3) 仅1件。器形与前式近似,唯口部两旁各有一附加堆纹的耳,腹部也较深。

(12)小口镂孔罐(D12;图三二;图版肆肆,4) 共3件。口小底大,如圆形袋状灰坑。近底部穿三孔,腹部印有篮纹,用途不详。

(13)器盖 绝大多数系小陶杯盖,大器盖仅占极少数。可分四式:

D13a(图三二:图版肆伍,1) 共2件。盖背隆起如球面,上有一环状纽。

D13b(图三二;图版肆伍,2) 仅1件。器形与前式近似,唯盖背较高。

D13c(图三二;图版肆伍,3) 共114件。短纽,系小陶杯盖,可置于D9a-d式小陶杯上使用。

D13d(图三二;图版肆伍,4) 共2件。长纽。用途与前式同。

2. 工具

(1)刀 绝大多数系由陶片改制,仅个别直接用陶土制成。陶质以细泥红陶为最多,泥质灰陶较少见。形制基本上有两侧带缺口和穿孔两种。缺口多在两侧的中部,也有少数在上部的。孔多由两面对穿,也有少数直穿或由两面挖成的,皆单孔。绝大多数都位于近背部的中间,仅有个别位于中央的。刃部多由两面磨成,单面者较少见,少数陶刀的刃部也有打制未磨的。此外,还有个别两侧不带缺口亦不穿孔的,也有穿孔未透又在两侧打成缺口的陶刀。前一种可能尚未完全制好,后一种当为原想用穿孔而后来放弃又改为在两侧打成缺口。可分四式:

1A(图版肆伍,5-8) 共28件。两侧带缺口,形状不一,有长方形、梯形、反梯形、带肩形等几种。

1B(图版肆伍,9、10) 共7件。无缺口及穿孔,有椭圆形与长方形两种。

1C(图版肆伍,11-14) 共52件。长方形,穿孔。T237:15一件系直接用陶土制成,孔直穿。

1D(图版肆陆,1、2) 共 13 件。圆背,穿孔。

(2)锛 由陶片改制,单面刃,穿孔。可分两式:

2A(图版肆陆,3) 仅 1 件。长方形。

2B(图版肆陆,4) 仅 1 件。梯形。

(3)瓶 形制互有不同,可分三式:

3A(图版肆陆,5) 仅 1 件。两端皆残,仅存中部,作长条形。由细泥红陶制成,表面附有细密的刺孔。

3B(图版肆陆,6-8) 共 8 件。实心球形,皆残存一半。由细泥红陶制成,表面划有方格纹或指甲纹,也有作圆点凹纹的。

3C(图三三,1;图版肆陆,9) 仅 1 件。空心球形,仅残存一半。由泥质灰陶制成,陶质较硬,表面有圆点凹纹。

以上各器的共同特点都是糙面,3A 式常见于陕西境内的仰韶文化遗址中,曾被推测为搓洗手用具,也可作为刮治皮革的用具[9]。3B、C 两式可能也具有同样的用途,过去曾被推测为玩具,但在仰韶文化遗址中较为常见,当是一种日常用具,玩具的说法是难以解释的。

(4)纺轮 有两种:一种系由陶片改制;另一种则直接用陶土制成。可分三式:

4A(图三三,2;图版肆陆,10、11) 共 68 件。由陶片改制,孔系两面对穿。

4B(图三三,3;图版肆陆,12、13) 共 15 件。由细泥红陶制成,孔直穿,边沿平整。

4C(图三三,4、5;图版肆陆,14、15) 共 2 件。由细泥红陶制成,作截尖圆锥形,但不甚整齐,孔直穿。素面或上下边沿有压印纹。

(5)弹丸(图版肆陆,16) 共 9 件。球形,制造较粗糙。

3. 装饰品 仅陶环一种。

(1)环 以灰陶占最大多数,红陶较少见,陶质都很细腻。器形完整者不多,有圆形、五角形、六角形、七角形、齿轮形等几种。剖面多呈圆形或椭圆形,也有少数呈三角形、半月形、长方形的。纹饰除素面磨光者外,有划纹、斜行方格纹、辫形纹以及乳丁纹等几种(图三四)。其中以素面与划纹占最大多数,余者皆不多见。此外,还有个别用红黑两种颜色彩绘的。可分七式:

1A(图三五,1-7;图版肆陆,17、18) 共 33 件。圆形,有素面、划纹、斜行方格纹、辫形纹等四种。

1B(图三五,8;图版肆陆,19;图版肆柒,5、7) 仅 1 件。圆形,周壁乳丁纹。

1C(图三五,9;图版肆陆,20) 共 2 件。五角形,仅有素面一种。

1D(图三五,10、11;图版肆陆,21、22) 共 9 件。六角形,有素面和划纹两种。

1E(图三五,12;图版肆柒,1) 共 6 件。七角形,仅有划纹一种。

1F(图三五,13、14;图版肆柒,2、3) 共 8 件。齿轮形,完整者未见,仅有素面一种。

1G(图三五,15;图版肆柒,4) 仅 1 件。残存一段,边上中间有一尖锥状的凸起物,两旁各有用泥条圈成的装饰。

4. 其他

(1)鸟头(图版肆柒,6) 仅 1 件。由细泥红陶制成。两眼甚大,上嘴尖已残,颈部有弦纹。

(2)钟(图三六,1;图版肆柒,8) 仅 1 件。由细泥红陶制成。器壁向下往外张,中空,上部有柄,肩部两旁各有一小孔通向壁内。素面,外表磨光。

(3)坠形器(图三六,2;图版肆柒,9) 仅 1 件。如圆柱状,两端皆圆头,一端穿有小孔,中部周壁向外凸出两旁亦各穿有一小孔,对称,不相通,用途不详。

(二)石器

1. 工具 制法有打制和磨制两种。质料系采用燧石、砂岩、板岩、石英岩、闪长岩、辉绿岩、玄武岩、片麻岩等几种。现按类分述如下:

(1)盘状器 圆形或椭圆形,多利用天然砾石加以打制,有的一面还保留着原来的岩面,也有个别利用石铲的残片加以改制而成。出土甚多,据不完全统计,共有 2230 多个。就灰坑的情况说,少者仅 1 个,多者竟达到 74 个。从出土的数量看,当为日常主要工具之一,但用途不详,可能是作为敲砸器用,有锋刃者可兼作刮削器用。按制法的不同,可分四式:

1A(图三七,1;图版肆柒,10、11) 共 1496 件。由一面垂直打下,边沿较平整而无锋刃。H363:05 一件系利用石铲残片改制,边沿一部分还保留着原来石铲的刃部。也有一件两面中央各有一个圆形凹坑,可能是准备改制石锤,钻孔未透而中止(图三七,5;图版肆柒,16)。

1B(图三七,2;图版肆柒,12) 共 559 件。边沿由一面斜行打成锋刃。

1C(图三七,3;图版肆柒,13、14) 共 183 件。边沿由两面交互打成锋刃。T344:78 一件系利用石铲残片改制,已残,一面中间有琢打痕迹。

1D(图三七,4;图版肆柒,15) 仅 1 件。利用石片由一面斜打成锐利的锋刃,部分仍保留着凸起的岩面,与以上各式用扁平砾石打成者不同。

(2)网坠 形状不一。可分两式:

2A(图版肆柒,17、18) 共 4 件。椭圆形,两侧带缺口。

2B(图版肆柒,19) 仅 1 件。长条形,中部有凹槽一周。

(3)刀 有打制及磨制两种,前者比较粗糙,后者多钻有单孔,仅有个别的标本是双孔的,也有少数先在两面划成一道长槽,然后再行穿孔,可分八式:

3A(图版肆捌,1-3) 共 23 件。两侧带缺口,一面保留原来的岩面,缺口多在两侧的中部,也有个别靠近刃部的。

3B(图版肆捌,4) 共 6 件。长方形,两侧无缺口。

3C(图三八,7;图版肆玖,9-11) 共 53 件。长方形,平刃或略成弧刃。

3D(图三八,8;图版肆玖,12)　共 3 件。长方形,凹刃。

3E(图版肆玖,13)　共 4 件。近椭圆形,平背,弧刃。

3F(图版肆玖,14)　仅 1 件。残存中部,穿双孔。

3G(图版肆玖,15、16)　共 8 件。弧背,平刃。

3H(图三八,9;图版肆玖,17、18)　共 2 件。系利用长方形石刀的残片改制而成,刃在短边。

(4)小石片　(图三七,12;图版肆捌,5)　共 2 件。由燧石上打下的略呈长三角形石片。打击点、半锥体以及疤痕都比较清楚,但缺少第二步加工的痕迹。两侧锋刃锐利,可能打下石片后即行使用,因而在两侧的锋刃上有明显的使用痕迹。

(5)锤　圆形,在中央由两面钻孔。可分四式:

5A(图三八,10;图版伍壹,1、2)　共 5 件。利用天然砾石钻孔而成,皆残缺一半。

5B(图三八,11;图版伍壹,3)　共 2 件。残存一段,器形与前式近似,唯孔径较大。

5C(图三八,12;图版伍壹,4)　共 5 件。皆残缺一小段,系利用石铲残片改制,边沿自两面交互打成锋刃。

5D(图三八,13;图版伍壹,5)　共 5 件。皆残存一半,磨光甚精细。

(6)斧　两面刃。制法系先将石料打成一定的形状(图版肆捌,6),然后再行磨光。仅有个别的穿孔。在磨制石斧中,有几件是利用天然的扁平小砾石磨成的。可分七式:

6A(图三七,6;图版肆捌,7)　共 4 件。长方形,平刃,横剖面略呈长方形。

6B(图三七,7;图版肆捌,8、9)　共 7 件。梯形,宽刃,横剖面略呈方形。

6C(图三七,8;图版肆捌,10)　共 4 件。皆残存下半段,窄刃,横剖面略呈椭圆形。

6D(图三七,9;图版肆捌,11)　仅 1 件。近长方形,孔未透,两面形成圆凹窝,横剖面呈椭圆形。

6E(图三七,10;图版肆捌,12)　仅 1 件。略呈长方形,刃部缺一大角,单孔,两面对穿,横剖面呈菱形。

6F(图三七,11;图版肆捌,13 - 15)　共 8 件。由天然砾石磨制,形状不一,椭圆形或近椭圆形。其中 H10∶13 一件顶部甚厚,纵剖面呈三角形,余者皆扁平。

6G(图版肆捌,16、17)　共 2 件。扁平小斧,单孔或双孔。T335∶01 一件孔未穿透。

(7)锛　单面刃。可分四式

7A(图三七,13;图版肆玖,1)　仅 1 件。长方形,平刃,横剖面呈长方形。

7B(图三七,14;图版肆玖,2)　共 2 件。近椭圆形,弧刃,横剖面呈椭圆形。

7C(图三八,1;图版肆玖,3) 仅1件。残存下半段,梯形,宽刃,横剖面呈长方形。

7D(图三八,2;图版肆玖,4) 仅1件。顶部窄小,平刃,仅在一面略为磨光。

(8)凿 可分三式:

8A(图三八,3;图版肆玖,5) 仅1件。长方形,单面刃,横剖面呈梯形。

8B(图三八,4;图版肆玖,6) 共2件。长方形,单面刃,横剖面呈长方形。

8C(图三八,5、6;图版肆玖,7、8) 共4件。近长方形,单面刃或两面刃,横剖面呈椭圆形。

(9)铲 完整者极少,多为残片。据不完全统计,灰坑与探方内共出有大小残片约130多件。从完整或已复原的器形看,小者长13.4厘米,大者长在29厘米以上。有的在近背部的中间,一面尚有琢打的痕迹,似为用来装柄的,至于如9c式铲身上部两侧,略加打制,可能是为了缚绳使木柄更加牢固。此外,还发现一件打制的残石铲,相当粗厚,当为一种未成品(图版伍拾,1),也说明了石铲的制法,系先将石料打成一定的形状,然后再进行磨光。可分四式:

9A(图三九,1;图版伍拾,2) 仅1件。平背,锋刃由两侧向前聚成尖形,背上已残缺一角。

9B(图三九,2;图版伍拾,3) 仅1件。器形与前式近似,唯器身较圆,一面近背部的中间有琢打痕迹。

9C(图三九,3;图版伍拾,4) 仅1件。近椭圆形,凹背,铲身较宽,两侧向前磨成圆刃,在铲身上部的两侧,微行打成缺口。

9D(图三九,4;图版伍拾,5、6) 仅1件。上部已残,圆刃,原来器身相当长(残长29厘米),根据其他残片观察,顶部当作弧形。

(10)纺轮(图三八,14;图版伍壹,6、7) 共15件。圆形,中间穿孔,皆由两面对穿,边沿多作弧形,个别也有平直的。

(11)球(图版伍壹,8、9) 共45件。大小不一,皆磨光。大者直径5.5厘米,小者仅3厘米,后一种可能兼作弹丸使用。

(12)磨杵 与磨盘同系研磨赤铁矿粉末的用具,无论杵面及盘面上均遗有赤铁矿的红色痕迹。可分两式:

12A(图版伍壹,10-12) 共3件。利用天然砾石作为磨杵,方柱形的两件(0:07,H329:10),磨面呈弧形凸起。另外一件(H304:05)略呈椭圆形,两面均已磨平。凡研磨面都光滑润整,附有红色痕迹。

12B(图版伍壹,13、14) 共2件。作束腰葫芦形,底端为研磨面,也附有红色痕迹。

(13)磨盘(图版伍壹,15;图版伍贰,1、2) 共3件。利用大块的天然扁平砾石制成,形状不一,表面磨平或凹入,都附有红色的痕迹。

2. 装饰品

(1)环(图版伍贰,3、4) 共2件。已残,皆磨制,剖面呈长方形或椭圆形。

(2)珠(图三八,15;图版伍贰,5) 仅1件。水晶制,形如算珠,孔由两面对穿。

(3)坠 质料除T234∶05一件系流纹岩外,其余皆为绿松石制成,均有穿孔。可分三式:

3A(图版伍贰,6-8) 共3件。椭圆形,剖面呈三角形或椭圆形,也有扁平的。

3B(图版伍贰,9、10) 共2件。长条形,扁平。

3C(图版伍贰,11) 仅1件。系利用绿松石的天然形状略为加工而成。

(三)骨、角、蚌、牙器

1. 骨器

(1)针 可分两式:

1A(图四〇,1;图版伍贰,12、13) 共5件。粗短。T235∶11一件针孔距顶端较远。

1B(图四〇,2;图版伍贰,14、15) 共12件。细长。

(2)锥 可分三式:

2A(图四〇,3、4;图版伍贰,16、17) 共4件。骨片锥,系利用骨片磨成锐尖。

2B(图四〇,5;图版伍贰,18) 共2件。利用猪的前肢骨劈去一半而磨成尖状,关节部分仍保持原状。

2C(图四〇,6;图版伍贰,19) 共3件。利用狗的腓骨,将其细端磨成尖状,其余部分未经加工。

(3)镞 镞身与铤部无明显的界限,绝大多数两端皆收缩成尖形,唯程度各有不同。可分六式:

3A(图四〇,9;图版伍叁,1) 共7件。扁平。

3B(图四〇,10、11;图版伍叁,2、3) 共27件。剖面呈三角形。

3C(图四〇,12、13;图版伍叁,4、5) 共15件。剖面呈半圆形。

3D(图四〇,14、15;图版伍叁,6、7) 共3件。剖面呈菱形。

3E(图四〇,16;图版伍叁,8) 共8件。剖面呈圆形。

3F(图四〇,17;图饭伍叁,9、10) 共11件。器形与前式近似,唯剖面呈椭圆形。

(4)尖状器(图四〇,7;图版伍叁,11) 仅1件。圆锥形,上部中空一段,或可附在柄上,用途不详。

(5)凿(图四〇,8;图版伍叁,12) 仅1件。长条形,扁平,上端由一面磨成刃,下端自一边磨成尖形。

(6)笄 是一种束发的用具,可分六式:

6A(图四〇,18;图版伍肆,1、2) 共8件。两端皆磨成尖形,剖面呈圆形。

6B(图四〇,19;图版伍肆,3) 共3件。平顶,下端磨成尖形,剖面呈圆形。

6C(图四〇,20;图版伍肆,4)　共 15 件。器形与 6A 式近似,唯剖面呈椭圆形。

6D(图四〇,21;图版伍肆,5)　共 23 件。器形与前式近似,唯器身扁平。

6E(图四〇,22;图版伍肆,6)　共 7 件。顶部略为收缩,下端磨成尖形,扁平。

6F(图四〇,23;图版伍肆,7、8)　共 5 件。平顶,下端磨成尖形,扁平。

(7)弧形饰　可分两式:

7A(图四〇,24、25;图版伍伍,1、2)　共 6 件。略成弧形。皆残缺,一端穿孔。
T203:13 一件弧起的一面有两道浅凹槽。

7B(图四〇,28;图版伍伍,3)　共 4 件。半圆形,两端各穿一孔。

(8)牙形饰(图四〇,26、27;图版伍伍,4、5)　共 4 件。顶端穿孔。T204 A:01 一件孔未穿透,两侧有小缺口。

2. 角器

(1)锥　可分两式:

1A(图四一,1;图版伍伍,6、7)　共 4 件。利用鹿角劈成一半而成,角面有明显的使用痕迹。

1B(图四一,2;图版伍伍,8)　共 2 件。利用鹿角的顶部截下一段而成,上有使用痕迹。

(2)凿(图四一,3;图版伍伍,9)　共 3 件。长条形,系利用鹿角切成一片磨制,刃部光滑并有使用痕迹。

(3)槌(图四一,4;图版伍伍,10)　仅 1 件。利用鹿角的分叉截成 T 形,中央穿方孔,每端皆行挖空,可能利用它来嵌入石器,而角槌作柄便于把握。

3. 蚌器

(1)笄(?)(图版伍伍,11)　仅 1 件。近菱形,一端折断,形如蚌镞,但边沿皆无锋刃,可能是笄的头部。

(2)指环(图版伍伍,12)　仅 1 件。圆形,出土(仰韶灰坑 49 内)时套在一具人骨架的左手的无名指上。

(3)坠　长条形,可分两式:

3A(图版伍伍,13)　仅 1 件。一端穿孔。

3B(图版伍伍,14)　共 2 件。两端各穿一孔。

(4)穿孔蚌壳　可分两式:

4A(图版伍伍,15、16)　共 2 件。单扇,利用淡水产的珠蚌壳在尾部磨孔而成,可能作为装饰用品。

4B(图版伍伍,18)　仅 1 件。单扇,利用蛤壳在尾部磨孔而成,用途与前式同。

4. 牙器　仅有牙饰一种。

穿孔牙饰(图版伍伍,17)　仅 1 件。利用猪的犬齿切成一半磨成,顶端穿孔,已残。

（四）自然遗物

有赤铁矿、家畜骨骼、鹿角、蚌壳等。

1. 赤铁矿　仅发现一小块，根据磨杵、磨盘以及一件小口瓶底部所遗留的痕迹看来，赤铁矿的粉末可能用之于装饰，因为彩陶中很少采用红色的颜料，可能不是做彩绘用的。

2. 家畜骨骼　多出自灰坑中，总的数量不多，都破碎不堪，难于统计。可识别者有猪、狗两种，以猪骨最多，狗骨次之，此外也见到羚羊角可能是猎获来的，当不是家畜。和龙山文化层相比较，不仅数量少，种类也少，可证明仰韶文化的家畜还具有若干原始性。

3. 鹿角　有少量破碎的鹿角及零星的鹿骨，可能是当时猎获品。

4. 厚壳蚌　仅有少量破碎的残片，从仰韶文化层中仅见蚌制的坠、笄、指环等，可见其尚未用之制造工具。

四　龙山文化遗物

（一）陶器

龙山文化遗物中，以陶片为最多，有少部分可以复原。现在按器物用途的不同，分为容器和非容器两类，叙述如下：

1. 容器

陶容器质料可分为夹砂粗灰陶、泥质灰陶、细泥红陶、细泥黑陶等四种陶系。其中以夹砂粗灰陶占绝大多数，泥质灰陶次之，细泥红陶又次之，细泥黑陶最少。纹饰有素面、篮纹、绳纹、划纹、弦纹、方格纹、附加堆纹和彩绘等。其中以篮纹为最多，素面、附加堆纹、绳纹等次之，弦纹方格纹和划纹最少。器形共复原60余件，计有碗、盆、杯、罐、瓶、灶、豆、鼎、斝等。

现在摘选三个灰坑（H551、H567、H568），把它们的陶系、纹饰、器形的总数和百分比列表如下，并加以说明。

龙山文化（灰坑551、567、568）陶系及纹饰统计表

陶系	夹砂粗灰陶						泥质灰陶					泥质红陶			细泥黑陶		总计
数量	2617						1208					81			35		3941
百分比	66.45						30.62					2.05			0.88		100%
纹饰	篮纹	素面	绳纹	附加堆纹	方格纹	划纹	篮纹	素面	绳纹	附加堆纹	划纹	素面	彩绘	方格纹	素面	弦纹	
数量	1779	502	120	125	55	36	404	620	65	78	41	34	36	11	30	5	3941
百分比	45.14	12.72	3.05	3.17	1.39	3.91	10.31	15.73	1.65	1.97	1.04	0.87	0.91	0.26	0.76	0.12	100%

龙山文化(灰坑 551、567、568)陶器器形统计表(以能看出器形者为限)

陶系	夹砂粗灰陶							泥质灰陶						泥质红陶		细泥黑陶			总计
器形	罐	盆	鼎	斝	灶	器耳	器盖	罐	盆	碗	杯	豆	器盖	盆	杯	罐	碗	器盖	
数量	496	12	32	10	3	19	3	198	16	3	2	3	35	5	9	6	1	1	854
百分比	58.08	1.41	3.74	1.16	0.35	2.23	0.35	23.18	1.89	0.35	0.23	0.35	4.08	0.59	1.05	0.7	0.12	0.12	100%

A. 夹砂粗灰陶系

陶土未经过淘洗,内羼入大量的细砂。制法全部是手制的,多采用泥条筑成法。平底的陶器是器壁与器底分别制成,然后由外面结合在一起,而用底部的边缘包在器壁上,痕迹非常明显,我们可以称之为“接底法”。表面压印篮纹或绳纹,主要是为了使陶质坚实。有的器形在压印纹饰以后,再在表面附加几条平行凹凸纹的带饰,除了加固器壁,兼有装饰的作用。篮纹多为不相连接的竖条或斜条,排列不甚整齐,显然是用木制的拍子印上去的。绳纹概为垂直平行,排列比较整齐。方格纹则作菱形凸起的方格纹,也可能是用木制拍子印上去的。盆形器的内部常有密集的竖行划纹,用途不详。陶质坚硬,表面作灰褐色,有的作黑灰色,有的作灰黄色或橙黄色。在同一陶器上颜色常不一致,而有深浅的变化,这是由于在烧窑过程中未能充分还原的缘故。这类陶质多用作炊器。器形可分为圜底罐、浅腹盆、深腹盆、大口罐、单耳罐、敛口罐、鼎、斝、灶、器盖等 10 种。兹依次分述如下:

(1)圜底罐(A1;图四二;图版伍陆,1) 仅发现一件,大口,唇外折,深腹圜底,似是置在陶灶土的炊器。

(2)双耳盆 腹壁较浅,两侧附加凹形或山字形的双耳。可分为三式:

A2a(图四二;图版伍陆,2) 仅发现一件。大口,作桶状,平底,腹部双耳已经脱落。

A2b(图四二,图版伍陆,3) 共 2 件。大口,直唇,腹壁向里斜行收缩成平底。

A2c(图四二;图版伍陆,4) 共 3 件。大口,腹部稍深作弧形,平底,器内壁满布竖行划纹。

(3)浅腹盆 大口外侈,浅腹,小平底如盘形,可分为两式:

A3a(图四二;图版伍陆,5) 仅 1 件,腹壁稍歪,不平整。

A3b(图四二;图版伍陆,6) 仅 1 件,底部微凹入。

(4)深腹盆 大口,唇外侈,深腹,平底,可分为三式:

A4a(图四二;图版伍柒,1) 仅 1 件,腹部较他式稍浅。

A4b(图四二;图版伍柒,2、4) 共 2 件,唇沿划成或捏成锯齿状。

A4c(图四三;图版伍柒;图版陆伍,3) 共 2 件。唇缘较宽,颈部微敛,腹壁作弧形。

(5)大口罐 器身作筒状,大口,颈部或微敛,直唇或外侈,深腹平底,腹壁上有平行

的带状附加堆纹,一般的器形较大,高 21.5－43 厘米。可分为两式:

A5a(图四三;图版伍柒,5;图版伍捌,1)　共 2 件,大口,直唇。

A5b(图四三;图版伍捌,2－4)　共 3 件,颈部微敛,唇外侈。个别标本的唇缘上压成不甚明显的锯齿纹。

(6)单耳罐(A6;图四三;图版伍玖,1;图版陆伍,5)　共 2 件。大口,唇外侈,颈部微敛,平底,器身作筒状,在颈与腹之间附有一耳。

(7)敛口罐　器形互有不同,一般都是小型的,可分为四式:

A7a(图四四;图版伍玖,2)　仅 1 件。作筒状,大口直唇,部分口缘向里收敛,直腹,平底,口缘下有对称的两孔。

A7b(图四四;图版伍玖,3)　仅 1 件。唇微外侈,腹壁外凸。

A7c(图四四;图版伍玖,4、5)　共 2 件。直唇,肩腹无显著的分界,腹部凸出。

A7d(图四四;图版伍玖,6)　仅 1 件。唇外侈,肩腹无显著的分界,最大宽度在肩部。

(8)鼎　都附有三个实心足。可分为二式:

A8a(图四四;图版伍玖,7、8;图版陆拾,1、2)　共 4 件。大口,直唇或微侈,鼓腹,圜底。

A8b(图四四;图版陆拾,3、4;图版陆壹,1)　共 3 件。大口,唇微外侈,平底。

除了以上可复原的 5 件外,还发现完整的或残缺的鼎足 7 件,其大小不等,形状不同(图版陆壹,2－6)。

(9)鬶　敛口,唇外侈,圜底,附三个圆锥形袋足。可分为两式:

A9a(图四五;图版陆贰,1、2)　共 2 件。唇沿上有一道折棱。

A9b(图四五;图版陆贰,3、4)　仅 2 件,唇外侈较显著,唇沿上有一道凹棱,腹部扁而向外凸出。

(10)灶(A10;图四五;图版陆叁,1、2)　共 2 件。灶身呈圆筒状,近底部有一灶门,接近口缘有 4 个相对称的灶眼,成椭圆形或圆形,当是出烟和通风地方。

(11)器盖(A11;图四五;图版陆叁,3、4)　共 2 件。均残缺,仅存筒状的纽部,犹可看出器身向外扩张的趋势,足见原器甚大。其中的一件纽身镂孔,纽顶划有十字划纹,边缘压成锯齿形(图版陆叁,3)。

B. 泥质灰陶系

陶土似未经过精细淘洗,间或含有较粗的砂粒。制法也全部是手制的,器壁与器底分别制成,然后接合在一起,痕迹很明显。口缘大多数经过慢轮修整,但不见轮制的痕迹。表面平整,少数表面磨光。陶质坚硬,多作灰褐色或黑灰色,有的同一个器物而颜色不一致。器形有碗、浅腹盆、浅腹折缘盆、深腹盆、杯、单耳罐、小口罐、尖底瓶、豆、器盖等十种。

(1)碗　大口,外侈,浅腹收缩成小底。可分为三式。

B1a(图四六;图版陆肆,1、2) 共 3 件,底部稍微向外凸出,作假圈足的形状。

B1b(图四六;图版陆肆,3) 仅 1 件。腹部稍深。

B1c(图四六;图版陆肆,4) 共 2 件。皆残缺,器形与 B1a 相似,底部附有圈足。

(2)浅腹盆(B2;图四六;图版陆肆,5) 仅 1 件。大口,浅腹,器壁微向外侈。

(3)双耳盆 大口,浅腹,腹壁微向里收缩成平底,腹部两侧附双耳,可分三式:

B3a(图四六;图版陆肆,6) 仅 1 件。浅腹,盆内有密集的竖行划纹。

B3b(图四六;图版陆肆,7) 仅 1 件。腹部向底部收缩的斜度较大,腹上部附两个向下斜伸的半圆形扁耳。

B3c(图四六;图版陆肆,8) 仅 1 件。深腹,腹壁弧形收缩成小平底,并在腹部附一对扁耳。

(4)深腹盆 大口,唇外侈或外折,深腹,平底。可分为三式:

B4a(图四六;图版陆伍,1) 仅 1 件。唇微外侈,表面不平整。

B4b(图四六;图版陆伍,2) 仅 1 件。大口,唇外折,口缘下附一条带饰。

(5)杯(B5;图四六;图版陆伍,3) 都是残片,可以看出是属于筒状的杯。器壁较薄,一般都在 0.2—0.3 厘米左右,有的在表面还遗有绘朱的痕迹,但花纹已脱落不清晰。

(6)小口罐 小口,长颈,宽肩,深腹,平底或尖底,表面饰篮纹。据底部不同,可分为两式:

B6a(图四七;图版陆陆,1) 仅 1 件。肩腹交界处棱角显著,平底。

B6b(图四八;图版陆陆,3) 仅 1 件。根据采集部分陶片予以复原,器身较长,底部作钝尖状。

(7)小口圆肩罐 与 B6a 式相似,肩部作弧形无棱角,可分为两式:

B7a(图四七;图版陆伍,6) 仅 1 件。唇缘有不明显凹棱,颈稍短,腹部有附加堆纹一道。

B7b(图四七;图版陆陆,2) 仅 1 件。与 B7a 式相似,但颈稍长,肩部最宽处向下移,器身较细长。

(8)豆(B8;图四八;图版陆陆,4) 仅存细高的豆把部分,豆已残破,不能复原,有的豆柄上还有圆形镂孔。

(9)器盖 共 3 件。都残缺不全。据盖纽的形状不同,可分为三式:

B9a(图四八;图版陆陆,6) 纽作菇状,顶部略凹入。

B9b(图四八;图版陆陆,5) 纽作长条形,两端向上伸出。

B9c(图四八;图版陆陆,7) 纽作不整齐的圆柱形,顶部印有不甚清晰的绳纹。

C. 细泥红陶系

陶质细腻。都是手制的,表面经过精磨,有光泽。陶壁较薄,一般厚度为 0.4 厘米,最薄的达 0.15 厘米。表面作红褐色,除素面外,在陶杯上还涂有紫红色的陶衣,涂抹痕很清楚,在口缘的里面也涂抹一条。另外,也有彩绘,用黑色绘成带状菱形纹,还有拍印的方格纹。器形有杯、三耳盆、敛口深腹盆等三种:

(1)杯　发现的大多数是残陶片,完整的或可以复原的只有4件。根据其不同形状,可分为二式:

C1a(图四九;图版陆柒,1-3)　共3件。全体作喇叭状,大口,唇外侈,底微凹。表面涂抹紫红色的陶衣。在72和79号墓各出土1件,在71号探方的龙山层中也发现1件可以复原的,此外在龙山灰坑中有较多的碎片。

C1b(图四九:图版陆柒,4)　仅1件。身呈圆筒状,大口,平唇,直壁,平底,器壁较厚,表面没有陶衣。

(2)三耳盆(C2;图四九;图版陆柒,5)　仅1件。直口,表面作凸棱的方格纹,在腹部饰有凸耳三个。

(3)深腹盆(C3;图四九;图版陆柒,6)　仅1件。敛口,唇外折,肩腹无显著的分界,腹壁弧形向里收缩成小平底,表面磨光,在肩部绘有黑色菱形带状纹。

这种彩陶与A8a式陶鼎(0:11)在同一灰坑中采集,据其他共出的遗物证明确系龙山时期的遗存。1958年春在山西省平陆县盘南村遗址的龙山灰坑中也发现同样的彩陶盆3件,器形、花纹完全相同,可以互为佐证。

D. 细泥黑陶系

仅发现几件残片。陶土细腻,未加羼和料。手制,表面磨光。陶壁厚度一般为0.5厘米。陶质坚硬。表面作纯黑或漆黑色,有光泽,陶胎中心则为灰褐色。器形有盆、敛口罐、小口罐、圈足碗、器盖等五种:

(1)盆(D1;图四九;图版陆柒,7)　共3件残片。皆存口缘部分,从口缘残片的弧度上看其器形大抵都是大口浅腹盆,唇稍外卷,表面磨光,器壁较薄,约在0.3厘米左右。

(2)敛口罐(D2;图四九;图版陆捌,2)　仅残片1件。属于口沿部分,敛口,唇稍外卷,陶质坚硬,表面磨光发亮。

(3)小口罐(D3;图四九;图版陆捌,1)　仅残片1件。存口颈部和肩部,小口,唇稍外侈,长颈,颈肩间有一道凸棱。

(4)圈足碗(D4;图四九;图版陆捌,3)　仅残片1件,存器底和圈足部分。

(5)器盖(D5;图四九;图版陆捌,4)　共残片2件。仅残存纽部,圆纽中央凹入如圈足状。

2. 非容器

(1)陶刀　利用陶片加工而成,都已残缺,可分两式:

1A(图版陆捌,6)　共2件。长方形,在一长边上打制成刃部。

1B(图版陆捌,5)　在刀身有一个圆孔,由两面穿透,惟器形不详,系利用仰韶的细泥红陶片制成。

(2)陶垫(图五〇,1;图版陆捌,7)　仅1件。扁平长方形,横剖面作半圆形,中空。泥质灰陶,表面磨光。这是制陶工具,可插入木棒垫在陶器内部,然后再在外面拍印纹饰。

(3)纺轮(图五〇,2;图版陆捌,8、9)　共6件。周边作棱状凸出,中间有一圆孔,由两面穿透。皆泥质红陶制成。一般直径都在3.3厘米左右。

(4)弹丸(图版陆捌,10)　共2件,火候较低,陶质稍软。

(5)陶珠(图五〇,3;图版陆捌,11)　仅1件。泥质灰陶。球形,中央穿孔,表面涂红色。应是佩带用的装饰品。

(6)陶管(图五〇,4;图版陆捌;12)　仅1件。泥质黑陶,中腰凹入,如陶器的圈足状,当是佩带用的装饰品,其形很像后来的耳珰。

(7)柱状器(图五〇,5;图版陆捌,13)　仅1件。泥质灰陶。作截尖圆锥形状。用途不详。

(二)石器

龙山文化中的石器,主要是磨制的,打制者仅有石刀一种。石质有板岩、砂岩、辉绿岩和闪长岩等。就用途和器形而言,生产工具有斧、锛、刀、镰、磨盘、杵等,武器有镞、叶形石片、弹丸,装饰品有石璜和石环等。现在分述如下:

1. 工具和武器

(1)斧　都是长方形厚斧,横剖面作钝角的长方形。可分四式:

1A(图五一,1;图版陆捌,14)　共3件。斧身厚大,磨制稍粗,琢制的痕迹尚未完全磨去,刃部磨制较细致。

1B(图五一,2;图版陆捌,15)　共6件。斧身横剖面作椭圆形、长方形或钝角长方形,顶端和刃部宽度相等。

1C(图五一,3;图版陆捌,16)　仅1件。刃部较宽,顶部及刃部皆因砍击而崩裂。

1D(图五一,4;图版陆捌,17)　仅1件。与1C式相似,磨制细致,刃部对称与斧身有显著的分界。

(2)锛　一般的形状均较小,都作扁平的长方形,横剖面也作长方形,单面刃。可分四式。

2A(图五一,5;图版陆捌,18、19)　共3件。1件顶端残缺,磨制精致。

2B(图五一,6;图版陆捌,20;图版陆玖,1、2)　共3件。与2A式相似,但背部稍隆起,棱痕不甚清楚,有点像东南沿海的有段石锛。

2C(图五一,7;图版陆玖,3)　共2件。顶端稍窄,刃部较宽,可能利用仰韶文化的石铲改制而成的。

2D(图五一,8;图版陆玖,4)　仅1件。顶残缺,磨制精致,单孔,可能是用有孔石斧改制成单面刃的,故暂列入锛类。

(3)刀　从制法上看有打制和磨制两种。可分三式:

　　3A(图版陆玖,5-10)　共10件。利用由砾石上打下的石片,先修成矩形,再在两侧凿成缺口;也有不加修整,在椭圆形的石片上凿出缺口的。总的特点较仰韶文化的打制石刀在刃部及边缘上加工稍多。

　　3B(图五一,9;图版陆玖,11-15)　共18件。完整的只有2件,其余都是残缺不全的。呈钝角长方形,单孔,刃在长边的一端。穿孔法有下列三种:①由单面钻;②从两面对钻;③两面用凹沟划透,或再在沟中穿孔。在18件标本中,以两面对钻的占多数,共10件,两面用凹沟划透法次之,共5件,单面钻的最少,仅3件。

　　3C(图五一,10、11;图版陆玖,16、17)　共2件。已残缺,作半月形,直背锋刃外凸。

　　(4)镰(图版柒拾,1)　仅1件。已残缺,作长条形,在一长边有刃。

　　(5)磨盘(图版柒拾,2)　仅1件。磨盘扁平,两端残破,正面因研磨而成凹槽。从形状较大、研磨面平整来看,和仰韶文化研磨赤铁矿的磨盘不同。

　　(6)磨杵(图版柒拾,3)　仅1件。利用天然砾石制成,在研磨面上附有亦铁矿的痕迹,背面有供握手用的鼓起的凸柄。

　　(7)镞(图五一,12、13;图版柒拾,4、5)　共19件。完整的共11件,残缺的有8件。皆呈三角形的薄片,其大小相差不多,一般长度都在3厘米左右。

　　(8)叶状石片(图五一,14;图版柒拾,6)　仅1件。全体呈叶形,一侧微经加工,可能是石矛的未成品。

　　(9)弹丸(图版柒拾,10)　共3件。由天然砾石稍加磨制而成。

　2. 装饰品

　　(1)璜(图五一,15、16;图版柒拾,7、8)　共4件。璜身两端各穿孔一个,孔由两面穿透,大部分两端犹保存折断的残痕,可能是用碎石环改制的,磨制精致。

　　(2)环(图版柒拾,9)　共2件。皆为残片,环身扁平,磨制精致,表面光滑。

　(三)骨、角、蚌、牙器

　1. 骨器

　骨器的数量很多,有各种不同的形式和用途,如作为工具用的有针、锥、匕、镞状骨片。作为武器用的有镞,作为装饰品用的有笄、梳等。兹分别说明如下:

　　(1)针　可分四式:

　　　1A(图五二,1;图版柒拾,16-18)　共13件。其中完整的有8件,单孔,有由一面钻透的,也有由两面钻透的,孔呈圆形,顶端有圆形、尖锥、平顶等三种形式,磨制精致。

　　　1B(图五二,2;图版柒拾,21)　仅1件。与1A式相似,惟穿孔法不同,由两面划沟法挖成椭圆形孔。

　　　1C(图五二,3;图版柒拾,19)　仅1件。横剖面呈长方形,只有尖部为圆形,单孔,由一面穿透,除尖部磨光外,其余部分制作较粗糙。

1D（图五二,4;图版柒拾,20） 仅 1 件。针身剖面成圆形,尖部成椭圆形,穿孔处扁平。

（2）锥 用家畜的骨片或肢骨磨制而成。可分三式:

2A（图五二,5;图版柒壹,1 – 3） 共 10 件。用骨片刮成。其中完整的有 4 件,形状不固定,大小不一,除尖端磨制精致外,锥身一般都未经磨制。

2B（图五二,6;图版柒壹,4、5） 共 3 件。系利用猪的腓骨略加磨成尖端。

2C（图五二,7;图版柒壹,6） 仅 1 件。尖部已残缺,锥顶呈帽状如钉头形,虽然很像骨笄,但因形状过大,故暂归入锥类。

（3）镞 可分四式:

3A（图五二,9;图版柒壹,7 – 9） 共 12 件。完整的有 9 件。残缺的 3 件。镞身作柱状,横剖面皆作圆形或椭圆形,大小不等,从 5.3 – 13 厘米。

3B（图五二,10;图版柒壹,10、11） 共 3 件。完整的 2 件。镞身作扁平菱形,铤部磨制稍粗糙。

3C（图五二,11;图版柒壹,12） 仅 1 件。扁平三角形,无铤。

3D（图五二,8;图版柒壹,13） 仅 1 件。镞身较长,铤与镞身有清楚的分界,铤的横剖面呈圆形,镞身横剖面成椭圆形。

（4）带锯齿的骨片（4A;图五二,12;图版柒壹,14） 仅 1 件。在三角形的骨片上两长边作锯齿形,同时在表面有不规则的裂纹,用途不详。

（5）笄 都是长条形,横剖面作圆形、椭圆形或扁平形,一端作尖状,顶端有变化。可分三式:

5A（图五二,13;图版柒壹,15、16） 共 6 件。完整的 5 件。顶端齐头。磨制精致。

5B（图五二,14;图版柒壹,17、19） 共 9 件。完整的只有 1 件。顶端作尖状,横剖面作扁的长方形。一部分笄身弯曲成弧形。

5C（图五二,15;图版柒壹,20） 共 2 件。均残缺,顶端雕成如钉头的帽状,笄身扁平。

（6）梳（图五二,16;图版柒壹,21） 仅 1 件。已残缺,尚保存着 4 个梳齿,系用骨片制成,犹遗有刻划的沟痕。

（7）匕（图五二,17;图版柒壹,22） 共 3 件。完整的 1 件,用骨片磨制呈扁平长方形的小骨板。

2. 角器

（1）凿（图五二,18;图版柒壹。24） 仅 1 件。系利用天然鹿角在尖端磨成刃部而成,其他部未经加工。

（2）锥（图五二,19） 仅 1 件。系用切开的鹿角片加以磨制而成。

3. 蚌器

(1)刀(图五二,20;图版柒拾,11)　仅1件。已残缺,中间有一孔,由两面凹沟法穿透。

(2)镞(图五二,21;图版柒拾,12)　共2件。尖端残缺,镞身作三角形,无铤。

(3)坠(图五二,22;图版柒拾,13)　共3件。坠成长方形或梯形,中间有一孔,由一面穿透,制造精致。

4. 牙器

均系利用野猪的犬齿制成。

(1)镞(图五二,23;图版柒拾,14)　仅1件。镞本镞末都成三角形的锐尖,中脊剖面成三角形,磨制精致。

(2)加工牙片(图五二,24;图版柒拾,15)　共5件。皆残缺,系用犬齿切成薄片,磨成锋刃,或可作为刀类使用。

(四)自然遗物

有家畜骨骼、兽骨、鱼骨、蚌壳等。

(1)家畜骨骼　在各灰坑中出土相当丰富。从数量上来讲,26个龙山灰坑所出土的家畜骨骼,远远超过168个仰韶灰坑所出土的总和,可见家畜的数量比仰韶文化大有增加。由于骨骼过于破碎,无法进行统计。可鉴别的有猪、狗、山羊、牛等,仍以猪骨为最多,牛仅见到几块残胫骨及尺骨,种别不详,可能是家畜。这里家畜的种类加多,特别是大家畜的出现,说明较仰韶文化是大有进步的。

(2)兽骨　野生动物的骨骼次于家畜,以鹿(*Cervus hortulorum* Swinhoe)为最多,可能是当时的主要狩猎对象,此外尚有少数的麝(*Moschus sp.*)、狐(*Vulpes vulpes* L.)、虎(*Felis tigris* L.)等残骨,当都是猎获来的。

(3)鸡骨　共4块,据中国科学院动物研究所郑作新先生鉴定,系鸡的大小腿骨及前臂骨。

(4)鱼骨　在552号灰坑中曾发现两个黄颡鱼(*Pelteobagrus fulvidraco*)的胸鳍刺,这种胸鳍刺在安阳小屯的殷代层中也曾发现过。是当时人类捕食鱼类的有力证据。

(5)厚壳蚌　有许多碎蚌片,可能是准备制作蚌器的原料。

五　东周文化遗物

东周时代的文化遗物发现很少,除7件铜镞外,其余都是破碎的陶片。现在把这些仅有的文化遗物,简述如下:

(一)陶器

发现的都是残陶片,陶质都是泥质灰陶。制法以轮制为主。表面作青灰色或灰褐色。陶片上的纹饰有绳纹、弦纹和暗纹三种,其中以绳纹占绝大多数。器形都不能复原,但从陶片中的口沿和器底部分,可知其器形有盆、罐和豆形器等。

(二)铜镞

可分为两式:

A. 双翼式(图五三,1) 仅 1 件。镞中部有脊,分镞身为左右两叶,后锋构成倒刺形的双翼,脊下有铤。

B. 三棱式(图五三,2-4) 共 6 件。镞身分三棱,向前聚成,镞末向后形成倒刺,长铤。

六 唐墓

在 T1 区内发现一座(图五四)。为南北向的洞室墓,南边有长方形的墓道。方向正南北。墓室作长方形,长 2.7、宽 0.7、高 2.4 米。墓道底部略为倾斜,呈阶梯状,长 2.5、宽 0.67、深 6.7 米。

棺已腐朽,据其木朽痕迹看,长 1.9、宽 0.61 米。仅有一具人架,为仰卧伸直葬,头北,脚南。随葬品皆置于头上及足下,骨架的下面压有开元通宝 43 枚。现将随葬品说明如下:

1. 头饰

共 14 件。可并为一组,加以简述。

铜钗(图版柒贰,1) 2 件。用铜丝曲成。

银钗(图版柒贰,2) 2 件。用银丝曲成。

螺钿花钗(图版柒贰,3、5) 4 件。在镂孔的菱形铜花上嵌有螺钿,共 12 朵,下面有铜丝缠绕的梗枝接在双齿的钗上。

骨梳(图版柒叁,1) 共 2 件。平面呈斧形,梳面用阴线刻有两个儿童,在儿童的服装上绘有金线。

玉饰(图版柒叁,2) 1 双。边缘作齿状的椭圆形,质洁白,表面有一对鸟纹,在鸟纹下还有植物花纹,有四孔系以铜丝。

鸳鸯形玉饰(图版柒叁,4、5) 1 对。绿褐色。

2. 铅人(图版柒叁,3) 共 2 件。一个保存较好,人的轮廓很清楚。

3. 项链 由很多小珠串成的,珠分扁圆形、椭圆形、菱形等种,质料采用玛瑙等矿物。

4. 漆盒 共 4 件。只有两个保存较好,呈正方形,四角圆钝,盒上下围一银圈。

5. 粉盒(图版柒叁,6) 仅 1 件。平面呈花瓣形,瓷质,表面敷白釉。

6. 小口陶瓶(图版柒贰,8) 共 3 件。小口平唇,细颈,肩腹没有明显的分界,平底,系泥质灰陶制成。

7. 敛口陶罐(图版柒贰,7) 仅 1 件。敛口,唇外侈,短颈,鼓腹,平底,泥质灰陶,表面涂朱,但多已剥落。

8. 砚台(图版柒贰,4) 仅 1 件。底附有呈长方形的矮足,砚面有墨色,可能是磨墨留下的痕迹。

9. 开元通宝　共 43 枚。

10. 铜镜(图版柒贰,9)　仅 1 件。圆纽平缘,镜面花纹较粗糙。

11. 铁锅　仅 1 件。仅残存二块铁片。

12. 铁器　仅 1 件。长身扁条形,一端成钝尖,一端成锐尖。用途不详。

13. 铁剪(图版柒贰,6)　仅 1 件。保存较好。

14. 小瓷碟(图版柒叁,7)　共 2 件。大口,圆唇,浅腹,平底,表面敷白釉。

在随葬品中,因有铁剪、骨梳、粉盆等,看出墓主人可能是妇女。据墓形及随葬品推测,其年代当属唐代中叶以后。

叁 三里桥

一 地理环境与工作概况

三里桥遗址在陕县城东关外,位于青龙涧北岸与庙底沟遗址相对,中间仅隔着一条宽约1400米的河谷。从整个遗址看来,是一块大体上成长条形的黄土台地,中部被两条大沟所切断,东边与南家庄相邻,中间也隔着一条大沟,西边是现代的村落,北边有一条现代通往城里的公路,南边即面临着青龙涧(图版玖陆)。

这个遗址也是在1953年最初调查的并发现了龙山文化层叠在仰韶文化层上面的地层证据[5]。遗址的总面积约180,000平方米,大体上东部以龙山文化为主,西部以仰韶文化为主,两者交错相叠着,在周围的断崖上都暴露着灰坑或灰层。这里的仰韶文化和龙山文化与对岸的庙底沟都有所不同。因此,我们便决定在此进行发掘,以便互相比较。共进行了两次发掘工作:第一次自1957年4月12日开始至8月7日结束,第二次自同年10月7日开始至11月20日结束。前后共发掘了1526平方米。发现有仰韶文化、龙山文化以及东周时期的窑址、灰坑、墓葬及其文化遗物。第一次工作人员有陈作良、徐殿魁、蒋忠义、邓德宝及东北人民大学单庆麟和西北大学贾德耀等6同志;第二次工作人员有陈作良、阳吉昌、叶小燕、唐士和、张长庆、蒋忠义、郑大成、温孟元、王兆莹等同志。

二 文化堆积

(一)地层情况

地层的交叠关系很清楚,它是龙山文化层压在仰韶文化层的上面,或者是龙山文化的灰坑打破了仰韶文化层。现以探沟2的西壁剖面为例,来加以说明:第1层,耕土,厚15－38厘米,出有少量仰韶、龙山及战国陶片。第2层,龙山文化层,按土色、土质的不同,可分为两小层:2A层,土呈黄褐色,质较松,厚15－60厘米,出土物除了龙山陶片外,还夹有少量的仰韶陶片。在此层的北边,被一条近代壕沟所打破,一直到了生黄土。2B层,灰土,质松,厚10－38厘米,出土物与2A层相同,但夹有少量的残兽骨。第3层,仰韶文化层,土呈浅黄色,质较硬,厚15－52厘米,出有仰韶陶片。在此层的中部,被龙山灰坑(H2)所打破。灰坑分为三层:1层,土呈黄灰色,质松,厚30－55厘米。2层,灰土、土质与上层同,厚12－39厘米。3层,土呈黄褐色,质较硬,厚70厘米。以上各层均出有龙山陶片和石器、骨器等遗物(图五五)。在遗址的东部,还有仰韶、龙山和东周三个时期的文化交叠层,但东周时期的堆积仅占很少的一部分。

从上述的地层交叠关系看来,它再一次地提供了仰韶文化和龙山文化的相对年代的证据。这与对岸庙底沟遗址的堆积情况也是完全一致的。

(二)建筑遗存

1. 仰韶文化

(1)窑址

仰韶文化陶窑共发现了 2 座。形制相同,结构较简单;可分为窑室与火膛两部分,前者近圆形,后者呈半圆筒形。现以 301 号窑为例,来加以说明:火膛向东,位于窑室的前面,方向为 108 度。残长约 1.17 米,前口较小,高 0.2、宽 0.46 米;向后逐渐扩大接连窑室,高 0.34、宽 0.76 米,底部向外略呈斜坡直至膛口。窑室的上部已破坏(距地表约 1.2 米露出),周壁垂直,残高 0.25 - 0.36 米,底部平坦未见窑箅,直径约 2.1 - 2.24 米。整个陶窑的底部经火烧的结果,形成一层厚约 7 - 10 厘米的青灰色的烧土面;窑壁部分则略呈红色,厚约 3 - 4 厘米(图五六)。窑内堆积仅一层,皆为灰土,质松,内夹有大量的仰韶陶片及红烧土碎块。

(2)灰坑

仰韶文化灰坑共发现了 47 个。有圆形和椭圆形两种:前者较少,计 17 个,后者居多,计 30 个。灰坑保存得完整者甚少,约占四分之一强,余者皆有打破关系。这些灰坑的形制与庙底沟大体相同,也是口大底小者占绝大多数,直壁如筒状者次之,而口小底大者仅占少数。

2. 龙山文化

(1)窑址

龙山文化陶窑发现 1 座(Y4)。它可分为前后两部分;前部为火膛,后部即窑室。火膛的口部略小于底部,东西 0.97、南北 0.6 米,底部较大,东西 1.2、南北 0.82 米。系一深 1.3 米的椭圆形袋状竖坑。窑室呈圆形,上部已被耕土破坏(距地表 0.1 - 0.28 米露出),直径 1.3、残高 0.38 米,周壁向上往里略呈弧形,底部有四条南北向平行的沟状火道,长 1.2 - 1.36、宽 0.11、深 0.12 - 0.17 米。在火膛与窑室之间有一个隔梁,因而火道作斜坡式经过隔梁通到火膛(中间两条直行,东边成 160 度,西边成 120 度拐弯)。这里值得注意的是,在窑室的壁上还遗有明显的建造时所留下的工具痕迹,也作双齿形,与庙底沟龙山灰沟(HG553)的木末痕迹相同。另外在火膛与窑室之间的隔梁上面,还有一个窑口,方向为 175 度,长 0.5、宽 0.6、残高 0.36 米。整个陶窑的周壁及底部,经火烧的结果变成一层坚硬的青灰色的烧土面,厚 5 - 9 厘米(图五七,1、3;图版柒肆、柒伍)。窑内堆积除第 1 层系耕土外,第 2 层,土呈黄褐色,质较硬,厚 0.14 - 0.2 米。第 3 层,土呈黄灰色,质较松,厚 0.3 - 0.36 米。以上两层均出有龙山陶片,其中火膛内尚夹有烧土、木炭、残兽骨以及陶坯等(图五七,2)。

(2)灰坑

龙山文化灰坑共发现了103个,其中圆形54个,椭圆形49个。形制与仰韶灰坑大体相同,唯坑壁较整齐,保存完整者不多,仅占四分之一弱。出土物以陶片为最多,其中有的灰坑还出有精制的骨器。

(三)墓葬

1. 仰韶墓葬

仰韶文化墓葬共发现了2座。都是长方形的浅竖穴,仰身伸直葬。现以墓107为例,来加以说明:墓口距地表0.5、长1.88、宽0.54、深0.45米。方向为330度,头向西北(图五八)。此墓系葬于仰韶文化层中,填土内仅出有仰韶彩陶一片。

2. 龙山墓葬

龙山文化墓葬发现1座(墓108)。系长方形的浅竖穴,方向210度。墓口距地表0.55米,长度不详,宽0.6、深0.35米。葬式为仰身伸直,头向西南,两足已被龙山灰坑(H296)所打破,无随葬品(图五九)。从地层上观察,此墓自上面的龙山文化层打破了下面的仰韶文化层。因此,我们可以断定它属于龙山的墓葬。

三 仰韶文化遗物

(一)陶器

1. 容器

共复原19件。陶质以细泥红陶为最多,夹砂粗红陶次之,泥质灰陶与细泥黑陶最少,而且都是不能复原的残片。纹饰除素面或磨光者外,有彩绘、线纹、划纹、附加堆纹及乳丁等几种。这里的彩陶数量很少,而且花纹也较简单。器形有钵、碗、盆、罐、器座等。现以灰坑6为例,将其陶系、纹饰及器形等列表统计如下:

仰韶文化(灰坑6)陶系及纹饰统计表

陶系	细泥红陶系					泥质灰陶系	细泥黑陶系	夹砂粗缸陶系			总计
数量	291					25	7	164			487
百分比	59.76					5.14	1.44	33.68			100%
纹饰	彩绘	线纹	划纹	乳丁纹	素面	素面	素面	线纹	划纹	附加堆纹	素面	
量数	12	45	4	2	228	25	7	41	5	8	110	487
百分比	2.47	9.24	0.83	0.41	46.82	5.34	1.44	8.42	1.03	1.65	22.59	100%

仰韶文化(灰坑6)陶器器形统计表(以能看出器形者为主)

陶系	细泥红陶系					泥质灰陶系		细泥黑陶系	夹砂粗红陶系		总计
器形	钵	碗	盆	罐	器座	盆	罐	罐	盆	罐	
数量	41	27	31	22	5	13	5	4	34	28	210
百分比	19.53	12.85	14.77	10.47	2.38	6.19	2.38	1.81	16.19	13.34	100%

A. 细泥红陶系 绝大多数系素面,磨光者少见。彩绘仅见于折沿盆及敛口盆的口沿上。在陶片中也发现有几片带白衣的彩陶。

(1)钵 大口,浅腹,圜底或平底。可分两式:

A1a(图六〇;图版柒陆,1a、b) 共3件。圜底,其中H310:05一件,底部中央穿有一孔,疑可作甑使用。

A1b(图六〇;图版柒陆,2a、b) 仅1件。底略平,底部印有乳丁,可能是制陶器放置在某种陶垫上所遗留下的痕迹。

(2)碗 大口,腹壁向下往里收缩成平底,但腹部和底部无明显的分界。可分两式:

A2a(图六〇;图版柒陆,3) 仅1件。浅腹。

A2b(图六〇;图版柒陆,4) 仅1件。器形与前式近似,唯腹部较深。

(3)浅腹盆 大口折沿,浅腹,平底。可分两式:

A3a(图六〇;图版柒柒,1) 仅1件。腹壁斜行向下往里收缩。

A3b(图六〇;图版柒柒,2) 仅1件。腹壁成弧形向下往里收缩,盆沿上绘有黑彩。

(4)敛口盆 敛口,腹壁向下往里收缩成平底。可分两式:

A4a(图六一;图版柒柒,3) 共2件。腹壁成弧形收缩。

A4b(图六一;图版柒柒,4、5) 共2件。器形与前式近似,唯底部收缩较甚,与腹壁有明显的分界。

(5)敛口罐(A5;图六一;图版柒柒,6) 仅1件。敛口,深腹,小平底。

(6)器座(A6;图六一;图版柒捌,1) 仅1件。侈口,束腰,下部略往外扩张。

B. 泥质灰陶系 仅有素面一种。器形可识别者有盆、罐,但都不能复原。

C. 细泥黑陶系 数量最少。陶胎略呈红褐色,外表纯黑,皆素面,器形可识别者仅有罐一种,也不能复原。

D. 夹砂粗红陶系 多为素面,施纹饰者甚少,有线纹、划纹、附加堆纹等几种。

(1)敛口罐 敛口,鼓腹,平底。可分两式:

D1a(图六一;图版柒捌,2) 仅1件。腹部向外凸出。

D1b(图六一;图版柒捌,3) 共2件。侈唇,腹壁略向外鼓出。

(2)筒形罐(D2;图六一;图版柒捌,4) 共2件。筒形,深腹,平底。

2. 工具

(1)刀 皆由陶片改制,完整者未见。可分三式:

1A 共7件。两侧带缺口,形与庙底沟仰韶文化1A式刀相同。

1B(图版柒玖,1) 共5件。长方形,穿孔。

1C(图版柒玖,2) 共3件。圆背,穿孔。

(2)纺轮　共9件。皆由陶片改制,形与庙底沟仰韶文化4A式纺轮相同。

3. 装饰品

环(图版柒玖,3)　共3件。圆形,仅有素面一种。

(二)石器

1. 工具

按制法的不同,分为打制与磨制两大类:

(1)刀　可分两式:

1A(图版柒玖,4)　共6件。两侧带缺口。

1B(图版柒玖,5、6)　共3件。长方形或椭圆形,两侧不带缺口。

(2)斧(图版柒玖,7)　共3件。长方形,圆刃,横剖面呈椭圆形。

(3)纺轮(图版柒玖,8)　共6件。圆形,孔由两面对穿,边沿皆平整。

(4)球(图版柒玖,9)　共4件。大小不一,皆磨光。大者直径达6,小者仅29厘米。后一种可能兼作弹丸使用。

(三)骨器

(1)针(图版柒玖,12)　共3件。细长,后端穿孔。

(2)锥(图版柒玖,10、11)　共2件。利用猪的肢骨磨成。

(3)笄(图版柒玖,13、14)　共2件。两端皆磨成尖形,剖面呈椭圆形。

(四)自然遗物

仅有少量的家畜骨骼。可识别的有猪狗两种,其他不详,也有少量的鹿骨和鹿角等。

四　龙山文化遗物

(一)陶器

1. 容器

共复原69件。陶质以夹砂粗灰陶与泥质灰陶为最多,夹砂粗红陶与细泥黑陶次之,泥质红陶最少见。这里陶器的轮制痕迹很清楚,约占总数的五分之一;其他绝大多数是泥条筑成法制成。至于陶鬲则显然采用了模制法,利用已经烧好的陶鬲作内模,因此在鬲的袋足及裆的内部均附有清晰的"反绳纹",而所制出的器形,也比较整齐和一致。在陶片中还发现有少量的蛋壳陶。纹饰以绳纹为最多(约占1/2),篮纹次之(约占1/5),方格纹较少(约占1/12)。素面或磨光者也大量出现,另外还有划纹、镂孔及附加堆纹等,但比例都很少。器形有杯、碗、盆、罐、甑、鬲、鬶、斝、器座等。现以灰坑3为例。将其陶系、纹饰及器形等列表统计如下:

龙山文化(灰坑3)陶系及纹饰统计表

陶系	夹砂粗灰陶系					泥质灰陶系					夹砂粗红陶系		细泥黑陶系		泥质红陶系		总计
数量	1708					1031					303		271		48		3361
百分比	50.82					30.68					9.02		8.07		1.43		100%
纹饰	绳纹	篮纹	方格纹	附加堆纹	素面	绳纹	篮纹	方格纹	镂孔	素面	绳纹	素面	划纹	素面	篮纹	素面	
数量	1138	327	34	21	188	527	273	20	6	205	95	208	31	240	38	10	3361
百分比	33.86	9.73	1.02	0.63	5.6	15.68	8.13	0.6	0.18	6.1	2.83	6.19	0.93	7.14	1.13	0.3	100%

龙山文化(灰坑3)陶器器形统计表(以能看出器形者为限)

陶系	夹砂粗灰陶系			泥质灰陶系					夹砂粗红陶系	细泥黑陶系		泥质红陶系		总计
器形	罐	鬲	斝	碗	盆	杯	罐	甑	罐	豆	罐	罐	鬶	
数量	525	196	19	35	59	37	154	17	84	41	87	37	2	1293
百分比	40.61	15.16	1.47	2.71	4.57	2.87	11.91	1.32	6.5	3.64	6.73	2.87	0.16	100%

A. 夹砂粗灰陶系 器形不多,表面多饰绳纹、篮纹,其他纹饰皆少见。

(1)圜底罐(A1;图六二;图版捌拾,1) 仅1件。深腹,圜底,上部已残,胎厚2.8厘米。

(2)单耳罐 敛口,单耳,腹壁向下往里收缩成平底。可分两式:

A2a(图六二;图版捌拾,2、3) 共2件。腹部略向外鼓出。

A2b(图六二;图版捌拾,4) 共2件。器形与前式近似,唯腹部更为鼓出。

(3)敛口罐 敛口,鼓腹,平底。可分两式:

A3a(图六三;图版捌贰,1) 仅1件。腹部略向外鼓出。

A3b(图六三;图版捌贰,2) 仅1件。器形与前式近似,唯腹部更为鼓出。

(4)鬲 敛口,三袋足。可分两式:

A4a(图六二;图版捌壹,1、2) 共7件。唇外侈,在口沿与腹部间有一个錾。

A4b(图六二;图版捌壹,3) 仅1件。器形与前式近似,唯不带錾,颈部两旁各有一道附加堆纹。

(5)斝(A5;图六二;图版捌壹,4) 共2件。由圜底罐下加三袋足而成,口部两旁各有一个短耳,以便握持。

B. 泥质灰陶系 器形较多,纹饰除绳纹、篮纹、方格纹外,还有镂孔,素面者多不磨光。

(1)碗(B1;图六三;图版捌贰,3、4) 共4件。大口,腹壁斜行向下往里收缩成平底。此碗若将其倒转过来,亦可作为器盖使用。

(2)浅腹盆(B2;图六三;图版捌贰,5) 仅1件。大口微敛,浅腹,小平底。

(3)深腹盆 大口,深腹,平底。可分四式:

B3a(图六三;图版捌叁,1) 共2件。口沿外侈,腹壁斜行向下往里收缩。

B3b(图六三;图版捌叁,2) 仅1件。器形与前式近似,唯底部成弧形往里收缩。

B3c(图六三;图版捌叁,3) 仅1件。器形与B3a式近似,唯口沿外折,腹壁略向外凸出。

B3d(图六三;图版捌叁,4) 共2件。器形与前式近似,唯腹壁折成棱角向外凸出。

(4)单耳杯(B4;图六四;图版捌叁,5) 仅1件。大口,单耳,腹壁斜行向下往里收缩成平底。

(5)双耳杯(B5;图六四;图版捌叁,6) 共5件。大口,双耳,腹壁下折往里收缩成平底。

(6)敛口罐 敛口,鼓腹,平底。可分四式:

B6a(图六四;图版捌肆,1) 仅1件。圆唇,腹部微向外鼓出。

B6b(图六四;图版捌肆,2、3) 共3件。器形与前式近似,唯口沿外折。

B6c(图六四;图版捌肆,4;图版捌伍,1) 共3件。器形与前式近似,唯口沿外侈,颈部稍高。

B6d(图六四;图版捌伍,3) 仅1件。与前式相似,唯腹部较深。

(7)单耳罐(B7;图六五;图版捌伍,4) 共2件。敛口,鼓腹,平底。在口沿与腹部间有一个耳。

(8)长颈罐 长颈,鼓腹,颈肩有显著分界,可分为两式:

B8a(图六四;图版捌伍,2) 共2件。口稍大,颈较矮。

B8b(图六五;图版捌陆,1、2) 共2件。口小,而颈部较长。

(9)小口罐 小口,折肩,腹壁向里收缩成平底,一般的器形均较大。可以分为两式:

B9a(图六五;图版捌陆,3) 共两件。肩部印有篮纹或抹平。

B9b(图六五;图版捌陆,4) 仅1件。形制与前式基本相同,但在陶坯制好以后,由肩部将器口与器身割开,使器口成为盖部。盖为用来盛置较大的什物,以免罐口过小不能置入。这种制法比较特殊,在一般陶器中还是相当少见的。

(10)甑 敛口,鼓腹,平底,底部及周围均有穿孔,可分为两式:

B10a(图六六;图版捌柒,1a、b) 共2件。腹部略向外鼓出。

B10b(图六六;图版捌柒,2a、b) 仅1件。底部显著往里收缩,腹部两旁各附凸耳,以便把持。

(11)瓶(B11;图六六;图版捌捌,1) 仅1件。小口、鼓腹、平底。

(12)豆(B12;图六六;图版捌捌,2、3) 共2件。大口折沿,腰部往里收缩,下部外侈形成圈足。

(13)平底鬶(B13;图六六;图版捌捌,4a、b) 仅1件。侈口带流,腹壁向下往外扩张成平底。底部附有三个矮足,在颈部与腹部间还有一个耳,器形甚为特殊。除鬶以外还发现一个盉的流部残片,作管状,其他部分可能和盉相似,暂附于此。

（14）器座（B14；图六七；图版捌捌，5） 仅 1 件。直口，向下往外扩张，形如不带器身的大圈足。

C. 夹砂粗红陶系 多为破片，复原器形仅有大口罐一种。

大口罐（C1；图六七；图版捌捌，6） 共 2 件。上部已残，深腹，向下往里收缩成平底。胎厚 3 厘米。

D. 细泥黑陶系 表面纯黑，陶胎中心仍呈灰褐色，器形经复原者不多。

（1）双耳罐（D1；图六七；图版捌玖，1） 共 3 件。小口，鼓腹，小平底。腹部两旁各有一个耳。

（2）双耳豆（D2；图六七；图版捌玖，2） 仅 1 件。由 B12 式豆在口部两旁各加一个耳。

E. 泥质红陶系 在各陶系中以它所占的比例最少。色泽不纯，常夹有灰斑。器形能复原者也不多。

（1）敛口罐（E1；图六七；图版捌玖，3） 共 3 件，敛口，腹部略向外鼓出，向下往里收缩成平底。

（2）鬶（E2；图六七；图版捌玖，4） 仅 1 件。侈口带流，下为三袋足，颈部附有一个耳。

2. 工具

（1）刀 共 6 件。长方形，穿孔。皆利用陶片改制。

（2）纺轮 共 9 件。由陶土制成，周边成弧形或棱角，体积较小，直径皆 3 厘米左右。

（3）陶垫（图版玖拾，1） 仅 1 件。系制陶工具。一面平整，一面弧起，中空，横剖面呈半圆形。与庙底沟龙山文化的陶垫相似。

3. 其他 鸟头塑像（图版玖壹，6） 仅 1 件，已残缺，为夹砂粗红陶，外面有一层黑衣，嘴作扁圆形，很像鸭的形状。

（二）石器

（1）斧（图版玖拾，8） 共 11 件。长方形，平刃或弧刃，横剖面呈长方形。

（2）锛（图版玖拾，4） 仅 1 件。体扁平，单面刃，一面中间有切割痕迹，可能系准备切成两半以改制石凿。

（3）刀（图版玖拾，2、3） 共 10 件。长方形，单孔，由两面对穿，皆磨制。

（4）镞 共 2 件。扁平三角形，皆磨制。形与庙底沟龙山文化石镞相同。

（三）骨、蚌器

A. 骨器

（1）针（图版玖拾，10） 共 4 件。细长，后端穿孔。

（2）锥（图版玖拾，5） 仅 1 件。利用骨片磨成。

（3）镞（图版玖拾，9） 共 7 件。三棱形，无铤。

（4）铲（图版玖拾,6、7;图版玖壹,1-4） 共7件。利用猪的下颌骨磨成,也有1件利用盆骨磨成。

（5）凿 共3件,利用动物的肢骨,劈开一部分,将一端磨成单面刃。

（6）笄（图版玖拾,11） 共6件。两端略磨成尖形,剖面呈椭圆形。

B. 蚌器

（1）刀 仅1件。长方形,单孔,由两面挖成,已残。

（2）蚌镰 共2件,其中1件的刃部作锯齿形。

（3）坠 仅1件。长条形,一端穿孔,已残。

（4）蚌笄（图版玖壹,5） 仅1件,笄身扁平,顶端粗大作椭圆形,附长三角形锐尖。

（四）自然遗物

家畜骨骼不多,而且破碎较甚。可以识别的有猪、狗、牛、羊等,以猪骨为最多。也有鹿骨、鹿角及厚壳蚌等。

五 东周文化遗物

战国灰坑共发现了6个,但保存得都不好。出土遗物甚少,除陶片外有三棱铜镞3件、残玉器1件。另外在T236探方内出铸有“安邑二釿”的魏国布币1件（图六八）。此外在这个时期的灰坑里还发现很多圆锥形的小陶器,火候不甚高,陶质较松软。过去在河南渑池县仰韶村也曾发现过同样的陶器,但被误认为仰韶文化的产物[6]。这里仅见于东周时期的灰坑中,在较早的文化层里绝无存在,其他东周遗址（如陕县李家窑等）也均有出土,可证明其确系东周时期的遗物。

肆　文化性质及年代

这次配合黄河三门峡水库修建工程,在庙底沟和三里桥两处遗址所进行的大规模发掘,不仅发现了丰富的考古资料,也解决了一些问题和提出不少的线索,对研究中国新石器时代考古学和复原我国原始社会的面貌,是具有一定意义的。

由于过去对新石器时代遗址缺少系统的发掘,对其文化性质及相互关系的分析上都不够明确,甚至于某些关键性的问题也没有彻底解决,使今天在综合研究上存在着很多困难。通过庙底沟与三里桥的发掘和分析,可以端正过去的某些错误概念。如根据层位关系再一次证明了仰韶文化和龙山文化的相对年代,说明仰韶早于龙山的实例不仅限于豫北,在豫西也是同样清楚的;关于仰韶和龙山的文化性质基本上也得到明确,特别是证明了两者之间有着密切的联系,对分期问题提供了新的证据,这些都是这次发掘的主要收获。现在准备根据上述两个遗址的发现结合过去的知识和我们的看法,来说明它们的文化牲质、年代和生产技术等,并提出一些问题,以便在今后的考古工作中去陆续解决。

一　庙底沟

(一)仰韶文化层

仰韶文化是 1921 年在河南渑池县仰韶村最初发现的一种新石器时代遗存,那里有精美的彩陶和石器共存,代表着黄河流域的一种早期文化。后来凡具有同样文化性质的遗址,都称为仰韶文化。又因为遗物中有彩陶,也有人称它为"彩陶文化"。彩陶文化这个概念是比较模糊的,因为彩陶的使用期间较长,从新石器时代到铁器时代都有存在,如果用它来作为文化的名称,是不够妥当的。所以还是称为"仰韶文化",比较适合一些。

严格地讲,仰韶文化所从而取名的仰韶村便不是一处典型的遗址,因为在过去的发掘工作中存在着极严重的缺点,许多关键性的问题都不能够弄清楚。当仰韶村的遗物发表以后,我国的考古工作者曾指出其中混有龙山文化的遗物[11],或认为可以分成早晚两期[12],而安特生自己却强调它们是共存的[13]。在解放后的一次调查中曾提出这里是一种"仰韶和龙山的混合文化"[14],但问题也还没有完全解决。不过我们知道,这种性质的遗存在黄河流域有广泛的分布,而彼此之间又具有许多共同的特征。在没有更适当的文化名称以前,"仰韶文化"这一称谓还是可以采用的。

据我们初步了解,在仰韶文化遗址中从文化性质上可以分成不同的若干类型,彼此之间也是有所区别的,如庙底沟和三里桥便可以各代表一种类型。而陕县和渑池县相连接,庙底沟和仰韶村相距不过 50 公里,无论从地理位置上以及文化性质上都有着比较密切的联系。当仰韶村遗址的文化性质还没有搞清楚以前,最低庙底沟遗址可以代表仰韶文化的一部分面貌。因此搞清了庙底沟遗址的内涵,自然也会反映出仰韶村遗址的具体面貌。现在我们以庙底沟的仰韶文化遗存为中心,来分析它的文化特征。

三门峡水库区内仰韶文化遗址的处数最多,面积也较大,如庙底沟遗址的面积约240,000平方米,几和陕县附近的现代大型村落相等,另外,在它的附近还有不少的仰韶文化遗址,这充分反映了黄河流域仰韶文化遗址分布稠密的一般情况。

庙底沟遗址所发现的两座房屋与其他仰韶遗址中所发现的相同,都是近方形的浅竖穴,门前有斜坡形的窄门道,周围墙壁及居住面上均有柱洞,可复原成一种木架结构四角尖锥的房屋。但在居住面内的四个柱洞下面垫有石柱础,却是其他仰韶房子中所没有的。它们将石柱础的使用年限更为提早,增添了中国建筑史上的新资料。居住面用草泥土铺成,表面坚实光滑,当是经过人类长期居住的结果。另在302号房子的居住面中羼有红烧土末,因而质地坚实并带有红颜色,这只是居住面的一种做法,有人把类似现象认为是用火烧成的[15],是不符合事实。屋内的火塘,可能是取暖的设备,并兼用以保存火种。像这样做较深的圆形竖穴,也是比较特殊的。

遗址中大量的灰坑都是当时的窖穴,一般比较粗糙,很少像龙山灰坑那样整齐,这也许是它的原始特征之一。这种窖穴可能是贮藏粮食用的,废弃以后就用垃圾填塞,当需要时就另掘新的使用,因而往往打破了已被填塞的窖穴。灰坑的相互打破关系虽然复杂,但相隔的年代并不很久;特别是在房子附近打破关系尤为复杂,说明它们和房子是有着密切关系的。过去曾有人认为这种窖穴是住人的土穴[16],并引用古文献上所谓"穴居野处"和"陶复陶穴"为证[17],由于仰韶房子的普遍发现,这种说法就更难于置信了。

墓葬只发现了1座,也许在遗址附近还有成群的葬地,可惜未曾发现。至于在4座灰坑内发现5具人骨,可能说明当时也利用废弃的窖穴埋葬死人。

在全部文化遗物中以陶片为最多,形制也比较复杂,据复原的690多件陶器,可以对仰韶文化的陶器得到较为全面的认识。陶器的质料以细泥红陶为最多,夹砂粗红陶次之,泥质灰陶仅占少数,而细泥黑陶尤少。至于少量的细泥白陶,是利用了不含铁素(或微量)的白色陶土;是否是高岭土,尚待化验证明[18]。因这类陶质仅限于彩陶,故暂时收入细泥红陶中。值得注意的是泥质灰陶和泥质黑陶所占的比例虽少,但已开了龙山文化陶器的先河。而细泥白陶当也是后来龙山及殷代白陶的先驱。一般的陶质都比较坚硬,尤以细泥红陶最为显著,据过去的研究,河南渑池仰韶村陶片的火候是在摄氏1300－1400度之间,而河南成皋秦王寨的陶片是在摄氏1100－1200度之间[19],则这里陶器的火候也不会差得很远。

陶器的制法主要采用泥条筑成法,口缘部分多经过慢轮修整。小形陶器如碗、杯、器盖等多用捏塑法制成,个别的口缘也经过慢轮修整。过去有人认为仰韶陶器是轮制的①,

---

① 见参考文献[19]。

可能是根据这种慢轮修整痕迹而产生的误解。

　　陶器表面的纹饰有线纹、篮纹、划纹、附加堆纹、布纹、席纹、镂孔和彩绘等,而以线纹为最多,彩绘次之,其他均较少。线纹也称为细绳纹,排列疏朗,和龙山及其以后的绳纹截然不同。篮纹往往与线纹交互为饰,很少单独使用的,比例虽小,但已开了龙山篮纹陶器的先河。附加堆纹的波浪形泥条,有的还起着器耳的作用。布纹和席纹系制陶时所用的垫布或席类压印的痕迹,并不是专门作装饰用的。镂孔多见于器盖的纽上,起着通风的作用;至于器座上的镂孔,则装饰的作用可能要多一些。彩绘陶片达到14.02%,说明在完整陶器中所占的比例应更多。有的仰韶遗址中,彩陶的比例往往很少,如三里桥仰韶层仅占2.47%,和这里比较就有显著的不同。与此彩陶片多寡的同时,在纹饰和器形上也有相应的差异,这或者代表着不同的时代。彩绘仅限于细泥红陶(包括少量的细泥白陶),表面打磨光滑,并有部分施有深红色及白色的陶衣。深红色陶衣稍多,富有光泽,有的仅施陶衣而不加彩绘,似是这里的特点(在夹砂粗红陶中也有几片带红衣的),在其他地区却比较少见;白色陶衣的数量更少,并多在口腹上涂有一段白衣,然后绘彩,这里不像渑池以东的仰韶遗址那样普遍(以成皋附近的遗址最为显著)。彩绘的颜料主要用黑色,很少用红色,兼用黑、红两种色料的更少见,并只限于白衣彩陶。彩绘主要绘在器腹上,也有绘在口缘上的,绝不见器内绘彩的。纹饰的图案比较复杂而富于变化,基本上是用条纹、涡纹、三角涡纹、圆点纹及方格纹等所组成,但在结构上缺乏固定的规律。花纹虽可以分成许多不同的单元,但这些单元很少固定不变,而互有增减,比较难于把它们固定的母题分析出来;同时某种图案的配合也不尽限于一定种类的器物上。以上这些情况都是这里的特征。从图案的整体结构上来观察,它具有地区上的特点,可能是以三门峡水库区为中心而遍布于渑池以西、晋南和关中等地区,相反的与渑池以东的仰韶遗址差别较大,如曲腹的碗、盆多,而陶鼎及白衣彩陶少见,以及富有豫西特征的窄条带状方格纹在这里也没有,这些都是值得注意的现象。另外所发现的三片绘有蛙形纹的彩陶片,同样的蛙爪也见于渑池县仰韶村①,在陕西华阴西关堡也发现过类似的蛙形纹,这与三片壁虎塑像和鸟头塑像都是当时的杰出的艺术作品。

　　陶器的器形有盘、碗、盆、杯、罐、盂、瓶、甑、釜、灶、鼎、器盖、器座等,其中以盆形器为最多。特别是A10 e-g的盆形器和A6b的碗形器是这里的特点,在渑池以东的遗址中却很少发现。从陶器的器形上也表现了当时的日常生活,如泥质陶系中的绝大部分是盛置的容器,尖底瓶可能是汲水的用具,在洛阳汉河南县城内所发现的尖底瓶[20]以及汉墓陶井明器上所附的尖底瓶等可作为有力的旁证。陶甑是一种蒸器,与粗陶的釜有密切的联系,当时吃的可能是整粒的蒸饭,粗陶釜是专门和陶甑一起使用的,否则像仰韶陶釜那样小口扁腹是不大适用于煮食物的。夹砂粗陶除盛置的容器以外,主要为炊器,如釜、鼎、灶等。鼎仅有 1 件，并且是由陶釜改制的(图二九;图版叁玖,4),可以证明这里虽有鼎的存在,但并不普遍,这与渑池以东的仰韶遗址中往往有较多的陶鼎成为一个显著对比。又如出土有数量相当多的器盖,说明了过去认为器盖是龙山文化产物的看法是不够正确的。在陶器中已有个别的圈足器(如 A7a、b 碗,从器形上看也很可能是器盖的一种),也有较多的圈足器座,可能是圈足器的前身。至于粗红陶的小杯,数量既多,形状又小,而许多小形的器盖(D13c - d),也可能是这类陶杯的盖子,其用途还难以解释。根据以上器形的观察,过去认为属于龙山文化特征的杯、圈足器、器盖等器物,在仰韶文化中已经萌芽了。

容器以外的陶制品中和陶刀大部分是用碎陶片改制的,也有用陶土制成一定的形状再入窑烧制的。陶网坠是渔网上的附属品。至于陶瓶可能是一种搓洗手具,或可兼作刮治皮革的工具,如 3A 式在陕西境内出土最多,至于 3B - C 式多见于豫西及晋南的仰韶遗址中,用途还不易肯定,但不可能是弹丸或玩具,尚待进一步研究。

石器中以打制石器为最多,而磨制石器仅占极少的比例,这也是仰韶文化的原始特征之一。打制石器中,最常见的是盘状器,至于用途尚难确定,其周缘有刃的(如 1B 式)或可作刮削器使用;而大多数钝边的(如 1A 式)或可作为敲砸之用。两侧带缺口的石刀和磨制石刀是当时的主要收割农具。少数的石网坠和陶网坠都间接说明了渔业的存在。此外还发现了两片燧石片,在刃上遗有清楚的使用痕迹,从制法上来看和细石器文化中的细石器非常近似。磨制石器中以刀、铲为最多。石铲多成碎片,完整的很少,一般的形状较大,铲身扁平,磨制细致,锋刃锐利,背部中央有一段糙面,有的在肩部两侧还打成凹痕,显然是为了适于附着木柄和缚绳而故意制成的,使用的情况当和今天的铁锹一般,是当时的挖土工具。除石铲以外也许还有木制的耕种工具,但我们并没有发现任何痕迹。斧、锛、凿的数量不多,个别的器物制作得比较粗糙。石斧可能是砍伐树木的主要工具,形状较小的也可以作为刀类使用。石锤可能是一种敲砸器。磨杵、磨棒是研磨赤铁矿的用具,在上面还附有赤铁矿的痕迹。这里的仰韶文化层中缺少磨制石镞,也是值得注意的现象。

骨器的数量不多,远不及龙山文化那样丰富,种类也比较简单,这可能与骨料的来源有关,由于家畜不多也就限制了骨器的大量出现。角器也不多,有针、锥、笄、凿等,一般没有什么特殊的形态;至于这里所发现的角槌却是仰韶文化中所少见的。

装饰品中的陶环、石环,直径都较小,可能是佩在身上的一种悬饰[21]。绿松石的石坠、水晶珠、骨制的牙形饰、蚌坠和穿孔猪牙等,可能是属于颈饰或佩在身上的悬饰。骨笄是束发的用具,说明当时人类已经不再披头散发了。弧形骨片可能与环类的用途相似。另外也发现了蚌制的指环,套在左手的无名指上,和现代的佩戴方法一致。这些都是日常使用的装饰品。在这里发现了赤铁矿的碎块,当是磨成粉末供装饰上使用的。

关于仰韶文化的年代,过去的说法认为属于新石器时代晚期,并拟出了它的绝对年代;虽各家说法不一,大体都定在公元前 2000 年左右,这与实际情况是有许多矛盾的。我们曾提出仰韶文化的年代可能稍早,其上限或者可以提到新石器时代中期[22],虽还缺乏比较有力的证据,但据最近发现的情况来看,仰韶、龙山都比较复杂,每个文化都经过了长时期的发展过程,因而将仰韶文化的开端适当地提早是有必要的。至于绝对年代问题,希望在不久的将来能用放射性碳素予以解决。由于仰韶文化发展的时间较长,每个阶段的文化面貌也不尽相同。据在三门峡水库区内的调查和发掘所了解的,大体上可以分为两种类型:一种是彩陶数量多,纹饰复杂,器形以曲腹的碗、盆为主,但不见圜底的钵形器;另一种是彩陶数量少,纹饰简单,有大量的圜底钵,不见曲腹的碗、盆等器形。庙底沟是属于前一种类型,三里桥则属于后一种类型。这两个遗址距离很近,但呈现了不同的文化面貌,显然是代表着不同的发展阶段。和庙底沟同样性质的仰韶文化遗存,在豫、晋、陕三省比较普遍。据已发表的资料来看,如山西境内的夏县西阴村[23]、万荣县荆村、[24]永济县盛金庄[25];陕西境内如长安县马王村、五楼、华阴县西关[26]、华县柳子镇①等地,都是属于这种类型的遗址。河南境内陕、灵宝两县也有不少同类的遗址[5],渑池县仰韶村基本上也属于这种类型,不过还具有渑池以东的仰韶遗址的因素。成皋附近的许多遗址,在文化性质上稍有区别,如点军台、青台②、秦王寨③等遗址基本上也可以归入前一种类型。它们的具体特征都是彩陶数量多,纹饰较复杂。它们和彩陶稀少、纹饰简单的另一种类型的遗址(以三里桥仰韶层为代表的),常常交错地存在。上述的两种类型的遗址孰早孰晚,一时还不容易解决。尽管过去对彩陶纹饰的发展规律有由简到繁的说法,而把纹饰简单的彩陶作为早期的遗存④,但我们认为相反的可能性还是相当大的。特别是庙底沟的仰韶文化遗存具有若干原始的性质,可能属于仰韶文化的早期形态。这个问题,还有待于今后的发掘工作中来求得解决。

仰韶人类是以农业生产为主的,如大量农业生产工具的发现便是一个有力的证据;同时像这样堆积丰富的大规模村落遗址,象征着人数众多的氏族公社经过长期的定居生活,没有农业生产是无法维持的。当时的农作物虽然没有发现,但在陕西西安半坡[28]和华县柳子镇⑤都发现过粟粒,而两侧带缺口或穿孔的石刀,也是收割粟类的主要农具[29],则这里也当以粟类为主的农作物。从缺乏研磨谷类的磨盘看来,说明当时并不将粟类研碎、去壳以后放在陶甑中蒸食,这种做法直到今天还继续存在着,可以说已有非常悠久的历史了。纺轮和陶器上所印的线纹及清楚的布纹,说明当时已有了纺织;从陶器器耳上所出现的布纹在1平方厘米内,经纬各为10根,和现代的粗麻布相似,可能也是采用麻作原料的。因为麻类直到殷周时期还是主要的纺织原料[30],则仰韶文化的纺织原料也非麻莫属了。家畜种类还很简单,所发现的骨骼以猪为主,狗次之,由于数量不多,又过于

---

① 见参考文献[15]图一,图版贰。
② 见参考文献[2]图七。
③ 见参考文献[10]图版一三八至一四九。
④ 见参考文献[11]页77,[27]。
⑤ 见参考文献[15]页73。

破碎,无法统计大体的比例,不过从量上来讲,远不如龙山文化那样丰富,这也可能是它的原始特征之一。少量的骨镞和石、陶网坠的发现,可以说明渔猎已降为辅助性的生产了。遗址中的某些遗物,如装饰品中的绿松石、水晶以及赤铁矿等都不是附近出产的,可能是从别的地方用交换的方式得到的。至于白衣彩陶则很可能是受了渑池以东的仰韶遗址的影响。这些现象至少可以说明,当时各氏族之间是有往来和接触的。当时的社会组织是属于母系氏族的繁荣时期,氏族成员在生产资料公有的基础上,共同生产平均分配,而当时的对偶家族还没有形成独立的经济单位,家庭经济是由数个家庭以共产制的基础来经营的。当时的大型房屋绝不是对偶家族的几个人所能完成的,而有赖氏族成员的共同协作,在这样的前提之下,母系氏族社会已达到了繁荣的时期。至于所发现的绘有蛙形的彩陶图案以及有壁虎塑像的陶器,是否象征着氏族的图腾或作为氏族的标帜,也还有待于进一步研究。总之,庙底沟的仰韶文化遗存,不仅明确了仰韶文化的基本性质,且对当时生产发展的研究,也提供了有力的线索。

(二)龙山文化层

龙山文化是 1928 年在山东历城县龙山镇城子崖最初发现的,那里有薄黑有光泽的黑陶与石器共存,它的文化性质与仰韶文化不同,因而定名为龙山文化。由于有黑陶的存在,也有人称它为"黑陶文化"。但"黑陶"并不能代表整个文化的面貌,容易造成误解,将它作为文化的名称是不够妥当的。

龙山文化是黄河流域继仰韶文化而兴起的一种新石器时代文化,这在河南、山西、陕西等地都发现有地层上的证据。但所谓龙山文化遗址,由于地理分布的不同,在文化性质上也有显著的差别;曾被分为山东沿海区、豫北区和杭州湾区[31]。也有把这种地区之间的不同认为是由于时代上的区别①。解放以来,有关龙山文化的考古资料逐渐增多,所表现的地方性差异也更加显著。为了容易区别起见,曾把河南陕西地区的龙山文化称为"河南龙山文化"和"陕西龙山文化"②,以便和沿海地区的典型龙山文化相区别③。尽管在名称方面还不够妥善,但不能否认它们在文化性质上是各有特征的。关于这些问题,希望今后能及早地予以解决。至于所谓的"河南龙山文化"主要分布在河南境内,与过去所谓的龙山文化豫北区[27]和辛村期④相当,豫北和豫西之间虽也有一些小的区别,但大体上属于同一个范畴。此外陕西境内的龙山文化虽接近于"河南龙山文化",但仍有所不同,可称其为"陕西龙山文化"。

庙底沟晚于仰韶文化的遗存,却不属于"河南龙山文化"的范畴,它具有新的特点,很像是从仰韶到龙山的一种过渡阶段。由于在文化性质上和龙山文化比较接近,故暂列入龙山

---

① 见参考文献[11]页 49。
② 见参考文献[22]页 46。
③ 见参考文献[22]页 46。
④ 见参考文献[11]页 49。

文化中而称它为庙底沟第二期文化以资区别。与庙底沟隔河相对的三里桥龙山层却属于
"河南龙山文化",这两者之间的不同,在研究龙山文化的分期问题上,提供了有力的线索。

　　三门峡水库区内据调查所发现的龙山文化遗址虽少,不过凡有仰韶文化遗址的地方
往往有龙山文化层交叠存在,只是由于地面上曝露得过少,不容易被发现而已。如历次
在庙底沟的调查中都没有注意到龙山层的存在,直到正式发掘时才开始被发现。在其他
遗址的发掘中也遇到许多同样的例子。三门峡水库区内龙山文化遗存的文化性质比较
复杂,包括所谓"庙底沟第二期文化""河南龙山文化"和"陕西龙山文化"三种类型,但总
的说来,遗址范围不若仰韶文化那样广大稠密,文化堆积也比较薄。现在以庙底沟的龙
山层为重点,来分析它的文化特征。

　　庙底沟的龙山层除了在 T500 区比较集中以外,其他各区都是只有比较零星的遗存。
其分布范围虽然也很广,但远不及仰韶层那样丰富,毫无例外地都压住或打破了仰韶层
或灰坑。

　　龙山房子仅发现一座带门道的袋形竖穴,在居住面及门道的台阶上均铺有草泥土和
白灰面,根据残存的柱洞,可以复原成尖锥顶的房屋。白灰面在豫北的龙山文化遗址中
是比较常见的,一般是直径约 4 米的圆形居住面,也铺有草泥土和白灰层,但没有墙壁和
柱洞的痕迹,也没有见到门道(以上也可能是由于工作中的疏忽致未发现),火塘在白灰
面的中心①,和庙底沟龙山房子的结构是有显著区别的。和庙底沟龙山层同样结构的房
子从前并不是没有发现过,只是没有搞清它的时代和结构。例如山西万荣荆村所发现的
便没有注意到柱洞和白灰面[32];河南郑州林山砦所发现的 14 号灰坑也没有注意到柱洞,
而所谓白色的硬土面当即是白灰面的遗存[33]。以上两处的发现都没有发表图或照片,根
据文字所描写的当和庙底沟所发现的龙山房子一致,但都被误作仰韶文化的遗存。

　　这里的窑址虽形状较小,但在结构方面却比较进步,如火膛不像西安半坡 3 号窑[34]
和三里桥等仰韶窑那样长,而是利用窄深的火膛,借火力向上的作用通过火道和火眼以
进入窑室的。根据残存窑壁的弧度看,它也许是圆顶的,可能烧到最后阶段封闭窑顶,使
陶器发生还原作用,因此在陶器中产生了大量的灰陶。同样的窑址也见于山西万荣荆
村,但发掘者误视为炉灶②,也见于郑州林山砦③,两者俱误视为仰韶文化遗存。荆村简报
的图中似有火眼,但林山砦简报的图中只有火道,文中也没有提到窑箅与火眼,不知根本
不存在还是发掘时没有注意。

　　龙山的窖穴以袋形为主,一般都比仰韶灰坑整齐,虽有少数互相打破,所隔的年代也很
近,但在出土的遗物上没有什么区别。此外在两座窖穴中还发现埋葬整齐的人骨,可能是

---

①　见参考文献[37]页 7。
②　见参考文献[24]页 105 – 106。
③　见参考文献[33]页 2,图二、三。

利用废弃的窖穴作墓葬坑,人骨的置放也比较整齐,不像仰韶文化墓葬那样杂乱无序。

在 T1 区所发现的 145 座墓葬,排列整齐,方向在 175－190 度之间,这里当是氏族成员的共同墓地。仅有两个墓(M72、99)出土红陶小杯,其他均无随葬品。这种红陶小杯多见于龙山灰坑中,在仰韶灰坑中却绝无存在。从地层上观察,这批墓葬都打破了仰韶层或灰坑,上面又被东周层所压住或打破,因而肯定了它们年代的上下限。结合两墓出土龙山遗物,又可以肯定它们全部是龙山墓葬。

在 553 号灰沟北壁,发现许多木制工具所遗留的痕迹。从遗有双齿的条痕观察,它的大体形状是木柄的一端分成双叉,用双齿的部分来掘土,在日本新石器时代遗址中曾发现过木耒实物[35]和殷周时期文字中的耒,形状相似,则这里当是使用"木耒"掘土所遗留下来的痕迹。在这里没有见到像仰韶文化那样的石铲,也可能被木铲或木耒等所代替。在三里桥的龙山层中发现过同样形式的"木耒"痕迹,这种木耒是殷周时期木耒的先声,是当时一种进步的生产工具。

在全部文化遗物中,以陶片为最多,共复原器物达 60 余件。陶器的资料以夹砂粗灰陶为最多,泥质灰陶次之,细泥红陶及细泥黑陶仅占极少数;特别是细泥黑陶在这里还不到 1%,和"河南龙山文化"大不相同。它们的陶质坚硬,火候当和仰韶文化陶器相差不远,尤以细泥红陶和仰韶文化相同,可以说明这个问题。前两种陶系的颜色从灰褐色以及黑灰色,往往在同一件器物上颜色也不一致,说明在烧窑技术上还比较原始。

陶器主要采用泥条制成法,口缘多经慢轮修整,但绝不见轮制的痕迹。此外也采用接底的办法,分别制成器身与器底,然后接合在一起,这种制法在仰韶文化中并不明显,但这里却相当清楚,在"河南龙山文化"的陶器中也有同样的例子。除夹砂粗灰陶以外,陶胎有薄达 0.2 厘米者,应是蛋壳陶的前身。器身表面的纹饰以篮纹为最多,表面磨光者次之,绳纹又次之,方格纹、划纹最少见。此外尚有附加堆纹、镂孔和彩绘等装饰方法。彩绘仅限于细泥红陶,且可分为两种:一种是在小陶杯的表面涂抹紫红色陶衣,由于陶衣不匀,有着涂抹的痕迹,在龙山灰坑中曾有多量出土,仰韶灰坑中绝未发现,过去在仰韶村也曾发现过,但误作仰韶遗物①;另外一种是在敛口的深腹罐上,绘以黑色的菱形带纹,虽非正式发掘,但确与龙山遗物共存。1958 年在山西平陆盘南村龙山灰坑中也获得 3 件同样的彩陶罐,但在庙底沟仰韶层或灰坑中却绝未见到同样器形或花纹的彩陶。这种彩陶片过去在仰韶村也曾发现过,但被误视为仰韶文化的彩陶②。此外在灰陶杯上也发现过绘朱的痕迹,系烧好陶器以后再在上面绘上红色花纹,与以上两种不同,可惜花纹脱落不清晰。根据以上的地层证据,证明了龙山文化中确有彩陶存在,则将"彩陶文化"作为仰韶文化的命名,越发显得不妥当了。

---

① 见参考文献[10]图版四三,17。
② 见参考文献[10]图版四三,18、19。

　　陶器中有较多的大型的陶器,特点也非常显著,有碗、盆、罐、杯、豆、鼎、斝、灶、尖底瓶等器形,其中有不少的陶器好像是承袭了仰韶文化器形发展而来的,尤以杯、罐、尖底瓶及鼎等较为突出。尖底瓶是仰韶文化中的典型产物,类似这里的尖底瓶也见于渑池县仰韶村[①],在陕西华阴横阵村也有碎片出土[②],都和仰韶文化的尖底瓶有很大区别,而又有比较密切的联系。涂有红陶衣的小杯是这里的特殊产物,和仰韶的粗陶小杯当也有一定的联系。值得注意的是它的器形、陶衣等和湖北京山屈家岭出土的所谓"蛋壳彩陶"也非常接近,或者可以说明两者之间多少有一些关系。双耳盆是新兴的器形,豆、鼎等开始增多,斝的出现无疑是后来陶鬲的前身。总之,从庙底沟第二期文化的陶器上来看,具有由仰韶到龙山的过渡形态是非常浓厚的。

　　石器中以磨制为主,打制石器的比例甚少,且仅限于两侧带缺口的打制石刀,除和仰韶石刀完全相同的以外,也多修成矩形,而边缘及刃部常有加工的痕迹。石斧数量较多,器形也多厚大,横剖面成矩形者尤为这里的特点,这种石斧可能是砍伐树木的主要工具,由于斧身的加大加重,当可增加工作的效率。过去曾把这类石斧视为仰韶文化的典型产物[③],现在无论在庙底沟或三里桥都仅见于龙山层中,据此也可以纠正过去的错误认识。锛的数量较少,一般的形状都较小,并发现三件背部微行隆起,很像东南沿海地区的有段石锛。石刀除长方形以外,更有半月形的,还出现了石镰,这两种虽发现不多,但证明它们确是在龙山文化中才开始产生的。特别是石镰的出现,象征了在农业生产上的进步。其他如较多石镞的发现也是仰韶文化中所没有的。从石器的制法和形状上来观察,都比仰韶文化有了显著的进步。

　　骨器颇为丰富,无论数量和种类都远超过了这里仰韶文化层所出的,可能与家畜大量出现和骨料来源日渐丰富有关。器形有针、锥、镞、笄、梳等,其中不少进步的形式,如5C式骨笄是殷代骨笄的先声;骨梳虽制作简单,但殷周时期的骨梳还是承袭了这个系统。角器仅有角锥、凿两种。蚌制的刀、镞开始出现。牙器以牙镞最为罕见,至于磨制的牙片可能作为刀类使用,都是仰韶文化中所没有的。

　　装饰品的数量不多,陶制的有用赤铁矿染过的陶珠和陶管(瑱?)。石璜可能是利用折断的石环所改制。以上的装饰品可能都与悬饰有关。

　　根据文化遗物的性质来分析,庙底沟第二期文化确不同于河南地区所习见的"河南龙山文化",我们可以从陶器上举几个例子来说明:如陶器全部是手制的,不见轮制的痕迹,也没有典型的黑陶。纹饰以篮纹为主,绳纹次之,方格纹极少见,并有彩陶共存。器形都具有它自己的特点,有斝无鬲,这些都与"河南龙山文化"不同。如盆、罐、尖底瓶等器形还承袭着仰韶文化的形制,而彩陶更为突出的证据。至于斝、鼎、罐、豆等器形也开

---

①　见参考文献[10]图版二二,1－2。

②　见参考文献[1]图四,4－5。

③　见参考文献[13]页48。

了"河南龙山文化"陶器的先河,而类似蛋壳陶陶片的大量出现也说明了这个问题,因此它可能是从仰韶到龙山的一种过渡性质的遗存,当属于龙山文化的早期。

关于这种类型的遗址并不是第一次发现,由于过去没有搞清楚地层,都当作仰韶文化来看待,以致没有引起应有的注意。通过庙底沟的发掘才第一次分析清楚,我们相信搞清这个阶段的文化性质,对中国新石器时代考古的研究上是有一定作用的。过去在仰韶村所发现的遗物中便含有这种类型的遗物,显著的例子如菱形带状纹的彩陶片、带红色陶衣的小杯和小口尖底瓶等①,其他如大口或敛口的深腹罐,也都是仰韶文化或"河南龙山文化"中所没有的②。山西万荣县荆村不仅有与庙底沟同样形状的房屋与窑址,所出土的斝、小口罐、圜底罐等也和庙底沟的器形基本相同③。上述二地因有仰韶文化的遗存,就把这种类型的遗物归入了仰韶文化。解放以后在洛阳孙旗屯和郑州林山砦也都发现过,虽发表的遗物不多,但据我们实地观察标本的结果,基本上都与庙底沟相同,而发掘者也都误视为仰韶文化。如孙旗屯是根据它打破仰韶灰坑而定为仰韶晚期[36],其中灰陶的盆、罐、豆等皆和庙底沟一致,至于发掘者称其有彩陶共存,但彩陶的性质不详,除可能混有仰韶彩陶片以外,也许还含有龙山文化的彩陶。林山砦不仅有与庙底沟同样的房子和窑址,而且双耳盆、小口罐等皆和庙底沟相似④。最近在山西平陆盘南村也发现了同样性质的遗存叠在仰韶层的上面,其基本性质和庙底沟一致,并复原了 3 件和庙底沟同样器形和纹饰的彩陶盆。在陕西华县柳子镇也发现了同类型的遗存叠在仰韶层上,陶器的器形也和庙底沟一致,但据发表的简报中却混有陶鬲⑤,可能是没有搞清地层而将较晚期的器物(如陕西龙山文化)混入本层内,不然,其他遗址中都没有发现过陶鬲,而柳子镇的发现是值得怀疑的。根据上述各地的发现,可以证明以庙底沟为代表的龙山遗存,确有它自己的特征,而代表着一定的发展阶段,在分布上也相当广泛,因此我们暂称它为庙底沟第二期文化。从地层堆积上证明它晚于仰韶文化,同时在文化性质上又比"河南龙山文化"具有若干原始性质,很可能"河南龙山文化"是从庙底沟第二期文化中所发展出来的。

这个时期的生产仍是以农业为主的,在生产工具上有了更显著的改进,虽没有仰韶文化所常见的石铲,但可能用木铲代替。此外发现了双齿木耒的痕迹;同样的痕迹也见于三里桥龙山层中,直到殷周时期还是一种主要的农具,和粗笨的石铲相比较,较多木制工具的出现是具有重大的进步意义的。收割工具中除了打制石刀和长方形单孔石刀以外,还多出了半月形石刀、蚌刀和石镰。不仅种类加多,如石镰是附柄使用的,较石刀更可以提高工作效率。从生产工具的发展上可以间接说明当时的农业生产上也比仰韶文

---

① 见参考文献[10]图版四三,17—19;二二,1 - 2。
② 见参考文献[10]图版九,4;十,3。
③ 见参考文献[24]图版三,2、4、5。
④ 见参考文献[33]图版壹,2、3、13。
⑤ 见参考文献[15]图版三,8、12。

化有更多的进步。农作物的种类还不清楚,当和仰韶文化相同,也应是以粟类为主的。其次家畜也占很重的地位,由于出土的家畜骨骼过于破碎,无法做比较正确的统计,不过从出土量上观察,家畜骨骼较庙底沟仰韶文化层空前增多,如 26 个龙山灰坑出土的家畜骨骼,远远超过了 168 个仰韶灰坑所出土的数量,由此可见其情况的一般了。不仅数量多,除猪、狗以外,也有不少的羊骨和几块牛骨,这些都说明当时的家畜是比这里的仰韶文化层发达。鸡骨的发现,还无法确定当时鸡是否为家禽。过去在辽宁旅顺羊头洼遗址中也曾发现过鸡骨[39],则从龙山文化时期开始饲养家鸡的可能性并不是没有的,但还待于更多的发现来证明。根据石、骨、蚌、牙等镞类和石网坠的存在,但数量不多,也发现了鹿、麝、狐、虎等骨骼和黄颡骨胸鳍刺,这些都表现了渔猎经济还是当时的一种辅助生产。从农业和家畜的进一步发展,象征着龙山文化的生产经济有了更大的提高。

从生产的进步上也反映了社会组织的变化,根据农业的进一步发展和家畜的大量出现当反映了由母系氏族社会向父系氏族社会的转化过程,如恩格斯所指出的:"随着畜群及其他新的财富底出现,在家庭里面便发生了革命。……谋生的工具是由男性所制造的,因而成了他的财产。畜群是新的谋生工具:它们的最初的驯养与以后对它们的照管都是男性的事情。……而把妇女排挤到第二位了"[37]。至于所发现的成群墓葬,有固定的方向及葬式,当是氏族成员的共同墓地。值得注意的是全部墓葬都是单人葬,不见仰韶墓葬那样多人合葬的现象①,也许象征着社会组织的变化,而以氏族为中心的合葬法逐渐被淘汰了,这些还有待于今后的发现与研究。从以上的事实证明,当时的经济基础已在变化,私有制逐渐萌芽,而由母系氏族向父系氏族过渡大约是以这个时期为转折点的,嗣后更向高度发展,而加速了原始氏族公社的解体。由仰韶文化到龙山文化的过渡,由于生产力的进一步提高,推动了社会组织的转化,因而所反映的物质文化也就起了根本性的变化。

二　三里桥

(一)仰韶文化层

三里桥遗址的面积较小,约为 180,000 平方米。在整个遗址内都有仰韶层的分布,在遗址东部仰韶层的上面还叠有龙山层,但它的分布却不及仰韶层那样广。由于发掘的重点放在龙山层的地方,因而仰韶文化的收获不如龙山文化丰富。

这里没有发现仰韶的房子,只发现了 47 个灰坑,它的形状和庙底沟仰韶层的大体相同,多被龙山灰坑所打破,保存完整者极少。陶窑共发现了两座,虽和西安半坡所发现的

---

① 在许多仰韶文化的葬地中除了单人葬以外,也有部分是多人合葬的,例如陕西西安半坡、宝鸡第四中学、华阴横阵村及山西永济东庄村都有 2 人或更多的人合葬;华县柳子镇安家堡合葬现象比较普通,在一墓中人骨有由 12 – 23 具者。这些合葬的现象可能说明是以母系氏族为中心的葬法,并且是比较普遍的。到了龙山文化这种现象比较少见。最低在庙底沟 145 座墓葬中并没有发现过合葬。这种现象也许还反映着社会组织的情况。

筒形窑有些近似[34]，但并不完全一致。这里的陶窑由长筒形火膛和圆形的窑室所构成，窑室周围有直立的窑壁，残高达 0.36 米，火膛和窑室都在同一个平面上，没有火道和窑算的痕迹。从残存的窑壁观察，原来的窑室当是敞口的，在烧窑过程中也容易使陶器发生氧化作用；长筒形的火膛除容纳燃料以外，并兼有火道的作用。从结构上来看，这种陶窑是比较原始的。此外还发现了两座墓葬，被压在龙山层的下面，而打破了仰韶层，都是长方形竖穴，仰身伸直葬，没有随葬品。

文化遗物总的特点和庙底沟仰韶层基本相同，但在陶器上的区别却比较显著。如这里的彩陶数量很少，占陶片总数的 2.47%，花纹也比较简单，器形仅复原了钵、碗、盆、罐、器座等。圜底陶钵是这里显著的特点，数量也很多，这在庙底沟仰韶层中却绝未见到过；相反的却缺少庙底沟仰韶层中所常见的曲腹的碗、盆（仅发现个别的曲腹盆，但不绘彩）。至于陶器上的彩绘多见于口缘上，腹部绘彩者却很少见到，从彩绘的部位以及结构上来观察，很像是一种退化的形式。石器和骨器的数量不多，器形也和庙底沟仰韶层近似。值得注意的是在这里没有发现过石铲的痕迹，这种情况和半坡也极为近似（半坡仅发现 1 块残片），是否已有其他种类的掘土工具（如木制工具）出现，还需要今后继续研究。

三里桥和庙底沟两个遗址隔河相对，距离很近，但仰韶层所表现的文化面貌却不相同，很清楚看出是属于互不相同的两种类型。三里桥的仰韶层不够典型，发现的器物也太少，难于进行分析，在比较上也有一定的困难。从总的文化特征上来看，和陕西西安半坡非常接近，如这里的陶窑、圜底钵、筒形罐都曾见于半坡，虽然彩陶纹饰不同，且半坡没有敛口盆，这些可能是地方性的关系。同样类型的仰韶遗存在水库区内也有很广泛的分布，经过发掘的遗址如陕县的七里堡和山西平陆盘南村都和三里桥仰韶层相同，而在陕西境内也有不少的仰韶遗址和半坡相同，因此我们相信三里桥的仰韶层和半坡可能是比较接近的，或可以暂归于同一种类型。同时这种类型的仰韶遗存往往与以庙底沟为代表的仰韶遗存交错存在，这显然是具有时代上的意义而不可能是由于地方性的关系。关于上述两种类型的仰韶遗存的相对年代，因为没有找到地层证据，一时还难以解决。不过我们相信以三里桥仰韶层为代表的遗存，虽然彩陶数量少，花纹比较简单，但不代表着原始形态，可能是晚于以庙底沟仰韶层为代表的遗存。

（二）龙山文化层

龙山层仅分布在遗址的东部，面积较小。在这里只发现过白灰面的残片，并没有见到房子。共发现了 103 个灰坑，以坑壁整齐的袋形灰坑为最多，打破关系也比较复杂，但所出土的遗物并没有什么区别，可能年代不会隔得太久。陶窑只发现一座，保存相当完整，在结构上和庙底沟龙山陶窑微有不同，前面有一个方形的深火口，通过火膛分成 4 股火道进入窑室，以火道中间的隔梁代替窑算，窑室呈圆形，残壁作弧状，高达 0.38 米，说明当时的窑室可能是圆顶的，烧到最后阶段可以封闭窑顶然后"饮水"促使陶器发生还原作用。不仅窑室较大，它的结构也比庙底沟龙山陶窑更为进步。这个陶窑系于生土中挖成,在窑壁上还遗有许多和庙底沟龙山层相同的木末痕迹,证明木末也是当时的主要挖土工具。墓葬仅发现了1座,也是长方形的竖穴,仰卧伸直葬,但头向与仰韶墓葬不同,无随葬品,因为由龙山层打破了仰韶层,故时代比较明确。

在全部文化遗物中以陶片为最多,共复原完整陶器69件。无论质料、制法、纹饰和器形的比例,都和庙底沟龙山层有很大的不同。陶质以夹砂粗灰陶和泥质灰陶为最多,夹砂粗红陶和细泥黑陶次之,泥质红陶最少见。陶器的颜色比较一致,灰陶中不见庙底沟第二期文化那样不纯的现象,这表明在烧窑技术上有了更大的改进。这里的轮制陶器约占全部陶器的1/5,也有少量的典型蛋壳陶,其他是采用了泥条制法。至于纹饰以绳纹为最多,篮纹次之,方格纹较少,素面或磨光的陶器也大量出现,划纹和镂孔也比较常见。器形有碗、盆、杯、豆、鬲、斝、甗、器座等,绳纹带鋬的陶鬲大量出现,斝很少见,并出现了甗,也有盉的流部残片,但未见鼎的痕迹;较多的带耳的罐、杯也是这里的特点,说明绝大部分器物都是属于典型的"河南龙山文化"陶器。其中的长颈罐(B8b)与山东日照两城镇所出土的一致[39],双耳罐(D1)也与两城镇所出土的近似①。其中某些陶器如A1,A3a、b,B6c等罐形器以及陶鬲均与陕西长安客省庄相接近,说明这里和东西的龙山文化遗存均有若干联系,但其基本性质还是属于"河南龙山文化"的范畴。根据仰韶村所出土的陶器中也有很多和这里相同的,说明它也包含了"河南龙山文化"的遗存。石器有斧、锛、刀、镞等,都是磨制的,未见打制石器,可能也是它的进步特征之一。骨器较丰富,磨制精致,有针、锥、笄、镞、铲、凿等,骨铲是利用家畜的下颌骨磨制而成,也是相当进步的生产工具。蚌器有刀、镰、坠、笄等。以上的石、骨、蚌等器物,基本上都是龙山文化中所常见的产物,如不见打制石器和出现了骨铲,都具有更进步的意义。

三里桥的龙山层是属于河南境内所常见的"河南龙山文化"的范畴,它比庙底沟第二期文化具有更进步的性质,而斝和若干罐形器(如A2a、B6b、B9a、B9b)等基本上还是承袭庙底沟第二期文化的陶器形制。而陶轮的出现推动了制陶技术的更高发展,也象征了制陶业更明确的分工,因此我们相信"河南龙山文化"是承袭庙底沟第二期文化发展而来的。希望在今后能够找到明确的地层证据来加以说明。根据三里桥遗址中的部分遗物和山东日照两城镇及陕西长安客省庄相同,或者可以说明三者在年代上是大体相等的,至于彼此之间的不同,可能是代表着地方性的缘故。

三　庙底沟与三里桥的关系

庙底沟和三里桥两个遗址隔河相对,中间是一条宽约1,400米的河谷。两个遗址都有仰韶、龙山和东周的堆积,但所表现的文化面貌却互不相同,它们绝不是代表地域上的

---

① 见参考文献[38]图版陆,1。

特点,而可能具有时代上的意义。不仅庙底沟和三里桥如此,即附近的陕县七里堡和山西平陆盘南村也都是同样的情况,这些现象对研究新石器文化的分期,提供了一些重要的线索。至于庙底沟和三里桥两个遗址的新石器文化内涵,在时代上可能有着交错的关系,其发展顺序可推断如下:

庙底沟(Ⅰ)→三里桥(Ⅰ)→庙底沟(Ⅱ)→三里桥(Ⅱ)

关于仰韶、龙山的相对年代是无可怀疑的,但是仰韶或龙山本身分期的孰早孰晚还缺乏地层上的证据,以上只是一种假设,可能中间还有间隔,每个阶段也未必是紧紧衔接的;仰韶或龙山发展阶段的假设是否妥当,也有待于今后工作去证实。

根据上述的假设,也会产生这样的一个疑问。庙底沟和三里桥两个遗址的同一文化内涵为什么会属于不同的时期? 并且它们的发展为什么会不相连续? 这或者可以用青龙涧的河道变迁来解释它。这里位于青龙涧的下游,河谷宽达 1,400 余米,河道是经常变迁的。如果河道靠南流,则居住在庙底沟的人类用水方便,但三里桥却距河道较远,用水比较困难;相反的,如果河道靠北流,则居住在三里桥用水相当方便,而居住在庙底沟却比较困难,也许当时人类由于追逐水源的关系也就不能够长期地定居在同一个地点。例如我们 1953 年及 1955 – 1956 年在陕县调查发掘时,青龙涧的河道主要靠在南边,有一股河道紧靠着庙底沟遗址,但在 1957 年夏季经过大水泛滥以后,主要的河道都转移到北边而靠近三里桥了。现代和古代的情况未必相同,但河道的变迁却是不可避免的,在追逐水源而向适当地点迁居的前提下,也就形成了隔河相对而在时间上又互有先后的两个遗址。

四 仰韶文化与龙山文化的关系

自从 1931 年在豫北安阳后冈发现关于仰韶和龙山的交叠证据以后,在豫西、晋南和关中等地都陆续有所发现,两者的相对年代已经是无可怀疑的了。但是两者间的关系,过去也有许多争论,大体上认为这两种文化的来源不同①,而很少注意到这两种文化之间是否具有渊源关系。

过去安特生在仰韶村遗址的发掘中存在着严重的缺点,甚至于连仰韶文化的基本性质都未能搞清楚,因此很多考古工作者都怀疑仰韶村是包含着不同时期的遗存。根据解放后试掘中所遇到的现象,曾提出它可能是属于"仰韶和龙山的混合文化",但还不能完全解决仰韶村遗址的根本矛盾。我们并不否认"混合文化"的存在,因为在两种文化互相

---

① 过去所发表的著作中,一般认为龙山文化起源于东方,由东向西发展并逐渐代替了仰韶文化。也有认为由于来源不同,两者接触后首先产生了"混合文化"。关于龙山文化的起源问题目前还不容易肯定,因为这些不同类型的龙山文化,它们的来源未必完全相同,这些问题还有待于今后解决。

接触的条件下,是有"混合"的可能性的。通过三门峡水库区的调查和发掘又提供了许多新的线索,使我们有必要来重新考虑仰韶和龙山文化之间的关系问题。首先应该肯定在仰韶文化中确有一些器物好像具有龙山文化的特点,但这并不一定是受了龙山文化的影响以后才开始产生的。因为某些器形可能在较早的时期便已经萌芽,经过发展到晚期才成为成熟的定型,甚至于在制法上也是互不相同的。例如仰韶文化中的黑陶以及类似蛋壳陶的陶片都没有轮制的痕迹,圈足器在仰韶文化中也已经产生了,但不普遍。从上述现象或者可以说明具有所谓龙山文化特点的某些陶器,在仰韶文化中已经萌芽,到龙山文化中才成为成熟的定型,如果承认龙山文化是继承仰韶文化而进一步发展的文化,则在仰韶文化中所谓有龙山文化的因素,也就不足为奇了,因此混合文化的提法,也就值得再考虑了。

仰韶村的遗物确也相当复杂,根据陕县庙底沟和三里桥发掘的结果来相互对照,可以看出仰韶村包括了不同的文化和不同的时期,计有和庙底沟同样的仰韶文化层(以彩陶片、尖底瓶片和石铲等为代表)[①]、庙底沟第二期文化(以菱形带状纹彩陶片、带红陶衣小杯、篮纹尖底瓶、镂孔豆、盆、甑、大口罐和鼎等为代表)[②]、"河南龙山文化"(以鬲、单耳杯和单耳罐等为代表)[③]、东周时期(以圆锥形小陶器和陶鬲为代表)[④]等四个不同时期,而包括庙底沟(Ⅰ、Ⅱ)和三里桥(Ⅱ、Ⅲ)两个遗址的内容。它们相距不过 50 公里,而遗物又相同,绝不会有所谓地方性的差异,主要的关键是安特生在仰韶村的发掘中把地层搞乱了,以致给仰韶文化的概念造成一定程度的混乱,许多年来未能够很好地解决。根据庙底沟和三里桥的发掘可以得到一个有力的反证。

---

① 见参考文献[10]图版二四;三六,1、6;四一;四二;四三,1－12;四四;五九,1。
② 见参考文献[10]图版二,3－6;九,4;十,2－4;十五,4－5;二十;二二;二八;四三;17－19。
③ 见参考文献[10]图版一,2－4;十一;十九,5、6。
④ 见参考文献[10]图版二,2;二七。

伍　结束语

这次配合三门峡水库工程在陕县所发掘的庙底沟和三里桥,是两个距离很近,而文化性质又相类似的新石器时代遗址。由于规模较大,资料丰富,不但解决了过去所存在的一些问题,同时也奠定了今后系统研究的基础。其中的许多重要线索是值得特别一提的。

一　庙底沟

庙底沟主要是新石器时代的仰韶文化堆积,也有少量的龙山文化堆积和极少量的东周时期堆积,此外还有少数的汉唐墓葬。

仰韶文化层的两座房子虽是仰韶文化的常见形式,但屋内4个柱洞的下面垫有石柱础却是这里的特点,并把石柱础的使用年限更提早了。也解决了红烧土居住面的形成不是由于火烧,而是用红烧土末羼入的结果。大量的灰坑对仰韶文化窖穴的一般形制提供了更多的证明。所复原的690多件陶器,则是豫西新石器时代遗址中的空前发现,使我们对仰韶陶器有了更全面的认识。无论从陶器的形制或花纹上都具有显著的特点,特别是纹饰复杂和数量丰富的彩陶,不仅具有一定的地理因素,也可能还代表着时代上的意义。生产工具中以打制石器为主,磨制石铲在这里也有不少的发现,骨器不多,家畜种类简单而数量少,这些都代表着它的原始形态,而可能属于仰韶文化比较早期的遗存。

这里的龙山层是这次工作中的重要发现,给我们第一次搞清了它的文化性质,可暂称它为庙底沟第二期文化,很可能为龙山早期或由仰韶到龙山的一种过渡性质的文化。虽仅发现1座房子,但也搞清了它的结构。其他如灰坑比较整齐,窑址构造完善,都是比较进步的现象。木末痕迹的发现,最低说明在龙山文化时期已开始使用它,并象征着一种进步的生产工具。成群的墓葬除阐明葬俗以外,其中大批的人骨将是人类学研究上的宝贵资料。陶器依旧采用手制,还没有出现轮制的方法。除大量的灰陶以外,也有少量的细泥红陶和个别的彩陶。从陶器的形制以及纹饰等若干因素来看,它上承袭着仰韶文化,下启发着龙山文化,过渡的性质是相当明显的。石器中打制者减少,骨器增多,蚌器开始出现,都说明了它们的进步性质。从生产工具上的进步也表现了农业生产技术的发展,从家畜种类与数量的增多,也表现了财富的不断积累,生产力的大大提高,更推进了社会的进一步发展。

东周时期的文化层仅分布在T1区内,并有较多的路土踏坏了龙山墓葬。但灰层不显著,遗物不多,仅有少量陶片和铜镞等,似属战国时期的堆积。西汉墓仅有葬幼儿的瓦棺及瓮棺两种。唐墓仅有1座,随葬品丰富,大约是唐代中叶以后的墓葬。

二　三里桥

三里桥也同样有仰韶、龙山和东周时期的堆积,但仰韶和龙山所代表的文化面貌却与庙底沟不同。

仰韶层中有保存完整而形制原始的陶窑。遗物不多,在陶器中缺乏庙底沟所常见的曲腹碗、盆,而出现了庙底沟所没有的圜底钵。彩陶纹饰简单,数量也大为减少,表现了彩陶的退化倾向。不见石铲可能为木制工具所代替。它的时代也许晚于庙底沟的仰韶文化层。

龙山文化层是属于典型的"河南龙山文化"的范畴,所发现的陶窑形制稍大,而结构也比庙底沟龙山窑进步,窑壁上有和庙底沟同样的木末痕迹。有较多的轮制陶器,并有典型的黑陶,但不见彩陶的痕迹。开始出现陶鬲及龙山文化的典型陶器。从许多迹象来看,它可能是承袭着庙底沟第二期文化而发展的。

东周时期堆积不多,出土有战国陶片和铜镞等,也发现了1枚"安邑二釿"的魏国货币,对时代提供了更明确的证据。

三　几点收获

通过庙底沟和三里桥两个遗址的发掘,不仅解决了仰韶和龙山文化的性质及其分期线索,而最重要的是解决了仰韶文化和龙山文化之间的关系问题。庙底沟第二期文化确是这次工作中的主要收获,不仅首次搞清了它的文化性质为今后研究铺平了道路,也了解它承袭着仰韶文化的若干因素,开了"河南龙山文化"的先声,显然是属于两者之间的过渡阶段。据此可以做这样解释:晋、陕一带的庙底沟第二期文化是从仰韶文化中发展出来的,而"河南龙山文化"和"陕西龙山文化"又是继承庙底沟第二期文化而继续发展的。至于"河南龙山文化"中有山东地区的典型陶器,也可能是受了山东地区龙山文化的影响。如果确可以这样解释的话,则山东地区的龙山文化很可能另有来源,这个问题还有待于进一步研究。

解决了由仰韶向龙山的过渡,等于阐明了中国古代文明的起源问题。我们的祖先从远古时代起经过仰韶、龙山,直到殷周,在黄河流域不断的发展而创造了高度的文化,那么,这次的发掘对证明中国古代文化发展的连续性方面,是具有重大意义的。

参考文献

［1］黄河水库考古工作队:《黄河三门峡水库考古调查简报》,《考古通讯》1956 年 5 期,第 1 -
11 页。

［2］黄河水库考古工作队:《一九五六年河南陕县汉唐墓葬发掘简报》,《考古通讯》1957 年 4 期,第
9 - 19 页。

［3］黄河水库考古工作队:《一九五六年秋季河南陕县发掘简报》,《考古通讯》1957 年 4 期,第 1 -
9 页。

［4］黄河水库考古工作队:《一九五七年河南陕县发掘简报》,《考古通讯》1958 年 11 期,第 67 -
79 页。

［5］安志敏、王伯洪:《河南陕县灵宝考古调查记》,《科学通报》1954 年 7 期,第 79 - 80 页。

［6］鹰部屋福平:《北方圈の冢》,第 23 页,图 10,1943 年。

［7］关野克:《日本住宅小史》,图 7 - 9,1942 年。

［8］М. Г. Левина, Л. П. Потапова Народы Сибири, Стр. 585,1956.

［9］安志敏:《古代的糙面陶具》,《考古学报》1957 年 4 期,第 76 页。

［10］J. G. Andersson, The Prehistoric Sites in Honan, *BMFEA* No. 19, Pl. 27, 1947.

［11］尹达:《中国新石器时代》,三联书店,第 98 - 108 页,1955 年。

［12］G. D. Wu, *Prehistoric Pottery in China*, p. 50, 1938.

［13］J. G. Andersson, Researches into the Prehistory of the Chinese, *BMFEA* No. 15, p. 72, 1943.

［14］夏鼐:《河南渑池的史前遗址》,《科学通报》2 卷 9 期,第 937 页,1951 年。

［15］黄河水库考古队华县队:《陕西华县柳子镇考古发掘简报》,《考古》1959 年 2 期,第 71 页。

［16］安特生:《中华远古之文化》,《地质汇报》第 5 号 1 册,第 14 页,1923 年。

［17］龙非了:《穴居杂考》,《中国营造学社汇刊》5 卷 1 期,第 57 - 68 页,1934 年。

［18］Anna O. Shepard, *Ceramics for the Archaeologist*, p. 107, 1957.

［19］阿尔纳:《河南石器时代之着色陶器》,第 8 页,1925 年。

［20］苏秉琦等:《洛阳中州路》,第 42 页,图版贰贰:1,1959 年。

［21］夏鼐:《河南成皋广武地区考古纪略》,《科学通报》2 卷 7 期,第 726 页,图 8,1951 年。

［22］安志敏:《中国新石器时代的物质文化》,《文物参考资料》1956 年 8 期,第 44 页。

［23］李济:《西阴村史前的遗存》,1927 年。

［24］董光忠:《山西万泉石器时代遗址发掘之经过》,《师大月刊》3 期,图版四、五,1935 年。

［25］张德光:《永济县金盛庄与石庄的新石器时代遗址》,《文物参考资料》1958 年 5 期,图一。

［26］石兴邦:《陕西渭水流域新石器时代的仰韶文化》,《人文杂志》2 期,图版一、四,3 - 5;图版五,
1,1957 年。

［27］梁思永:《小屯龙山与仰韶》,《庆祝蔡元培先生六十五岁纪念论文集》,下册,第 563 - 564 页,

1935 年。

〔28〕考古研究所西安工作队:《新石器时代村落遗址的发现——西安半坡》,《考古通讯》1955 年 3 期,第 15 页。

〔29〕安志敏:《中国古代的石刀》,《考古学报》第 10 册,第 42 页,1955 年。

〔30〕安志敏:《中国史前时期之农业》,《燕京社会科学》2,第 48 - 49 页,1949 年。

〔31〕梁思永:《龙山文化——中国文明史前期之一》,《考古学报》第 7 册,第 10 - 11 页,1954 年。

〔32〕卫聚贤:《中国考古小史》,第 59 页,1933 年。

〔33〕河南省文化局文物工作队第一队:《郑州西郊仰韶文化遗址发掘简报》,《考古通讯》1958 年 2 期,第 1 - 2 页。

〔34〕考古研究所西安半坡工作队:《西安半坡遗址第二次发掘的主要收获》,《考古通讯》1956 年 2 期,第 29 页,图版贰:2,3。

〔35〕森本六尔:《日本农耕文化の起源》,图 13,1941 年。

〔36〕河南文物工作队第二队:《洛阳涧西孙旗屯古遗址》,《文物参考资料》1955 年 9 期,第 60 - 61 页。

〔37〕恩格斯:《家庭、私有制和国家的起源》,第 155 页,1954 年,人民出版社本。

〔38〕刘敦愿:《日照两城镇龙山文化遗址调查》,《考古学报》1958 年 1 期,图版陆,3。

〔39〕金关丈夫等:《羊头注》,第 97 - 99 页,图 9,1942 年。

双语版后记

　　《庙底沟与三里桥》是中华人民共和国成立以来中国科学院考古研究所(1977年改属中国社会科学院)最初的几本考古报告之一,1959年出版之后,即引起国际学术界的关注。原因在于庙底沟二期文化的发现,使中原地区史前文化的连续性得以证实,20世纪三四十年代构建的所谓仰韶文化在西、龙山文化在东的二元对立学说,受到了极大挑战。

　　这本报告出版之后不久,即发生了"文化大革命",中国的考古研究举步维艰,且差不多处于与外界隔绝的状态。《庙底沟与三里桥》很可能主要是通过张光直先生的《古代中国考古学》(耶鲁大学出版社,1963,1968和1977)受到西方读者注意的。从保存下来的通信看,开始这项翻译工程的时间,至少可以上推到1980年。1980年7月2日,美国宾夕法尼亚大学人类学系教授波西尔给夏鼐先生写信,说他本人和纽约美国自然博物馆的瓦特·费尔赛维思博士合作翻译了《庙底沟和三里桥》一书,他已经同北卡罗莱纳州的卡罗莱纳科学出版社联系出版事宜,对方表示有意出版此书。同年9月13日,夏鼐在回复波西尔的信中这样说:"来信收到了。我们高兴地获悉Fariservis博士已将《庙底沟与三里桥》一书译成英文,这对介绍新中国的考古成果以及增进中美两国考古学者的相互了解,是有极大好处的。因此我和该书的作者,愉快地接受在美国出版的建议。"又说:"为了出版的方便,我们可以提供该书的图版照片。不过这些照片我们只此一份,希望制版以后,请将原照片还给我们。如果你们同意上述办法,请与安志敏教授直接联系,以便寄去。"1981年1月21日,波西尔写信向安志敏索要照片,并把此信附给夏鼐,以便让他知道事情的进展,同时还把他的新著《印度河的古代城市》一书寄赠考古所图书室。同年2月19日,安志敏给波西尔回信说:"您给夏鼐所长和我的来信都收到了,并承蒙寄来大作《印度河的古代城市》一书,谨此致谢。《庙底沟与三里桥》一书的全部图版照片(图版壹—玖贰),已由海邮寄上,请查收。由于这份图版照片是考古所保存的完整资料,用完后请尽早退还给我。关于译文的定稿,我想不必看了,因为我相信您会译得很好,并对您的好意表示感谢。"在波西尔的上述来信中,我们知道他正在准备《庙底沟与三里桥》的最终译稿,并表示如果安志敏愿意看译稿的话,他可以把稿子寄过来。

　　为什么翻译这部报告,为什么费了许多时间和人力最后没有在美国出版,现存的档案都没有给予足够的说明。1980年12月22日,波西尔致信斯坦福大学的丁爱博教授(Albert E. Dien),对出版这部报告的原因做了稍微的说明。他说,他正在编辑一套有关古代考古遗址的"早期文明丛书"(暂定名),目的是把世界上最伟大、最重要的考古发现介绍给英文世界的读者,每本书的字数大约不超过 40,000 – 50,000 字。他透露他已经介入《庙底沟和三里桥》这部专刊的翻译工作达数年之久。这本书是在瓦特·费尔赛维思教授的指导下由西雅图华盛顿大学的几个中国人完成的。目前译稿就在他的手里,稍经加工即可出版。他还提及此事已得到夏鼐和安志敏先生的支持,他们愿意提供原版照片以便在美国出版。信中还提到张光直教授是他的朋友,张答应在不久的将来愿意提供一本关于安阳的性质相同的书籍。波西尔写信的原因,不是寻求经费方面的帮助,而是因为他刚刚知道(据同年 10 月 15 日丁爱博教授拟出版《中国考古文摘》寻求译文帮助的公开信)丁爱博计划出版 1972 – 1981 年间《考古》和《文物》杂志所发表重要论著的长篇摘要,他希望这个计划不要与《庙底沟与三里桥》的翻译撞车。

波西尔教授是南亚考古专家,对哈拉帕文明深有研究,但他对中国考古并不熟悉。主持翻译此书的瓦特·费尔赛维思教授曾经参加过第二次世界大战,战后从日本返回美国才成为职业考古学家。他的田野工作主要在巴基斯坦,也是哈拉帕文明考古的专家。不过他的兴趣广泛,写过介绍早期人类的洞穴壁画、古代埃及甚至蒙古高原的不少通俗性作品。他为什么对《庙底沟与三里桥》发生兴趣,我们并不清楚,也许是因为波西尔教授编辑"早期文明丛书"的邀请;而波西尔知道这部报告,推测应该是通过张光直先生。

1981 年 1 月 22 日,波西尔致函张光直,不仅把寄给安志敏的信附给他,让他了解考古研究所允诺可以在美国出版该书并愿意提供原版照片的情况,还请求张光直为英文版写一篇序言,以便读者了解更多的背景资料。1 月 27 日,张先生回信,答应为英文版写序,但同时希望再了解一下翻译此书的原委、过程和译者。三天之后,波西尔教授回信,说此书的初稿是在费尔赛维思教授指导下由西雅图的一群中国学生翻译的。初稿很"生硬",因此他将与 Cheng Mei Chang 合作在当年夏天把译稿加工完善。6 月 2 日,波西尔教授催问序言,同时告诉张光直他正在和一个叫 June Li 的女士加工译稿,希望可以在本年秋季定稿云云。

张先生的序言,拖了很久,一直到 1981 年 7 月 13 日才寄给波西尔教授。这篇序言,把张先生对庙底沟和三里桥遗址的理解以及报告发表 20 多年来他由新材料的发现而得到的新认识,做了简要的阐发。这是中国考古学学术史上的一篇重要文献,于今发表,距离当初张先生撰写此文,又过了 30 年。本书最后的打印稿,是 1987 年完成的。负责抄写的人告诉波西尔教授加利福尼亚科学出版社应付 96 小时的打印费,于此可知书稿也曾交付加利福尼亚科学出版社。

后来因何原因没有付印,我们无从知悉。

2009 年河南省文物考古研究所的马萧林博士在美国考古年会上巧遇波西尔,波西尔说到这本尚未出版的英文译稿。随后波西尔把初稿、修改稿和最后的定稿、原书照片以及他同夏、安、张、丁等几位先生的通信等一并寄给马萧林。马萧林又把邮包原封不动地转交给我,于是我们便启动了这个双语版的计划。

《庙底沟和三里桥》是第二部被美国考古学家翻译的中国考古报告。第一部是《城子崖》,曾于 1956 年在美国出版。《城子崖》是中国的第一本田野考古报告,也是迄今为止唯一被翻译成英文在国外出版的考古发掘报告,不过,由于流传不广,国内很少有人知道。

《庙底沟与三里桥》至今还经常被人引用,其在中国考古学史上的价值毋庸在此赘述。不过,中文版早已售罄,如果能够把中文与英文对照出版,使国内外读者一册在手,都能使用,又使更多的青年学子知道如何用另外一种语言表述某种考古现象或考古遗物,则幸何如也!

本书张光直先生序言由陈星灿翻译成中文。全书文字由孙丹、付永旭录入,陈起通读全书并加以校补。最后全书经陈星灿通校。由于编校者的水平有限,错谬之处,在所难免,敬请读者指正。此书出版,首先感谢波西尔教授惠赐英文译稿,感谢为翻译此书作出贡献的费尔赛维思教授及其他知名、不知名的译者和编校者,也感谢马萧林先生费心把译稿及原书照片送还给我们。2010 年正值考古研究所建所 60 周年,今年又逢仰韶文化发现 90 周年,本书既是对考古研究所建所 60 周年的纪念,也是对夏鼐、安志敏等已故前辈学者的缅怀。本书出版,得到河南省渑池县人民政府的部分经费资助,谷艳雪同志为此书出版花费许多心血,在此一并致谢。

陈星灿

2011 年 6 月 19 日于考古研究所

Miaodigou and Sanliqiao

Foreword

Kwang-chih Chang

The archaeological report on Miaodigou and Sanliqiao, now translated into English and published here, was an important milestone in the history of the Neolithic archaeology of China. The readers of this book may find useful a brief review of the historical context in which the original report had appeared.

In the late 1940s, just prior to the establishment of the People's Republic of China, the Neolithic archaeology of China may, in essence, be summarized by two words: Yangshao and Longshan. The former, name of a village in Mianchi county of western Henan, where the first Neolithic site of China was excavated in 1921 by J.G. Andersson, exemplified a "Late Neolithic" culture, estimated to date from the 3rd millennium B.C. and characterized by painted red pottery and round, polished stone celts. It occurred in the loessic highlands of western North China, mostly in the provinces of western Henan, Shanxi, Shaanxi, and Gansu. Longshan, on the other hand, was the name of a town in central Shandong province, in eastern North China, where a Neolithic site was excavated in 1928, that had been used to designate a second "Late Neolithic" culture, characterized by thin, lustrous, black pottery and square, polished adzes.

The Yangshao and the Longshan culture as archaeological entitles had indeed been well established, in the late 1940s, through a small series of sites, few of which had been excavated, but their respective dates and geographical areas of distribution and their interrelationship had not been clearly understood. Andersson, who had investigated more Yangshao culture sites than any other scholar, believed that this culture came into western North China in the middle of the 3rd millennium B.C., probably from western Asia. Li Ji (Li Chi) and Liang Siyong (Liang Ssu-yung), leaders of the archaeological team that excavated the site at Chengziya, in Longshan, considered that Longshan culture native Chinese whose geographic orientation was eastern and coastal. These two cultures, one western and one eastern, had seemed to meet in the province of Henan, where archaeological sites had been found that yielded cultural relics characteristic of both cultures-mainly both painted and black potsherds. These "mixed sites" were logically looked at as the archaeological localities where the two cultures had come into contact.

Miaodigou, had it been studied in the late 1940s, would probably have been classified as one of those mixed sites. But in the 1950s the archaeological scene had been changed drastically and a reassessment of Neolithic archaeology, necessitated by the new circumstances, brought about a new cultural alignment, to which the sites of Miaodigou and Sanliqiao had materially contributed.

With the establishment of the new People's Republic, two developments were consequential to the archaeological scene. The first was the rapid progress of many construction projects of major scale throughout the country, which led to accidental discoveries of numerous archaeological sites from every prehistoric and historic period. The second development pertains to the laws and regulations that had been enacted and promulgated nationally for the protection of cultural relics. Archaeologists must now work alongside engineers in construction projects, and accidental finds must also be dealt with.

In the 1950s one of the most important industrial projects was the construction of a number of reservoirs along the Yellow River of North China for hydroelectric and irrigation purposes. Among these was the Sanmen Gorge Reservoir, near Sanmenxia, in northwestern Henan. A Sanmen Gorge Reservoir Archaeology Team was organized by the Institute of Archaeology, of the Chinese Academy of Sciences, and the team was active during the period of 1955-1959. Both Miaodigou and Sanliqiao had been found and excavated during this period as a result of project-related surveys.

The characteristics of the various cultural materials at Miaodigou and Sanliqiao, and the stratification of the cultural strata represented, are described in this monograph. Briefly, the situation was like this: At Sanliqiao, a small village on Shan county in north-western Henan, a Yangshao culture and a characteristic Longshan culture (of the usual Henan variety) were found. At Miaodigou, another village in the same county, only 1400m south of Sanliqiao, two cultures were also found in stratigraphic relationship. The earlier culture, Miaodigou I, is Yangshao. The later culture, Miaodigou II, has characteristics of both Yangshao and Longshan, similar to the so-called "mixed "sites of the late 1940s. The chronological alignment of the three cultures involved in the two sites were shown to be as follows:

Yangshao(Miaodigou I and Sanliqiao I)

"Mixed culture"(Miaodigou II)

Longshan(Sanliqiao II)

This shows that the so-called "mixed culture" sites were in fact "transitional ",i. e., representing a new stage of Neolithic culture in a continuous sequence of cultural development that begins with Yangshao and goes on into Longshan. This seemingly small bit of conclusion had nevertheless transformed North China Neolithic archaeology. Instead of serving as the meeting ground of the two contemporary prehistoric cultures, one originating in the west and the other in the east, the Yellow River valley in Henan now takes the role of the cradle of a prehistoric civilization, apparently ancestral to the historic Chinese civilization, which underwent its own internal development and change. It is no accident that in 1959, the year the Miaodigou and Sanliqiao monograph was published, several papers appeared in which the thesis of a continuous development of a single prehistoric Chinese culture was presented, including: "Shi lun Huanghe liuyu xinshiqi shidai wenhua (A tentative discussions of the Neolithic cultures of the Yellow River Valley)",by An Zhimin (in *Kaogu* 1959/10,pp.559-565); "Huanghe liuyu yuanshi shehui kaogu yanjiu shang de ruogan wenti(Some issues in the archaeological study of the primitive society in the Yellow River Valley)",by Shi Xingbang(in *Kaogu* 1959/10,pp.566-570); "Guanyu zhongyuan xinshiqi shidai wenhua de jige wenti(Several issues in the Neolithic cultures of the central Plains)", by Xu Shunzhan (in *Wenwu* 1960/5,pp.36-39);and "Zhongguo xinshiqi shidai wenhua duandai(Chronology of the Neolithic cultures in China)",by myself (in *Bulletin of the Institute of History and Philology,Academey Sincia*,30.1959,pp.259-309).

Miaodigou and Sanliqiao were not the only sites where the Yangshao-Miaodigou II-Longshan sequence of continuous development had been established; other sites in western Henan investigated in the late 1950s, notably Wangwan in Luoyang, had also been brought to light. But the sites reported on this monograph were the most thoroughly excavated and they continue to serve as the type localities of both Yangshao (of the Miaodigou phase) and Miaodigou II cultures, and the development sequence characterized above remains valid for the western Henan area today.

But we have since 1959 benefitted from more than twenty years of additional archaeological research in China, and some of our views of the Chinese Neolithic archaeology have become quite different from those held at the time of this monograph's publication. It may be useful also to mention a few of these new developments to which the data from Miaodigou and Sanliqiao still pertain.

1. Chinese scientists began to determine radiocarbon dates of archaeological samples in the 1960s, and they began to publish them in 1972, thus bringing about a revolution in our knowledge concerning the prehistoric chronology of China. In his most recent comprehensive treatment of the subject, "Tan-14 ceding niandai he zhongguo shiqian kaogu xue(Carbon-14 dates and Chinese prehistoric archaeology)"(*Kaogu* 1977/4, pp.217-232), Xia Nai, director of the Institute of Archaeology, the Chinese Academy of Social Sciences, places the Yangshao culture into the period of 5000-3000 B.C., and the Longshan culture into the period of 2800-2300 B.C. The latter, in Xia's terminology, includes an earlier (Miaodiogu II) and a later (Henan Longshan) phase.The dates from Miaodigou and an adjacent site fit well within these general ranges:

    1. Miaodigou I (Yangshao)

      ZK110 5030±100 BP(half-life 5568) or 3910±125 BC(tree-ring calibrated)

      ZK112 4905±170 BP(half-life 5568) or 3545±190 BC(tree-ring calibrated)

    2. Miaodigou II(Miaodigo II)

      ZK111 4140±95 BP(half-life 5568) or 2780±145 BC(tree-ring calibrated)

    3. Wangwan II (Longshan, Henan phase)

      ZK126 3838±95 BP(half-life 5568) or 2390±145 BC(tree-ring calibrated)

The last date was derived from a sample from the Longshan stratum at Wangwan in Luoyang, which is to the east of Shan county and whose Longshan culture closely paralleled that of Sanliqiao. (All the above dates are cited in the Xia Nai paper of 1977, except for ZK112, which is seen in *Kaogu*, 1978/4). As additional dates accumulate from North China, and from western Henan in particular, our Neolithic chronology for the Miaodigou and Sanliqiao sites will become more refined and precise, but the above dates give us a pretty good idea.

2. If Miaodigou and Sanliqiao were instrumental in the initial establishment of a continuous sequence of cultural development in prehistoric China, archaeological

research throughout North China subsequent to the publication of this monograph has served to amplify and expand that cultural continuum. Although Miaodigou I represents only a late, local phase of Yangshao culture, it has long been known that Yangshao culture as a whole went back to at least 5000 B.C. in both Shaanxi and northern Henan. Now, since the late 1970s, a series of even earlier sites has been brought to light in southern Hebei, central Henan ,and the Wei River Valley in Shaanxi and easternmost Gansu; these sites, represented by Cishan in southern Hebei and Peiligang in central Henan, are carbon-dated to the 6th millennium B.C., and their cultural remains are precedent to Yangshao culture in many aspects. We are now rather close archaeologically to the beginning stages of the Chinese agricultural ways of life in the Yellow River valley.

3. It is now clear that the excavations of Miaodigou and Sanliqiao began to account for the origin of the Longshan culture of Henan. But how about the Longshan cultures of Shandong and other coastal regions? An Zhimin and Shi Xingbang, in their 1959 discussions on the Yangshao-Longshan sequence, were both careful enough to make it clear that the Miaodigou evidence applied only to the Henan Longshan culture, and that the origin of the Longshan culture of Shandong remained unknown.

In an effort to seek to explain the origin of the Longshan culture of Shandong, as well as to explain the similarities of Miaodigou II and several apparently contemporary cultures, in 1959 I proposed to formulate the concept of the Longshanoid–a supraregional cultural horizon characterized by both developmental and stylistic features common to the prehistoric cultures across a vast area of China-primarily the Miaodigou II culture of Henan, the Qinglianggang culture of Jiangsu, the Qujialing culture of Hubei, and the early Liangzhu culture of Zhejiang. Since no antededant culture had at that time been found in any of the regions involved except for Henan, I speculated that the whole horizon may have resulted from an explosive expansion of the Longshanid from its Henan basis, an expansion of both culture and population resulting from internal forces released by the agricultural revolution in the Northern Chinese Nuclear Area.

This thesis of the Longshanoid origins has now proved to be highly improbable. In the first place, radiocarbon chronology has not shown that Miaodigou II is the earliest member culture of the Longshanoid. More importantly, cultures antecedent-and in all cases probably precedent-to the coastal Longshanoid cultures have now come to light.

On the other hand, the development and stylish similarities of the many Longsha-noid culture-the above named, plus several others newly recognized-that are more or less contemporaneous remain an important fact that has to be explained. It looks that the horizon indicates a vast sphere of interaction-to borrow the terminology of the late Joseph Caldwell-which had by then been formed of several antecedent cultures that were rooted in different areas of China. This new thesis I have recently presented in an *American Scientist* paper (Volume 69, number 2, March-April 1981, pp.148-160).

4. The further development of the Henan Longshan culture, as represented by Sanliqiao II, is now an important topic for wide discussion in Chinese archaeology. There are in fact so many Henan Longshan culture sites now that this culture can be further divided into at least three local phases-the central and western Henan Long-shan phase, the northern Henan phase, and the eastern Henan phase. The first, the central and western Henan phase, characterized by Wangwan II, is generally regard-ed as being ancestral to the Erlitou culture, carbon-dated to the several centuries on both sides of 2000 B.C., which many scholars now identify with the Xia civilization in the cultural continuum first established by Miaodigou and Sanliqiao is now tied into the historic continuum of the Chinese civilization. The significance of that fact is immense and self-evident.

These new development made it abundantly clear that the Neolithic archaeology of North China has entered into a stage of sophistication and richness that was not foreseeable in 1959, when the Miaodigou and Sanliqiao monograph was published. But the monograph played a crucial role in fostering these developments, and the archaeological facts it contains are still current and important. The English transla-tion will surely help place the book among the archaeological classics of the world.

TABLE OF CONTENTS

FIGURES

PLATES

Color Plate: Painted pottery basin and jar of the Yangshao culture from Miaodigou

28   Fine red basins and *zeng* steamer of the Yangshao culture from Miaodigou

29   Fine red *zeng* steamers of the Yangshao culture from Miaodigou

30   Fine red *zeng* steamer, cups, *yu* basin, and jar of the Yangshao culture from Miaodigou

31   Fine red jars of the Yangshao culture from Miaodigou

32   Fine red jars and bottles of the Yangshao culture from Miaodigou

33   Fine red bottles, vessel covers, and vessel stand of the Yangshao culture from Miaodigou

34   Fine red vessel stands and grey plate, bowls, and basin of the Yangshao culture from Miaodigou

35   Grey basins of the Yangshao culture from Miaodigou

36   Grey basin and jars of the Yangshao culture from Miaodigou

37   Grey vessel covers, fine black jars, and coarse, sand-tempered red jars and *fu* cauldron of the Yangshao culture from Miaodigou

38   Potsherds with molded geckos of the Yangshao culture from Miaodigou

39   Coarse, sand-tempered red *fu* cauldrons, *zao* stoves, *ding* tripod, and plate of the Yangshao culture from Miaodigou

40   Coarse, sand-tempered red bowls and basins of the Yangshao culture from Miaodigou

41   Coarse, sand-tempered red basin, cups, and *yu* basins of the Yangshao culture from Miaodigou

42   Coarse, sand-tempered red jars of the Yangshao culture from Miaodigou

43   Coarse, sand-tempered red jars of the Yangshao culture from Miaodigou

44   Coarse, sand-tempered red jars of the Yangshao culture from Miaodigou

45   Coarse, sand-tempered red vessel covers and pottery knives of the Yangshao culture from Miaodigou

46   Pottery implements and ornaments of the Yangshao culture from Miaodigou

47   Pottery and stone artifacts of the Yangshao culture from Miaodigou

48   Stone implements of the Yangshao culture from Miaodigou

49   Stone implements of the Yangshao culture from Miaodigou

50   Stone spades of the Yangshao culture from Miaodigou

51   Stone hammers and so forth of the Yangshao culture from Miaodigou

52   Stone and bone artifacts of the Yangshao culture from Miaodigou

53   Bone arrowheads and so forth artifacts of the Yangshao culture from Miaodigou

54   Bone hairpins of the Yangshao culture from Miaodigou

55   Bone, antler, shell, and tooth artifacts of the Yangshao culture from Miaodigou

56   Coarse, sand-tempered grey jar and basins of the Longshan culture from Miaodigou

57   Coarse, sand-tempered grey jars of the Longshan culture from Miaodigou

58   Coarse, sand-tempered grey jars of the Longshan culture from Miaodigou

59   Coarse, sand-tempered grey jars and *ding* tripods of the Longshan culture from Miao-digou

60   Coarse, sand-tempered grey *ding* tripods of the Longshan culture from Miaodigou

61   Coarse, sand-tempered grey *ding* tripods of the Longshan culture from Miaodigou

62   Coarse, sand-tempered grey *jia* tripods of the Longshan culture from Miaodigou

63   Coarse, sand-tempered grey *zao* stoves and vessel covers of the Longshan culture from Miaodigou

64   Grey bowls and basins of the Longshan culture from Miaodigou

65   Coarse, sand-tempered grey basins and jar and grey basin, cup, and jars of the Longshan culture from Miaodigou

66   Grey jars, *dou* pedestal , and vessel covers of the Longshan culture from Miaodigou

67   Fine red cups, basins, and fine black basins of the Longshan culture from Miaodigou

68   Pottery and stone artifacts of the Longshan culture from Miaodigou

69   Stone adzes and knives of the Longshan culture from Miaodigou

70   Stone, bone, shell, and tooth artifacts of the Longshan culture from Miaodigou

71   Bone awls and so forth of the Longshan culture from Miaodigou

72   Artifacts from Tang dynasty tomb M100 at Miaodigou

73   Artifacts from Tang dynasty tomb M100 at Miaodigou

74   Pottery kiln Y4 of the Longshan culture at Sanliqiao

75   Pottery kiln Y4 of the Longshan culture at Sanliqiao

76   Fine red *bo* bowls and bowls of the Yangshao culture from Sanliqiao

77   Fine red basins and jar of the Yangshao culture from Sanliqiao

78   Fine red vessel stand and coarse, sand-tempered red jars of the Yangshao culture from Sanliqiao

79   Pottery, stone, and bone artifacts of the Yangshao culture from Sanliqiao

80   Coarse, sand-tempered grey jars of the Longshan culture from Sanliqiao

81   Coarse, sand-tempered grey *li* tripods and *jia* tripod of the Longshan culture from Sanliqiao

82   Coarse, sand-tempered grey jars and grey bowls and basin of the Longshan culture from Sanliqiao

83   Grey basins and cups of the Longshan culture from Sanliqiao

84   Grey jars of the Longshan culture from Sanliqiao

85   Grey jars of the Longshan culture from Sanliqiao

1 *INTRODUCTION*

The combined task of controlling floods, and diverting the water into irrigation systems along the course of the Yellow River, is one of the great engineering projects the Chinese people are doing in their struggle against nature. This project, guided by the Communist Party, will entirely change the natural features of the area through which the Yellow River flows, making this long river, a plague for thousands of years, a productive one. The Sanmen Gorge Reservoir is an important part in the first stage of this combined project to prevent flood, generate electricity, and improve irrigation. Its construction began on April 13, 1957. The beautiful dream of the Chinese people for thousands of years to see a "clear Yellow River" is becoming a reality.

The Yellow River is the cradle of China's civilization. The Sanmen Gorge Reservoir, located in the triangular region in the bend of the River, has been an important center of communication since ancient times, occupying an important political, economic and cultural position. In order to learn more about the ancient cultural remains in the Sanmen Gorge Reservoir area, protective measures and excavations were carried out before the water was stored. The Yellow River Reservoir Archaeological Team was formed and organized jointly by The Chinese Academy of Sciences and the Ministry of Culture in October, 1955. The deputy director of the Institute of Archaeology, Chinese Academy of Sciences, Dr. Xia Nai, organized and led the team in the investigations. In the course of the exploration, 211 ancient sites, 73 tombs, and 13 momuments were discovered[1]. The finds in this region not only were rich, but also spanned different periods in time. They may be regarded as the epitome of a phase in Chinese history, hence extremely valuable for understanding the formation and development of ancient Chinese civilization.

Since 1956, sites excavated in conjunction with the constructions of the city of Sanmenxia and centered in Shan county, Henan, include: Neolithic sites of Miaodigou and Sanliqiao, burials of the State of Guo in Shangcunling, tombs of the Eastern Zhou, Han and Tang dynasties at Houchuan, and tombs of Han and Tang at Liujiaqu, all rich in archaeological finds. [2-4] Since 1959, there were also trial and full excavations in the three provinces in the Reservoir area of Henan, Shanxi, and Shaanxi, resulting in some very important archaeological finds.

These excavations have changed the face of a formerly empty Chinese archaeological research; and raised many questions. The grand works planned by the government under the ideals of Socialism are opening new paths for archaeology, of which the construction of Sanmen Gorge Reservoir was a prime example. These projects reveal to us that it is only under the great leadership of a Socialist government that Chinese archaeology can move forward; and only through the cooperation with the great construction of Socialism that our eyes may see further, our findings may grow.

This report forms the second volume of the Yellow River Reservoir Archaeological Report, and includes the two Neolithic sites at Miaodigou and Sanliqiao. Other excavations will be edited and published as monographs or single articles.

This report was written jointly by An Zhimin, Zheng Naiwu and Xie Duanju. Parts 1, 2-I, 4 and 5 were written by An Zhimin while section II-(II)-ii, II-(III), IV, V and VI of part 2 were written by Xie Duanju and the rest by Zheng Naiwu. Proofreading was initially done by An Zhimin and the final editing and corrections by Mr. Xia Nai. The Russian and English abstracts were translated separately by Zhang Yidong and Wang Junming. The animal bones were examined by Mr. Jia Lanpo of the Institute of Vertebrate Paleontology, the Chinese Academy of Sciences.

During the process of investigation and excavation, we were assisted by the people's committee from the provincial, city and county levels, in the three provinces of Henan, Shanxi and Shaanxi, as well as the Sanmen Gorge Engineering Bureau. To them we owe our thanks.

2 *THE MIAODIGOU SITE*

I. Geography and Excavation Procedures

The Miaodigou site is situated southeast of Nanguan in Shan county, an area rich in ancient remains. We will begin with brief introduction to the geography of Shan county. Shan county was formerly part of Shan prefecture in western Henan, bordered in the north by the Yellow River, and is parallel to Pinglu county in Shanxi. The famous Sanmen Gorge is about twenty-five kilometers east of the county seat. Following the construction of the Sanmen Gorge Reservoir and the hydro-electric power station, the new city of Sanmenxia developed on the plain near Huixingzhen, a town east of the county seat.

There are many rivers in the Shan county. Aside from the Yellow River, there are two other major rivers, one of these is the Qinglongjian, also called the Tuo River in the *Shuijingzhu* (the 6th century *Commentary on the Water Classics*). The classic records that the Tuo River "originates in Tuo mountain, flowing northwestward; it passes the west of the Shan county seat, and flows northwestward into the River (Yellow River)". The Qinglongjian spans across Shan county separating the county seat from Nanguan. At present, both the busy city center and railway station are on the south bank of the Qinglongjian. The part of the city on the north bank is not as prosperous. The other major river is the Canglongjian, also called the Qiao River in the *Shuijingzhu*. It says that the Qiao River "originates in a mountain called Changcheng, commonly known as Zhigan mountain. These were names given at different times. The mountain is eighty *li* (half kilometer) south of the county seat, and its river separates into two streams which merge together, flowing northwestward and into the Yellow River". Canglongjian also enters the Yellow River near the county seat. There are many small tributaries which drain into these above mentioned rivers. On the banks of all these tributaries, sites from the Neolithic and earlier periods are found. Because of the converging rivers and fertile land, this area was suitable for settlement and production in ancient times. In the area near Shan county seat, especially, the land is bounded by the Yellow River in the north, while receiving two rivers, the Qinglongjian and Canglongjian. Therefore, geographically, it is very important and many large sites with complex chronologies are concentrated in the vicinity of Shan county seat (Fig. 1). Many sites, including Miaodigou (Yangshao, Longshan, and Eastern Zhou), Sanliqiao (Yangshao, Longshan, and Eastern Zhou), Qilipu (Yangshao, Longshan, Yin, Eastern Zhou, and Han) are found here. Across the Yellow River in Pinglu county in Shanxi lies the village of Pannan (Yangshao, Longshan, and Eastern Zhou). Because of the above mentioned conditions we centered our work in Shan county, beginning with Miaodigou and Sanliqiao. Since 1958, we have also started the excavation of other sites.

Miaodigou site is on the south bank of the Qinglongjian, and east of the Shan county railway station. It is situated on a relatively flat loess plain which is divided by two north-south ravines. The ravine to the west is commonly known as Miaodigou, and is more than forty meters deep. Many caves were dug in its sides. It is the center of Miaodi village. The ravine to the east is commonly called Cilonggou, also more than forty meters deep. At the bottom of the ravine is a small stream which originates more than twenty kilometers away in Yaotou. The section of the ravine between Yaotou and Chendong is called Huoshaoyanggou. The lower part beyond Chendong is called Cilonggou. The perennial stream, flowing from south to north, joins the Qinglongjian. It is probably the Dugushui described in the *Shuijengzhu*, "flowing from the nearby streams in the south and enters the Tuo in the north". The Qinglongjian cuts into the northern border of this area, causing erosion and forming a cliff about forty meters high. The Long-Hai Railroad runs in an east-west direction near the banks. Hanzhuang, to the south, is a loess tableland more than twenty meters high with field terraces on its sides.

Thus, Miaodigou is fenced from the north by the "Jian" river (Qinglongjian) and Hanzhuang in the south, while bounded by the ravines in both east and west, forming a roughly rectangular plain. The Neolithic sites are mainly scattered on this plain. Sites are also found in the area near the Jian River, on the east bank of the Cilonggou (Pl. XCIII) where it joins Qinglongjian. This triangular area must have been a good area for Neolithic settlement and production. On the cliffs of the two east and west ravines and on both sides of the Longhai Railway traces of ash and ash pits are exposed. The total area of this site is 240, 000 square meters, much larger than even the big villages near Shan county. Across the river on the north bank is the Neolithic site of Sanliqiao, some 1400 meters away and separated by a broad valley.

Most of the area of Miaodigou is farmland with the present day village centered in the western part of the site and around the caves dug in the ravines. Only one building remains on the site, a temple dedicated to the Earth Goddess, now converted into the Miaodigou

Primary School. "Miaodi" or Miaodigou actually refers to the village on the western part of the site. For convenience we have named the entire area surrounding the site Miaodigou. The term "Miaodi" had an early origin which is definitely related to the temple of the Earth Goddess. An inscription from this temple dated to the Ming dynasty, 18th year of Chenghua (1482) states, "about one *li* or so south of the prefecture is a temple called Earth Goddess, recorded in various local annals. It was built in the 2nd year of Dading by a local man named Gao Da, and was therefore commonly known as the Gao Family Temple. In our present dynasty, the 25th year of Hongwu, Hongnongwei director Zhou Jian rebuilt it. Many families resided near the temple, two-thirds belonging to the Gao. From ancient times to the present, the Gao family has cared for the temple." During excavation we have also found a piece of land deed in red ink, dating to the 16th year of Hongzhi in the Ming dynasty (1503), "The person who is from the two *li* western border of Shan county in Henan now lives at Miaodi". Hence we know that the name Miaodi was used as early as the Ming Dynasty.

This site was first discovered in the autumn of 1953 by the Henan Archaeological Investigation Team of the Institute of Archaeology in the Chinese Academy of Sciences. [5]The Yellow River Reservoir Archaeological Team, in its general survey and reexamined investigations, made many significant explorations. Due to its size and the rich finds, we chose this site to train our staff, as well as to start the first large scale excavation, laying a foundation for our future work.

Two excavations were completed at Miaodigou, the first being from September 31 to December 6, 1956. We first made 103 exploratory pits on the east side of the site, each measuring four by four meters and numbered T1-100 (Three additional pits were added, and simply included in the T1 area, see Pl. XCIV). Next, fifty-three pits were dug on the west side, and numbered T100-150 (Including three additional pits, simply designated as area T100).

The second excavation began on March 26 and ended on July 25, 1957. There were forty more pits dug on the west side and numbered T203 to T285 (not consecutively numbered and as before, were also appended, simply called area T200). To the west of the central part of the site, seventy-two pits were dug and numbered T301-359 (with eleven pits of different sizes appended, and simply called area T300, see Pl. XCV). In the westerly part of the site, only three pits were dug. The work was stopped because of the existence of man-made caves. These were numbered T401-T403 (abbreviated as area T400). In the triangular region on the east bank of the Cilonggou, a fragment made from the Longshan culture was found and twenty-seven pits were dug on the eastern side of this area, and numbered T551-566 (including eleven appended pits of different sizes called simply area T500). These two excavations totalled 280 pits and extended over 4480 square meters.

We found 168 ash pits and two houses of the Yangshao culture; 26 ash pits, one house and an area for pottery manufacture from the Longshan culture; and 156 tombs, mostly belonging to the Longshan culture. This Neolithic site contained finds mainly from the Yangshao culture followed by those of the Longshan culture. The stratigraphy of the site demonstrates this to be true. A thin cultural stratum from the Eastern Zhou and some burial remains from the Han and Tang dynasties were also found. Their distribution and preservation are discussed in detail in the next chapter.

The excavation of the Miaodigou site was done on a large scale, bringing together a huge staff from the very beginning. During 1956, it numbered seventy-five people, including members of the Institute of Archaeology of the Chinese Academy of Sciences, twenty numbers from the central government's Culture Ministry, various provincial cultural relics administrations, museums and other units; as well as a teacher at Northwest University. There were forty-one staff from the Institute of Archaeology, who were inexperienced; thus the project was significant to their training. The second excavation only had twenty-six people, but because of their experience, the work improved both in quality and quantity despite the reduced number of participants. Participants who were in both the excavations of autumn, 1956 and spring 1957 are: An Zhimin, Wu Ruzuo, Hong Qingyu, Zheng Naiwu, Xie Duanju, Yang Jichang, Zheng Xiaomei, Ye Xiaoyan, Liu Zengkun, Wang Zhaoyan, Wang Yufu, Ren Yumei, Dong Xizhen, Hai Dihua, Song Ruizhen, Shi Guishan, Shen Shuzhen, Wen Mengyuan, Zhang Changqing, Wu Jiyuan, Wang Zhaoying, Bai Rongjin, Deng Wenzhang, Zhi Yuanhong among others; others who participated in the 1956 excavation include Chen Zuoliang, Wang Kelin, Gao Donglu, Zhao Ruiting, Zhao Hongde , Zhong Ling, Zhang Ziming, Wang Qiteng, Bi Baoqi, Gong Qiongying, Li Jin, Xu Diankui, Zheng Dacheng, Shi Chubao, Wang Xiuqing, Zhao Zijie, Wang Jiqing, Jiang Zhongyi, Dai Fuhan, Yang Bintao, Zhang Guohui, Gao Hongqi, Zhao Rongguang, Zhang Qingxia, Deng Debao, Guan Qisheng, Liu Yongcai, Pang Zhongwei, Xu Jue, Tang Shihe, Du Yusheng, Ao Chenglong, Guo Ren, Cheng Mingfa, Xu Bingkun, Zhang Ji, Zhao Qi, Yun Xizheng, Zhang Shouzhong, Luo Shaomu, Zhang Caijun, Sun Weichang, Xu Qingquan, Bao Enli, Li Zhongyi, Zhu Zhicheng, Zhu Guochen, Ou Ze, Zhao Zhixiang, Liang Renzhi, Jia Deyao; additional people who joined the 1957 excavation are Zhang Zhenbang and Ding Liulong.

II. Cultural Deposits

(I) Discription of the Strata

Excavation of the site was divided into six areas. The pits all measured four by four meters (except in the appended pits). The grid system was oriented in the north-south direction except for area T500, which is slightly askew because of the topography. The grid was numbered from north to south, and east to west, covering an area of 4480 square meters. Although stratigraphic conditions in each section were different, they can generally be grouped into three kinds: Those belonging to the Yangshao culture, those with superimposed Yangshao and Longshan strata and those with superimposed Yangshao and Warring States strata. We will discuss each area separately.

i. Area T1   We discovered thirty-six ash pits from the Yangshao culture; one kiln, and 145 tombs from the Longshan culture, one tomb from the Tang dynasty; and two other tombs of unknown dates. There were also modern ditches, one on the north side and the other on the east. Some modern tombs were found on the southern side (Pl. XCIV). Stratification of the deposits here generally shows the Warring States stratum on top of the Yangshao stratum. Only in the western side of the site, near the Longshan kiln, was found part of a stratum from the Longshan culture. The Longshan burials were either disturbing the Yangshao cultural stratum and ash pits, or were on top of the ash pits. The burials were rather orderly, suggesting this to be the public cemetery for a clan. Let us take the wall from the south side of pits T8, 18, 28, 38 as examples to illustrate the strata condition.

The first stratum is the plough zone, 0.15-0.3 meters thick. Deposits included potsherds from the Yangshao and Warring State period, mingled with some tiles of the Han dynasty as well as some modern potsherds. The second stratum is from the Warring States, and contained yellowish brown soil that was harder, 0.3-0.5 meters thick. Deposits included potsherds from the Warring States as well as potsherds and disk-shaped objects from the Yangshao culture. A modern ditch had broken through the eastern side of the stratum right down to the layer of virgin soil. The third stratum is from the Yangshao culture, but it has been interrupted by five Longshan burials. According to differences in color and soil quality it may be divided into two sub-strata: Stratum 3A with greyish, soft soil that was 0.25-0.3 meters thick; stratum 3B with reddish brown, harder soil, containing a small amount of lime concretion and was 0.35-0.56 meters thick. Deposits included potsherds, broken pottery ring and stone disc-shaped objects from the Yangshao period (Fig. 2:1).

ii. Area T100   We discovered forty-two ash pits from the Yangshao culture, and two from the Longshan culture. A crooked modern ditch, spanning east-west, cuts through the southern part of this area. Some modern tombs were also scattered here. Aside from the Yangshao stratum, we found Two Longshan ash pits, (H27, 35) that had apparently broken into a Yangshao pit.

iii. Area T200   We discovered: Five ash pits from the Yangshao culture, one round area with a hard surface, one ash ditch, one roadside ditch, as well as an ash pit from the Longshan period. The Yangshao ash ditch (HG201) was originally a natural ditch, wending from the northeastern part of the excavation area towards the southwestern side. The top of the ditch was 2.35 meters below the surface, and 4.75-7 meters wide. It was 3.5-5 meters wide at the bottom, and 4.2 meters deep. Deposits from the ditch can be divided into five strata including different soil colored greyish brown, yellowish brown, reddish brown, and silt. The density of the soil was quite loose. Artifacts from this ditch all belonged to the same period. The roadside ditch (LG201) was also a natural ditch, wending from the southern half of the excavation area to the east side. Its top was 1.3-1.5 meters below the site surface, 3-4.6 meters wide. It is 2.4-2.9 meters wide at the bottom, with a depth of 2-3.4 meters. In the ditch, there were many strata of road soil of different colors, such as yellowish brown, reddish brown and greyish black. Deposits from this area all belonged to the same period. Aside from the Yangshao stratum, a Longshan ash pit (H202) had intruded into the Yangshao roadside ditch on the southern side of this area.

iv. Area T300   We discovered eighty-three ash pits, two houses and one tomb from the Yangshao period; one ash ditch, three coffin jars and one tile coffin from the Han dynasty, two tombs of uncertain date, as well as several modern tombs (Pl. XCV). The deposits in this area mostly belong to the Yangshao culture with the exception of a very thin Han stratum to the north and a north-south Han ash ditch.

v. Area T400   The excavated area measured only forty-eight square meters. Deposits from the plough zone downwards belong to the Yangshao culture.

vi. Area T500   We discovered two ash pits and one ash ditch from the Yangshao period; twenty-three ash pits and two ditches from the Longshan period; several modern tombs. The deposits were mainly from the Longshan period; in some instances we have also found the Longshan stratum on top of the Yangshao, and the Longshan ash pits intruded those of the Yangshao. This may be illustrated by the east wall profiles of the three pits, T558, 560 and 562: Stratum one was the plough zone, 0.08-0.2 meters thick, containing some modern potsherds. The second stratum belonged to the Longshan culture. The yellowish, brown, loose soil was 0.24-0.35 meters thick. It contained Longshan potsherds and even some Yangshao potsherds. Below this stratum were two ash pits, one on top of the other. The top pit (H567), of Longshan affiliation, can be divided into three layers. The first layer may, again, be divided into two sub-strata according to different colors and soil qualities. Sub-stratum 1A consisted of yellowish grey, loose soil, and was about 0.15 meters thick. Sub-stratum 1B consisted of greyish black soil that was even looser in quality than in previous strata, and was 0.1-0.2 meters thick. The second layer was yellowish grey, with a soft texture, and was 0.2-0.5 meters thick. The soil of the third layer was similar in color to that of the previous layer. However, it was harder with a thickness 0.15-0.36 meters. Longshan potsherds were found in each of the above layers mingled with a few Yangshao potsherds. Ash pit H571 (below pit H567) of Yangshao origin can be divided into two layers. The first was of mixed yellow soil, loosely packed, with a thickness of 0.51 meters; the second was of dark grey soil, loosely packed, with a thickness of 0.24 meters. Yangshao potsherds were excavated from both layers. Layer three, of Yangshao, was of reddish brown loose soil, 0.45-0.75 meters thick. Yangshao potsherds were found here. Below this layer was an ash ditch (HG552) of Yangshao origin. It had been filled with slightly greyish red soil which was comparatively hard. It was 0.75-1 meters deep. A small amount of Yangshao potsherds was excavated here (Fig. 2:2).

(II)Architectural Remains

i. Yangshao Culture

(i) Houses

Altogether, two houses from the Yangshao period were discovered within area T300. Both were broken into by the north-south ash ditch (HG301) of the Han dynasty, as well as by several Yangshao ash pits. From the remains of these houses, we can see their original dimensions, and that their structures were basically the same. They were north-south rectangular shallow pits, with a narrow sloping entrance to the middle of the south side. Inside, not far from the door was a circular oven. In the center, four post holes were found with foundation stones below. The walls of these shallow pits were plastered with a layer of straw and mud. Post holes were distributed at equal intervals around the top edge of the walls. Their numbers differed between houses. No foundation stones were found beneath. On the bottom of the shallow pit, a layer of straw and mud covered the floors. Let us separately discuss the two houses.

House F301 was found within the area of the seven pits, T311A, 321, 321A, 321B, 331,

331A and 331B. The upper deposits of the house were evident only at 0.36-0.53 meters below the present ground surface. The house was about 6 meters from east to west, and about 7.86 meters from south to north. The outline of the house was apparent only after the entire surface was excavated. Aside from the southwest part which was disturbed by a Han ash ditch (the walls, deposits, and floor were all disturbed), the western side, the southeast corner of the south wall, as well as the east corner of the entrance interrupted by Yangshao ash pits H376, 305, and 323, the rest of the house was in reasonably good condition (Fig. 3:1) (Pl. II:1).

The house was oriented at 206°. The entrance was 2.84 meters long by 0.6-0.72 meters wide, sloping at 11°. The two extant walls measured 0.43-0.76 meters high. Both the walls and the sloped entrance were plastered with a layer of straw and mud 7-14 cm thick. The roughly rectangular living area immediately adjoined the entrance. The southern side was 7.42 meters long by the north 6.8 meters, 6.18 meters in east side and 6.27 meters in the west. The floor was covered with greyish white straw and mud 7-14cm thick, and quite hard (Fig. 3:3).

The straw and mud plaster on the four extant walls of the shallow pit was 6-8 cm thick. The highest wall was 0.68 meters while the lowest was 0.34 meters. Thirty-seven post holes remained. The four in the center of the house formed a square and were used to support the roof. They all had foundation stones underneath except hole No. 4 which was completely ruined. These post stones were made of naturally eroded gravel, smooth on two sides (Fig. 3:4). The remaining thirty-three post holes were systematically arranged around the four walls. Some of the holes were evident outside of the walls while others were on the inside. They were placed vertically or at an angle to the ground. The southern wall appeared to have only vertical post holes while the other three walls included both kinds. The widest angle from the vertical was 16.5°. The diameter of the largest hole was 24 cm and the smallest was 14 cm. When the posts were placed in the holes, a filling of mud and straw was added to reinforce the posts. Cross sections show that the holes were vertical while the traces of the post dried in them were slanted. A small amount of charcoal appeared on the earth filling of these holes, probably remnants of the rotted posts. Several other holes contained Yangshao potsherds and fragments of animal bones. These were probably deposited later, after the house was abandoned. The position, size and depth of each post hole are in the Posthole Registration Table of Yangshao House F301.

Posthole Registration Table of Yangshao House F301

(Unit:Meter)

Location		Number	Opening Diameter	Base Diameter	Posthole Depth		Note
					Above Floor	Below Floor	
Central Area of the Interior of the House	SE	1	0.23	?	/	0.03-0.07	
	NE	2	0.23-0.25	?	/	0.035-0.065	
	NW	3	0.27	?	/	0.05-0.055	
	SW	4	?	?	/	?	Destroyed, no post stone found
South Wall (East Part)		5	0.17	0.14	0.26	0.525	
		6	0.18	0.14	0.3	0.47	
		7	0.16	0.12	0.29	0.43	
		8	0.17	0.11	0.25	0.47	
		9	0.19	0.12	0.21	0.36	
East Wall		10	0.18	0.14	0.44	0.35	The posthole was a bit slanted to the interior with some broken animal bones
		11	0.21	0.18	0.4	0.72	The posthole was 6.5° slanted to the interior with potsherds
		12	0.14	0.12	0.35	0.59	The posthole was 5° slanted to the interior
		13	0.16	0.15	0.3	0.49	The posthole was a bit slanted to the interior with potsherds
		14	0.17	0.16	0.3	0.62	
		15	0.16	0.13	0.25	0.67	
		16	0.17	0.13	0.31	0.51	The posthole was a bit slanted to the interior with potsherds
		17	0.16	0.14	0.28	0.46	The posthole was 14.5° slanted to the interior
Northeast Corner		18	0.16-0.2	0.1-0.11	0.15	0.68	The posthole was 16° slanted to the interior with potsherds
North Wall		19	0.17	0.16	0.12	0.48	The posthole was a bit slanted to the interior
		20	0.16	0.15	0.2	0.42	With potsherds
		21	0.18	0.12	0.3	0.59	
		22	0.14	0.12	0.25	0.49	The posthole was 8° slanted to the interior
		23	0.18	0.105	0.35	0.6	The posthole was a bit slanted to the interior
		24	0.2	0.15	0.38	0.34	The posthole was 16.5° slanted to the interior
		25	0.18	0.15	0.2	0.37	
		26	0.18	0.16	0.29	0.48	
		27	0.17	0.16	0.16	0.55	The posthole was a bit slanted to the interior

Continuation of the Last Table

Location	Number	Opening Diameter	Base Diameter	Posthole Depth		Note
				Above Floor	Below Floor	
Northwest Corner	28	0.18	0.17	0.2	0.48	The posthole was 8° slanted to the interior with potsherds
West Wall	29	0.19	?	0.12	0.48	The posthole was a bit slanted to the interior
	30	?	0.14	0.45	0.46	The posthole was a bit slanted to the interior
	31	0.18	0.15	0.46	0.5	The posthole was a bit slanted to the exterior
	32	0.19	0.13	0.46	0.3	The posthole was a bit slanted to the exterior with potsherds
Southwest Corner	33	0.17	?	0.49	0.6	The posthole was a bit slanted to the interior
South Wall (West Part)	34	0.17	0.14	0.49	0.4	The posthole was a bit slanted to the interior
	35	0.17	0.16	0.3	0.48	
	36	0.19	0.17	0.35	0.46	
	37	0.17	0.12	0.31	0.5	With potsherds

The fireplace was in the center of the house, facing the entrance. It was a circular pit, 1.24 meters deep, with a diameter of 1.17 meters at the top and 0.91 meters at the bottom. Traces of firing were left on top, while the dwelling floor was greenish black. The inner side and bottom of the pit showed a layer of hard red fired earth 3-6 cm deep, becoming harder with depth, perhaps because of long periods of firing. The deposits in the pit were divided into five strata. The first contained slightly red and hard soil and 5-15 cm thick. No artifacts were found here. The second stratum was of loosely packed yellow soil, 18-32 cm thick. Its upper part contained a small layer of stones and mud, probably used to fill the fireplace when it was in disuse. Five stone discs of different sizes were excavated here. The third stratum contained loose, yellowish grey soil, 0.26-0.51 meters thick. Yangshao potsherds were found there. The fourth stratum consisted of a grassy grey soil, loosely packed, and 0.17-0.3 meters thick. Only a small amount of Yangshao potsherds were excavated from this layer. The fifth stratum was a loose, greyish black soil, 0.1-0.28 meters thick. No artifacts were found there (Fig. 3:3).

The roof and walls of the house had fallen in filling up the interior and surrounding areas. This filling was 0.8 meters below the ground surface, and 18-37 cm thick. It was yellow, loosely packed in the top and more densely at the bottom. This stratum contained grass roots which may be the remnants of the straw and mud used on the roof and walls.

The deposits in the house can be divided into seven strata. The first was the plough zone, the second contained reddish brown soil (Han dynasty), and the strata below them were all Yangshao deposits. The third stratum of greyish black soil included some loose yellow soil and red burnt soil. It was loose in quality, and 5-43 cm thick. The area of the deposit was about the same as the area of the house, with a portion crossing the house's north boundaries. The fourth stratum was of loose, grey soil, 5-23cm thick. It was piled up within the house limits. The fifth stratum of yellow soil, was loose, and 5-20 cm thick and also within the house limits. The three layers just described were remnants of the fallen-in roof and walls. Yangshao potsherds were found, among which some stone discs and bone arrowheads were recovered in the third stratum. The sixth stratum of mud and straw also contained remnants of the roof and walls (see the previous paragraph about the roof and walls). The seventh stratum can be subdivided into three sub-levels according to different colors and qualities of soils. Sub-stratum 7A was 8-30 cm thick. Its upper soil was slightly red and relatively hard, while the soil in the lower part was yellow and loosely packed. This sub-level was contained within the house. The deposits in the east edge of the north side and in the entrance were higher than in the other areas. Sub-level 7B was a loose, greyish black soil, 3-6 cm thick, and also contained within the house. Layer 7C was 10-20 cm thick, and generally similar to layer 7A. However, it was in this level that the post holes in the center of the house began to show. Yangshao potsherds and fragments of shell hairpins (?) were found. All of these three sub-levels were formed before the house fell in, and probably contained deposits from the period of occupation (Fig. 3:2).

House F302 was found within pits T347, 348, 349, 357, 358, and 359. It is about 25.2 meters from house F301. The upper deposits of the house were exposed, beginning at about 0.12-0.2 meters from the surface. From north to south, the deposits covered 6.2 meters (east to west measurement is unclear). This house was preserved in a similar way as house F301, except the east side was broken by an ash ditch of the Han dynasty destroying all the walls, deposits, and living area of the shallow pit. The west side and the front part of the entrance were respectively broken by Yangshao ash pits H383 and 391. These parts were more seriously disrupted (Fig. 4:1; Pl. II:2).

The house was oriented at 205°. The remaining entrance was 2 meters long, 0.48 to 0.54 cm meters wide with its original surface destroyed (virgin soil has been exposed). The two remaining walls were 0.63 meters high, plastered with a layer of mud and straw about 15 cm thick. The composition of the dwelling floor was slightly different from that of house F301. Aside from the mud and straw, it contained bits of a red fired earth with a smooth surface, brownish red color, firm and hard and 2 cm thick. From the remains, we see the shape of the dwelling floor was similar to that of house F301, slightly rectangular. The remaining height of the south side was 6 meters, of the north side was 3.4 meters, of the west side was 4 meters. The section between the entrance and the fireplace was destroyed. Near the entrance, a broken stone knife was found. Between the dwelling floor and the bottom of the shallow pit, there was another hard layer of mud and straw, 10 cm thick. It is probable that this was the original floor for this house, the brownish red floor on top being reinforced after the original floor was destroyed (Fig. 4:3).

The walls of the shallow pit were all plastered with mud and straw 3-4 cm thick, with the remaining height ranging from 0.34 meters to 0.63 meters. Twenty-one post holes were found, three in the center of the house (formerly four, one was destroyed by a Han ash ditch); all had the smooth, flat, gravel post bases (Fig. 4:4). The four walls contained eighteen vertical holes with mud and straw filling in the spaces between the posts and the walls. None of the wall holes contained any ash soil or artifacts, except for a broken stone axe and ash soil deposits in bottom half of hole No. 9. The position, size, and depth of every post hole can be found in the Posthole Registration Table of Yangshao House F302.

Posthole Registration Table of Yangshao House F302

(Unit:Meter)

Location		Number	Opening Diameter	Base Diameter	Posthole Depth		Note
					Above Floor	Below Floor	
Central Area of the Interior of the House	SE	1	0.22-0.27	?		0.19	
	SW	2	0.28-0.33	?		0.13	
	NW	3	0.23	?		0.12	
South Wall (East Part)		4	0.22-0.24	0.07	0.4	0.62	
		5	0.22-0.26	0.1	0.4	0.78	
		6	0.28-0.3	0.1	0.43	0.58	
North Wall		7	0.24	0.1	0.24	1.05	
		8	0.26	0.11	0.2	0.5	
		9	0.22-0.26	0.09	0.17	1	A broken stone axe was found at 0.6 m below the surface
		10	0.2-0.23	0.1	0.18	0.45	
		11	0.22-0.26	0.11	0.19	0.85	

Continuation of the Last Table

Location	Number	Opening Diameter	Base Diameter	Posthole Depth		Note
				Above Floor	Below Floor	
West Wall	12	0.22-0.26	0.12	0.21	0.5	
	13	?	0.16	?	0.92	The upper part was broken into by ash pit No.386
	14	?	0.14	?	0.97	Same
	15	?	0.11	?	0.7	Same
	16	?	0.1	?	0.41	Same
Southwest Corner	17	0.24	0.12	0.5	0.75	
South Wall (West Part)	18	0.23	0.13	0.58	0.76	
	19	0.18-0.23	0.08	0.4	0.76	
	20	0.16	0.1	0.4	0.87	
	21	0.19	0.08	0.44	0.74	

The position and shape of the fireplace were similar to the fireplace in house F301. The top diameter was 1 meter, while the bottom diameter was 0.76 meters, with a depth of 0.71 meters. The interior and bottom of the pit were plastered with mud and straw (slightly different from the fireplace in house F301). This plaster, having been burnt, has become red-fired earth. It was 3-10 cm thick. Burnt traces were found near the opening of the fireplace. The deposits here may be divided into two strata: The first consisted of a yellow plaster, hard in quality and 5-46 cm thick, formed when the roof of the house collapsed. Only a few Yangshao potsherds were found here. The second stratum contained loosely packed ashes 2-26 cm thick, formed whe n the fireplace was in use. Only three shards of Yangshao pottery were found.

After falling in on the dwelling floor, the roof and walls formed a deposit 25-40 cm thick at 0.7-0.78 meters below the present ground surface. A small deposit containing some Yangshao potsherds, made of yellow mud and straw was also found in the northwest corner of the house.

The deposits in the house can be divided into three strata. Again the first stratum was the plough zone. The other two strata both contained deposits attributing to the Yangshao culture. The second stratum can be divided into four sub-levels on the basis of color and soil density. Sub-level 2A contained a very fine ash soil, 10-38 cm thick. Sub-level 2B was consisted of a black ash soil, fine in quality and 3-5 cm thick. These two levels were found in the south part of the house. Sub-level 2C was of coarse, greyish brown soil, 12-48 cm thick. Sub-level 2D, a combination of lime concretion and yellow soil, was coarse and 10-30 cm thick. These two levels were in the northern half of the house. In all four sub-levels, Yangshao potsherds were found. The third stratum, of mud and straw, was formed when the roof and walls collapsed (see the above paragraph dealing with roof and walls). The dwelling floor of this house was under the third stratum. No other deposits were found (Fig. 4:2).

It is difficult to reconstruct the structures of the houses described above due to a lack of good deposits from the roof. However, some ideas may be gleaned from Neolithic houses discovered in other Asian countries, or comparatively from the complete structures of existing primitive houses. The common characteristics of houses F301 and F302 are: An almost square, shallow, vertical pit, four wooden posts with post bases in the center of the dwelling floor, and a sloping entrance to the south of the door. Similar houses have been discovered at Banpo, in Xian, Shaanxi province (although the posts at Banpo have no foundation stones). We might say that it is a basic form of Yangshao houses. Firstly, similar structures can be found in the primitive houses of Asia such as those of the Ainu people from Sakahlin Island in Russia. Their houses were also square, shallow pits with vertical walls. The conical roofs were made of slanted beams supported by four pillars in the center of the dwelling area, and plastered with a thick layer of mud and straw on the outside. The external appearance of the house appeared to be round with a conical roof. [6] Houses found in the Neolithic sites in Japan were also shallow pits with vertical walls, and four posts standing inside the structure. They were reconstructed with heavy eaves, as in the shapes of the ceramic house models of haniwa (ancient Japanese burial objects in pottery and placed around the tomb), and the depictions of houses on bronze mirrors and bells. [7] Whether these sources are completely reliable is a matter worth considering. Although the Yangshao houses at Miaodigou have four posts, their structures were probably quite different from those other Neolithic houses. This is because the post holes on the walls of house F302 were all vertical; even those of house F301 did not slant very much. Thus it would have been impossible to build conical or four-cornered roofs with slanted posts from the ground. According to our observations, the post holes along the walls supported both the roof and the walls, while the four posts inside the house were mainly for the support of the roof, which was a four-cornered, conical shape. The wooden posts along the walls, standing vertically of slightly slanted towards the center of the pit formed a surrounding wall (Figs. 5, 6). Similar houses can still be found in Siberia, in the birch bark houses of the Khanti Clan.[8] Therefore, we believe that our reconstruction is fairly accurate. The mud and straw deposits found in the house were probably remnants of the roof and walls, since it was a common practice to plaster walls and roofs with mud and straw.

In addition to these two houses, we have also found a round, hard-packed area (F207) in pit T227. It was 2.2 meters from the ground surface, with a diameter of 1.5-1.65 meters, and was 6.5-13 cm thick. Its surface was yellowish brown. Near the center, but slightly towards the southeast a post hole with a top diameter of 21-23 cm, bottom diameter of 11 cm was found. The bottom of this hole, which was 22 cm deep, had a deposit of light yellow mud, with a great deal of straw, about 8 cm thick. The upper parts of soil was greyish brown. To the south and a bit west of this hard surface, there was a section of road soil, forming a slope from north to south. Both on the surface and around it were scattered mud and straw deposit, which may be part of the remains from the upper part of the house. Judging from the remains of this building, which covered a very small area and were simple overall in structure, we think it was probably a conical shed, supported by a central post. It must have been a place of storage and not suitable for habitation. Furthermore, a Yangshao road ditch (LG201) ran to the east of this hard surface, while an ash ditch (HG201), again from the Yangshao period, ran to the northwestern side. The little shed was thus located on a small mound of earth between these two ditches.

(ii) Ash Pits

We discovered 168 ash pits of the Yangshao culture, generally of two types: Sixty-five oval pits and 103 circular pits. The ash pits were scattered over most of the entire site (Since the excavated part area T400 was only 48 square meters, no ash pits were found). The greatest concentration of ash pits was area T300. For example, within an area of 100 square meters west of Yangshao house F301, more than twenty ash pits were found. Their interrelationships were quite complex. In one case, seventeen pits were connected together.

Only forty-two of the pits were well-preserved, about one-forth of the total excavated Yangshao pits in this site. The pits intersect each other, at the least two, and the most seventeen as stated above. Aside from this, a number of these ash pits were interrupted by ash ditches (HG201) and road ditches (LG201) of the Yangshao period and also ash ditches of the Han dynasty (HG301). A few have been disturbed by modern tombs or pits of later periods.

The ash pits were all different in size. Generally, the opening diameter was 2-3 meters; but individual variations ranged from as large as 5.7 meters to as small as 0.54 meters. The general depth was between 1 and 2.5 meters; however, the deepest variation was 3.9 meters, and the shallowest 0.45 meters. The inside walls of these pits were uneven and could be divided into three types according to their tilt: those with wide openings and narrow bottoms, resembling the shape of a Chinese *dou* bushel, were in the majority. Pits with vertical walls and shaped like buckets were the next most common and those with small openings and wide bottoms, like the shape of a sack, were fewest (See the table following I, II for comparisons of the different types)

Statistic Table of the Types of Yangshao Ash Pits (I)

Type Shape	Wide Openings and Narrow Bottoms	Vertical Walls	Narrow Opening and Wide Bottoms	Total
Circular	74	18	11	103
Percentage	71. 85	17. 48	10. 68	100%

Statistic Table of the Types of Yangshao Ash Pits (II)

Type Shape	Wide Openings and Narrow Bottoms	Vertical Walls	Narrow Opening and Wide Bottoms	Total
Oval	51	11	3	65
Percentage	78.47	16.93	4.62	100%

The bottom portions of these ash pits were usually smooth and flat, though there were few very uneven ones. There were four pits where the walls and bottom were covered with straw and mud, 10-20 cm thick. Some of the bottoms revealed many unusual, small, and shallow holes. Since these were uncommon, we cannot explain their original function.

The soils in these pits varied in color and density. The strata of deposits varied from ten to one. The finds were generally very rich in these pits except for a few of the smaller, shallower ones. Most of the finds were potsherds; however, there were also some stone, bone and antler objects and other natural remains.

In nine of the ash pits, human and domesticated animal bones were discovered, in addition to the usual cultural remains. It is possible that because the ash pits were deserted, they were used for burials at that time. Four of the ash pits contained human skeletons; three had skeletons of dogs; and another two had skeletons of pigs (one of which also contained a dog skeleton). Most of the skeletal remains were neither complete nor well-preserved. The number of skeletons excavated from each ash pit is listed on the following table.

Table of Skeletons Excavated From Yangshao Ash Pits

Ash Pit Number	Human Skeletons	Pig Skeletons	Dog Skeletons	Condition of Preservation
12			1	Incomplete
22		1	3	Incomplete
25	2			One is complete, the other is incomplete
40		1		Incomplete
41			1	Incomplete
44			4	Incomplete
49	1			Incomplete
51	1			Incomplete
62	1			Incomplete

From the table, we find that the human skeletons were not mixed with those of the domesticated animals in the same pit (whether this is due to inadequate excavation or some other cause can only be decided by further investigations). Two pits will be used as examples for discussion.

Ash pit H22 was located within pits T128 and 133, had its opening at 1 meter from the ground surface. The diameter of its top was 2.4 meters and its bottom 3 meters with a depth of 1.75 meters. It was a circular, sack-like pit with a narrow opening and wide bottom. The north side was slightly broken by another Yangshao ash pit (H44). The deposits were divided into two strata: The first stratum, of red soil, was 1.5 meters thick. Yangshao potsherds and broken animal bones were found here. On the east side, at the bottom of the stratum, that is, the top of stratum two, and 1.5 meters from the opening of the pit, a poorly preserved skeleton of a dog was found. The second stratum of greyish black soil was 0.25 meters thick. The cultural finds from this stratum were similar to the above stratum. In the central part of this stratum an incomplete skeleton of a pig was found; while disorderly skeletons of dogs were discovered on the south and southwest sides (Fig.7:1).

Ash pit H25 was located in pit T123, and 1.85 meters from the surface. Its opening diameter was 1.4 meters, the bottom diameter was 2.2 meters, and the depth 0.75 meters. It was also a circular, sack-like ash pit with a small opening and large bottom. The northeast side of this pit has been slightly broken by two other Yangshao ash pits (H40, 43). Only one layer of deposit, 0.75-1 meter thick, was in the pit. The soil was yellowish grey. This stratum had yielded Yangshao potsherds and fragmentary animal bones; and 0.4 meters from the opening, a human skeleton was found. The skeleton was located in the central portion of the pit, its head oriented towards the north, lying face down. The right hand was raised up high with palm facing down. The left hand was raised and bent. Both legs were bent to the left with heel crossing, left over right (Fig. 7:2). Another human skeleton was found, 0.8 meters from the top of the pit. This one was close to the northeast side of the pit. Its head was oriented towards the east, and the legs to the west. It was laid on its back with the left hand bent and raised upward. The right hand was missing. The legs were crossed with the left femur over the right (Fig. 7:3). Immediately below the skeleton was raw, yellow soil.

Human remains from three other ash pits also differed in posture. Some were fully extended, lying on their backs while others were lying on their sides with the limbs bent. One skeleton excavated from ash pit H49 (incomplete and in disorder) wore a complete and delicate ring made of shell on his ring finger (H49:01).

Most of the 168 Yangshao ash pits were joined to each other because they had broken through each other. Of interest to us is whether there was chronological order among these pits. For this purpose, we have selected more than twenty pits, circular and oval, that were clearly broken through to each other, and one Yangshao ash ditch (HG201) to make some preliminary comparisons. The results showed that the artifacts in these ash pits do not show any significant differences, as far as shapes and patterns were concerned; therefore, the ash pits can not be too far removed from one another in time.

ii. Longshan Culture

(i) Houses

We discovered a house of the Longshan culture in area T500. It had broken into a Yangshao ash pit (H552), and was also partially disturbed by a Longshan ash stratum and tombs of later periods but still fairly well preserved. It consisted of a circular, sack-like pit with a white floor made of lime at the bottom. There was a stair-like entrance on the east side. Around the vertical walls of the pit, there were some regularly arranged post holes (Fig. 8; Pl. III: 1).

The bottom diameter of the house was 2.7 meters, with walls 1.24 meters high. The opening was smaller than the bottom. The house was dug into virgin soil with the bottom covered by a 0.4 cm thick layer of mud and straw. On top of this, a very smooth lime surface, 0.3-0.5 cm thick, served as the dwelling floor. The lime covering on the western half had come off, revealing the mud and straw plaster below. In the center, slightly inclined to the north, was a post with a diameter of 0.08 meters and a depth of 0.15 meters, filled with potsherds, and mud and straw that was used to stabilize the wooden posts. The walls were still smooth and tidy and although they had been partially burnt showing a hard, light grey surface, the area from the dwelling floor to 6 cm above the wall base was plastered with a layer of lime 0.1 cm thick.

A deep earthern niche, semi-circular in shape and rising 8 cm above the dwelling floor, was found on the southwest wall. It was 0.45 meters high, 0.4 meters wide and 0.5 meters deep. The surrounding soil had turned into red fired earth and a few burned clay fragments were remained on the white lime surface in the vicinity. This was probably where the kitchen stove was placed.

On the east side of the house was a narrow, rectangular entrance, oriented at 330°, and 0.74 meters long by 0.56 meters wide. There was also a stairway, 0.28 meters high, plastered with mud and straw and white lime.

Around the top of the pit, about 0.2 meters from the opening, was a row of post holes. Because of later disturbances, only ten survived. The holes, buried in virgin soil, were 0.38 meters deep, conical in shape, with a diameter of 0.09 meters. They inclined slightly inward at 8°. Greyish brown soil filled the holes with no trace of wood.

The interior of the house was completely filled with grey soil that may be divided into three strata. The first was loose, greyish brown soil, 0.41 meters thick. The second stratum of yellowish grey soil, was harder, and 0.27-0.34 meters thick. The third stratum of grey soil was relatively loose, and partially mixed with mud and straw plaster, with a thickness of 0.11-0.14 meters. The strata with cultural finds contained only remains of the Longshan culture.

From the outlines, it is possible to reconstruct a pointed, conical roofed house. Thick wooden posts in the central part of the dwelling floor support the center of the roof. The posts along the wall not only supported the roof but also served as the wall frame. Because the post holes around the house slanted inwardly only slightly, the original posts were probably vertical. The roof and walls were probably plastered with the usual mud and straw (Figs. 9, 10).

(ii) Kiln Site

Only one kiln site had been discovered in T94, and it was in fairly good condition. It consisted of the kiln chamber, fire opening, firing cavity, firing tunnel, and kiln grid. The fire opening, firing chamber and firing tunnel were dug out in virgin soil and plastered with a layer of mud and straw. Other parts like the kiln grid were also made of this plaster, and have turned to a hard, red-fired earth after firing (Fig.11; Pl. III: 2).

The kiln chamber was round and 2 meters below the earth's surface. Its diameter was 0.93 meters from south to north, 0.78 meters from east to west. The walls were all broken down, with the remaining height of the east wall at 0.48 meters. The curve of the walls may point to a dome-shaped top for the kiln.

The oval-shaped fire opening was attached to the west side of the kiln chamber. It was 0.4 meters long and 0.26 meters wide. The firing chamber was a vertical, rectangular pit, 0.94 meters long by 0.6 meters wide by 0.96 meters deep.

The firing tunnel separated into eight branches, leading upwards from the firing chamber to the bottom of the kiln chamber. Three branches entered the central part of the kiln chamber. The flanking branches again divided into three or four sub-branches. These firing tunnels were all different in length and width; the general measurements were 0.1-0.36 meters long by 0.07 meters wide by about 0.08 meters high. In the kiln grid on the flanking firing tunnels were some shallow semi-circular pits which may have been old fire ways. The grid was made by plastering mud and straw on top of the firing tunnel to a thickness of 0.16-0.3 meters, with twenty-five firing holes. The firing holes had wide bottoms and narrow openings, all different in size, from 0.23 meters to 0.03 meters.

The soil filling in the upper part of the kiln and in the firing chamber had yielded many potsherds and much red-fired earth. Most of the potsherds dated to the Longshan period although a few were from the Yangshao period. According to the stratification and excavated finds, it is certain that these remains were the Longshan culture.

(iii) Ash Pits

We discovered a total of twenty-six Longshan ash pits, all of which were in area T500, except for H27 and H35 in area T100, and H202 in area T200.

The ash pits were either circular, or oval. The circular type again can be divided into two kinds: A narrow opening with wide bottom; and a wide opening with narrow bottom. We have found seventeen of the first kind and five of the second, varying in size and depth: opening diameter ranges from 1.6-3.39 meters; the bottom diameter from 2-4.42 meter; and the depth from 0.31-2.61 meters. The sack-shaped ash pit, with small opening and wide bottom, was mostly prevalent among the Longshan pits. The walls of these pits, having been smoothed, were generally in better and more orderly shape.

Only four oval ash pits had been discovered, all with wide top and narrow bottom. The opening diameter ranged from 2.5-2.65 meters; the bottom from 2.15-2.32 meters; and the depth from 1.1-2.7 meters.

There were interlinked thirteen Longshan ash pits: Six Longshan ash ditches break into contemporary ash pits; and seven Longshan ash pits break into Yangshao ash ditches. Thus, some Longshan pits, after broken into Yangshao ash ditches were in turn broken by ash pits of the same period. The extreme example showed six ash pits adjoined to one another in an area of only 96 square meters. Only four ash pits were complete. The excavated finds show that these Longshan ash pits were not far removed from one another in time.

The cultural deposits in the strata of these ash pits were different. A representative ash pit

(H563) may be used for our discussion. The first stratum of loose, light grey silt was 0.3 meters thick. The second stratum, of loose, dark grey soil was 0.12-0.32 meters thick. A hard, yellowish brown soil containing mud and straw from the third stratum was 0.17-0.18 meters deep. The fourth stratum of loose, greyish brown soil was 0.13-0.6 meters thick. The fifth stratum of a loosely packed greyish black soil was 0.04-0.24 meters deep. The sixth stratum was greyish yellow, and harder in quality, and 0.2-0.32 meters deep. The seventh stratum of brown soil was hard in quality, and partially mixed with mud and straw. It was about 0.2-0.6 meters deep. The eight and last stratum had looser, yellowish brown soil, and was 0.1-0.53 meters deep. Only Longshan remains were found.

A skeleton was excavated from each of the two sack-like ash pits. In ash pit H35, the skeleton was found on the north side of the second stratum. It had been buried with limbs extended supinely, head to the east and feet to the west, turned 120°, face looking southward. The head was lower than the feet. On the whole, it was fairly well preserved. The skeleton in ash pit No.202 was also found on the north side of the second stratum. It was well preserved except for the skull and fingers on the left hand, which were broken. The body was also buried supinely, head to the east and feet to the west. Its orientation was 95°, face facing upward. No funerary objects were found in either.

The burial method and orientation of these two skeletons were similar. It is possible that abandoned pits were used to bury the dead. At any rate, these Longshan skeletons were buried in a more orderly way than were their Yangshao counterparts.

On the north wall of HG553, we have also discovered many traces of a tool used by the Longshan people, most of which includes a tight concentration of incised, cross lines. After careful examination, we found that these incisions were made by some sort of double-pronged instrument. The diameter of each tooth appears to be 4 cm while the distance between them was also 4 cm, although some were as far apart as 6 cm. The length of the instrument was not entirely clear, perhaps around 20 cm. We have chosen groups of relatively clearer lines, and copied them on paper (Fig.12). We have also made a plaster mould of these incisions (Pl. XCII). This instrument may be similar to the wooden *lei* shovel used during the Yin and Zhou dynasties.

(III)Tombs

Altogether, 156 tombs have been found, including one Yangshao tomb (M307), 145 Longshan tombs, four Han dynasty tombs (M301, 302, 303, 305), one Tang dynasty tomb (M100) and five tombs from unidentified periods (M34, 136, 142, 149, 304).

The tombs were located in the eastern and central portions of Miaodigou, in areas T100 and T300. In area T100, the tombs were numbered from 1 onwards. Of the total 149 burials here, there were 145 Longshan tombs, one Tang tomb, and three tombs of unknown dates. This was undoubtedly the burial grounds of the Longshan people, their tombs closely together and arranged in an orderly manner. In area T300, the tombs were numbered beginning with 301. They included four Han dynasty tombs, one Yangshao tomb, and two tombs of unknown date, making a total of seven.

Of the 156 tombs, four of the Han dynasty, one of Yangshao and eighteen of Longshan were destroyed. The rest of the 127 Longshan tombs have yielded generally well-preserved human skeletons, providing a wealth of materials for the study of human physical characteristics of this period.

We shall discuss the tombs chronologically.

i. Yangshao Cultural Tombs

The only Yangshao burial (M307) was on the east side of the entrance to house F301. It was a rectangular tomb pit with vertical walls and a depth of 1.24 meters. Because it had been interrupted by Yangshao ash pit (H323), and the entrance to a house (F301), the extent of the tomb was not very clear.

Only the skull, ribs, and right arm bones of the human skeleton were remained. The skeleton was supine, head pointing north and facing east, with an orientation of 180°[1]. No traces of buried objects were found here. It is notable that the skeleton in this tomb was special in that it was placed with head raised, neck bent, and right arm also bent in an inclined posture. The other bones have been lost (Fig.13).

Although no burial objects were found, the interruption by the Yangshao house and ash pit (H323) points to the probability that it could not be later than this period.

ii. Longshan Cultural Tombs

The total number of Longshan burials discovered was 145. All of the tombs were rectangular pits, with vertical walls. The tomb outlines were quite clear, the usual length being 1.8-1.9 meters and width being 0.41-0.51 meters, while the depth varied from 1-2 meters. Since some tombs had been broken into by modern ditches and others destroyed by the road soil of the Eastern Zhou period, the original depth cannot be adequately determined by the present depth.

Most of the human burials were well preserved. 127 burials yielded complete skeletons, while another eighteen did not due to later disturbances. No traces of burial objects were

---

1   The orientation should be 0°. —editor

found in any of these tombs.

All of the tombs were single burials, oriented north-south with the head to the south[2], feet to the north and the orientation between 175-190°. From this it is obvious that there was a system of burial at that time. There were two types of burials: Extended and flexed. We have found 138 extended burials, and two flexed burials, while five examples cannot be determined because of later disturbances.

There were no apparent system governing orientation of the body in the extended burial and arms were also placed in different postures. Six burials were with right arm placed alongside the body and left arm resting on the pelvis, while two burials were with both hands on the pelvis, one on top of the other. The rest showed both arms placed alongside the body.

In the flexed burials, the bones were more seriously decomposed than in the extended burials. Their heads pointed to the north, facing either east or west, with arms either lying straight beside the body, or bent at the elbows inwards, with the hands on the pelvis. The legs were bent at different angles. In tomb M19, the leg bones bent slightly to the east at about 110°; while in tomb M143, the leg bones were also slightly bent to the east the right leg were bent at 150° while the left was at 160°.

Usually there were no burial objects in the tombs, except for a small pottery cup recovered from each of the two tombs (M72 and M99). The cup from tomb M72 was placed between the arm and the ribs, while the one from tomb M99 was beside the right arm (Fig.14).

All these tombs had broken into the Yangshao stratum and were deep in the virgin soil (Fig.2:1). Some tombs were even on top of the Yangshao ash pits; therefore, aside from Longshan potsherds, there was also a lot of Yangshao potsherds mixed in. The upper parts of the burial opening were just under the Eastern Zhou stratum. Layers of road soil had destroyed the human skeletons in the Longshan tombs. Hence we can determine the early and late boundaries of the dates of these Longshan tombs. Small pottery cups, like those excavated from the tombs M72 and 99 were also found in the Longshan ash pits. Thus from the stratification and burial objects, we can ascertain that these tombs belonged to the Longshan period.

iii. Han Dynasty Tombs

There were burials in coffin jars and one in a tile coffin (M301). The tile coffin was made up of joining two tiles with cord impression decorations together. The skeletons had disintegrated into powder. The tombs holding coffin jars were irregular, rectangular pits with vertical sides, varying in depth. The burial pit M302 was 2.7 meters long by 0.7-1.14 meters wide and 1.55

2　The orientation is not consistent with the Figure 14. —editor meters deep. The orientation of tomb M303 was 268°, the length 1.7 meters, the width 0.97 meters, and the depth 2.18 meters.

No burial objects were found in either the jar coffins or the tile coffins; therefore, these tombs were possibly used for the burial of children during the Western Han Dynasty.

III. Yangshao Cultural Remains

(I) Pottery

More than 690 pieces of Yangshao pottery were reconstructed. According to their functions, they may be divided into containers, cooking utensils, tools, ornaments, and toys.

i. Containers and Cooking Utensils

These were daily utensils of the time. They can be divided into four related wares: fine red ware, grey ware, fine black ware and coarse sand-tempered red ware. Besides plain-faced or polished wares, the decorations included painted motifs, linear patterns, basket patterns, incised patterns, string patterns, cloth patterns, mat patterns, as well as decorations in appliqué or open work. These decorations were not only used by themselves, but also together with two or three other designs. Vessels that are identifiable include cups, plates, bowls, basins, jars, *yu* jars, bottles, *zeng* steamers, *ding* tripods, *fu* cauldrons, *zao* stoves, vessel covers and vessel stands.

The following tables list the wares, decorations, and vessel shapes of potsherds excavated from the four Yangshao ash pits rich in such examples.

Table of the Sum Total of Ware Families and Decorations of the Yangshao Culture
(Ash Pits H5, 10, 363,387)

Ware Family	Fine red ware					Grey ware		Fine black ware	Coarse sand-tempered red ware					Total
Amount	9169					1663		4	5246					16082
Percentage	57.02					10.34		0.03	32.62					100%
Decorations	Painted motifs	Linear patterns	Basket patterns and linear patterns	Cloth patterns	Plain	Decorations in appliqué	Plain	Plain	Linear patterns	Linear patterns and incised patterns	String Patterns	Decorations in appliqué	Plain	
Amount	2254	4741	76	3	2095	12	1651	4	3441	168	23	146	1468	16082
Percentage	14.02	29.48	0.48	0.02	13.03	0.08	10.27	0.03	21.4	1.05	0.15	0.91	9.13	100%

The Table of the Sum Total of Pottery Vessel Forms of the Yangshao Culture
(Ash Pits H5, 10, 363, 387) (Limited to those with recognizable forms)

Ware Family	Fine red ware						Grey ware				Fine black ware	Coarse sand-tempered red ware								Total
Vessel forms	Bowl	Basin	Jar	Bottle	*Zeng* steamer	Vessel cover	bowl	Basin	Jar	Vessel stand	Jar	Cup	Bowl	Basin	Jar	*Fu* cauldron	*Zao* stove	Vessel cover		
Amount	521	3126	1089	3125	3	11	92	924	119	2	4	12	87	1027	3754	3	3	4	13906
Percentage	3.75	22.48	7.84	22.48	0.03	0.08	0.67	6.65	0.86	0.02	0.03	0.09	0.63	7.39	27	0.03	0.03	0.03	100%

A. Family of Fine Red Pottery

This is a fine, delicate ware. Most of the clay used for this ware seems to have been well levigated except for a small portion which still contains sandy grains.

The vessels were all hand-made. Except for the small cups and vessel covers that were mold made, all vessels were made by coiling. There are still obvious traces of the technique in the interior walls of some vessels. Most of the rims were formed with the help of a slow wheel and are, therefore, very regular and have the characteristic wheel striations left on them. After being formed, the vessels underwent a delicate procedure of grinding and polishing. Some were impressed with linear patterns or basket patterns.

This is a hard ware, usually red or orange in color. Some individual specimens are partly greyish brown or have grey spots on them due to incomplete oxidation. Also, a small portion of this ware is similar to the white painted ware which we have temporarily included in this family. Kaolin clay may have been used for this ware but proof will have to await chemical examination.

Most of the plain pottery was carefully polished although some was rather coarsely done with deep traces of the rubbing process. A few bowls and basins show a dark red or white slip. The red-slipped ware is glossy, and often has only the slip, color painting on this ware was relatively uncommon. The white-slipped ware is extremely rare. Mostly the white slip covered the rim and the main body of the vessel; color designs were drawn on it, most of the potteries containing both red and black patterns belong to these white-slipped wares.

The decorations used include: painted motifs, linear patterns, basket impressions, incised patterns, cloth patterns, mat patterns, decorations in appliqué and open work.

The most common color used for the painted motifs was black; red is rarely seen; and a combination of red and black is even more uncommon. The patterns were generally painted on the main body of the vessel. Some basins show painted motifs along the rims; but none show painting on the interior. The composition of the designs is quite complex, and lends itself to transformations; it was developed from the basic motifs of lines, whirls, triangular whirls, round dots and squares (Pls. IV-VIII). These designs can be divided into two groups in terms of composition: The first was composed of several symmetrical units, with different or a symmetrical unit inserted in the overall design. This was often due to the lack of planning before the design was painted; any left over space that the motif did not cover must be filled in by an inserted design. Certainly there were cases where units were inserted purposely for the sake of variety. The other groups of design was composed of beautiful continuous patterns, where individual motifs transformed into different shapes, intersecting one another, making it very difficult to find the beginning or end of the pattern (Figs.15, 16).

The first group is often seen on bowls and rarely on basins and jars. The second design is often seen on basins, and rarely on jars, and never on bowls. As for animal representations, only the frog motif was found on fragments of basins with constricted rims; one fragment shows the complete animal, while two other pieces show bits of the head, front paw, thigh and rear limb (Pl. IX: 1-3). These animals were vividly drawn, which is rarely seen on painted pottery.

There are also combined designs of painted motifs and linear or incised patterns found on fragments of the rims of basins and jars (Pl. VII: 5, 6). Sometimes a section of incised pattern was rubbed smooth; a white slip was then applied, and painted motifs added. This has only been found on fragments of the body of some small mouth bottles, and rarely. (Pl. VII: 9, 11). Slanted linear patterns were often found on bottles and jars. Horizontal or slanted basket patterns were seldom employed alone; instead they were used in alternate rows with the linear motif. This is often seen on bottles and *zeng* steamers. The incised pattern was always arranged in parallel lines, and applied to basins and jars. Decorations in appliqué usually include wave-like clay strips and round cake form. The wave-like designs were also functional as handles when they were attached on the sides of basins. The cloth pattern was found on the bottle handles and on decorations in appliqué. This was made by pressing cloth onto the vessel before it was fired, to form the cloth pattern on the wet clay (Pl. VIII: 11). The mat pattern is seen on the handles of bottles. Again the motif of a mat was pressed onto these handles before they were luted on to the vessel (Pl. VIII: 12, 13). The open work patterns were only found on the handles of vessel covers. The latter three designs were probably not for ornamentation. The attached parts included not only handles of bottle and vessel covers, but vessel handles in the shape of a bird's head (Pl. IX: 4-6); although we cannot determine the type of vessel to which these handles belong.

The shapes of the following vessels were reconstructed: cups, plates, bowls, basins, jars, *yu* jars, bottles, *zeng* steamers, vessel covers, and vessel stands.

(1) Round-bottomed jars (A1; Fig.17; Pl. X: 1)

Only one was found. It was a constricted mouthed vessel with a deep body and round bottom. Linear pattern was used over the whole vessel with nine convex buttons on the body.

(2) Plate (A2; Fig.17; Pl. X: 2)

Only one fragment of a plate was discovered. It was a shallow vessel with a wide opening, vertical sides, and a flat bottom. There were some painted designs on the sides.

(3) Shallow-bellied bowls (A3; Fig.17; Pl. X: 3-7; Pl. XI: 1, 2; Pl. XII: 2-7)

Altogether there were twenty two examples. The mouths were wide; the bodies were shallow; and the sides curved downwards from the rim narrowing to a flat bottom. They were both plain and painted.

(4) Deep-bellied bowls

These vessels had wide openings, deep bodies, and flat bottoms. They were all painted usually with simple patterns on the rims; sometimes the body was also painted. They can be divided into two types:

A4a (Fig.17; Pl. XI: 3-5)

There were four examples. The sides of the bowl curved downwards and narrowed towards the bottom. H327:06 was painted with a red design.

A4b (Fig.17; Pl. XI: 6)

Only one was found. The lower sides of the body showed an inward curve, and tapered to a small flat bottom.

(5) Wide-mouthed bowls

These vessels had wide mouths, and sides narrowing to flat bottoms. They were plain or painted. The plain ones were usually not polished carefully; so that there were even some deep traces of burnishing left on the body walls. These vessels may be divided into three types:

A5a (Fig.17; Pl. XII: 1)

There were six examples. The sides tapered slightly towards the lower portion of the vessel. The bottom diameter was about three-fourths of the opening diameter.

A5b (Fig.17; Pl. XIII: 2)

There were five examples. The sides curved downwards; the bottom was everted in a ring-like foot.

A5c (Fig.17; Pl. XIII: 3, 4)

There were three examples. The sides showed only a slight curve.

(6) Curved-bellied bowls

This type had a wide open mouth. The vessel walls curved downwards and inwards toward a narrow, flat bottom. They were both plain and painted, and may be divided into two types:

A6a (Fig.17; Pl. XIII: 5-7; Pl. XIV: 1-7; Pl. XV: 1, 2)

There was a total of twenty-nine pieces. The shape of this variety is similar to that of the previous type; however, the curve of the sides is very pronounced. T24:12 combined black and red painting; one stripe and dots in the center portion of the vessel were painted in black, while two other stripes were in red.

A6b (Fig.17; Pl. XV: 3-7;Pl. XVI: 1-7;Pl. XVII: 1-7;Pl. XVIII: 1, 2)

There were ninety-five pieces. The walls showed the reversed curve and narrowed to the bottom.

(7) Ring-based bowls

The sides from the rim downwards, tapered towards the bottom which was either flat or round, and had a ring base. From the shape of these vessels, it appears possible that they were also used as covers. They were both plain and painted. There were two types.

A7a (Fig.18; Pl. XVIII: 3)

Only one was found. It had a flat bottom and notches around the base.

A7b (Fig.18; Pl. XVIII: 4)

Only one was found. It had a convex, round bottom, short ring base, and painted decorations on the body.

(8) Shallow-bellied basins

These had wide mouths and flat bottoms. Most of them had a plain surface but a few were painted along the rims. These were individual variations where the body of the vessel was painted. This can be divided into four types:

A8a (Fig.18; Pl. XVIII: 5)

There were six examples. The rims flared outward. Some were painted on the rims while others were not.

A8b (Fig.18; Pl. XIII: 1)

There were three examples. It was similar to the former variety; only the rims were more widely flared.

A8c (Fig.18; Pl. XIX: 1)

There was only one example. The lip of the rim curled outwards and the sides had a slight curve, narrowing to the bottom.

A8d (Fig.18; Pl. XIX: 2)

There was only one example. This was similar to A8c except for a greater curve on the sides.

(9) Constricted-mouthed basins

The rims were constricted with walls tapering towards a flat bottom. In addition to plain and painted designs, some basins were decorated with incised patterns around the rim and the body of the vessel; or a pair of decorations in appliqué was added on each side of the body. There were nine types:

A9a (Fig.18; Pl. XIX: 3, 4)

There were three examples. They had slightly constricted openings and shallow bodies. Aside from plain ones there were some with painted designs on the body.

A9b (Fig.18; Pl. XIX: 5, 6; Pl. XX: 1)

There were nine examples. The mouth was somewhat narrowly constricted and the body tapered to the bottom.

A9c (Fig.18; Pl. XX: 4)

There were four examples. The shape was similar to A9b except that the mouth was given a thickened rim.

A9d (Fig.18; Pl. XX: 2, 3)

There were two examples. It was similar to A9c. The exception was that the rim was relatively more constricted.

A9e (Fig.19; Pl. XXI: 1)

There were four examples. The rim was everted, and the body was fairly deep.

A9f (Fig.19; Pl. XXI: 2)

There were three examples. The shapes were similar to A9e; however, the sides tapered only slightly downwards.

A9g (Fig.20; Pl. XXI: 3)

Only one example was found. The lower part of the vessel wall had an inward curve.

A9h (Fig.20; Pl. XXI: 4)

There was only one example. It was similar to A9g, except that its opening was smaller.

A9j (Fig.20; Pl. XXII: 1)

There was only one example. It had a globular body, with a flat bottom.

(10) Deep-bellied basins

This type had a slightly flaring rim, a deep body, sides which tapered towards a flat bottom. In addition to plain and painted designs, some vessels were decorated with incised patterns near the rim and around the top portion of the body. Sometimes decorations in appliqué were placed on two sides of the body. Individual examples show orderly, impressed designs around the body. We can divide this into nine types:

A10a (Fig.20; Pl. XXII: 2)

There were three examples. All of them had wide mouths with sides tapering to the bottom.

A10b (Fig.20; Pl. XXII: 3)

There were three examples. The vessel shape was similar to A10a except for a distinct curve in the sides.

A10c (Fig.20; Pl. XXII: 4)

There was only one example. It had a wide mouth and a globular body. The sides form a break, and then tapered to a small bottom.

A10d (Fig.20; Pl. XVIII: 6; Pl. XXII: 5; Pl. XXIII: 1-3)

There were thirty examples. The shape was similar to A10c except that the body walls (did not show a distinct break) were arced and tapered to a small bottom.

A10e (Fig.21; Pl. XXIII: 4, 5)

There were eleven examples. The shape is similar to that of A10c except that the break in the sides was not as pronounced.

A10f (Fig.21; Pl. XXIV: 1-4)

There were seventeen examples. The vessel shape was similar to A10e.The body, however, bulged slightly.

A10g (Fig.21; Pl. XXIV: 5,6; Pl. XXV: 1-5; Pl. XXVI: 1-2; Pl. XXVII: 1)

There were fifteen examples. The vessel shape was similar to A10f; like the previous model, the body bulged slightly.

A10h (Fig.21; Pl. XXVII: 2)

There was only one example. The body showed an obvious bulge.

A10j (Fig.21; Pl. XXVII: 3)

There were only two examples. The vessel shape was similar to A10h. However, it had a deeper body.

(11) Oval-shaped basins

This type was oval with straight or slanted walls and a flat bottom. There were two types, both lacking in decoration.

A11a (Fig.21; Pl. XXVII: 4)

There was only one example. It had a level rim and vertical walls.

A11b (Fig.21; Pl. XXVII: 5)

Again there was only one example. The rim was slightly flared, and the vessel walls expanded outward so that the flat bottom was larger than the mouth.

(12) Tubular basins

These vessels were tubular with a deep body and flat bottom. All of the examples were undecorated. This can be divided into four types:

A12a (Fig.22; Pl. XXVIII: 1)

There were two examples. This variety had a large mouth and sides which were gradually constricted toward the bottom.

A12b (Fig.22; Pl. XXVIII: 2)

There was one example. It had a thick-rim and nearly straight walls.

A12c (Fig.22; Pl. XXVIII: 3)

There was only one example. The rim curled outwards with straight walls.

A12d (Fig.22; Pl. XXVIII: 4)

There was only one example. The rim was slightly everted while the walls showed a small bulge.

(13) *Zeng* steamers

These vessels were basin shaped with bodies that were plain, or decorated in the basket pattern. These can be divided into four types:

A13a (Fig.23; Pl. XXVIII: 5a, b)

There was just one example. It had a wide mouth. The straight walls tapered toward a flat bottom. There were four symmetrically placed oval holes in the bottom.

A13b (Fig.23; Pl. XXIX: 1a, b)

There was only one example. It had a wide mouth, with a rolled rim and sides which tapered toward a flat bottom. There were also four symmetrically placed oval holes in the bottom.

A13c (Fig.23; Pl. XXIX: 2a, b)

There was only one example. Its shape is similar to type A13a; but the lip curled outwards, and its bottom showed seven holes.

A13d (Fig.23; Pl. XXX: 1a, b)

There was only one example, similar to type A13b. However, there were eight round holes in the bottom of this.

(14) Cups

They had wide mouth with vertical or slanted sides, and flat bottoms. They can be divided into two types:

A14a (Fig.22; Pl. XXX: 2)

There was only one example. It had a shallow body, the lower portion of which was decorated with a few incised patterns.

A14b (Fig.22; Pl. XXX: 3)

There were two examples. This type showed a deep body, and a saw tooth pattern pressed onto the rim. On either side of the rim was a handle. Linear patterns covered the whole body.

(15) *Yu* basins (A15; Fig.22; Pl. XXX: 4)

There was only one example. It had a narrow mouth, convex body, and a flat bottom. There was a short handle placed horizontally on either side of the inner wall.

(16) Constricted-mouthed jars

They had a constricted mouth, a bugled body which tapers to a flat bottom. Aside from the plain and the painted kinds, some vessels had an incised pattern or decorations in appliqué on the body. They were divided into three types:

A16a (Fig.22; Pl. XXX: 5)

There was just one example. Its rim curled outward.

A16b (Fig.22; Pl. XXXI: 1)

There was only one example. The rim was slightly everted.

A16c (Fig.24; Pl. XXXI, 2, 3)

There were two examples. The shape of this type is similar to A16b. However, it had a short neck and no everted lips.

(17) Long-necked jars

These vessels had a long neck, and a convex body, which tapered toward a flat bottom. These jars were either plain or painted; and some combined incised designs with the painted motifs. They can be divided into three types:

A17a (Fig.24; Pl. XXXI: 4)

There was only one example. It had an everted lip, and its exterior was covered with a dark red slip, polished to a luster.

A17b (Fig.24; Pl. XXXII: 1)

There was only one example, similar to type A17a. However, the neck was longer here.

A17c (Fig.24; Pl. XXXII: 2)

There was only one example. It had a slightly slanted lip and the body was in convex curve.

(18) Bottles

There were two types: One with a pointed bottom, and one with a flat bottom. Both types are narrow-mouthed, and a few have handles. Most of the decoration showed a pressed on basket pattern on the body, with pressed on linear patterns all over it. In some cases, the designs near the bottom were wiped smooth. There were few examples showing just the basket or the linear design. We have also reconstructed another shape from some rim fragments-a gourd shape-showing a short neck and heavy lip, a long neck and a curved rim (Pl. XXXII: 3-6). However, we do not know which kind of vessel they belong to. The fragments of the long-necked, curved rim kind were painted, powder of a red dye was found on the inner and outer walls. This powder was probably from a red iron ore (Pl. XXXII: 7). The bottles can be divided into two types:

A18a (Fig.24; Pl. XXXII: 8, 9)

There were five examples, all with pointed bottoms.

A18b (Fig.24; Pl. XXXIII: 1, 2)

There were five examples with flat bottoms.

(19) Vessel covers

Mostly the fragments were so broken that only very few reconstructions are possible. In some only the top knob remained. There are four types:

A19a (Fig.24; Pl. XXXIII: 3)

There was only one example. The vessel cover was globe shaped with the lip curling outwards. The knob was wide on top and narrow below.

A19b (Fig.24; Pl. XXXIII: 4).

There was only one example. Only the knob was found. It had a round top, and a long neck, which had four round holes symmetrically bored through. Impressed patterns systematically done were found all around the top edge.

A19c (Fig.24; Pl. XXXIII: 5)

There was only one example. Again only the knob survived. It had a pointed top, and the lower broken part showed traces of burnishing. Perhaps after this knob was broken from the cover, it was burnished for another purpose. Linear patterns covered the top.

A19d (Fig.25; Pl. XXXIII: 6)

There was only one example. It had a wide mouth; its upper part tapered to a narrow hole. On either side was a decoration in appliqué. If it were turned upside down, it could be used as a funnel, thus it was probably intended for both uses.

(20) Vessel stands

These were used to support vessels with round bottoms. There were three types:

A20a (Fig.25; Pl. XXXIII: 7)

There was only one example. Both ends of the vessel were level and the waist was slightly constricted,

A20b (Fig.25; Pl. XXXIV: 1)

There was only one example with an everted mouth and slender waist. One end of the vessel was smaller than the other.

A20c (Fig.25; Pl. XXXIV: 2)

There were two examples. This type had a constricted mouth. Its body expanded towards the lower part of the vessel. There was no bottom on this type of stand. The body was decorated with a linear pattern, and four oval holes, which were oriented on a slant and arranged symmetrically around the stand.

B. Family of Grey Pottery

The clay for this ware did not go through the delicate levigating process nor was it adulterated by temper material. The surface was usually unpainted and polished, and seldom with patterns. The patterns included basket marks, incised patterns, decorations in appliqué, and open work. The decorations in appliqué usually appeared on the two sides of the basin body both as decoration and as vessel handles; the incised pattern was often seen on the neck of the long necked jar; the basket pattern was mostly seen on wide-mouthed bowls; while the open work was often seen on the handle of vessel covers. The colors were grey and greyish brown. The vessel shapes included plate, bowl, jar, vessel cover and vessel stand.

(1) Plate (B1; Fig.25; Pl. XXXIV: 3)

Only one example was found. It had a wide mouth, shallow body and flat bottom.

(2) Wide-mouthed bowl (B2; Fig.25; Pl. XXXIV: 4)

There was only one example. It had a wide mouth and walls that curved into a flat, narrow bottom.

(3) Curved-bellied bowls

These bowls had a wide mouth and a body that curved in towards the bottom forming a flat base. There were two types:

B3a (Fig.25; Pl. XXXIV: 5)

There were six examples. The curve of the body wall was not very obvious.

B3b (Fig.25; Pl. XXXIV: 6)

There was only one example. The body wall had a wide curve which reversed itself, tapering to a very small bottom.

(4) Shallow-bellied basins

These basins had wide mouths and protruding rims. The walls curved in towards the flat bottom. There were three types:

B4a (Fig.25; Pl. XXXIV: 7)

There were fourteen examples. The vessels narrowed towards the bottom in a slight arc curve.

B4b (Fig.25; Pl. XXXV: 1)

There was only one example. The body was curved at the top, and then narrowed towards the bottom in a relative straight line.

B4c (Fig.26; Pl. XXXV: 2)

There was only one example. Its shape is similar to B4b, but with a deeper body.

(5) Constricted-mouthed basins

They had a narrow mouth and body walls curved downwards to a flat bottom. There were four types:

B5a (Fig.26; Pl. XXXV: 3)

There were two examples. The lip was curved and turned in, slightly narrowing.

B5b (Fig.26; Pl. XXXV: 4)

There was only one example. Here the lip just slightly narrowed inwards.

B5c (Fig.26; Pl. XXXV: 5)

There were six examples. The lip was curved inward. There was a section of decorations in appliqué on either side of the body.

B5d (Fig.26; Pl. XXXVI: 1)

There were two examples. The shape of these vessels was similar to the B5c except that this type was much bigger, the height being 49cm, the opening diameter 70cm, the bottom diameter 25cm, and the thickness of the ware was 1.2cm.

(6) Constricted-mouthed jars

This type had a narrow mouth, bulged sides and a flat bottom. It can be divided into three types:

B6a (Fig.27; Pl. XXXVI: 2)

There was only one example. The lip did not curl outwards, but was a simple, flat one.

B6b (Fig.27; Pl. XXXVI: 3)

There was only one example. The shape was similar to B6a; only the lip curled slightly outwards, and the body was more bulging.

B6c (Fig.27; Pl. XXXVI: 3)

There was one example. It is similar to B6a except that lip curled slightly outwards.

(7) Long-necked jar (B7; Fig.28; Pl. XXXVII: 1)

Only one fragment of the rim was discovered. The vessel shape was similar to A17c. There were some incised patterns around the neck.

(8) Vessel covers

The recovered parts are mostly fragments of the knobs. Very few could be reconstructed. They can be divided into four types:

B8a (Fig.28; Pl. XXXVII: 2)

There were four examples. The knob fragment had a short neck and round top decorated by a row of impressed designs on the edge.

B8b (Fig.28; Pl. XXXVII: 3)

There were two examples. This knob fragment also had a round top and long neck.

B8c (Fig.28; Pl. XXXVII: 4)

There were five examples. Knob fragments showed a conical top, with an orderly network of small holes all over it, edged by a row of impressed notches.

B8d (Fig.28; Pl. XXXVII: 5)

There were five examples and they were shaped like upside-down bowls. The tops of the knob were hollow. There were obvious traces showing where the knob was luted on to the rest of the cover.

(9) Vessel stands (B9; Fig. 28; Pl. XXXVII: 6)

There were three examples. They were round with slender waists. As in a semi-conical manner, the upper rim was smaller than the lower.

C. Family of Fine Black Pottery

Very little of this pottery was discovered in the Yangshao strata. Both the outside and the inside of the ware were black and the paste was grey to reddish brown. The only reconstructed shape is a jar with a round bottom. We have discovered a rim fragment with the relief of a gecko on it, done vividly. However, the anterior part of its body no longer remained. (Pl. XXXVIII: 1)

(1) Round-bottomed jar (C1; Fig.28; Pl. XXXVII: 7).

Only one example was found. It had a vertical rim, round shoulder, bulging body, and round bottom.

D. Family of Coarse, Sand-tempered Red Pottery

This ware is very coarse, containing a great deal of fine sand. The most common decorative motif was linear pattern, all placed in a slant and often seen on jars and *fu* cauldrons. The next most common was plain vessels, mostly basins. Incised patterns, string patterns and decorations in appliqué were seldom seen, incised patterns and decorations in appliqué were combined with the linear motif, while string patterns were seen only on individual jars, *ding* tripods and *fu* cauldrons. We have also found a round bottom jar of this coarse red ware covered with a dark red slip, a specimen we seldom came across. We also discovered two rim fragments with reliefs of geckos on them; one was more or less complete while the other was missing a tail. (Pl. XXXVIII: 2, 3).The vessel shapes included cups, plates, bowls, basins, jars, *yu* jars, *ding* tripods, *fu* cauldrons, *zao* stoves, and vessel covers.

(1) Round-bottomed jar (D1: Fig.28; Pl. XXXVII: 8)

There was only one example. It had a broken rim, a deep body and a round bottom. The exterior was covered with a dark red slip, and had been polished to a luster.

(2) *Fu cauldrons.*

These vessels had a small mouth, a level or sloping shoulder, and a round bottom. There were four types:

D2a (Fig.28; Pl. XXXVII: 9)

There was only one example. It had a sloping shoulder and a bulging body.

D2b (Fig.28; Pl. XXXIX: 1)

There was only one example. It also had a sloping shoulder. The vessel was first made with a round bottom; and before it was fired, it was pressed down, making a small flat base.

D2c (Fig.28; Pl. XXXIX: 2)

There were four examples. The slope of the vessel shoulder is small compared to D2b.

D2d (Fig.29; Pl. XXXIX: 3)

There was only one example. It had a level shoulder.

(3) *Ding* tripod (D3; Fig.29; Pl. XXXIX: 4)

There was only one example collected near the site. It was made by attaching three flat legs to a type D2c *fu* cauldron. The lower parts of the legs were broken.

(4) *Zao* stove (D4; Fig.29; Pl. XXXIX: 4)

There was only one example. Its body was like a pitcher shape, with a fire door in the front and three short legs below. Near the rim on the inner wall, there were three convex knobs, which could have been used to support *fu* cauldrons.

(5) Plate (D5; Fig.29; Pl. XXXIX: 7)

There was only one example. It had a wide mouth, a shallow body, straight walls and a flat bottom.

(6) Wide-mouthed bowls

From its wide mouth, the sides tapered to a flat bottom. They can be divided into four types:

D6a (Fig.29; Pl. XL: 1)

There was only one example. It had a shallow body.

D6b (Fig.29; Pl. XL: 2)

There were two examples. The shape was slightly deeper than D6a.

D6c (Fig.29; Pl. XL: 3)

There were four examples. The body wall narrowed slightly towards the bottom which was quite big, about three-fifths the size of the opening diameter.

D6d (Fig.29; Pl. XL: 4)

There were two examples. The mouth was slightly constricted, and the body wall tapered to the bottom which was only one half the size of the opening diameter.

(7) Shallow-bellied basins

They were wide-mouthed, shallow bodied and flat bottomed. They can be divided into three types:

D7a (Fig.29; Pl. XL: 5)

There were two examples. The rim was turned outwards and the walls tapered downwards.

D7b (Fig.29; Pl. XL: 6)

There was only one example. Its shape was similar to D7a; however the wall of the body tapered less.

D7c (Fig.29; Pl. XL: 7)

There was only one example. The lip was turned outwards and the body wall arched and tapered downward.

(8) Deep-bellied basins

This type had a wide mouth, and a deep flat bottom. They can be divided into two types:

D8a (Fig.30; Pl. XL: 8).

There was only one example. The body was tapered inwards toward the bottom.

D8b (Fig.30; Pl. XLI: 1)

There were two examples. The shape was similar to D8a. Here, however, the body was a bit more globular.

(9) Cups

All of the cups were small and mostly decorated with a linear pattern. Very few were plain. Of the excavated pottery cups were the most numerous, and some were even complete. There were four types:

D9a (Fig.30; Pl. XLI: 2)

There was a single example. It had a wide mouth, and tapered to a flat bottom.

D9b (Fig.30; Pl. XLI: 3, 4)

There were 124 examples. The shape included an everted mouth and the body walls tapering slightly to a flat bottom. Near the bottom, was a ring of small, round or oval shaped pits.

D9c (Fig.30; Pl. XLI: 5, 6)

There were two examples. The mouth was everted with straight sides, and a flat bottom. A row of deep oval-shaped pits appeared near the bottom of some.

D9d (Fig.30; Pl. XLI: 7)

There were four examples. The type was tubular, with a deep body, and a flat bottom.

(10) *Yu* basins

It had a narrow mouth, bulging sides, and a flat bottom. There were two types:

D10a (Fig.30; Pl. XLI: 8)

There was a single example. The body wall was slightly bulging.

D10b (Fig.30; Pl. XLI: 9)

There was only one example. The shape was similar to D10a. Only the body was more globular. A short knob was placed horizontally on each side of the inner wall of the vessel.

(11) Constricted-mouthed jar

The characteristics included a constricted mouth, globular body, and a flat bottom. There were ten types:

D11a (Fig.30; Pl. XLII: 1)

There was one example. It had a slightly constricted mouth and the body walls tapered in towards the bottom.

D11b (Fig.30; Pl. XLII: 2)

There were four examples. The shape was similar to D11a, except that the body walls tapered more acutely.

D11c (Fig.30; Pl. XLII: 3)

There were five examples. The body wall was slightly arced in the upper portions; below the middle it curved inwardly and tapered.

D11d (Fig.31; Pl. XLII: 4)

There was one example. It had a narrow mouth and an obvious globular body.

D11e (Fig.31; Pl. XLII: 5)

There was one example. Its shape was similar to D11d except that the rim was not everted.

D11f (Fig.31; Pl. XLII: 6)

There was one example. The bulge in the body formed an angle, then continued to taper downwards to a flat bottom.

D11g (Fig.31; Pl. XLIII: 1)

There was one example. The mouth was slightly constricted while the body wall tapered to the bottom.

D11h (Fig.31; Pl. XLIII: 2, 3)

There were five examples. The body bulged slightly and tapered to the bottom.

D11j (Fig.31; Pl. XLIII: 4; Pl. XLIV: 1, 2)

There were four examples. The vessel shape was similar to D11h, except that the body was a bit more globular.

D11k (Fig.32; Pl. XLIV: 3)

There was one example. The vessel shape was similar to D11j, but on each side near the top was a pair handles, and the body was a little deeper.

(12) Constricted-mouthed jars with open work (D12; Fig.32; Pl. XLIV: 4)

There were three examples. They had a constricted mouth and large bottom, a shape similar to the round sack-like ash pit. There were three holes placed around the bottom. The walls were decorated with basket patterns. The function of these jars is not known.

(13) Vessel covers

Most of the covers were for pottery cups, and covers for larger vessels are very few. There were four types:

D13a (Fig.32; Pl. XLV: 1)

There were two examples. The back of the cover had a globular shape and a loop handle was placed in the center.

D13b (Fig.32; Pl. XLV: 2).

There was one example. The shape was similar to D13a, except that its back is higher.

D13c (Fig.32; Pl. XLV: 3).

There were 114 examples. They had short knobs, and were also covers for small pottery cups, suitable for use with the cup types D9a-d.

D13d (Fig.32; Pl. XLV: 4).

There were two examples. They had long knobs. Their function was similar to D13c.

ii. Implements

(1) Knives

Most of the knives were remade from potsherds, although several were made directly from clay. The ware was mainly of the fine red ware, while the grey ware was rare. Structurally, there were two kinds of knives: One with notches on both sides of the blade; the other with a hole in the top center of the blade. The notches were usually in the central part of both sides of the blade; a few were in the upper half. Mostly the holes were made by pecking from both sides, although a few were made by piercing through only one side. All blades showed a single hole, placed mainly near the centre of the back of the blade, except for individual variations that were at the center. The edges were usually made by grinding down on both sides, and rarely on just one side. A few of the pottery knives showed that the blades had not been sharpened. Other knives found, included some with neither notches nor holes, and some with incomplete holes and notches on the sides. The former kind was probably unfinished; and the latter group may indicate a change in design, first with the hole then changing to the notches. There were four types:

1A (Pl. XLV: 5-8)

There were twenty-eight examples. This type showed the notches on both sides and various shapes including, trapezoidal, rectangular and shouldered shapes.

1B (Pl. XLV: 9, 10)

There were seven examples. There were neither holes nor notches, on this type, which were in oval and rectangular shapes.

1C (Pl. XLV: 11-14)

There were fifty-two examples. The type had a rectangular shape with a pierced hole. Knife T237:15 was made directly from clay with the hole drilled directly through the sides.

1D (Pl. XLVI: 1, 2)

There were thirteen examples. The type had rounded backs and a drilled hole.

(2) Adzes

These implements were made from potsherds and have a single cutting edge, with a pierced hole at one end. They can be divided into two types:

2A (Pl. XLVI: 3)

There was one example. It had a rectangular shape.

2B (Pl. XLVI: 4)

There was one example and it had a trapezoidal shape.

(3) Pitted tools

The various types can be divided into three types:

3A (Pl. XLVI: 5)

There was one example. Both ends were broken with only the central portion remaining, and it was rectangular. It was made of fine red pottery with holes closely pierced all over the surface.

3B (Pl. XLVI: 6-8)

There were eight examples. This type was a solid spherical shape; but they were all broken with only half of each surviving. They were made from fine red pottery of relatively hard clay, with a trellis or fingernail pattern on the surface, or with a concave dot pattern.

3C (Fig.33: 1; Pl. XLVI: 9)

There was one example. It had a hollow spherical shape of which only a half remained. It was made from grey pottery that was rather hard. Its surface had a pattern of concave dots.

The common characteristic of those implements in type 3A, B, C is a coarse surface. Type 3A was often seen in the Yangshao sites within Shaanxi province. It had been suggested that its function was rubbing and washing the hands or for scraping leather. [9] Types 3B and 3C probably had the same function. In the past, they were thought to be toys; but since they were often found in the Yangshao sites, they must be of daily use also. The theory that they were toys is difficult to explain.

(4) Spindle whorls

There were two kinds: One was made from potsherds, and the other directly from clay. They can be divided into three types:

4A (Fig.33: 2; Pl. XLVI: 10, 11)

There were sixty-eight examples. These were made from potsherds and the holes were pierced from both sides.

4B (Fig.33: 3; Pl. XLVI: 12, 13)

There were fifteen examples. They were made of fine red pottery with the holes drilled straight through. The edges were smooth and neat.

4C (Fig.33: 4, 5; Pl. XLVI: 14, 15)

There were two examples. They were made of fine red pottery, in a flat, conical shape. They were not very neatly done, and were directly drilled through. Except plain surface, there were impressed patterns on the surface around the upper and lower edges.

(5) Pellets (Pl. XLVI: 16)

There were nine examples. They were ball-shaped and concisely made.

iii. Ornaments

There was only one kind of pottery rings.

(1) Rings

Most of the rings were made of grey pottery; the red ware was seldom seen, but the quality of both was very fine. Not many were complete; the shapes included circular, pentagon, hexagon and heptagon and cog-like. Their cross-sections were commonly round or oval, with only a few triangular, half-mooned, or rectangular examples. Aside from polished, plain surfaces, there were also decorations, with incised patterns, a slanting checkered pattern, a braid-like pattern, and nipple pattern (Fig.34). The most often seen were the plain-surfaced ones and ones with the pattern incised. There were also a few painted with red or black. There were seven types:

1A (Fig.35: 1-7; Pl. XLVI: 17, 18)

There were thirty-three examples. The type was a round shape, with plain surface or three kinds of decoration: Incised pattern, slanting checkered pattern, and a braided pattern.

1B (Fig.35: 8; Pl. XLVI: 19; Pl. XLVII: 5, 7)

There was only one example. It was round with the dotted protruding pattern all over the surface.

1C (Fig.35: 9; Pl. XLVI: 20)

There were two examples. The type was five-sided with no decoration.

1D (Fig.35: 10, 11; Pl. XLVI: 21, 22)

There were nine examples. These were six-sided, with both plain and incised surfaces.

1E (Fig.35: 12; Pl. XLVII: 1)

There were six examples. They were seven-sided with only incised patterns.

1F (Fig.35: 13,14; Pl. XLVII: 2, 3)

There were eight examples. This type had an undecorated surface in a cog-like shape. No complete example of this type had been found.

1G (Fig.35: 15; Pl. XLVII: 4)

There was one example. It was partly broken. In the center of the edge was a cone-like, protruding element; on either side was a decoration formed by clay stripes.

iv. Miscellaneous

(1) Bird head (Pl. XLVII: 6)

There was one example. It was made of fine red pottery and had very large eyes; its upper beak was broken; the neck had ringed grooves.

(2) Bell (Fig.36: 1; Pl. XLVII: 8)

There was only one example. It was made of the fine red ware. The vessel wall flared downwards; its body was hollow, and it had a handle on top with small holes on either side of the shoulder. It had a plain and brightly burnished surface.

(3) Pendant (Fig.36: 2; Pl. XLVII: 9)

There was only one example. It was shaped like a round post with rounded ends, and one end had a small hole. The convex middle section had a hole on either side, placed symmetrically, but not connecting. The function of this object is not known.

(II) Stone Artifacts

i. Tools

These were made by both flaking and grinding. Different kinds of stone used include: flint, sandstone, slate, quartz, diorite, diabase, basalt, and gneiss. We will discuss them according to their classifications.

(1) Disc-shaped tools

Round or oval, most of these were made by flaking natural gravel; on the reverse side of some, the original stone surface still remains. There were also some made by reworking a broken piece of stone spade. Many of these tools have been excavated, their incomplete total being more than 2, 230. All ash pits have at least one of these tools, and at most seventy-four. From their sizable number, they might have been used for daily use; but their function is not known. They could have been used as hammers or those with blades could have been scrapers. According to the different manufacturing techniques, they can be divided into four types:

1A (Fig.37: 1; Pl. XLVII: 10, 11)

There were 1,496 examples. These were made by flaking on one side vertically. The sides were quite even, but blunt. Number H363:05 was made by re-shaping a broken piece of stone spade, so that one part of the edge is still the original blade of the stone spade. There was also one tool with a round concave pit on both sides of the center. It could have been an unfinished stone hammer (Fig.37: 5; Pl. XLVII: 16) .

1B (Fig.37: 2; Pl. XLVII: 12)

There were 559 examples. A cutting edge was formed by flaking at an angle.

1C (Fig.37: 3; Pl. XLVII: 13, 14)

There were 183 examples. This type was flaked from both sides to make a sharp edge. Number T344:78 was made by reshaping a fragment from a stone spade. It was broken but the middle of one side retained traces of having been pecked and flaked.

1D (Fig.37: 4; Pl. XLVII: 15)

There was one example. This specimen was made by flaking at an angle on one side, with a piece of stone to form a sharp edge. Parts of its original rock surface still remain in convex shapes. This is different from the other types which were flaked with gravel to flatten sides.

(2) Net sinkers

They were all different shapes; and may be divided into two types:

2A (Pl. XLVII: 17, 18).

There were four examples. They were oval with notches on both sides.

2B (Pl. XLVII: 19).

There was one example. It was long and narrow with a groove around the center.

(3) Knives

Some knives were made by flaking and others by grinding. The former was usually coarser than the latter. The ground knives usually had a single hole through the blade; only a few had two holes. Some examples were first carved with a long groove on each side, and then the holes were made. There are eight types:

3A (Pl. XLVIII: 1-3)

There were twenty-three examples. Notches were found on both sides. The original stone is apparent on one side. Most of the notches were placed on the central parts of both sides; in a few cases, they were close to the cutting edge.

3B (Pl. XLVIII: 4)

There were six examples. They were rectangular with no notches.

3C (Fig.38: 7; Pl. XLIX: 9-11)

There were fifty-three examples. They were rectangular with flat or slightly arced cutting edges.

3D (Fig.38: 8; Pl. XLIX: 12)

There were three examples, rectangular in shape with concave cutting edges.

3E (Pl. XLIX: 13)

There were four examples. They were nearly oval in shape, with flat backs and arced cutting edges.

3F (Pl. XLIX: 14)

There was one example. Only the central part survived with two holes.

3G (Pl. XLIX: 15, 16)

There were eight examples. They have arced backs and flat cutting edges.

3H (Fig.38: 9; Pl. XLIX: 17, 18)

There were two examples. They were remade from fragments of rectangular stone knives. The blade was on the shorter side.

(4) Flakes (Fig.37: 12; Pl. XLVIII: 5)

There were two examples. They were roughly triangular flint flakes. The striking platforms, cones of percussion and positive bulbs of percussion were all quite clear, but there were no traces of retouching. The blades on both sides were sharp. They were probably used immediately after being detached as traces of use are obvious on both edges.

(5) Hammers

They were round in shape with a hole drilled through the middle. There were four types:

5A (Fig.38: 10; Pl. LI: 1, 2)

There were five examples. The hole was drilled through natural gravel. All of the examples were half broken.

5B (Fig.38: 11: Pl. LI: 3)

There were two examples. Only one section was left. The shape was similar to 5A except that here the diameter of the hole was large.

5C (Fig.38: 12; Pl. LI: 4)

There were five examples. A small section was missing from each example. They were made from fragments of stone spades, with edges chipped into sharp blades by alternately striking on both sides.

5D (Fig.38: 13; Pl. LI: 5)

There were five examples. Only half of each remained. They were highly polished and of a fine quality.

(6) Axes

The stone was first shaped properly (Pl. XLVIII: 6), and then highly polished. Only some have holes in their blades. In the polishing process, some of these axes were worked on by small, flat pebbles. There were seven types:

6A (Fig.37: 6; Pl. XLVIIIL: 7)

There were four examples. The type was rectangular with a flat cutting blade. The cross-section was roughly rectangular.

6B (Fig.37: 7; Pl. XLVIII: 8, 9)

There were seven examples. The type was trapezoidal with a broad blade. The cross-section was roughly square.

6C (Fig.37: 8; Pl. XLVIII: 10)

There were four examples. Only the lower portions were remained. They had narrow blades with a cross-section that was roughly oval.

6D (Fig.37: 9; Pl. XLVIII: 11)

There was one example. It was nearly rectangular, and the holes were not completely drilled through. The cross-section was oval.

6E (Fig.37: 10; Pl. XLVIII: 12)

There was only one example. It was slightly rectangular with a large portion missing in the blade. A single hole was made by working from both sides. The cross-section was lozenge shaped.

6F (Fig.37: 11; Pl. XLVIII: 13-15)

There were eight examples. They were made from natural gravel and were of several different shapes such as oval and semi-oval. H 10:13 is very thick on top with the vertical section showing a triangular shape. All the others were flat tools.

6G (Pl. XLVIII: 16, 17)

There were two examples. They were small, flat axes with single or double holes through the blade. On T335:01 the holes have not been completely drilled through the blades.

(7) Adzes

There were four types:

7A (Fig.37: 13; Pl. XLIX: 1)

There was only one example. It was rectangular with a flat blade and a rectangular cross-section.

7B (Fig.37: 14; Pl. XLIX: 2)

There were two examples. The shape was nearly oval, with a convex blade, and an oval cross-section.

7C (Fig.38: 1; Pl. XLIX: 3)

' There was one example. The only remaining half was trapezoidal, with a broad blade, and a rectangular cross-section.

7D (Fig.38: 2; Pl. XLIX: 4)

There was one example. The top was narrow with a flat blade. Only one side shows slight polishing.

(8) Chisels

They can be divided into three types:

8A (Fig.38: 3; Pl. XLIX: 5)

There was only one example. It was rectangular with one cutting edge on one side. The cross-section was trapezoidal.

8B (Fig.38: 4; Pl. XLIX: 6)

There were two examples. They showed a rectangular outline, a one-sided blade, and a cross-section that was rectangular.

8C (Fig.38: 5, 6; Pl. XLIX: 7, 8)

There were four examples. The shape was nearly rectangular, with a one-sided or bifacial blade. The cross-section was oval.

(9) Spades

Mostly fragments with only a few complete examples found. According to our incomplete count, about 130 fragments have been excavated from ash pits and excavation pits. Judging from the complete or reconstructed examples, the small spades were 13.4 cm long, while the large ones were more than 29cm long. Some show traces of chipping on one side near the central part of the back; this seems to have been used for fixing the handle. Some, like type 9C, were chipped on the upper part of both sides, probably for tying and securing a wooden handle.

We also discovered a broken chipped stone spade, rather coarse and thick, indicating that it was unfinished (Pl. L: 1). This also illustrated that the first step in manufacturing was to shape the tool, and then polish it. There were four types:

9A (Fig.39: 1; Pl. L: 2)

There was one example. It had a flat back with a pointed blade. A corner was missing from its back.

9B (Fig.39: 2; Pl. L: 3)

There was one example. Its shape was similar to 9a, except the body was more round. On one side there were traces of chipping near the center of the back.

9C (Fig.39: 3; Pl. L: 4)

There was only one example. It was nearly oval with a concave back. The body of the shape was quite broad. The two sides were ground to form a rounded blade. On both sides of the body, slight notches were made.

9D (Fig.39: 4; Pl. L: 5, 6)

There was only one example. The upper part was broken. It had a round blade; the body was rather long; the remaining length was 29 cm. Judging from extent fragments, the top part must have been convex.

(10) Spindle whorls (Fig.38: 14; Pl. LI: 6, 7)

There were fifteen examples. They were round with holes pierced through the middle from both sides. Most of the edges were curved, although a few were flat and straight.

(11) Balls (Pl. LI: 8, 9)

There were forty-five examples of various sizes, but all were polished. The larger ones had a diameter of 5.5 cm while the smaller ones were only 3 cm, and were probably used as sling balls.

(12) Pestles

Pestles and mortars were both used for grinding red iron ore into powder. Traces of this red iron remained on the mortars and the pestles. They may be divided into two types:

12A (Pl. LI: 10-12)

There were three examples. The pestles were made from natural gravel. Two of them were squarish (0:07, H329:10), with the pounding surface convex. The remaining one, H304:05, was slightly oval with both sides ground flat. Each grinding surface was smooth with the traces of red iron on it.

12B (Pl. LI: 13, 14)

There were two examples. Both were shaped like bottle guards with a narrow waist. The bottom grinding surface showed traces of red iron.

(13) Mortars (Pl. LI: 15; Pl. LII: 1, 2)

There were three examples. They were made from large pieces of natural flat gravel. The shapes were all different, and the surfaces were either flat or concave. Traces of red iron were seen on all of them.

ii. Ornaments

(1) Rings (Pl. LII: 3, 4)

There were two examples, both broken. They were polished, with a cross-section rectangular or oval.

(2) Bead (Fig.38: 15; Pl. LII: 5)

There was only one example. It was made of rock crystal and shaped like abacus bead. The hole was drilled from both sides.

(3) Pendants

All were made of turquoise except T234:05, which was made of rhyolite and they all had holes on them. They may be divided into three types:

3A (Pl. LII: 6-8)

There were three examples. The shape was oval with a triangular or oval cross-section. There were some flat ones.

3B (Pl. LII: 9, 10)

There were two examples. They were long and flat.

3C (Pl. LII: 11)

There was one example. It was worked along the natural shape of the turquoise.

(III) Bone, Antler, Shell, and Tooth Artifacts

i. Bone artifacts

(1) Needles

They can be divided into two types:

1A (Fig.40: 1; Pl. LII, 12: 13)

There were five examples, which were broad and short. No. T235:11 is the one whose hole was rather far from the top.

1B (Fig.40: 2; Pl. LII: 14, 15)

There were twelve examples. All were narrow and long.

(2) Awls

There were three types:

2A (Fig.40: 3, 4; Pl. LII: 16, 17)

There were four examples. The so-called bone fragment was made from sharpened pieces of bone.

2B (Fig.40: 5; Pl. LII: 18)

There were two examples. The front leg bone of a pig was split up and sharpened, leaving part of the joint still in its original shape.

2C (Fig.40: 6; Pl. LII: 19)

There were three examples, made from a dog's fibula, sharpened at the narrow end. The rest of the bone was not worked on.

(3) Arrowheads

There was no obvious division between the trunk and the sharp point of the arrowheads. In most cases, both ends were constricted to a point with differences in the degrees of pointedness. There were six types:

3A (Fig.40: 9; Pl. LIII: 1)

There were seven examples which were all flat.

3B (Fig.40: 10,11; Pl. LIII: 2, 3)

There were twenty-seven examples, all with a triangular cross-section.

3C (Fig.40: 12, 13; Pl. LIII: 4, 5)

There were fifteen examples, with a semi-circular cross-section.

3D (Fig.40: 14, 15; Pl. LIII: 6, 7)

There were three examples, with a diamond-shaped cross-section.

3E (Fig.40: 16; Pl. LIII: 8)

There were eight examples, with a round cross-section.

3F (Figure 40: 17; Pl. LIII: 9, 10)

There were eleven examples. The shape of this type was similar to 3E except that its cross-section was oval.

(4) Pointed Implement (Figure40: 7; Pl. LIII: 11)

There was only one example. It was conical and hollow in the upper part, probably for the purpose of attaching a handle. Its use is unclear.

(5) Chisel (Fig.40: 8; Pl. LIII: 12)

There was only one example. It was a long flat shape with one end sharpened into a cutting edge, while the other end was sharpened to a point.

(6) Hairpins

They were used for holding the hair in place. They may be divided into six types:

6A (Fig.40: 18; Pl. LIV: 1, 2)

There were eight examples. Both ends were sharpened to a point, and the cross-section was round.

6B (Fig.40: 19; Pl. LIV: 3)

There were three examples, with flat tops and sharpened lower ends. Their cross-section was round.

6C (Fig.40: 20; Pl. LIV: 4)

There were fifteen examples. Their shapes were similar to 6A except that the cross-section was oval.

6D (Fig.40: 21; Pl. LIV: 5)

There were twenty-three examples. The shape was similar to 6C except that it was flat.

6E (Fig.40: 22; Pl. LIV: 6)

There were seven examples. The top was slightly narrowed, and the lower end was sharpened to a point. They were all flat.

6F (Fig.40: 23; Pl. LIV: 7, 8)

There were five examples. They had flat tops, pointed ends, and a flat cross-section.

(7) Arc-shaped ornaments

They may be divided into two types:

7A (Fig.40: 24, 25; Pl. LV: 1, 2)

The were six examples. This type had an arch shape. None were found complete, but all had a hole at one end. On the convex side of T 203:13 there were two shallow grooves.

7B (Fig.40: 28; Pl. LV: 3)

There were four examples. They were semi-circles with a hole on each end.

(8) Tooth-shaped ornaments (Fig.40: 26, 27; Pl. LV: 4, 5)

There were four examples. Each one had a hole on the top end. In No. T204A:01, the hole was not drilled through, and there were small notches on both sides.

ii. Antler Artifacts

(1) Awls

They can be divided into two types:

1A (Fig.41: 1; Pl. LV: 6, 7)

There were four examples. They were made by splitting a deer antler in two. The surface of the implement showed traces of use.

1B (Fig.41: 2; Pl. LV: 8)

There were two examples. They were made by cutting off the point of a deer's antler. Traces of use were apparent.

(2) Chisels (Fig.41: 3; Pl. LV: 9)

There were three examples. They were slender, and were made by cutting and grinding a piece of a deer's antler. The blade was smooth and showed traces of use.

(3) Hammer (Fig.41: 4; Pl. LV: 10)

There was only one example. It was made by cutting a T-shape at the point where the deer's antler branches out. A square hole was made at the center while each end was hollowed out, probably so that it could be set into a stone tool. Thus the antler portion was really a convenient handle for such a hammer.

iii.Shell Artifacts

(1) Hairpin *(?)* (Pl. LV: 11)

There was only one example. It was nearly diamond shape with one end broken. Its shape was similar to that of a shell arrowhead, except that the edges were sharp. This artifact might be the head of a hairpin.

(2) Ring (Pl. LV: 12)

There was one example. It was round, and was found around the third finger of the left hand of a skeleton in Yangshao ash pit No. 49.

(3) Pendants

They were long and narrow and may be divided into two types:

3A (Pl. LV: 13)

There was one example, with a hole on one end.

3B (Pl. LV: 14)

There were two examples. Each had one hole on both ends.

(4) Shells with holes

There were two types:

4A (Pl. LV: 15, 16)

There were two examples. This type consisted of a hole at one end of the shell of a fresh water mother-of-pearl. It was probably intended to be an ornament.

4B (Pl. LV: 18)

There was only one example. It was made by piercing a hole on the end of one side of a clam shell. Its use was probably similar to that of 4A.

iv. Tooth Artifact

There was only one example, intended as an ornament. It had a hole at the top (Pl. LV: 17) and was made by grinding a pig's canine tooth that was split up. It was broken when found.

(IV) Natural Remains

Including red ochre, bones of domesticated animals, deer antlers, and clam shells

i. Red Ochre

Only a small piece was discovered. From traces left on the pestles, mortars, and on the bottom of a narrow-mouthed bottle, it seems that the powder of this red ocher was probably used for decoration. Since that red was seldom used on painted pottery, this might not have been used as a paint.

ii. Bones of Domesticated Animals

Most of these were taken from the ash pits. The total number is small since the bones were all broken up; it is difficult to determine the exact number. Those which can be identified include bones of pigs and dogs, with the pig bones in the majority. Antlers of antelopes, which were not domesticated, were also found. When compared with the Longshan remains, the total number of bones was small, and the species represented were fewer. This proves that in Yangshao culture, there were only few domesticated animals.

iii. Deer Antlers

There were a few broken pieces of deer antler and fragments of deer bone. They were probably results of a hunt.

iv. Thick Shells

Only a few fragments of shells were found. From the Yangshao stratum, we have only pendants, a hairpin, and a ring made from shells, indicating that the use of shells for making real tools had not developed yet.

IV. Longshan Cultural Remains

(I)Pottery

Of the Longshan remains, potsherds were the most numerous and a small portion of them can be reconstructed. According to the different functions of the vessels, we have divided them into containers and non-containers.

i.Containers

Pottery containers were made of four kinds of wares: A coarse grey ware, a fine grey ware, a fine red ware, and a fine black ware. The coarse grey ware was the most common, seconded by the fine grey ware, followed by the fine red ware, and lastly the fine black ware. The decorations included plain surface, basket patterns, cord impressions, incised patterns, string patterns, a checkered motif, decorations in appliqué, and painted motifs. The basket patterns was the most common, followed by the plain surface, decorations in appliqué, and the cord impressions; and lastly the string patterns, checkered patterns, and the incised patterns. More than sixty vessel forms were reconstructed including the bowl, basin, cup, jar, bottle, *zao* stove, *dou* pedestal, *ding* tripod and *jia* tripod.

Three ash pits (H551, H567, and H568) were selected for study and a table comparing the total number and percentage of wares, decorations and vessel forms were made (96b).

Table of the Sum Total of Pottery Ware Families and Decorations of Longshan Culture

(Ash Pits H551, 567, 568)

Ware Family	Coarse, sand-tempered Grey Ware	Grey ware	Red ware	Fine black ware	Total
Amount	2617	1208	81	35	3941
Percentage	66.45	30.62	2.05	0.88	100%

Decorations	Basket patterns	Plain	Cord impressions	Decorations in appliqué	Checkered patterns	Incised patterns	Basket patterns	Plain	Cord Impressions	Decorations in appliqué	Incised patterns	Plain	Painted motifs	Checkered patterns	Plain	String Patterns	Total
Amount	1779	502	120	125	55	36	404	620	65	78	41	34	36	11	30	5	3941
Percentage	45.14	12.72	3.05	3.17	1.39	0.91	10.31	15.73	1.65	1.97	1.04	0.87	0.91	0.26	0.76	0.12	100%

The Table of the Sum Total of Pottery Vessel Forms of Longshan Culture

(Ash Pits H551, 567, 568) (Limited to those with recognizable forms)

Ware Family	Coarse ,sand-tempered Grey Ware							Grey Ware						Red Ware		Fine Black Ware			Total
Vessel forms	Jar	Basin	*Ding* tripod	*Jia-* tripod	*Zao* stove	Vessel handle	Vessel cover	Jar	Basin	Bowl	Cup	*Dou* pedestal	Vessel cover	Basin	Cup	Jar	Bowl	Vessel cover	
Amount	496	12	32	10	3	19	3	198	16	3	2	3	35	5	9	6	1	1	854
Percentage	58.08	1.41	3.74	1.16	0.35	2.23	0.35	23.18	1.89	0.35	0.23	0.35	4.08	0.59	1.05	0.7	0.12	0.12	100%

A.Coarse, sand-tempered Grey Ware

The clay for this ware was not levigated so that it contained a large amount of fine sand. All of the vessels were hand made, mostly by the coiling method. The walls and flat bottoms were made separately, and then attached to each other on the outside with the edge of the bottoms folded up on to the vessel walls, leaving an obvious mark. This technique we will call the "bottom connecting method".

The surface of these vessels was marked with the basket or cord impressions, mainly used to strengthen the ware. Some vessels were first pressed with the decorations, and then had a few parallel bands with a pitted pattern luted on to the upper part. This was used to strengthen the vessel wall, and also for decoration. Basket impressions were usually unconnected lines, straight or slanted, randomly arranged, and obviously formed by wooden beaters. The cord pattern was better arranged in vertical parallel lines. The checkered pattern was a convex diamond shape and was probably also formed by wooden beaters. Many straight incised patterns appeared on the interior of basin-like vessels, but their use is unknown. The ware is hard, with a greyish brown surface. Other colors include dark grey, greyish yellow, or orange. Often the color appears inconsistent even on the same vessels with different shades showing. This was due to inefficiencies in the firing process.

This ware was mostly used for cooking vessels. The ten vessel forms include a round-bottomed jar, shallow-bellied basin, deep-bellied basin, big-mouthed jar, single-handled jar, narrow-mouthed jar, *ding* tripod, *jia* tripod, *zao* stove, and vessel cover. They will be discussed individually as follows:

(1) Round-bottomed jar (Al; Fig.42; Pl. LVI: 1)

Only one was found. It had a wide mouth, with a slightly flaring rim and a deep round bottom. It seems to have been a cooking utensil for the pottery *zao* stove.

(2) Double-handled basins

It had a shallow bottom, with two luted on handles in a convex shape, or in the shape of the " 山 (mountain)" character. There were three types:

A2a (Fig.42; Pl. LVI: 2)

Only one example was found. It had a wide mouth, a barrel shape and a flat bottom. Both handles on the sides had broken off.

A2b (Fig.42; Pl. LVI: 3)

There were two examples. This type had a wide mouth, straight rim and a wall which tapers downwards to the small flat bottom.

A2c (Fig.42; Pl. LVI: 4)

There were three examples. The type had a wide mouth, deep and relatively arch-shaped sides, terminating in a flat bottom. The inner wall was covered with vertical incised patterns.

(3) Shallow-bellied basins

These vessels had a wide, everted mouth, shallow body, and a small, flat bottom, like a plate shape. There were two types:

A3a (Fig.42; Pl. LVI: 5)

Only one example was found. The body wall was unevenly formed and quite irregular.

A3b (Fig.42; Pl. LVI: 6)

There was one example. The bottom of this vessel was slightly concave.

(4) Deep-bellied basins

These basins had a wide mouth, everted lip, deep body and a flat bottom. They may be divided into three types:

A4a (Fig.42; Pl. LVII: 1)

There was a single example. The bottom was shallower than the others.

A4b (Fig.42; Pl. LVII: 2, 4)

There were two examples. A saw tooth configuration was incised or molded unto the lip.

A4c (Fig.43; Pl. LVII; Pl. LXV: 3)

There were two examples. The lip was wider than the others, the neck was slightly narrowed, and the wall had an arch shape.

(5) Wide-mouthed jars

The vessel body was tubular with a wide mouth. The neck area may be slightly narrowed, with either a straight or everted lip, a deep body, and a flat bottom. The wall had luted on designs of parallel bands. Generally the vessels were relative large, from 21.5-43cm high. They can be divided into two types:

A5a (Fig.43; Pl. LVIII: 5; Pl. LVIII: 1)

There were two examples. They had a wide mouth and straight rim.

A5b (Fig.43; Pl. LVIII: 2-4)

There were three examples. The neck was narrow and the rim everted. In some, the rim was pressed with an unclear saw tooth pattern.

(6) Single-handled jars (A6; Fig.43; Pl. LIX: 1; Pl. LXV: 5)

There were two examples. These vessels had a wide mouth, everted rim, slightly narrow neck, flat bottom, tubular body, with one handle luted on, between the neck and the body.

(7) Narrow-mouthed jars

They were of different shapes and were generally small. They may be divided into four types:

A7a (Fig.44; Pl. LIX: 2)

Only one example was found. It was tubular with a wide mouth and straight lip. Part of the rim narrows inwards. The sides were straight, bottom flat, and there were two symmetrical holes under the rim.

A7b (Fig.44; Pl. LIX: 3)

There was one example. The lip was everted and the wall convex.

A7c (Fig.44; Pl. LIX: 4,5)

There were two examples. They had a straight rim with no clear separation between the shoulder and the body. The wall was convex.

A7d (Fig.44; Pl. LIX: 6)

There was one example. This vessel had an everted rim and no clear separation between the shoulder and the body. The widest dimension was at the shoulder.

(8) *Ding* tripods

They each had three solid legs. There were two types:

A8a (Fig.44; Pl. LIX: 7, 8; Pl. LX: 1, 2)

There were four examples. They had a wide mouth, straight or slightly flared lip, rounded side and bottom.

A8b (Fig.44; Pl. LX: 3, 4; Pl. LXI: 1)

There were three examples. They had a wide mouth, slightly flared rim, and a flat bottom. Aside from five reconstructable pieces, seven other tripod legs, complete or broken, were found. They were different sizes and different shapes (Pl. LXI: 2-6).

(9) *Jia* tripods

This vessel had a constricted mouth, flared rim, and round bottom. Three conical, bag-shaped legs were attached to its bottom. There were two types:

A9a (Fig.45; Pl. LXII: 1, 2)

There were two examples. The lip had a folded edge.

A9b (Fig.45; Pl. LXII: 3, 4)

There were two examples. The lip was obviously everted with a groove running around it. The body was flattened and bugles towards the middle.

(10) *Zao* stoves (A10; Fig.45; Pl. LXIII: 1, 2)

There were two examples. The body was tubular with a stove door at the bottom. There were four symmetrically placed, round or oval holes placed to the rim. There were smoke and ventilation passages.

(11) Vessel covers (A11: Fig.45; Pl. LXIII: 3, 4)

There were two examples. Both were broken leaving only the tubular knobs. From the knobs we can make out the expanding shapes of the covers, and that their original size was quite large. The knob body of one was incised with crossed lines on the top, and a sawtooth pattern on the edge (Pl. LXIII: 3).

B. Grey Ware

The clay for this ware did not appear to have been thoroughly levigated as it contained coarse grains of sand. All vessels were hand made. The vessel wall and bottom were made separately and then connected together, leaving obvious marks on the vessel. Mostly the rims were reshaped on slow wheels; however, wheel-made signs were not apparent. The surface was smooth and a few were highly burnished. The ware was hard, mostly greyish brown or dark grey in color. The color was not consistent on some of the vessels. Vessel forms included the bowl, shallow-bellied basin, shallow-bellied basin with an angular edge, deep-bellied basin, cup, single-handled jar, small-mouthed jar, pointed-bottom bottle, *dou* pedestal, vessel cover, and others.

(1) Bowls

They were shallow with wide mouths, and small bottoms. The sides flare outwards and up-wards. There were three types.

B1a (Fig.46; Pl. LXIV: 1, 2)

There were three examples. The base of these vessels was shaped to form a small ridge all around the bottom.

B1b (Fig.46; Pl. LXIV: 3)

There was a single example. It had a deeper bottom than the others.

B1c (Fig.46; Pl. LXIV: 4)

There were two examples. Both were broken. The vessel form was similar to B1a, with a ring base attached all around the bottom.

(2) Shallow-bellied basin (B2: Fig.46; Pl. LXIV: 5)

There was one example. This vessel had a wide mouth, shallow belly and slightly flaring sides.

(3) Doubled-handled basins

These vessels had a wide mouth, shallow belly and a slight taper from top to bottom. Two handles were attached to opposite sides of each vessel. They may be divided into three types:

B3a (Fig.46; Pl. LXIV: 6)

Only one example was found. It had a shallow belly with many straight incised lines on its inside wall.

B3b (Fig.46; Pl. LXIV: 7)

There was just one example. This vessel had walls with a greater slope than the others. There were two semi-circular flat handles attached to the body.

B3c (Fig.46; Pl. LXIV: 8)

There was one example. This vessel had a deep belly and arc-shaped wall which narrowed to a small flat bottom. There was a pair of flat handles attached to the sides.

(4) Deep-bellied basins

These vessels had a wide mouth, a flared rim, a deep belly and a flat bottom. They may be divided into three types:

B4a (Fig.46; Pl. LXV: 1)

There was one example. This vessel had a slightly flared rim. The surface appears irregular.

B4b (Fig.46; Pl. LXV: 2)

There was one example. This vessel had a wide mouth, a flared rim, and a luted on band of decoration below the rim.

(5) Cups (B5; Fig.46; Pl. LXV: 3)

They were all broken. It is conceivable that they were tubular cups. The body wall was quite thin, between 0.2-0.3cm. Some show signs of red paint on the surface; but the pattern have all disappeared or are unclear.

(6) Small-mouthed jars

These vessels had small mouths, long necks, wide shoulders, and deep bellies with bottoms that were flat or pointed. There were basket impressions on the surface. According to the different shapes of their bottoms, they may be divided into two types:

B6a (Fig.47; Pl. LXVI: 1)

There was one example. This vessel showed an obvious angle between the shoulder and the body. The bottom was flat.

B6b (Fig.48; Pl. LXVI: 3)

There was one example. The reconstruction from potsherds shows that the body was longer than the others, and the bottom had a blunted point.

(7) Small-mouthed, round-shouldered jars

These vessels were similar to B6a except that the shoulder was rounded rather than angular. There were two types:

B7a (Fig.47; Pl. LXV: 6)

There was only one example. It had a subtle curve on the inside of the rim, a short neck, and a luted on design on the body.

B7b (Fig.47; Pl. LXVI: 2)

There was one example. This was similar to B7a, but had a longer neck. The shoulder had also a greater curve, and the vessel body was longer.

(8) *Dou* pedestals (B8; Fig.48; Pl. LXVI: 4)

The *dou* pedestals were broken and could not be reconstructed. On some of the remaining thin, tall bases, a pattern of round holes were apparent.

(9) Vessel covers

A total of three were found, but all were broken. They may be divided into three types according to the different shapes of their knobs:

B9a (Fig.48; Pl. LXVI: 6)

It was of a mushroom shape, and slightly concave at the top.

B9b (Fig.48; Pl. LXVI: 5)

The knob was a long strip, with both ends stretching up and out.

B9c (Fig.48; Pl. LXVI: 7)

The knob was of an irregular post shape; faint cord marks showed on the top.

C. Fine Red Ware

This was a delicate ware. All of the vessels were hand made and were very well burnished to a glossy finish. The walls were quite thin, generally about 0.4 cm, the thinnest being 0.15 cm. The surface was reddish brown. In addition to the plain wares, a crimson slip was added to the cups, leaving very clear brush marks, often a single line of slip was painted around the inside of the rim. There were also painted motifs, in rows of black, lozenge pattern, and pressed checkered patterns. The three kind of vessel forms included the cup, the triple-handled basin, and the narrow-mouthed and deep-bellied basin.

(1) Cups.

Most of the finds were potsherds with only four of the cups capable of being reconstructed. They may be divided into two types according to shapes:

C1a (Fig.49; Pl. LXVII: 1-3)

There were three examples. They all had a trumpet shape, wide mouth, flaring rim, and a slightly concave bottom, and were all covered by a crimson slip. One cup was excavated from each of Tombs 72 and 79, and another cup which also may be reconstructed, was found in the Longshan stratum of excavation pit No. 71. More potsherds were found in the Longshan ash pits.

C1b (Fig.49; Pl. LXVII: 4)

Only one cup was found. It was tubular with a wide mouth, flat rim, and relatively thick straight walls, flat bottom, and no slip on the vessel surface.

(2) Triple-handled basin (C2; Fig.49; Pl. LXVII: 5)

There was one example. The basin had a vertical rim. The surface was decorated by a checkered pattern. The body was decorated with three handles.

(3) Deep-bellied basin (C3; Fig.49; Pl. LXVII: 6)

There was one example. This vessel had a constricted mouth and flared rim, without any obvious separation between the shoulder and the body. The body wall had an arch-like outline tapering inwards to a small flat bottom. The surface was burnished and smooth. On the shoulder was a painted rhomboid pattern.

This type of painted pottery and the type A8a *ding* tripod (0:11) was found within the same ash pit. As other excavated finds show, they were from the Longshan period. For example there were three other vessels of exactly the same shape and painted decoration found in the Longshan ash pits at the site of Pannan village in Pinglu County, Shanxi province, in the spring of 1958.

D. Fine Black Ware

Only a few sherds of this were found. It was delicate, unadulterated ware. The vessels were hand made, and burnished on the surface. The general thickness of the ware was about 0.5cm, hard and glossy, in pure black or lacquer black. Under the surface the ware was greyish brown in color. There were five vessel forms: Basin, narrow-mouthed jar, small-mouthed jar, ring-based bowl, and vessel cover.

(1) Basins (D1; Fig.49; Pl. LXVII: 7)

A total of three broken pieces were recovered. All of them were rim sherds. Judging from the arc of the fragments, these vessels were wide-mouthed, shallow-bellied basin with a slightly flaring lip, and smoothly burnished surface. They had a rather thin wall of about 0.3cm.

(2) Narrow-mouthed jar (D2; Fig.49; Pl. LXVIII: 2)

There was only one fragment of this type. It was from the flared rim of a vessel with a narrow mouth. The ware was hard, and its surface shows a luster.

(3) Small-mouthed jar (D3; Fig.49; Pl. LXVIII: 1)

There was one piece of potsherd left. It was a part of the rim, neck, and the shoulder. It showed that the vessel had a constricted mouth, slightly flared rim, and a long neck, with a protruding break between the neck and the shoulder.

(4) Ring-based bowl (D4; Fig.49; Pl. LXVIII: 3)

One broken piece of this type was found. It was part of the vessel bottom and the high ring base.

(5) Vessel covers (D5; Fig.49; Pl. LXVIII: 4)

Two broken covers were found. Only the parts of the knob remained. The center of the round knob was concave so that it was like a ring base.

ii. Non-containers

(1) Pottery knives

These implements were made by reworking potsherds. All of the knives were broken. There were two types:

1A (Pl. LXVIII: 6).

There were two examples. They were rectangular, with the blade flaked on one of the long sides.

1B (Pl. LXVIII: 5).

There was a hole in this knife drilled from both sides. Its shape is   unclear. It was made of the fine red ware of the Yangshao period.

(2) Pottery anvil (Fig.50:1; Pl. LXVIII: 7)

Only one anvil was found. It was hollow with a flat rectangular shape, and a semi-circular cross-section. It was a grey ware which was highly burnished. This tool was used in pottery making. It was put onto a wooden stick and placed inside the pottery vessel; then patterns were pressed onto the exterior of the vessel.

(3) Spindle whorls (Fig.50:2; Pl. LXVIII: 8, 9)

There were six examples. The side was slightly convex; there was a round hole, drilled from both sides in the center. All the examples were made of red ware with an average diameter of about 3.3cm.

(4) Pellets (Pl. LXVIII: 10)

There were two examples. They were heated at a low temperature, and therefore the ware was slightly soft.

(5) Pottery bead (Fig.50:3; Pl. LXVIII: 11)

Only one example was found. It was a grey ware, spherical, with a hole drilled in the center, and painted red on the surface. It was probably worn as an ornament.

(6) Pottery tube (Fig.50:4; Pl. LXVIII: 12)

There was one example. It was a black ware, with a concave side, like the ring-base of pottery vessels. It was probably a kind of ornament, its shape being very similar to the later *zhen* earring.

(7) Cylindrical object (Fig.50:5; Pl. LXVIII: 13)

Only one example was found. It was made of a grey ware and appears to be a section from a conical-shaped object. Its use is unknown.

(II) Stone Artifacts

The stone implements from the Longshan period were chiefly made by polishing and grinding. The only flaked tools were stone knives. The different kinds of stone used included slate, sandstone, diabase and diorite. Classified by their function and shape, the productive tools included axes, adzes, knives, a sickle, a mortar and a pestle; while the weapons included arrowheads, a leaf-shaped stone object, and pellets. The ornaments included semi-annular *huang* pendents and rings. Let us separately discuss these objects:

i. Tools and Weapons

(1) Axes

All of these were thick and rectangular, with a blunt-angled rectangular cross-section. They can be divided into four types:

1A (Fig.51:1; Pl. LXVIII: 14)

There were three examples. The axe body was thick and big. The grinding was coarsely done, leaving chisel scars not completely polished away. The work seemed to be finer on the cutting edge.

1B (Fig.51:2; Pl. LXVIII: 15)

There were six examples. The cross-sections of these axe bodies were oval, rectangular, or blunt-angled rectangular. The top end and the blade were equal in width.

1C (Fig.51:3; Pl. LXVIII, 16)

There was one example. The blade was wider than the others. The top part and the blade were broken due to use.

1D (Fig.51:4; Pl. LXVIII: 17).

This one example was similar to 1C. It was delicately made. The cutting edge was symmetrical and clearly separated from the axe body.

(2) Adzes

They were, in general, smaller than the axes, all flat and rectangular with a rectangular cross-section as well. The cutting edge was ground down on one side only. There were four types.

2A (Fig.51:5; Pl. LXVIII: 18, 19)

There were three examples. One of these was broken on the top. The grinding work was delicate.

2B (Fig.51:6; Pl. LXVIII: 20; Pl. LXIX: 1, 2)

There were three examples. They were similar to 2A, but with a slight bulge on the back; the angle of the curve was not too visible. They were somewhat similar to the stepped stone adzes found along the coasts of southeast China.

2C (Fig.51:7; Pl. LXIX: 3)

There were two examples. The top end was narrower than the blade. They could have been refashioned from the stone spades of the Yangshao period.

2D (Fig.51:8; Pl. LXIX: 4)

There was one example. It had a broken top, and was carefully made. There was a single hole drilled from both sides. This could have been remodeled into a single-sided blade from a stone axe with a hole; so it is temporarily classified as an adze.

(3) Knives

They were made either by flaking or by grinding. There are three types:

3A (Pl. LXIX: 5-10)

There were ten examples. These tools were simply chipped gravel. First, the gravel was shaped into rectangles, and then both ends were chipped away. Some of the gravel was not shaped into rectangles, but directly worked on while still maintaining the oval shape. There were more finishing on the blades and edges on these tools than on those of the Yangshao period.

3B (Fig.51:9; Pl. LXIX: 11-15)

There were eighteen examples. There were only two complete specimens, all the rest being broken. The appearance was rectangular with a blunt corner and a single hole. The cutting edge was on the long side. The hole was made in three different ways: 1) Drilled from one side; 2) drilled from both sides; 3) both sides were gouged into concave grooves and the hole was at times drilled in the groove. Of the eighteen samples, ten of them had holes drilled from both sides; five had holes drilled in the concave grooves; and three had holes drilled from one side only.

3C (Fig.51:10, 11; Pl. LXIX: 16, 17)

There were two examples. Both of these were broken and were in half-moon shape. They had a straight back with a curved blade edge.

(4) Sickle (Pl. LXX: 1)

A single, broken sickle was found. It was rectangular with a cutting edge on the long side.

(5) Mortar (Pl. LXX: 2)

Only one was found. It was flat and broken at both ends, with its main face showing a concave trough made due to grinding. Its large size and smooth grinding surface were different from the mortar of the Yangshao period which might have been used as grinding red ocher.

(6) Pestle (Pl. LXX: 3)

There was only one example. It was made from natural gravel. Traces of red ochre were found on the grinding surface. A convex handle was on the back.

(7) Arrowheads (Fig.51:12, 13; Pl. LXX: 4, 5)

A total of nineteen were found. Altogether, eleven were complete and eight were broken. They were triangular and thin, and all about the same size, with an average length of 3 cm.

(8) Leaf-shaped stone object (Fig.51:14; Pl. LXX: 6)

Only one example was found. It was leaf-shaped with one side slightly worked on. It could have been an unfinished stone spear.

(9) Pellets (Pl. LXX: 10)

The three pellets found were made by grinding natural gravel.

ii.Ornaments

(1) *Huang* pendants (Fig.51:15, 16; Pl. LXX: 7, 8)

Four examples were found. On either side of the pendant, a hole was drilled from both sides. On most of them, the two sides showed traces of breakage. They were perhaps remodeled from fragments of stone rings and carefully polished.

(2) Rings (Pl. LXX: 9)

There were two examples. Both were fragments. The ring body was flat, well polished, and had a smooth surface.

(III) Bone, Antler, Shell, and Tooth Artifacts

i. Bone Artifacts

There were a great many bone artifacts, with different shapes and functions. Tools included needle, awl, dagger, and arrowhead-like pieces; there were weapons such as bone arrowheads; and ornaments such as hairpins and combs. Let us discuss them individually.

(1) Needles

There were four types:

1A (Fig.52:1; Pl. LXX: 16-18)

There were thirteen examples. Eight of these were complete. Each needle had a single round hole, drilled either from one side or from both sides. The top end was either round, pointed or flat in shape. The needles were delicately made.

1B (Fig.52:2; Pl. LXX: 21)

There was one example, which was similar to 1A except that the hole was drilled differently. The oval-shaped hole was made by first carving a groove on each side, and then drilling the hole.

1C (Fig.52:3; Pl. LXX: 19)

There was one example. Its horizontal cross-section was rectangular, and only its pointed end was round. There was a single hole, drilled from one side. The pointed end was ground smooth; but the rest was less delicately made.

1D (Fig.52:4; Pl. LXX: 20)

There was one example with a round horizontal cross-section. Its pointed end was oval, while the end with the hole was flat.

(2) Awls

Awls were made by grinding bone fragments or limb bones of domesticated animals. There were three types:

2A (Fig.52:5; Pl. LXXI: 1-3)

There were ten examples; of which there were four complete awls, made by scraping bone fragments. They were of various shapes and sizes. The pointed end was well-worked but the body was mainly left unpolished.

2B (Fig.52:6; Pl. LXXI: 4-5)

There were three examples. They were made by grinding a pointed end on the fibulas of pigs.

2C (Fig.52:7; Pl. LXXI: 6)

There was one example. The pointed end of this awl was broken. Its top was of a cap shape, like a nail-head. Although it looked very much like a bone hairpin, its shape was too large for it. Hence it was classified as an awl for the time being.

(3) Arrowheads

They may be divided into four types:

3A (Fig.52:9; Pl. LXXI: 7-9)

There were twelve examples. Nine of these were complete while three were broken. The body of the arrowhead was cylindrical and the horizontal cross-section was either round or oval. The arrowheads were of different sizes, ranging from 5.3-13cm.

3B (Fig.52:10; Pl. LXXI: 10, 11)

There were three examples. Of these, two were complete. The body was flat and the shaft was roughly ground.

3C (Fig.52:11; Pl. LXXI: 12)

The shape was flat and triangular; no shaft.

3D (Fig.52:8; Pl. LXXI: 13)

There was one example. The arrowhead body was quite long. There was an obvious separation between the body and the shaft. The horizontal cross-section of the body was oval, while the shaft was round.

(4) Bone artifact with sawteeth (4A; Fig.52:12; Plate LXXI: 14)

There was one example. The sawteeth pattern was notched along the two long sides of this triangular bone piece. Also there was an irregular, cracked pattern, on the surface. The use was unknown.

(5) Hairpins

All of the hairpins were long and narrow. The horizontal cross-section was either round, oval, or flat. One end was always pointed, while the top was in various shapes. There are three types:

5A (Fig.52:13; Pl. LXXI: 15, 16)

There were six examples; of these five were complete. The top end was blunt and flat. They were delicately polished.

5B (Fig.52:14; Pl. LXXI: 17, 19)

There were nine examples; only one of them was complete. The top end was pointed while the horizontal cross-section was flat and rectangular. Part of the body bent like an arc shape.

5C (Fig.52:15; Pl. LXXI: 20)

There were two examples and both were broken. The top end was carved into a cap-like nail head, while the body was flat.

(6) Comb (Fig.52:16; Pl. LXXI: 21)

There was one broken example. The comb was made of bone. Only four teeth remained, with traces of carving.

(7) Rectangular plates (Fig.52:17; Pl. LXXI: 22)

There were three examples. The only complete one was made by grinding a small bone fragment to a flat rectangular plate.

ii. Antler Artifacts

(1) Chisel (Fig.52:18; Pl. LXXI: 24)

There was one example. It was made from a deer antler; the blade was ground from the pointed tip of the antler. The rest was untreated.

(2) Awl (Fig.52:19)

There was one example. It was made by grinding a split deer antler.

iii. Shell Artifacts

(1) Knife (Fig.52:20; Pl. LXX: 11)

There was one example. The knife was broken, with a hole in the middle that was drilled from both sides.

(2) Arrowheads (Fig.52:21; Pl. LXX: 12)

There were two examples. The point was broken. The arrowhead body was triangular; there was no shaft.

(3) Pendents (Fig.52:22; Pl. LXX: 13)

There were three examples. The shell pendent was either rectangular or trapezoidal, with a hole in the center drilled from one side. They were delicately made.

iv. Tooth Artifacts

All of these artifacts were made from the canine teeth of boars.

(1) Arrowhead (Fig.52:23; Pl. LXX: 14)

There was one example. Both ends were triangular with sharp points, and the cross-section of the middle part was also triangular. It was delicately polished.

(2) Treated tooth fragments (Fig.52:24; Pl. LXX: 15)

There were five examples and all were broken. They were made by cutting the canine teeth into thin pieces, then grinding them into sharp blades. They could have been used as knives.

(IV) Natural Remains

These included bones of domesticated animals, wild animals, fish and also shells.

i. Bones of Domesticated Animals

The finds of domesticated animal bones in ash pits were quite rich. The number excavated from twenty-six Longshan ash pits was much higher than the total from 168 Yangshao pits, indicating that the domestication of animals greatly increased in the Longshan period. There is no way to account for the total number of bones due to their fragmentation. We can identify the bones of the pig, dog, goat, and cattle, with pig bones being the most common. Only a few broken fragments of shinbone and humerus of the cattle were found. The type of cattle cannot be distinguished, but these were probably domesticated ones. The number of different species of domesticated animals showing increase, especially in the appearance of larger domesticated beasts, indicates that the Longshan culture was more advanced than the Yangshao culture.

ii. Animal Bones

The bones of wild animals were fewer. Among the wild animals, most of the bones were deer (*Cervus hortulorum* Swinhoe), indicating that they were probably the most commonly hunted. There were also a few fragments of the musk deer (*Moschus* sp.), fox (*Vulpes vulpes* L.), and tiger (*Felis tigris* L.). They were probably all hunted.

iii. Chicken Bones

There were four pieces found. Mr. Zheng Zuoxin of the Institute of Zoology at the Chinese Academy of Sciences identified them to be the thigh legs, and forearm bones.

iv. Fish Bone

The base of two pectoral fins of the Huangsangyu or Yellow-head fish (*Peltoebagrus fulvidraco*) were found in ash pit 552. This base part of the pectoral fin had also been found in the Shang dynasty stratum at Xiaotun, in Anyang. This is strong evidence for fishing.

v. Thick Oyster Shells.

There were many broken oyster shells, which could have served as raw material for making tools.

V. Eastern Zhou Cultural Remains

Very few remains of the Eastern Zhou period were found. Aside from seven bronze arrow-heads, there were only potsherds. Let us now briefly describe the findings:

(I) Pottery Vessels

The finds were all potsherds and the pottery was a grey ware. The vessels were mainly wheel-made, and appear greyish blue or greyish brown, with cord and string patterns and near-invisible patterns. Among these motifs the cord pattern was the most popular. None of the vessels could be entirely reconstructed; but from fragments of rims and bottom parts we see the pottery forms included the basin, jar, and stemmed cup.

(II) Bronze Arrowheads

They may be divided into two types:

A: Double-winged Type (Fig.53:1)

There was one example. A ridge separating the body of the arrowhead into two sides ran down the center. The back blades formed two inverted wings. Below the ridge was a shaft.

B: Triangular Type (Fig.53:2-4)

There were six examples. The body of the arrowhead was consisted of three corners that gathered in a forward-facing point. The back blade faced backwards like an inverted thorn with a long shaft.

VI.Tang Dynasty Tomb

One Tang tomb was found within Area T1 (Fig.54). It was a tunneled tomb chamber with a true north-south orientation. On the south side was a rectangular tomb passage. The tomb chamber was rectangular, 2.7 meters long, 0.7 meters wide and 2.4 meters high. The bottom part of the tomb passage was slightly tilted and stairs-like. It was 2.5 meters long, 0.67 meters wide, and 6.7 meters deep.

The coffin had disintegrated, but vestiges of the decayed wood show that it was 1.9 meters long and 0.61 meters wide. Only one human skeleton was found. It was buried supinely, body extended, with the head to the north and the feet to the south. All burial objects were found either around the head or under the feet. There were forty-three pieces of coins of the *Kaiyuan*

Tongbao type under the skeleton. The buried objects included:

(1) Hair ornaments

A total of fourteen found, and may be grouped as described below:

a. Bronze hairpins (Pl. LXXII: 1)

There were two examples, both made by bending bronze wires.

b. Silver hairpins (Pl. LXXII: 2)

There were two examples made by bending silver wires.

c. Hair ornaments with mother-of-pearl inlay (Pl. LXXII: 3, 5)

There were four examples. The total of twelve lozenge-shaped bronze flowers inlaid with mother-of-pearl. The firm branch entwined by bronze was extended into the two prongs on the ornaments.

d. Bone combs (Pl. LXXIII: 1)

There were two examples shaped like an axe. The combs were decorated with two children in intaglio. Their costumes were painted with golden lines.

e. Jade ornaments (Pl. LXXIII: 2)

There was one pair of these ornaments found. There was a sawtooth oval rim. The jade was a pure white. A pair of symmetrical birds was atop a flowering branch motif. There were also four holes with bronze wires threaded through them.

f. Jade mandarin ducks (Pl. LXXIII: 4, 5)

There was one pair found. They were greenish brown in color.

(2) Lead figurines (Pl. LXXIII: 3).

There were two examples. The better preserved one showed the outlines of the figure clearly.

(3) Necklaces

It was consisted of many small beads of different shapes: Flat, round, oval, and rhombic, in a mineral substance like agate.

(4) Lacquered boxes

There were four examples. Only two were in relatively good condition. They were square with four rounded corners, and on the top and bottom was a silver brace.

(5) Powder box (Pl. LXXIII: 6)

Only one example was found. The surface was petal shaped. It was porcelain and covered with a white glaze.

(6) Small-mouthed vases (Pl. LXXII: 8)

There were three examples. They were made of a grey ware. They each had a small mouth, flat rim, and narrow neck with a flat bottom. There was no obvious separation between the shoulder and the body of the vases.

(7) Narrow-mouthed pottery jar (Pl. LXXII: 7)

Only one example was found. It had a narrow mouth, flaring rim, short neck, bulging body, and flat bottom. It was made of a grey ware and painted with red slip, most of which had disappeared.

(8) Ink slab (Pl. LXXII: 4)

Only one example was found. Two short rectangular feet supported the slab, which showed some black color on its surface. This was perhaps remnants of the ground-up ink.

(9) *Kaiyuan Tongbao* coins

A total of forty-three was found.

(10) Bronze mirror (Pl. LXXII: 9)

There was just one example. The mirror was flat and round with a round knob. The decorations on its top surfaces were quite coarse.

(11) Iron pot

Only one example was found, with two broken metal pieces left.

(12) Iron object

Only one example was found. The body of this tool was a long, flat stripe. One end was blunt while the other was sharp. Its use is not known.

(13) Iron scissors (Pl. LXXII: 6)

Only one example was found, but it was well-preserved.

(14) Small porcelain plates (Pl. LXXIII: 7)

There were two examples. They had a wide mouth, round lip, shallow body and flat bottom. The surface was covered with a white glaze.

Due to the presence of the iron scissors, bone comb, and powder box among the burial objects, it is possible that the individual in the tomb was a female. Judging by the shape of the tomb and the burial objects, the tomb dates from the middle Tang period onwards.

3 *THE SANLIQIAO SITE*

I. Geography and Excavations Procedures

The Sanliqiao site is beyond the east gate of the Shan county seat, on the north bank of the Qinglongjian River, facing the site of Miaodigou: There exists only a valley of about 1,400 meters wide between them. The overall appearance of the site is that of a long, loess terrace, with its center cut by two large ditches. Sanliqiao is neighbored to the east by the village of Nanjiazhuang, also with a ditch lying between them; to its west is the present day village; to its north is a modern highway that passes through the city; and to its south is the Qinglongjian River (Pl. XCVI).

The preliminary investigation of this site was undertaken in 1953, when excavation revealed a Longshan stratum super-imposed on the Yangshao stratum. [5] The total area of this site is about 180,000 square meters. The eastern part contains mainly Longshan cultural finds, while the Yangshao finds dominate the western part. Both intercept and interrupt each other. Ash pits and ash layers were exposed in the surrounding cliffs. It was found that the Yangshao and Longshan cultures represented here were different from those at Miaodigou on the opposite bank. Therefore, we decided to excavate here so as to set up a comparison with the other site. Excavations were carried out on two occasions: From April 12 to August 7, and from October 7 to November 20, 1957. The total area excavated was 1,526 square meters. We discovered kiln sites, ash pits, tombs and other cultural remains of the Yangshao and Longshan cultures, as well as of the Eastern Zhou period. The six members who worked on the first dig are: Chen Zuoliang, Xu Diankui, Jiang Zhongyi, Deng Debao, Shan Qinglin of Northeast People's University, and Jia Deyao of Northwest University. Those who worked on the second dig are: Chen Zuoliang, Yang Jichang, Ye Xiaoyan, Tang Shihe, Zhang Changqing, Jiang Zhongyi, Zheng Dacheng, Wen Mengyuan, and Wang Zhaoying.

II. Cultural Deposits

(I) Discription of the Strata

The interrelationship of the strata was very clear: Longshan strata were found on top of the Yangshao layer, or it could be said that the Longshan ash pits intruded into the Yangshao layer. Let us explain using the cross-section of the west wall of excavation ditch 2: The first level of ploughed earth was 15-38cm thick, and yielded a few Yangshao, Longshan and Warring States (Eastern Zhou) potsherds. The second was a Longshan stratum, and may be divided into two sub-layers according to the soil color and texture. Sub-layer 2A, of yellowish brown soil, was loose in texture, and 15-60 cm thick. It yielded not only Longshan potsherds but a few Yang-shao potsherds as well. On the north side of this stratum, a modern ditch had cut down to the virgin loess. Sub-layer 2B was of loose grey earth, 10-38 cm thick, and yielded similar arti-facts as in 2A with the addition of a few broken animal bones. The third stratum, a Yangshao stratum, was of hard, light yellow earth, 15-52 cm thick. Yangshao potsherds were found here. The middle part of this stratum was interrupted by a Longshan ash pit (H2). The ash pit was divided into three layers: The first contained yellowish grey, loose soil, and 30-55 cm thick. The second had a grey soil, similar in texture as the previous layer, and 12-39 cm thick; the third was a hard, yellowish brown soil, 70cm thick. Artifacts such as Longshan potsherds, stone tools and bone tools were found in all three layers of the ash pit (Fig.55). The eastern part of the site contained a crisscrossed cultural stratum of the Yangshao, Longshan and East-ern Zhou periods. However, remains, from the Eastern Zhou were few.

The stratification described above was another evidence of the relative dates of the Yang-shao and Longshao cultures. This is also consistent with the stratigraphic conditions at Miao-digou on the opposite bank.

(II) Architectural Remains

i. Yangshao Culture

(i) Kiln Site

Altogether two pottery kilns of the Yangshao period were found, with similar designs and simple structures. The kilns were divided into two parts, the kiln chamber and the fire cham-ber. The former was round, while the latter was semi-cylindrical. Let us take kiln Y301 as an example. In front of the kiln chamber was the fire chamber, facing east, with an orientation of 108°. The remaining length was about 1.17 meters. The smaller front opening was 0.2 meters high and 0.46 meters wide. Towards the back, the fire chamber expanded, gradually connecting with the kiln chamber which was 0.34 meters high and 0.76 meters wide. The bottom of the fire chamber gradually sloped downwards to its opening. The upper part of the kiln chamber was broken (it was exposed at about 1.2 meters below the earth's surface). The surrounding perpendicular walls had a height of 0.25-0.36 meters. The bottom was flat with no kiln grill present. The diameter was about 2.1-2.24 meters. The bottom of the entire kiln was a layer of bluish-grey, fired earth, about 7-10 cm thick, formed by the constant heat. Parts of the kiln walls were red, 3-4cm thick (Fig.56). Inside the kiln, there was only one stratum, consisting of grey earth, loose in texture, where a lot of Yangshao potsherds and broken pieces of red fired clay were found.

(ii) Ash Pits

Altogether, forty-seven Yangshao ash pits were found. They were of two types, circular and oval; seventeen of the former and thirty of the latter were discovered. Only a few of them, about one-fourth of the total, were well conserved. The rest were all broken through to each other. The shapes of these ash pits were more or less similar to those of Miaodigou. Most of them had a wide opening and small base; then, some had the straight cylindrical walls; finally there were those with a small mouth and a wide base.

ii. Longshan Culture

(i) Kiln Site

One Longshan pottery kiln (Y4) was found. It was divided into two parts, the fire chamber in the front, and the kiln chamber in the back. The opening of the fire chamber was a bit smaller than the bottom part. It measured 0.97 meters east to west, and 0.6 meters north to south. The bottom was larger and measured 1.2 meters east to west and 0.82 meters north to south. The fire chamber was an oval, bag-shaped, vertical pit. The kiln chamber was circular in shape; the upper part was broken at the plow zone (it was exposed at 0.1-0.28 meters from the earth's surface). Its diameter was 1.3 meters and the remaining height 0.38 meters. The upper parts of the surrounding walls inclined slightly inwards, like an arch. On the bottom there were four north-south, parallel, ditch-like fire passages, each 1.2-1.36 meters long, 0.11 meters wide, and 0.12-0.17 meters deep. There was a divide between the fire chamber and the kiln chamber, so that the fire passage to the fire chamber passed through the divide with a slope (the two middle passages were straight; the one in the east bent at 160°; and the one in the west at 120°). Most noteworthy were the obvious marks on the walls, left from the time when the kiln was built. They were also double-pronged marks, similar to those left by a wooden shovel in the Longshan ash ditch at Miaodigou (HG553). There was another kiln opening on top of the divide between the fire chamber and the kiln chamber, oriented at 175°. It was 0.5 meters long, 0.6 meters wide, with a remaining height of 0.36 meters. On the surrounding walls and base of the whole kiln was a layer of hard, bluish grey, fired earth formed from the constant heat. The layer was 5-9 cm thick (Fig.57:1, 3; Pls. LXXIV, LXXV). The deposit inside the kiln was consisted of a first layer of ploughed earth, a second layer of hard, yellowish brown soil, 0.14-0.2 meters thick, and a third layer of loose, yellowish grey soil, 0.3-0.36 meters thick. Both the second and the third layers yielded Longshan potsherds. The firing chamber contained some fired earth, charcoal, broken animal bones, and unfired pottery vessels (Fig.57:2).

(ii) Ash Pits

Altogether, 103 Longshan ash pits were found. Fifty-four of them were circular, and forty-nine were oval. Their shapes were more or less similar to those of the Yangshao period, except that the walls of the Longshan pits were more regular. Very few of the ash pits – less than one-fourth – were completely preserved. Potsherds were the most common finds in the ash pits, although some delicately made bone objects were also found.

(III) Tombs

i. Yangshao Cultural Tombs

Altogether, two Yangshao tombs were found, being rectangular, shallow vertical pits. The burial posture was supine. We shall take tomb M107 as an example for discussion. The tomb opening was 0.5 meters from the earth's surface; its dimensions were 1.88 meters long by 0.54 meters wide by 0.45 meters deep. The orientation of the burial was 330° with the head pointed toward the northwest (Fig.58). This burial was found within the Yangshao stratum. However, only one piece of Yangshao painted potsherds was found in the earth fill.

ii. Longshan Cultural Tomb

Only one Longshan tomb was found (tomb M108). It was also a rectangular, shallow, vertical pit, oriented at 210°. The Tomb was 0.55 meters from the earth's surface; its length was not known; it was 0.6 meters wide, and 0.35 meters deep. The burial posture was supine, with the head facing southwest; both legs were broken by the intruded Longshan ash pit (H296). There were no burial objects found (Fig.59). Judging from the stratification, this tomb had fallen from the Upper Longshan stratum onto the lower Yangshao layer. Therefore, we can conclude that this tomb belonged to the Longshan culture.

III. Yangshao Cultural Remains

(I) Pottery

i. Containers

Altogether there were nineteen reconstructed examples. The majority of those fine red ware, followed by a more coarse red ware, and then a fine grey ware and a small amount of fine black ware, the latter two were mainly broken pieces that could not be reconstructed. Aside from plain and polished surfaces, decorations included painted motifs, linear patterns, incised patterns, decorations in appliqué, and nipple patterns. There was very few painted pottery here. The decorative patterns were simple. Vessel shapes included: *Bo* bowls, bowls, basins, jars, vessel stands, and so on. We have made a table of pottery wares, decorations, and vessel forms from ash pit H6 to give a comparative summary:

Table of Total Pottery Ware Families and Decorations of the Yangshao Culture (Ash Pit H6)

Ware Family	Fine Red Ware					Grey Ware	Black Ware	Coarse, Sand-tempered Red Ware				Totals
Amount	291					25	7	164				487
Percentage	59.76					5.14	1.44	33.68				100%
Decorations	Painted	Linear pattern	Incised pattern	Nipple pattern	Plain	Plain	Plain	Linear pattern	Incised pattern	Decorations in appliqué	Plain	
Amount	12	45	4	2	228	25	7	41	5	8	110	487
Percentage	2.47	9.24	0.83	0.41	46.82	5.34	1.44	8.42	1.03	1.65	22.59	100%

Table of the Pottery Forms of Yangshao Culture Ash Pit H6 (Limited to those distinguishable)

Ware Family	Fine Red Ware					Grey Ware		Fine Black Ware	Coarse,Sand-tempered Red Ware		Totals
Ware Form	*Bo* Bowl	Bowl	Basin	Jar	Vessel Stand	Bowl	Jar	Jar	Bowl	Jar	
Amount	41	27	31	22	5	13	5	4	34	28	210
Percentage	19.53	12.85	14.77	10.47	2.38	6.19	2.38	1.81	16.19	13.34	100%

A. Fine Red Ware

Most of these were plain, and very few were polished. Painted motifs were only found on some basins, several pieces of painted pottery with white slips were found among the potsherds of this type.

(1) *Bo* bowls

These had a wide mouth, a shallow body, and a round or flat bottom. There were two types:

A1a (Fig.60; Pl. LXXVI: 1a, b)

A total of three vessels were found. They all had round bottoms. In vessel H310:05, there was a hole drilled in its bottom center. It was possibly used as a steamer.

A1b (Fig.60; Pl. LXXVI: 2a, b)

Only one example was found. The bottom was flat and stamped with the nipple pattern. These marks were probably left by a certain kind of beater used in the manufacturing of pottery.

(2) Bowls

They had a wide mouth. The body wall tapered inward to a flat bottom, with no obvious separation between the body and the bottom. There were two types:

A2a (Fig.60; Pl. LXXVI: 3)

Only one example was found. It had a shallow body.

A2b (Fig.60; Pl. LXXVI: 4)

Only one example was found. Its shape was similar to A2a, but it had a deeper body.

(3) Shallow-bellied basins

These vessels had a wide mouth, with rolled rim, a shallow body, and a flat bottom. They may be divided into two types:

A3a (Fig.60; Pl. LXXVII: 1)

There was only one example. The body wall slanted downwards and tapered to the bottom.

A3b (Fig.60; Pl. LXXVII: 2)

There was just one example. The sides formed an arc shape, and tapered to the bottom. Black painted motifs appeared along the rim.

(4) Constricted-mouthed basins

These had an inwardly turned rim with the body wall sloping inward to a flat bottom. There were two types:

A4a (Fig.61; Pl. LXXVII: 3)

Two examples were found and the body arced and tapered downwards.

A4b (Fig.61; Pl. LXXVII: 4, 5)

Two examples were found. The vessel shape was similar to A4a but the bottom tapered downwards greatly and showed a clear separation from the body wall.

(5) Constricted-mouthed jar (A5; Fig.61; Pl. LXXVII: 6)

There was only one example found. It had an inwardly turned, constricted mouth, a deep belly, and a flat bottom.

(6) Vessel Stands (A6; Fig.61; Pl. LXXVIII: 1)

Only one example was found. It had a flared mouth, narrow waist, and a slightly flaring lower portion.

B. Grey Ware

The vessels were all plain surfaced. There appeared to be basins and jars, but neither could be reconstructed.

C. Fine Black Ware

There was the least number of this ware. The interior of the body was slightly reddish brown, but the exterior was pure black, both were plain with no decorations. The only recognizable ware type was jar, but it also could not be reconstructed.

D. Coarse, Sand-tempered Red Ware

These were mostly plain surfaced, with only a few decorated. The few decorative motifs included the linear patterns, incised patterns and decorations in appliqué.

(1) Constricted-mouthed jars

These each had a constricted mouth, a bulging body, and a flat bottom. There were two types:

D1a (Fig.61; Pl. LXXVIII: 2)

Only one example was found. The body was convex.

D1b (Fig.61; Pl. LXXVIII: 3)

There were two examples. They were flared-lipped, with a slightly convex body.

(2) Tubular jars (D2; Fig.61; Pl. LXXVIII: 4)

There were two examples. They were tubular with a deep body and a flat bottom.

ii. Tools

(1) Knives

All were made from potsherds and none of them were complete. They may be divided into three types:

1A

Seven examples were found, with chipped notches on both ends. They were similar in shape to the Yangshao knife 1A at Miaodigou.

1B (Pl. LXXIX: 1)

There were five examples. They were rectangular with a hole.

1C Pl. LXXIX: 2)

There were three examples. They had round backs and a hole.

(2) Spindle whorls

There were nine examples made from potsherds. Their shape was similar to the Yangshao spindle whorl Type 4A at Miaodigou.

iii. Ornaments

Rings (Pl. LXXIX: 3)

A total of three rings were found; they were round and plain.

(II)Stone Implements

i. Tools

They may be divided into two kinds, those that were made by chipping and those that were made by grinding.

(1) Knives

They may be divided into two types:

1A (Pl. LXXIX: 4)

A total of six were found. Both ends were notched.

1B (Pl. LXXIX: 5, 6)

A total of three examples were found. They were rectangular or oval, with no notched ends.

(2) Axes (Pl. LXXIX: 7)

A total of three examples were found. They were rectangular with a round blade. The cross-section appeared oval.

(3) Spindle whorls (Pl. LXXIX: 8)

A total of six examples were found and they were round, with a hole drilled from both sides. The edges were smooth and even.

(4) Balls (Pl. LXXIX: 9)

There were four examples. They were all of different sizes, and highly polished. The largest diameter was 6 cm, and the smallest was 2.9 cm. The small ones might have been used as pellets.

(III) Bone Artifacts

(1) Needles (Pl. LXXIX: 12)

There were three examples. They were thin and long, with a hole at one end.

(2) Awls (Pl. LXXIX: 10, 11)

There were two examples. They were ground from the limb bone of a pig.

(3) Hairpins (Pl. LXXIX: 13, 14)

There were two examples. Both ends were ground to a point. The cross-section was oval in shape.

(IV) Natural Remains

There were very few skeletons of domesticated animals found. The only recognizable were the pig and the dog, and the rest unknown. There were also a small number of deer bones and antlers.

IV. Longshan Cultural Remians

(I) Pottery

i. Containers

A total of sixty-nine vessels were reconstructed. A coarse, sand-tempered grey ware and a grey ware were the most popular, followed by a coarse, sand-tempered red ware, and a fine black ware; the fine red ware was the most uncommon. About one-fifth of the vessels were turned on the wheel, leaving very clear marks on the vessels. Most of the rest were made by coiling. However, the *li* tripods were obviously mould-made – an already fired pottery tripod worked as the inner mould – thus, clear "reverse cord impressions" were apparent on the inside of the leg and hip. The vessel forms made this way were consistent in size and uniform in shape. A small amount of egg-shell pottery was found among the potsherds. The most popular decoration was the cord patterns (about one-half); followed by the basket impressions (about one fifth) and then the checkered pattern (about one twelfth). There were also many plain or highly polished examples, and pottery with incised patterns, open work, and decorations in appliqué; however, these only account for a small minority. The vessel forms included cups, bowls, basins, jars, *zeng* steamers, *li* tripods, *gui* vessels, *jia* tripods, vessel stands and others. We have listed in a table a comparative summary of vessels taken from ash pit H3, as an example.

The Table of the Sum Total of Pottery Ware Families and Decorations of Longshan Culture(Ash Pit H3)

Ware Family	Coarse, Sand-temptered Grey Ware					Grey Ware					Coarse, Sand-tempered Red Ware		Fine Black Ware		Red Ware		Total
Amount	1708					1031					303		271		48		3361
Percentage	50.82					30.68					9.02		8.07		1.43		100%
Decorations	Cord patterns	Basket patterns	Chec-kered patterns	Decora-tions in appliqué	Plain	Cord patterns	Basket patterns	Chec-kered patterns	Decora-tions in appliqué	Plain	Cord patterns	Plain	Incised patterns	Plain	Basket patterns	Plain	
Amount	1138	327	34	21	188	527	273	20	6	205	95	208	31	240	38	10	3361
Percentage	33.86	9.73	1.02	0.63	5.6	15.68	8.13	0.6	0.18	6.1	2.83	6.19	0.93	7.14	1.13	0.3	100%

The Table of the Sum Total of Pottery Vessel Forms of Longshan Culture (Ash Pit H3)(Limited to those with recognizable forms)

Ware Family	Coarse, Sand-tempered Grey Ware			Grey Ware					Coarse Sand-tempered Red Ware	Fine Black Ware		Red Ware		Total
Vessel Forms	Jar	Li Tripod	Jia Tripod	Bowl	Basin	Cup	Jar	Zeng Steamer	Jar	Dou Pedestal	Jar	Jar	Gui Vessel	
Amount	525	196	19	35	59	37	154	17	84	41	87	37	2	1293
Percentage	40.61	15 16	1.47	2.71	4.57	2.87	11.91	1.32	6.5	3.64	6.73	2.87	0.16	100%

A. Coarse, Sand-tempered Grey Ware

The few vessel forms were mostly decorated with the cord and basket impressions. Other patterns were rare.

(1) Round-bottomed jars (A1; Fig.62; Pl. LXXX: 1)

There was one example. It had a deep body, round bottom, with a broken upper part. The body was 2.8 cm thick.

(2) Single-handled jars

This had a narrow neck and a single handle. The sides tapered downwards to a flat base. It may be divided into two types:

A2a (Fig.62; Pl. LXXX: 2, 3)

There were two examples. The body bulged slightly.

A2b (Fig.62; Pl. LXXX: 4)

There were two examples. Its shape was similar to A2a, although the body was more bulging.

(3) Constricted-mouthed jars

These had a narrow mouth, bulging body, and a flat base. They can be divided into two types:

A3a (Fig.63; Pl. LXXXII: 1)

This single example had a slightly bulging body.

A3b (Fig.63; Pl. LXXXII: 2)

This single example was similar to A3a, but with a great bulge in the body.

(4) *Li* tripods

These vessels had a narrow neck, with three bag-like legs. They can be divided into two types:

A4a (Fig.62; Pl. LXXXI: 1, 2)

There were seven examples. They had a flared lip, with a handle between the rim and the body.

A4b (Fig.62; Pl. LXXXI: 3)

There was just one example. Its shape was similar to A4a except that it had no handle, but had luted on designs on either side of the neck.

(5) *Jia* tripods (A5; Fig.62; Pl. LXXXI: 4).

There were two examples. Three bag-like feet were added to a round-bottomed jar, to form this vessel. One short handle placed on each side of the mouth for holding convenience.

B. Grey Ware

There was quite a variety of vessel forms in this group of ware. Besides cord and basket impressions, and checkered patterns, there were also holed patterns on these wares. They were mostly plain wares, most of which were not burnished.

(1) Bowls (B1; Fig.63; Pl. LXXXII: 3, 4)

There were four examples. They had a wide mouth with the sides sloping inwards to a flat base. This type of bowl may be used as a vessel cover when turned over.

(2) Shallow-bellied basin (B2; Fig.63; Pl. LXXXII: 5).

There was one example. This vessel had a large mouth with a slightly inverted rim. The body was shallow, and the base was flat and small.

(3) Deep-bellied basin

These had a large mouth, deep body, and a flat base, and may be divided into four types:

B3a (Fig.63; Pl. LXXXIII: 1)

Two examples were found. The rim had a pronounced flare and the body tapered inwards.

B3b (Fig.63; Pl. LXXXIII: 2)

There was one example. Its shape was similar to B3a, but the lower part of the body was arc shaped and contracted inwards.

B3c (Fig.63; Pl. LXXXIII: 3)

There was one example. Its shape was similar to B3a, except that the rim was flared, and the body was slightly convex.

B3d (Fig.63; Pl. LXXXIII: 4)

There were two examples. Their shapes were similar to B3c but there was an obvious convex angle in the bulging body.

(4) Single-handled cup (B4; Fig.64; Pl. LXXXIII: 5)

There was one example. This vessel had a large mouth and a single handle. The body sloped inwards and tapered to a flat bottom.

(5) Double-handled cups (B5; Fig.64; Pl. LXXXIII: 6)

There were five examples. This type had a large mouth and a pair of handles. The body wall sloped downwards, and then tapered at an angle to a flat bottom.

(6) Constricted-mouthed jars

These had a narrow mouth, bulging body, and a flat bottom. They maybe divided into four types:

B6a (Fig.64; Pl. LXXXIV: 1)

There was one example. It had a round lip and a slightly bulging body.

B6b (Fig.64; Pl. LXXXIV: 2, 3)

There were three examples. The vessel form was similar to B6a, except for an outward bending rim.

B6c (Fig.64; Pl. LXXXIV: 4; Pl. LXXXV: 1)

There were three examples. Their shape were similar to B6b, but the rim was everted and the neck higher.

B6d (Fig.64; Pl. LXXXV: 3)

There was one example. It was similar to B6b, but it had a deeper body.

(7) Single-handled jars (B7; Fig.65; Pl. LXXXV: 4)

There were two examples. The vessel had a constricted mouth, bulging body and a flat bottom. A handle was placed between the rim and the body of the vessel.

(8) Long-necked jars

The vessel had a long neck, bulging body, and an obvious division between the neck and the shoulder. They may be divided into two types:

B8a (Fig.64; Pl. LXXXV: 2)

There were two examples. They had a relatively wide mouth with a short neck.

B8b (Fig.65; Pl. LXXXVI: 1, 2)

There were two examples. They had a small mouth but a relatively long neck.

(9) Small-mouthed jars

The vessel had a small mouth, an angular shoulder, below which the body tapered to a flat bottom. In general they were quite large. There were two types:

B9a (Fig.65; Pl. LXXXVI: 3)

A total of two examples were found. The shoulder section was either stamped with a basket pattern or was smooth.

B9b (Fig.65; Pl. LXXXVI: 4)

There was one example. Its shape was basically similar to B9a; however, the vessel, in biscuit form was severed at the shoulder, between the vessel mouth and the vessel body. Thus the severed portion was used as a cover, allowing large objects that would otherwise be stuck at the small opening to enter the jar. This was an unusual way of making the vessel, rarely found among the pottery vessels.

(10) *Zeng* steamers

It had a narrow mouth, bulging body, and a flat bottom. There were holes on the bottom and around the base. The vessel may be divided into two types:

B10a (Fig.66; Pl. LXXXVII: 1a, b)

There were two examples. The body was slightly bulging.

B10b (Fig.66; Pl. LXXXVII: 2a, b)

There was one example. The bottom of this vessel tapered inwardly; a pair of convex handles was luted on each side of the body for functional purposes.

(11) Vase (B11; Fig.66; Pl. LXXXVIII: 1)

Only one example was found. It had a small mouth, bulging body, and a flat bottom.

(12) *Dou* pedestal (B12; Fig.66; Pl. LXXXVIII: 2, 3)

There were two examples. This vessel had a wide mouth with folded rim. The body tapered to the waist, below which it flared outwards, forming a round base.

(13) Flat-bottomed *gui* vessel (B13; Fig.66; Pl. LXXXVIII: 4a, b)

Only one example was found. The everted lip had an open spout. The body wall expanded towards the base to form a flat bottom where three short legs were attached. There was one handle between the neck and the body. The vessel shape was unusual. Besides this *gui* we have found a piece of the spout of the *he* vessel type in a tubular shape. We have temporarily included it here due to their similarity.

(14) Vessel stand (B14; Fig.67; Pl. LXXXVIII: 5)

Only one example was found. It had a straight rim, and the body curved outwards to a wide ring base.

C. Coarse, Sand-tempered Red Ware

Most of this ware was found as broken potsherds. The only reconstructable vessel was the large-mouthed jar.

Large-mouthed jars (C1; Fig.67; Pl. LXXXVIII: 6)

Two examples were found. The upper part of the vessel was already broken. The vessel was deep and tapered downwards to a flat bottom. The body was 3 cm thick.

D. Fine Black Ware

The surface of this vessel was pure black, but the interior of the vessel was greyish brown. Not many of the vessels were restored.

(1) Double-handled jars (D1; Fig.67; Pl. LXXXIX: 1)

There were three examples. Each had a small mouth, bulging body, and a small flat bottom, and a handle on either side of the body.

(2) Double-handled *dou* pedestal (D2; Fig.67; Pl. LXXXIX: 2)

There was one example. It was in the same shape as the B12 *dou* pedestal with a pair of handles added near the mouth.

E. Red Ware

This was the least popular pottery. The color was not pure, and was often mixed with grey spots. Not many of the vessels can be reconstructed.

(1) Constricted-mouthed jars (E1; Fig.67; Pl. LXXXIX: 3)

There were three examples. The vessel had a constricted mouth with a slightly bulging body that tapered downwards to a flat bottom.

(2) *Gui* tripod (E2; Fig.67; Pl. LXXXIX: 4)

Only one example was found. It had an everted mouth with an open spout, and was supported by three pocket legs. There was a handle on the neck.

ii. Tools

(1) Knives

There were six examples. They were rectangular with a hole drilled through. They were all from potsherds.

(2) Spindle whorls

There were nine examples. They were made of pottery clay and had sides that were either curved or angular. They were rather small, with a diameter of about 3 cm.

(3) Pottery anvil (Pl. XC: 1)

Only one was found. It was used in pottery manufacturing. One side was straight and regular, while the other was convex. It had a hollow center and the cross-section was a semi-circle. This tool was similar to that of the Longshan period from Miaodigou.

iii. Other Artifacts

A molded figure of a bird head (Pl. XCI: 6)

There was only one found and it was broken. It was made of the coarse, sand-tempered red ware, with a thin black slip on the exterior. The bird's mouth was round and flat, suggestive of a duck.

(II) Stone Implements

(1) Axes (Pl. XC: 8)

Altogether, eleven were found. They were rectangular with a straight or curved blade, and a rectangular cross-section.

(2) Adze (Pl. XC: 4)

Only one was found. Its body was flat and thin, with a one-sided cutting edge. There were cut marks in the middle of one side. The tool was probably going to be split into two to become stone chisels.

(3) Knives (Pl. XC: 2, 3)

There were ten examples. They were rectangular, with a single hole drilled from both sides. All were made by grinding.

(4) Arrowheads

Two were found. They were flat and triangular, and were all polished. They were similar in form to those of the Longshan period at Miaodigou.

(III) Bone and Shell Artifacts

A. Bone Artifacts

(1) Needles (Pl. XC: 10)

There were four examples. They were long and thin with a hole drilled near the end.

(2) Awl (Pl. XC: 5)

Only one example was found. It was ground from a piece of bone.

(3) Arrowheads (Pl. XC: 9)

Seven examples were found. They were triangular with no tangs.

(4) Spades (Pl. XC: 6, 7; Pl. XCI: 1-4)

Seven examples were found. These were made by grinding the mandible bone of a pig. However, one was made by grinding the pelvic bone.

(5) Chisels

Altogether three were found. They were made from limb bones of animals, by splitting a section and polishing one end to form a single sharp edge.

(6) Hairpins (Pl. XC: 11)

Six were found. Both ends of these hairpins were ground to form sharp points. They had an oval cross-section.

B. Shell Artifacts

(1) Knife

Only one was found. It was rectangular with a single hole, drilled from both sides. It was broken.

(2) Shell Sickles

Two were found. One of them had a sawtooth edge.

(3) Pendant

Only one example was found. It was shaped like a long strip, with a hole drilled at one end. It was also broken.

(4) Shell Hairpin (Pl. XCI: 5)

Only one example was found. The body of the pin was flat and smooth while the top end was thick and large and in an oval shape. There was a long, sharp triangular point at the end.

(IV) Natural Remians

There were not too many skeletons of domesticated animals found. All of them were badly broken up. The distinguishable species included the pig, the dog, the cattle, and the sheep; pig bones were the most popular. There were also deer bones and antlers and thick oyster shells found.

V. Eastern Zhou Cultural Remians

Altogether, six ash pits of the Warring States period were found, none of them well preserved and excavated finds were very few. Besides potsherds, we found three triangular bronze arrowheads and one broken jade object. Within the excavation area of T236, we also found a piece of bronze spade coin of the Wei Kingdom, with an inscription of "*An Yi Er Jin*" (Fig.68). There were also conical pottery vessels found in the ash pits of this period. They were fired at a low temperature, and therefore, were loose and soft. Similar pottery vessels were found at the Yangshao village in Mianchi county, Henan, although they were mistaken to be products of the Yangshao period. [16] These vessels were found only in Eastern Zhou ash pits and did not appear in any earlier strata. Other Eastern Zhou sites such as Lijiayao have yielded similar vessels, which gives evidence of their existence in the Eastern Zhou period.

4 *CULTURAL CHARACTERISTICS AND CHRONOLOGY*

The large scale excavations at the sites of Miaodigou and Sanliqiao, undertaken in connection with the construction of the Sanmen Gorge Reservoir on the Yellow River, were extremely meaningful. They have not only provided a wealth of archaeological materials, but have also answered many questions and offered some clues for the future archaeological studies of the Neolithic Period in China, and for the reconstruction of China's primitive society.

Due to the lack of systematic excavations of Neolithic sites in the past, analyses of the cultural characteristics and relationships between Neolithic sites have been vague. Some key problems were not resolved, so that we encounter many difficulties in our present attempt to synthesize our investigations. The excavation and analysis of Miaodigou and Sanliqiao will correct some of the misleading concepts of the past. For example, the stratigraphic studies have given further proof that the Yangshao culture preceded the Longshan culture, and that the fact was not limited to the area of Northern Henan, but existed in Western Henan as well. These excavations have given greater distinction of the basic characteristics of the Yangshao and Longshan culture, as well as giving new proof to their intimate interrelationship and insight into their chronologies. These were the major contributions of the excavations.

In the following page we shall synthesize past studies and our own observations, based on the excavations of the two sites, to attempt to explain the cultural characteristics, chronologies and productive abilities of the cultures, as well as raise some new questions for future research.

I. Miaodigou

(I) Yangshao Cultural Stratum

The Yangshao culture, a vestige of the Neolithic period, was first discovered at Yangshao village in Mianchi county, Henan, in 1921. It is an early culture along the Yellow River, characterized by delicate, painted pottery existing alongside stone artifacts. In time, all prehistoric sites with similar cultural characteristics were assigned to the Yangshao culture. It has also been called "painted pottery culture" by some, because of the painted pottery found among the remains. This name, however, is not accurate, since the painted pottery had existed for a long time, from the Neolithic Period to the Iron Age. Therefore, it is not correct to use it to describe one specific culture. Rather, the more preferable name is "Yangshao culture".

Strictly speaking, Yangshao village, from which the name "Yangshao culture" derives, is itself not a typical site. Because of severe weaknesses in past excavations, many problems of significance remain unclear. When the first Yangshao finds were published, many Chinese archaeologists pointed out there were Longshan remains in the mix[11], others felt that the finds could be separated into early and late periods[12], but J. G. Andersson insisted that the two cultures were contemporaneous.[13] A study after 1949 suggested that the site showed a kind of "combined culture of Yangshao and Longshan"[14], but the problem is not thoroughly resolved yet. We do know, however, that the characteristics of the site were found in many other sites along the Yellow River. So until a proper name is found, we can use the term "Yangshao Culture".

According to our preliminary understanding, there appear several different cultural types within the Yangshao sites; and the sites are all distinctive. For example, Miaodigou and Sanliqiao each could represent one type. Since Shan county and Mianchi county are connected to each other, and the distance between Miaodigou and Yangshao village being only fifty kilometers, the two sites are inevitably closely related both cultural and geographically. While the cultural characteristics of the original Yangshao village site are not entirely clear, the Miaodigou site can at least represent a part of the Yangshao culture. Therefore, by working out clearly the contents of the Miaodigou site, we will naturally arrive at specifics of the Yangshao village site. We shall focus on the Yangshao remains at Miaodigou to analyze their cultural characteristics.

The Sanmen Gorge Reservoir area contains the most sites of Yangshao culture. The sites are also the largest; Miaodigou being about 240,000 square meters, is almost equal in size to the large modern villages in the Shan county. There are also a few other Yangshao sites around Miaodigou, fully indicating a rather dense distribution of Yangshao sites along the Yellow River.

The two houses found on the Miaodigou sites are similar to those in other Yangshao sites. They are all made with shallow pits, near square in shape, with a sloping, narrow entrance way leading to the door. Post holes exist on all the floors and surrounding walls may help reconstruct a kind of wooden frame structure with a conical roof on four corners. However, the foundation stones under the four post holes on the dwelling floor of the Miaodigou house are not seen in any other Yangshao house. This point reveals an earlier use of foundation stones, adding insight to the history of Chinese architecture. The dwelling floor is covered with straw and mud, forming a solid and smooth surface. This is the result of long periods of human habitation. The floor of house F302 contains a powdery red fired earth, giving it a hard surface with a shade of red. This was only one method of floor construction. However, some people believe that it was the result of firing.[15] This does not tally with the facts. The fire pit inside the house was possibly used for heating, and for keeping alive cinder. This kind of deep cylindrical pits were quite unusual.

Most of the ash pits in the site were used as storage at the time and were generally quite irregular, seldom as neat as the Longshan ash pits. This may be one of its more primitive traits. This kind of pit may be used for storing food. It was filled in with rubbish when abandoned, and when new pits were dug when they were needed, they often cut into the already filled storage pits. Although the relationship of these intersecting pits is complicated, these pits were never too far apart in time. The relationship of the intersecting pits is even more complicated near the house, indicating a close relationship between the ash pits and the house. In the past, some scholars believed that this kind of storage pit was a human dwelling[16], quoting phrases like "living in the caves in the wilderness" and "kiln-like huts and caves"[17] from the ancient literature as proof. Since houses of the Yangshao culture have been found in abundance, the theory has become harder to believe.

Only one tomb was discovered, although there may be many more around the Miaodigou site, still undiscovered. The five human skeletons found in the four ash pits show the abandoned pits could have been used as places of burial.

Most of the cultural remains were potsherds, with quite complex shapes. A relatively thorough understanding of Yangshao pottery vessels can be obtained from the 690 pieces of reconstructed vessels. From the materials used, the fine red ware was the most common, followed by a coarse red ware; grey ware accounted for a minor potion, and the fine black ware was the rarest. The few of the fine white pots were made of white clay with little or no iron; whether this is kaolin or not has yet to be confirmed chemically.[18] We have temporarily placed this pottery with the fine red ware, because it was limited to painted pottery. It is notable that although the amount of grey and black ware was small, the early development of Longshan pottery had begun. The fine white ware was also significant of the later Longshan and Yin dynasty white pottery. Generally, the quality of the ware was rather hard, especially in the fine red ware. Based on past research we know that the Yangshao potsherds from Mianchi, Henan were fired at a temperature between 1300-1400 ℃ ; and those from Qinwangzhai in Cheng-gao, Henan were fired between 1100-1200℃ .[19] Thus the firing temperature of the pottery here would not differ greatly.

The method of pottery making was mainly by coiling and the rim was often reshaped on a slow wheel. Small vessels such as bowls, cups and vessel covers were usually made from moulds; but some rims were trimmed on the slow wheel. In the past, the Yangshao pottery was thought to have been made on the wheel (see Reference 19) a misunderstanding which was probably caused by traces left by the reshaping wheel.

The pottery surface was decorated with linear patterns, basket impressions, incised patterns, and decorations in appliqué, cloth and mat impressions, open work, and painted motifs. The most common was the linear patterns; followed by painted motifs; the rest were quite rare. The linear impressions, also called fine cord impressions, were widely spaced, and entirely different from the cord impressions of the Longshan and later periods. The basket impressions were usually interlaced with linear impressions, and seldom appeared alone, Although there are few examples, those independent examples marked the beginning of basket impressions in Longshan pottery. The luted on wave-like strips were sometimes used as vessel handles. The cloth and mat impressions were made by the cloth and mat beater during the manufacturing process and were not made especially as decorations. The hollow-outs were mostly found in the knobs on the top of vessel covers; they were used for ventilation. The holes on the vessel stands, however, were perhaps more for decoration. Painted pottery pieces occupy as much as 14.02 percent, indicating that they probably would have an even greater percentage within complete vessels. Some Yangshao sites have very few painted pottery. For example, at the Sanliqiao Yangshao stratum, only 2.47 percent were painted potsherds. There is an obvious difference. Just as there is a difference in the numbers of painted pottery found, there is also a big difference in decorations and vessel forms, perhaps indicative of different periods.

Painted motifs were restricted to the fine red ware (and a few of the fine white ware), the vessel surface was highly burnished with portions of it covered by a very thin crimson or white slip. The crimson slip was slightly more common and had a rich gloss. Some vessels had only the slip, and no painted motif, apparently a characteristic of this area (some of the coarse red ware contained pottery with red slip), rarely seen elsewhere. Pottery vessels with white slip were fewer; the white slip was applied to the rim and body areas, the pottery were then painted. The feature was not as common here as in the Yangshao sites east of Mianchi (Especially near the site of Chenggao). The paint color was mainly black, and very seldom red. Even fewer vessels showed a combination of black and red, and limited to the white-slip painted types. Most of the painted motifs were done on the vessel bodies and rims, but never on the interior walls.

The decorative patterns were relatively complicated and rich in variety. They were basically composed of stripes, whirls, triangular whirls, dots, and checkered forms. But there were no regularity to their arrangement. Although the patterns could be divided into groups, it is rather difficult to analyze the individual motif of these patterns, since these motifs often interacted with other motifs in a transformed pattern. Also, certain patterns were not restricted to the same type of vessels.

The above observations are particular to this site. As a whole, the structure of these patterns shows some regional traits. These characteristics have probably spread from the central regional of the Sanmen Gorge Reservoir to the areas west of Mianchi, to southern Shanxi, and central Shaanxi. However, these characteristics differ greatly from those in the Yangshao sites to the east of Mianchi. For example, there were many bent belly bowls and basins, but only a few of the *ding* tripods and the white slipped painted pottery. Also, the narrow, ribbon-shaped checkered patterns, characteristic of western Henan, do not appear here. These are significant observations.

The frog-shape designs on the three pieces of painted potsherds found here were similar to the frog feet designs found at Yangshao village in Mianchi county (See references 10, Pl. XLI: 14, 27) and also the frog-shaped patterns at Xiguanbu in Huayin, Shaanxi province. This frog design and the three pieces with the lizard motif as well as the molded bird's head were all outstanding works of art at that time.

The pottery vessel forms included plate, bowl, basin, cup, jar, *yu* basin, bottle, *zeng* steamer, *fu* cauldron, *zao* stove, *ding* tripod, vessel cover and vessel stand. Among these, the basin-shaped vessels were the most numerous. Types A10 e-g of basin-shaped vessels and types A6b of bowl-shaped vessels were characteristic of this area, and very seldom found in the sites east of Mianchi. We have learnt about the daily life of the time from the shapes of the pottery vessels: For example, most of the vessels made from a mud-based ware were containers. The pointed-bottom bottle might have been a vessel for drawing water. Similar vases found at the county seat of Luoyang of the Han Dynasty, [20] along with the pointed-bottom vases attached to the pottery well models in Han tombs support this idea. The pottery *zeng* steamer was closely related to the coarse pottery *fu* cauldron. The cauldron was probably used together with the steamer to steam whole grains of millet. The small-mouthed, flat-bottomed cauldrons of Yangshao were not suitable for cooking food. Aside from containers, the coarse sand-temperted ware was used mainly as cooking vessels, such as the *fu* cauldron, *ding* tripod, and *zao* stove. There was only one *ding* tripod found, and it was remodeled from a pottery *fu* cauldron (Fig.29; Pl. XXXIX, 4), and showed that while *ding* tripods existed in this area, they were not common. This is in sharp contrast to the Yangshao sites east of Mianchi where pottery tripods were common. Also, the large number of excavated vessel covers shows that past observations—that they were products of the Longshan culture—are incorrect. Vessels with deep ring-base were found (like bowls A7a, b, both looking like they could have been a type of vessel cover). There were also quite a few stands, which might have been the prototype of the deep ring-based vessels. Many pieces of small cups made of coarse red ware were found together with many small vessel covers (D13c-d), which could have been used as covers for them. Their function is still difficult to explain. From the above observations, we see that the cup, the ring-based vessel, and the vessel cover, which were considered to be characteristic of the Longshan culture, already had their beginnings in the Yangshao culture.

Most of the pottery knives and non-containers were remade from broken potsherds. Some knives were made directly from clay and then fired. The pottery net sinker was an accessory to the fishing net. A pottery tool which might have been a hand tool for rubbing and washing, or for scraping leather, was found in abundance as Type 3A in the Shaanxi province, while Type 3B-C were mostly found in the Yangshao sites in western Henan and southern Shanxi. Their function is still difficult to determine, although they cannot be pellets or toys. A further study is needed.

Most of the stone utensils were made by flaking, and very few by grinding. This is also one of the primitive characteristics of Yangshao culture. The most commonly chipped stone tool was a dish-like object. Its use is still unclear. The type with a sharp edge all around (Like type 1B) may have been used for scraping and chipping. The blunt-edged type (Type 1A) may have been mostly used for knocking and smashing. The stone knife with notches on both ends, and the ground stone knives were the main harvesting tools. The small number of stone and pottery net sinkers found hinted the existence of fishing. Two pieces of flint were found with clear usage marks on their edges. They appear to have been made the same way as the microlithic tools of the microlithic cultures.

Most of the stone artifacts made by grinding were knives and spades. Almost all of the spades were broken with very few complete examples. They were generally large with the spade body flat and finely ground to a sharp edge. There was a coarse section on the backside center, and some examples have notches on both sides of the shoulder. Clearly, these notches were made purposely in order to attach a wooden handle with binding ropes. They could then have been used as digging tools the same way as we use modern shovels. There may have been wooden ploughing tools, but we did not find any. Only a small number of axes, adzes and chisels were found, each one rather coarsely made. The larger stone axes were probably used for cutting trees, while the smaller ones could have been used as knives. The stone hammer could have been a pounding and smashing tool. The stone pestle and mortar were tools for grinding red iron ore, traces of which can be found on the tools. There were no ground stone arrowheads found in the Yangshao stratum. This is a point worth noting.

There were few bone artifacts, fewer than in the Longshan culture and much simpler in form. This may be related to the availability of the bones. The production of bone artifacts was limited since there were few domesticated animals. There were also not many antler objects: Needles, awls, hairpins, chisels among others; none of them with any characteristic shape. The antler hammer discovered here is rarely seen among the Yangshao sites.

Ornaments such as pottery and stone rings are relatively small, and may have been worn as suspended ornaments.[21] Turquoise pendants, crystal beads, tooth-shaped bone ornaments, shell pendants, and drilled pig's teeth may have been neck ornaments or body pendants. The bone hairpin was used for holding the hair in place, indicating that people no longer allowed their hair to hang loosely. The arc-shaped bone pieces were probably used like rings. There was also an oyster shell ring found on the skeleton's ring finger, worn the same way as today. These were all ornaments for daily use. The fragments of red iron ore found here must have been ground to powder and used for cosmetic purposes.

The Yangshao culture was thought, in the past, to belong to the late Neolithic Period. Its definite date was argued by many, but determined to be around 2000 B.C. This is contradictory in many respects to reality. We have suggested that the Yangshao culture may be of an earlier date, perhaps as early as the Middle Neolithic period[22], although strong evidence is still lacking. This seems probable, since recent discoveries reveal that both the Yangshao and Longshan cultures were very complex, indicating a long period of development. As far as the specific date is concerned, we hope that radio carbon may be used to solve the problem. Because the Yangshao had developed through a long period of time, its cultural appearance varied in time. According to our investigations and excavations in the Sanmen Gorge Reservoir area, there appears to be two different types: One type exhibits many painted vessels with complex decorations and vessel forms of mainly curved bowls and basins, but not round-based bowls; the other type has few painted vessel with simple patterns, and many round-bottomed bowls, but no curved bowls or basins.

Miaodigou belongs to the former type and Sanliqiao the latter. Even though these two sites are geographically close to each other they reveal very different phases of the same culture, obviously representing different stages of development. The Miaodigou type of Yangshao re-mains is more common in Henan, Shanxi, and Shaanxi. Within Shanxi, sites of the same type are: Xiyincun in Xia county[23], Jingcun in Wanrong county[24] and Shengjinzhuang in Yongji county[25]. Within Shaanxi, there are Mawangcun and Wulou in Changan county, Xiguan of Huayin county[26], and Liuzizhen in Hua county(See reference 15, Fig.1; Pl. II). Quite a few other sites of this type were found at Shan and Lingbao counties in Henan.[5] The village of Yangshao in Mianchi also basically belong to this group, although it includes some elements of the Yangshao sites to the east of Mianchi. The many sites around Chenggao are slightly dif-ferent culturally, though sites like Dianjuntai, Qingtai (See reference 21, Fig.7) and Qinwang-zhai (See reference 10, Pls. 138-149) basically belong to the first type. Their basic character-istics include a large amount of painted pottery with complex patterns. This type was often interlocked with the second type of Yangshao sites, which has very few painted pottery and simple patterns (Represented by the Yangshao stratum at Sanliqiao). It is still uncertain which of these two sites is the earlier. The old theory of cultural development from the simple to the complex would have assigned the type of simple patterns as the earlier period. (See references 11, p. 77, 〔27〕) However, we consider that there is a serious possibility for the reverse to be true since the Yangshao remains at Miaodigou show many primitive aspects and may thus be-long to an earlier Yangshao period. This problem can only be solved by future excavations.

The Yangshao people were chiefly agricultural, as proven by the discovery of so many ag-ricultural tools. The large village sites with rich remains also indicate a long period of tribal settlement, which could not be maintained without agricultural production.

Although we have not discovered any crops of the time, at Banpo in Xian, [28] Shaanxi, and Liuzizhen in Hua County (See references 15, p. 73), millet grains and stone knives with notched ends or drilled holes have been found. They were the main tools for harvesting millet. [29] Thus, millet was probably the main agricultural crop at these sites. The lack of grain grind-ing tools shows that these grains were not ground, but simply steamed in a steamer without removing the husks. This method of cooking still exists today. We can say it has an extremely ancient history.

Spindle whorls and pottery vessels with linear and cloth patterns indicate that there was spinning and weaving. The cloth pattern on pottery handles showed ten threads each of the warp and woof within one square cm. This is similar to modern coarse linen, and the material could have been hemp. Since hemp was the main material for spinning and weaving until the Shang and Zhou periods, [30] the raw material for spinning and weaving in the Yangshao period was very likely hemp.

The species of domesticated animals were not numerous. Most of the bones were of the pig, followed by those of the dog. Because of the small numbers of finds and their fragmented conditions, it is impossible to summarize and compare them. However, in terms of excavated bones, the Longshan culture exceeds the Yangshao culture. This may also be one of the primitive characteristics of the Yangshao culture.

The very few numbers of bones arrowheads and net sinkers made of stone and pottery show that fishing and hunting were of secondary importance in food production. Some things, such as the turquoise, crystal and red iron ore used for making ornaments were not from local sources. They could have been imported through bartering. The painted wares with white slips could have been influenced by the Yangshao sites east of Mianchi. At the very least, these points show that there were contacts between the different clans. It was a matriarchal society at its height. Every member of the clan was required to share equally in the work and in the distribution of products. The economy was based on the sharing of properties, since no independent economic units were formed by the families. The economy was sustained on the basis of sharing by several families. The large houses could not have been built by only members of related family, but rather through the cooperation of members of the whole extended clan. Under such conditions, the matriarchal society had reached its peak. Whether the painted pottery vessels with the frog motif and the luted on lizards designs represent the totem or symbol of a clan still require further study. On the whole, the Yangshao remains at Miaodigou not only clarified the basic characteristics of the Yangshao culture, but have also given strong evidence concerning the development of contemporary production.

(II) Longshan Cultural Stratum

The Longshan culture was first discovered in the Chengziya on the town of Longshan in Licheng county, Shandong province, in 1928. A thin lustrous black pottery ware and stone objects were found here. Their cultural characteristics were different from the Yangshao culture, thus it was named the Longshan culture. It was also called the "black pottery culture", due to the presence of the black ware. However, "black pottery" does not adequately describe the entire culture, and is misleading. Therefore, the name "Longshan culture" was used in this report.

The Longshan culture is a Neolithic culture found along the Yellow River. It had succeeded the Yangshao culture, as supported by stratigraphic evidence in Henan, Shanxi, and Shaanxi. However the so-called Longshan sites differ in many ways from each other, because of their different geographical locations. They have been divided into the Shandong coastal type, the northern Henan type, and the Hangzhou bay type.[31] These variations had also been considered to be the result of chronological differences. (See reference 11, p.49) After 1949, archaeological material concerning Longshan culture gradually increased, revealing more of the regional differences among the sites. In order to distinguish one from the other, the Longshan culture in Henan and Shaanxi were named the "Henan Longshan culture" and the "Shaanxi Longshan culture" respectively. (See reference 22, p.46) Thus they were distinguished from the typical Longshan culture found along the sea coast (See references 22, p.46). Although the names are not completely satisfactory, we cannot deny that each type has special characteristics. We hope to solve this problem in the near future.

The so-called "Henan Longshan culture" is found mainly in the Henan province, and is the same Longshan culture found in northern Henan[27] and Phase Xincun. (See references 11, p. 49). There is a slight difference between the northern and western Henan types, although they belong to the same category. And, although the Longshan culture in Shaanxi province is very similar to the "Henan Longshan culture", there are still differences that set them apart; therefore it is called the "Shaanxi Longshan culture".

Post-Yangshao finds at Miaodigou do not belong to the category of "Henan Longshan culture". They show characteristics that appear to be transitional from the Yangshao to the Longshan. We will include these finds in the Longshan culture for the time being, since they are closer culturally to Longshan characteristics; we have distinguished it with the name, Miaodigou II Culture. The Longshan stratum at Sangliqiao, across the river from Miaodigou, belongs to the "Henan Longshan culture". The difference between these two sites is important for studying the chronology of the Longshan culture.

Excavations show that even though few Longshan sites were found in the Sanmen Gorge Reservoir area, where there is a Yangshao site, there often exist Longshan strata; they were only hard to find due to the rarity of exposure above ground. Various past investigations of the Miaodigou site did not expose any Longshan stratum until the proper excavations began. This was true at other sites. The Longshan sites within the Sanmen Gorge Reservoir were culturally complex, and had incorporated the so-called "Miaodigou II", the "Henan Longshan culture" and the "Shaanxi Longshan culture". However, on the whole, the excavation area is not as large or dense as that of the Yangshao culture, and the strata are also thinner. We shall focus on the Longshan stratum at Miaodigou to analyze the cultural characteristics of the Longshan culture.

The Longshan remains in Miaodigou Area T500 were rather concentrated, but all the other areas had only scattered remains. Although in area coverage, the Longshan strata at Miaodigou could be considered extensive, in quality of finds, they are not as rich as those of the Yangshao strata. Without exception, the Longshan strata were either directly above the Yang-shao strata, or had broken into them.

Only one Longshan house was found. It was a pocket pit with a door passage. The dwelling floor and the passage stairs were all covered with straw, mud and lime. From the remaining post holes, the house may be reconstructed to one with a conical roof. Lime covered floors have often been seen in the Longshan houses of northern Henan, generally on a round dwell-ing floor with a diameter of about 4 meters. This area was covered with straw, mud and lime, but there were no signs of walls, post holes or door passages (Also probably due to hurried excavations of the past). The hearth was in the center of the dwelling floor (See references 37, p. 7), very different in plan than the Longshan house at Miaodigou. This is not to say that houses with the same structure as those at the Miaodigou Longshan stratum had never been found, only that their dates and plans were not clearly analyzed. For example, one such house was found at Jingcun in Wanrong county, Shanxi, where any post holes and lime surface went unnoticed. [32] Another similar case was in ash pit H14 at Linshanzhai in Zhengzhou, Henan, where post holes were unnoticed. The so-called "white hard earth" must have been the remain-ing lime surface such as at Miaodigou. [33] Neither of these two sites reports had any accompa-nying figures or photographs. And according to the written description, they should have been similar to the Longshan house at Miaodigou, although both were mistakenly thought to belong to the Yangshao culture.

Although the kilns at Miaodigou were smaller, they had a more advanced structure. For ex-ample, the firing chamber was not as long as those at either the No. 3 kiln[34] in Banpo, Xian or the Yangshao kiln in Sanliqiao. Instead, a narrow and deep firing chamber was used to force the fire upwards to pass through the firing tunnel, pressing it into the kiln chamber. Judging from the curvature of the remains of the kiln walls, the kiln chamber should have been round-topped. The kiln top was closed during the last stage of firing, acting as a reducing agent on the pottery vessels; hence, a large amount of grey ware was produced among the pottery. A similar kiln was found at Jingcun in Wanrong, Shanxi, but was mistaken as a *zao* stove by the excavator (See reference 24, p.105, 106); another was found at Linshanzhai in Zhengzhou (See references 33, p.2, Figs.2, 3). In both cases, they were mistaken as remains of the Yang-shao culture. In the brief report on Jingcun, the figures appear to show firing holes. In the fig-ure from the brief report on Linshanzhai, there were only figures of a firing tunnel, and no kiln passage or firing tunnels were mentioned in the text. We do not know whether these things were absent, or whether they were missed by the excavators.

The Longshan pits were generally bag shaped, and were tidier than the Yangshao ash pits. Although a few of the pits cut into each other they were not far apart in time, and the excavated remains were not significantly different. Because of the discovery of neatly buried human skeletons in two of these pits, we may assume that the abandoned pits were used for burials. The burials were not as disorderly as those of the Yangshao culture.

The arrangement of the 145 tombs in Area T1 was quite orderly with an orientation between 175-190°. This must have been the communal graveyard for members of the clan. Only two tombs (M72, 99) contained small cups of the red pottery ware. All of the rest were without any burial objects. These small red-ware cups were often found in the Longshan ash pits, but never in the Yangshao ash pits. Stratigraphically, these tombs have broken through the Yangshao strata or Yangshao ash pits, and were in turn, pressed down and interrupted by the Eastern Zhou stratum. Thus, their chronology is certain, and together with the evidence of Longshan remains from the two tombs, all 145 tombs are considered to belong to the Longshan culture.

On the north wall of ash ditch HG533, traces of wooden tools were found. From the traces of double-pronged strips, they appeared to be wooden handles split into a double prong at one end. The double-pronged part was used for digging the soil. Similarly shaped wooden shovels were also found in Neolithic sites in Japan. [35] The shape is like the shovel character *lei* of the Yin-Zhou periods. Thus, these traces were probably left by the wooden *lei* shovel turning the earth. No stone spades like those of the Yangshao culture were found here; perhaps they were replaced by wooden spades or *lei* shovels. Similar traces left by "the *lei* shovel" were found in the Longshan stratum at Sanliqiao. This kind of shovel was the forerunner of the Yin-Zhou wooden *lei* shovel, and was an advanced productive tool of the time.

Most of the remains were potsherds and more than sixty vessels were reconstructed. Most of the pottery was of the coarse, sand-tempered grey ware, followed by the fine grey ware, and very seldom the fine red ware or fine black ware. Very little of the fine black ware was found, totaling less than one percent. This is very different from the "Henan Longshan culture". The ware was hard and required about the same heat to fire as the Yangshao wares. This property is especially noted in the fine red ware, which was similar to pottery found in the Yangshao culture. The grey wares range in color from greyish brown, to dark grey, with the color varying on the same vessel, showing that the firing skill was still rather primitive.

The pottery vessels were mainly made by coiling, with the rims reshaped on a slow wheel, without any evident traces of the wheel. In some cases the vessel bodies and bottoms were made separately, and then luted together. This technique of pottery making was not apparent in the Yangshao culture, but was very clear here. Similar techniques have been found in the

"Henan Longshan culture". Except for the coarse sand-tempered ware, vessel bodies were as thin as 0.2 cm. These were probably the forerunners of egg-shell pottery.

The most common decoration on the vessel body was the basket impressions, followed by a highly burnished surface, and then by cord patterns; the least common were the checkered patterns and incised patterns. Other forms of decorations were decorations in appliqué, open work, and painted motifs. The painted motifs were found only on the fine red ware. They may be divided into two types: One type was the result of a red purplish slip added on to the tops of small pottery cups. The slip was unevenly added, leaving marks of rubbing. Many pieces of this type were excavated from Longshan ash pits and none from Yangshao ash pits. They were found at Yangshao village, but were incorrectly taken to belong to the Yangshao culture. (See reference 10, Pl. 43: 17) The second type showed a painted band of black lozenge pattern on the constricted mouth of a deep-bodied jar. Although this type had not been properly excavated, it had definitely existed alongside Longshan remains. Three similarly painted pottery jars were found in the Longshan ash pit at Pannan village in Pinglu, Shanxi in 1958. However, this type was not found at the Miaodigou Yangshao strata or ash pits. They were found at Yangshao village, and were mistaken to be of Yangshao origin. (See reference 10, Pl. 43: 18, 19) Traces of red paint were also found on the grey ware pottery cups of the Longshan period. The designs were added to the surface of the vessels after firing. This technique differed from the other two types. Unfortunately, the patterns on these vessels were faded and unclear. From this stratigraphic evidence, it is certain that painted pottery existed in the Longshan culture, and thus, it becomes increasingly inaccurate to call the Yangshao culture the "painted pottery culture".

Among Longshan pottery vessels, there were a relatively large number of big vessels with distinct characteristics. They included bowls, basins, jars, cups, *dou* pedestals, *ding* tripods, *jia* tripods, *zao* stoves, and pointed-bottom bottles. Many of these seem to have been developed from the vessel forms of the Yangshao culture, particularly the cup, jar, and pointed-bottom bottles. The pointed bottom bottle was a typical product of the Yangshao culture. It was found at Yangshao village in Mianchi county (See reference 10, Pl. 22: 1-2.), and fragments were excavated at Hengzhen village in Huayin, Shaanxi (See reference 1, Fig.4: 4-5). These Longshan examples are very different from the pointed-bottom bottles of the Yangshao period, yet they were closely related to each other. The small cup with red slip was special to this Longshan area, and must have been related to the small coarse cups of the Yangshao period. It is notable that the vessel shape and the slip of the small cup were very similar to the so-called "egg-shell painted ware" found at Qujialing in Jinshan, Hubei province. There were at least some relationships between these two. The double-handled basin was a relatively new vessel shape. The *dou* pedestal and *ding* tripod became more common and the *jia* tripod was undoubtedly the forerunner of the later *li* tripod pottery. As a whole, the pottery vessels of the Miaodigou II Culture show clear patterns of transition from the Yangshao culture to the Longshan culture.

The stone objects were mostly made by grinding, and very few by flaking. The latter were limited to knives with notched double ends. Aside from stone knives that were similar to the Yangshao equivalents, there were ones that were shaped into rectangles with marks of additional work on the edges and the blades. There were quite a lot of stone axes, most large and thick, with characteristic rectangular cross-sections. This kind of stone axe could have been the primary woodcutting tool. It would be a more efficient tool than its predecessors because of a larger and heavier body. This type of stone axe was thought to be typical of the Yangshao culture (See reference 13, p. 48). However, we now know that it was only found in the Longshan strata of Miaodigou and Sanliqiao. There were fewer adzes found and they were relatively smaller. Three adzes with slightly raised backs were found, very similar to the stepped adzes found along the southeast coastal region. Besides rectangular stone knives, there were half-moon shaped knives and stone sickles. Not many of these latter two were found, but it was proof that they were only first introduced in the Longshan culture. The appearance of the stone sickle especially, indicates an improvement in agricultural production. The appearance of many arrowheads was also unheard of in the Yangshao culture. In terms of the manufacturing process and the shapes of stone tools, we see a noticeable advancement from the Yangshao culture.

There was quite a wealth of bone objects, surpassing Yangshao bone objects both in quantity and in variety. Perhaps this was due to an increase in the number of domesticated animals, hence a richer source for bones. The objects included needles, awls, arrowheads, hairpins, and combs, many of which had advanced shapes. For example, the Type 5C bone hairpin was the forerunner of bone hairpins of the Yin dynasty. And despite the simple shape of the comb, the Yin-Zhou bone combs were continued in this tradition. In terms of antler objects, there were only awls and chisels found. Oyster shell knives and arrowheads began to appear. Among tooth-based objects, arrowheads were seldom seen. The ground tooth pieces were perhaps used as knives. None of these objects were found in the Yangshao culture.

There were not many ornaments found. Pottery ornaments included pottery beads dyed with red iron ore and pottery tubes (*zhen* earrings?). The stone *huang* pendant was perhaps made from a broken stone ring. All of these ornaments were probably some form of pendant.

After an analysis of the characteristics of the cultural remains, the Miaodigou II Culture appears quite different from the "Henan Longshan culture". A few examples from the pottery vessels will illustrate this. At Miaodigou, all pottery vessels were hand made with no traces of the wheel. The typical black pottery was not found. Vessels were mainly decorated with basket impressions, followed by cord impressions, and then the checkered patterns. These coexisted with painted pottery. The vessel forms all had their own characteristics. There was the *jia* tripod and no *li* tripod. And while pottery such as the basins, jars, and pointed-bottom bottles inherited the forms of the Yangshao culture, the painted pottery proved that it was a continuation of the Yangshao Culture. All of these Miaodigou characteristics are different from the "Henan Longshan culture". The existence of the *jia* tripod, *ding* tripods, jars and *dou* pedestals gave a preface to what was to come in the "Henan Longshan culture"; the large amount of egg-shell pottery potsherds also enforces this point. Thus, there were objects of a transitional phase, from the Yangshao to the Longshan periods, and so belonged to the early period of the Longshan culture.

This is not the first time that sites with this kind of characteristics were found. In the past, when the stratification was not clearly analyzed, they had all been assigned to the Yangshao culture. The first clear analysis was carried out at Miaodigou. We believe that understanding the cultural characteristics is definitely a step forward in the archaeological study of Neolithic China. In the past, remains with similar type were found at Yangshao village. Some obvious examples were the painted potsherds with the band of lozenge design, the small cups with red slip, and pointed-bottom bottles, among others (See reference 10, Pl. 43: 17-19; Pl. 22: 1-2). Other objects, such as deep-bellied basins with a constricted mouth, were not found in the Yangshao culture or the "Henan Longshan culture" (See reference 10, Pl. 9: 4; Pl. 10: 3). In Jingcun, in Wanrong county, Shanxi province, there were not only houses and kiln sites that were similar to those at Miaodigou, but also the *jia* tripod, small-mouthed jar, and round-bottomed jar, which were of the same basic forms as those at Miaodigou (See reference 24, Pl. 3: 2, 4, 5). Because Yangshao remains were found in both places, this kind of artifacts was assigned to the Yangshao culture. From 1949, similar remains were also found in Sunqitun in Luoyang, and Linshanzhai in Zhengzhou. Although the remains were being published in a very brief way, according to our on-site observations, their characteristics were basically the same as that in Miaodigou. However, the excavators had mistaken them to be from the Yangshao culture. For example, Sunqitun was assigned to the late Yangshao period because the stratum had broken into the Yangshao ash pits.[36] Among the objects, the grey ware basin, jar and *dou* pedestal were all similar to objects from Miaodigou. The excavators had reported the existence of painted wares, though the quality of the wares was not known. Thus, these potsherds could be a mixture of painted wares from both Yangshao and Longshan. At Linshanzhai, not only were the houses and kiln sites similar to those at Miaodigou, the double-handled basin, small-mouthed jar and other vessels were also similar (see reference 33; Pl. 1: 2, 3, 13). Recently, the same kind of Miaodigou type remains was found in the stratum above the Yangshao layer at Pannancun in Pinglu, Shanxi. Three painted basins with the same shape and pattern as those from Miaodigou were reconstructed. Remains with similar typology were found above a Yangshao stratum at Liuzizhen in Hua county, Shaanxi province. However, the brief report stated that there were pottery *li* tripods mixed in with the other remains (See reference 15, Pls. 3: 8, 12). They could have been later period vessels (such as those found in the Shaanxi Longshan culture) that were accidentally mixed into this stratum. If this is not so, this discovery in the Liuzizhen would be suspicious, since the *li* tripod had not been found at other contemporaneous sites.

Based on the finds from other sites, we may conclude that the Longshan remains at Miaodigou were representative of some special characteristics, a particular period of development, and was fairly widespread. For now, we shall name it the Miaodigou II Culture. Stratigraphically, it is later than the Yangshao culture, and yet it is a bit more primitive than the "Henan Longshan culture". Thus the "Henan Longshan culture" probably developed from the Miaodigou II.

This period was still dependent on mainly agricultural production, but there were obvious improvements on the productive tools. There was no stone spade, such as those seen in the Yangshao culture; it was possibly replaced by a wooden one. Traces of the double-pronged wooden *lei* shovel were found; they were also seen in the Longshan stratum at Sanliqiao. It had been the main farming implement until the Yin-Zhou period. Compared to the large, clumsy stone spades, the appearance of more wooden tools implies a great deal of improvement. Besides the chipped stone knife and the rectangular single-holed stone knife, the tools for harvesting included the half-moon shaped stone knife, the shell knife, and stone sickle. Not only had the variety of the tools increased, but also their efficiency. For instance the use of the stone sickle with a handle was much more efficient than using the stone knife. This development in farming tools indirectly shows that agriculture was more advanced than in the Yangshao period. The kinds of crops harvested are still not fully known, but they were probably similar to those of the Yangshao culture, which were mainly millets. Domesticated animals also occupied an important position. A proper account of the animal bones is impossible because of the fragmentary condition of the bones. However, there were many more bones here than there were in the Miaodigou Yangshao stratum. The bones of domesticated animals recovered in twenty-six Longshan ash pits far outnumbered those excavated from 168 Yangshao ash pits. And the variety of species found in the Longshan ash pits was also greater. There were many sheep bones and even some cattle bones in addition to pig and dog bones. This shows that domestication of animals in the Longshan period was more developed than in the Yangshao period. Chicken bones were also found, but we have not yet determined whether the chickens were domesticated. It is certainly not impossible for the Longshan culture to have had domesticated chickens, since chicken bones had also been found at the site of Yangtouwa in Lüshun, Liaoning in the past. However, evidence is needed to confirm this.

There were a small number of stone, bone, shell, and tooth arrowheads and stone net sinkers found; also found were the bones of deer, musk deer, fox, and tiger, forehead bones and the base of the fish's pectoral fin. These indicate that fishing and hunting were still part of this culture's livelihood. The developments in agriculture and animal domestication signify that the Longshan culture had raised their productive economy to a higher level.

The change in social organization is reflected in this development in productivity. The transition from a matriarchal society to a patriarchal society is shown by a further development of agriculture with a greater number of domesticated animals. As Engles pointed out, "The herds and the other new objects of wealth brought about a revolution in the family. ··· Gaining a livelihood had always been the business of the man; he produced and owned the means therefore. The herds were the new means of gaining a livelihood, and their original domestication and subsequent tending was his work. ···forced the woman into second place."[37]

The discovery of groups of tombs revealed a definite orientation and burial style. They should have been common burial for the clan. It is important to note that all of the burials were single interments; there were no group burials like those found in Yangshao tombs (A number of Yangshao graveyards had multiple burials along with single burials; examples: at Banpo in Xian, Shaanxi; No. 4 Middle school in Baoji; Hengzhen in Huayin; Dongzhuang village in Yongji, Shanxi province. All of these tombs had two or more burials. At Anjiabu of Liuzizhen, in Hua county, group burial was quite common. Each tomb contained 12-23 skeletons. This kind of group burial may be said to be reflective of a matriarchal society, and was rather common. By the Longshan period, group burial was seldom seen, at least not in 145 tombs at Miaodigou. This type of phenomenon might also reflect the organization of the society). The phenomenon is worth noting as it may indicate the change in social organization, where the clan-centered group burial gradually becomes eliminated. Indeed this has yet to be discovered and studied. As the facts show, the economic foundation of the Miaodigou culture was changing: The beginning of private property. It marks the transition from a matriarchal to a patriarchal society. As this process developed, it led to the breakdown of the primitive clan community. From the Yangshao culture to the Longshan culture, a change in social organization began because of developments in production. The material culture reflects this fundamental change.

II. Sanliqiao

(I) Yangshao Cultural Stratum

The Sanliqiao site is relatively small in area, with 180,000 square meters. Yangshao strata are spread all over the site, with those in the eastern portion of the site covered by Longshan strata, which are less extensive. Because the main excavation was carried out on the Longshan layers, artifacts recovered from the Yangshao strata were not as numerous as those from the Longshan culture.

There were no Yangshao houses found here; however, there were forty-seven ash pits discovered. The shapes of these pits are more or less the same as those in the Yangshao layers at Miaodigou. Most of them were broken by one or more Longshan ash pits, and very few were complete. Two pottery kilns were found, and were similar to the cylindrical kilns found in Banpo, [34] Xian, but not entirely the same. They had a long tubular firing chamber, a round kiln chamber, around which were vertical walls, and a remaining height of 0.36 cm. The firing chamber and the kiln chamber were on the same plane without any sign of a firing tunnel or kiln grid. Judging from the remaining kiln walls, the original kiln chamber should have had an opening, which would have enabled the vessels to undergo oxidation while they were exposed to the high heat of the kiln chamber. The long tubular firing chamber was used as a firing tunnel as well as for storing fuel. Structurally, this type of pottery kiln is rather primitive.

Two tombs were found below the Longshan stratum. Both had broken into the Yangshao stratum. They were rectangular, vertical pits, where the bodies were placed in an extended supine position with no accompanying objects.

The general characteristics of the cultural remains are basically similar to those from the Yangshao strata at Miaodigou. However, the differences are obvious in the pottery vessels. For example, there was relatively few painted pottery, about 2.47% of the total. The patterns were comparatively simple, and the shapes included only the *bo* bowl, bowl, basin, jar, and vessel stand. The *bo* bowl with a round bottom was found in abundance and is special to this site; it was not found in the Yangshao strata at Miaodigou. On the other hand, the curve-bellied bowls and basins (only a few curve-bellied basin was found, but they were unpainted), which were commonly seen in the Yangshao strata at Miaodigou, were not found at Sanliqiao. The painting was usually done on the rim, seldom on the body of the vessel. From the positioning and composition of the painting, it appears somewhat backward in style.

The numbers of stone and bone artifacts found were few, and their shapes were similar to those in the Yangshao strata at Miaodigou. No sign of the stone spade was found here, as was almost the case at Banpo, where only one broken piece was found. Whether there were other kinds of digging tools (such as wooden tools) requires further investigation.

The sites of Sanliqiao and Miaodigou stand on opposite sides of the river, and close to each other. However, judging from the remains, their cultures were very different, indicating that they were of two different types. The Yangshao layer at Sanliqiao cannot be regarded as typical, and because only a few vessels were recovered, it was difficult to analyze or even use in comparison. Its general culture characteristics are very similar to the Banpo site in Xian, Shaanxi. For example, the pottery kiln, round-bottomed *bo* bowl, and tubular jar found at Sanliqiao were also found in Banpo, although the patterns on the painted wares were different at the two sites. There was no constricted-mouthed basin found at Banpo. These were perhaps due to local differences. Similar types of Yangshao remains are quite widespread within the Reservoir area. Excavated sites such as Qilipu in Shan county, Henan and Pannan in Pinglu, Shanxi, are similar to the Yangshao strata at Miaodigou. And many Yangshao sites in Shaanxi are similar to the Banpo site. Therefore we believe that the Yangshao strata at Sanliqiao and Banpo are very close to each other, and for the time being, may be grouped in the same type.

Often this kind of Yangshao remains was interlocked with the representative Yangshao remains of Miaodigou, pointing obviously to a chronological relationship, and not a geographical one. As for the relative dates of these two Yangshao types, they are still unresolved because of a lack of stratigraphic evidence. Nevertheless we believe that the Yangshao finds at Sanliqiao do not represent a primitive phase, despite the scarcity of painted pottery wares and their simple designs; rather they should be considered later than the Yangshao remains represented by Miaodigou.

(II) Longshan Cultural Stratum

The Longshan stratum was limited to a small area in the eastern part of the Sanliqiao site. No houses were found except for a few broken pieces of white plaster. Altogether, 103 ash pits were found, mostly pocket-shaped ash pits with well-dug, smooth walls, and very complex interrelationships. However, the excavated remains from the pits are not very different, perhaps indicating that they were not far apart in time.

Only one pottery kiln was found, almost completely preserved. It is slightly different in structure from the Longshan pottery kiln at Miaodigou. A square and deep fire opening is in the front. The firing tunnel divides into four passages that pass through the firing chamber and enter the kiln chamber; a beam in the center of the firing tunnel substituted the kiln grid. The kiln chamber was probably round. Its remaining walls exhibited an arc shape, and were 0.38 meters high. This indicates that the kiln chambers of the time might have had round tops and could have been closed at the last stage of firing, so that the pottery would "drink water" to cause a reduction. The kiln chamber was not only large, but its general structure appeared more advanced than the Longshan pottery kiln at Miaodigou. This kiln was made by digging a pit in the virgin soil. Traces left by the wooden *lei* shovel, much like those found in the Longshan strata at Miaodigou, were found on the kiln walls, indicating that these wooden *lei* shovels were one of the main digging tools of the time.

Only one tomb was found: A rectangular pit with vertical walls. The skeleton was again supinely extended, but the head was oriented differently than in Yangshao tombs. There were no burial objects. Because the Longshan stratum had broken into the Yangshao layer, its chronological position is quite clear.

Out of all the cultural remains, potsherds form the majority with a total of sixty-nine reconstructed vessels. They were different from the Longshan vessels at Miaodigou in terms of quality, manufacturing method, and decoration. The most common was a coarse, sand-tempered grey ware and a grey ware, followed by a coarse, sand-tempered red ware and a fine black ware; and the least common was the red ware. The colors on the pottery vessels are quite consistent, with no impure colors as the grey ware which appeared in the Miaodigou II Culture had. This shows some improvement in the firing technique. Wheel-made pottery vessels made up one-fifth of the pottery ware. There were also some typical egg-shell pottery and the rest were made by coiling. The most common decoration was the cord patterns, followed by the basket impressions, and then checkered motifs. There were also many plain surfaced or burnished vessels, incised designs and decorations in appliqué were also commonly seen. Vessel forms included the bowl, basin, cup, *dou* pedestal, *li* tripod, *jia* tripod, *gui* vessel, vessel stand and so on. A great number of *li* tripods with handles and cord impressions were found, while there were very few *jia* tripod; the *gui* tripods appeared. There were also spout fragments of the *he* vessel, but there was no *ding* tripod found. Jars and cups with handles were characteristic to this area. Most of these vessel forms typologically belong to the "Henan Longshan Culture". The long-necked jars (B8b) found here are similar to those from the town of Liangchengzhen in Rizhao, Shandong. [38] The double-handled jar (D1) is also similar to the ones from Liangchengzhen (see reference 38; Pl. 6: 1). Other vessels, such as the jar types A1, A3a, A3b, B6c and the *li* tripod, are similar to those at Keshengzhuang in Xian, Shaanxi, indicating that the remains found here were related to the Longshan remains to the east and west of Sanliqiao. However, the basic characteristics still lie within the "Henan Longshan Culture". Furthermore, many of the pottery vessels from the Yangshao village are similar, meaning that the Yangshao village also contained some remains from the "Henan Longshan Culture".

Stone tools included the axes, adzes, knives, and arrowheads, all of which were made by grinding and polishing. None was made by chipping; this fact may be one of the features of improvement. The bone artifacts were more varied and better made; they included needles, awls, hairpins, arrowheads, spades and chisels. The spade was made by polishing the mandibles of domesticated animals. It was also an advanced tool for production. Oyster shell objects included knives, sickles, pendants, and hairpins. These stone, bone, and oyster shell artifacts were all common products of the Longshan culture. The disappearance of chipped stone tools and the appearance of bone spades are meaningful indications of further progress.

The Longshan stratum at Sanliqiao belongs within the bounds of the "Henan Longshan Culture", commonly found in the Henan province. It possesses characteristics that are more advanced than the Miaodigou II Culture; although the *jia* tripod and some of the jars (such as type A2a, B6b, B9a, B9b) were basic continuations of the Miaodigou II vessel forms. The appearance of the pottery wheel further developed the skill of pottery making and signified a clearer division of labor in pottery making. Thus, we believe that the "Henan Longshan Culture" developed out of the Miaodigou II, and hope that further stratigraphic evidence will be found to support this.

Since some of the remains from Sanliqiao are similar to those from Liangchengzhen in Rizhao, Shandong, and from Keshengzhuang in Xian, Shaanxi, the three may be about the same age, while the difference among them may be local attributes.

III. Relationship between Miaodigou and Sanliqiao

The sites of Miaodigou and Sanliqiao are on opposite sides of a river, divided by a 1,400 meter wide valley. Both sites contain strata from the Yangshao, Longshan, and Eastern Zhou periods; and yet they appear culturally different. The differences were not geographical but rather differences in time. This is not only true at Miaodigou and Sanliqiao, but also at nearby Qilipu in Shan county, and Pannancun in Pinglu, Shanxi. These phenomena are useful for studying the chronology of the Neolithic period.

Regarding the contents of the Neolithic culture at Miaodigou and Sanliqiao, there may be interlocked relationships in terms of time. The order of their development was deduced as follows:

Miaodigou (I)→Sanliqiao (I)→Miaodigou (II) →Sanliqiao (II)

The relative dates of the Yangshao and Longshan cultures cannot be disputed, however, stratigraphic evidence for sub-dividing each period into earlier or later phases is still lacking. The above deduction is only a hypothesis. There may be intervening stages between each phase of development. Whether our theory on the development stages of the Yangshao or Longshan culture is correct must be proved by future studies.

According to the above hypothesis, some questions are raised: Why did similar cultural content at Miaodigou and Sanliqiao belong to different periods? And why were their developments discontinuous? Perhaps the change in the course of the Qinglongjian may explain. The sites are on the lower portions of the Qinglongjian, with a river valley of more than 1400 meters wide dividing them. This river has been known to frequently change course. When it flowed south, it was convenient for the people at Miaodigou to use water, and difficult for the Sanliqiao settlement, which would be quite far from the river course. Conversely, when the river changed course and flowed north, it became convenient for the people at Sanliqiao and difficult for those at Miaodigou. Hence, people at the time would probably move to follow the water source. In 1953, and 1955-1956, when we were excavating at Shan county, the Qinglongjian flowed mainly along the south, close to the Miaodigou site; but after the flood in the summer of 1957, the river moved its course northwards, and flowed near Sanliqiao. Although the situation in ancient times might not be the same as the present, changes in the river course were still inevitable. Under these circumstances, the settlements move to the most suitable location depending upon the water supply. Thus, the two sites, on opposite sides of the valley, were occupied at different times.

IV. Relationship between Yangshao and Longshan Cultures

Ever since 1931, when the evidence of the alternating relationship of the Yangshao and Longshan cultures was found at Hougang in Anyang, northern Henan, similar evidence has been found in western Henan, southern Shanxi, and in Shaanxi. Thus there is no doubt regarding the relative chronology of these two cultures. However, the relationship between the two has raised many arguments in the past. Most archaeologists agree that these two cultures derived from different origins (It was generally considered in past publications that the Longshan culture originated in the east and developed westward, displacing the Yangshao culture. Others thought that the two cultures had different origins, but formed a "mixed culture" after the two cultures met. At the present, it is still not possible to determine the origin of the Longshan culture because it included different types, which may not all have the same origin. These are problems to be resolved in the future), but they failed to look for the source of their relationship.

Andersson's excavation of the Yangshao village contained many serious mistakes. This resulted in the inability to define the basic structure of the Yangshao culture. Thus many archaeologists suspect that the findings of the Yangshao village site are from different periods. Exploratory excavations after 1949 suggested a "mixed Yangshao and Longshan culture", though this did not solve the fundamental contradictions present at the Yangshao village site. We do not deny the existence of a "mixed culture" because this was a possibility had the two cultures met under the right conditions.

With the many clues resulting from the investigation and excavation of the Sanmen Gorge Reservoir area, we have to reconsider the relationships between the Yangshao and Longshan cultures. It is certain that some vessels of the Yangshao culture have the same characteristics as some of those of the Longshan period, though the latter might not necessarily have influenced the former. Some of these vessel forms might have started earlier and then developed into distinctive types later on, which could have resulted in differences in pottery making techniques. For example the black pottery and egg-shell like wares of the Yangshao culture show no signs of being wheel made; and although ring-based vessels were introduced and made in the Yangshao culture, they were not common. Therefore, it maybe suggested that certain pottery vessels of the Longshan culture had their beginnings in the Yangshao culture but became mature forms in the Longshan. If we acknowledge that the Longshan culture is a continued development of the Yangshao culture, it would not be unusual to see Longshan elements in the Yangshao culture. Hence the theory of a mixed culture needs reconsideration.

The finds at the Yangshao village are very complicated. When compared to the findings at Miaodigou and Sanliqiao, it is clear that the Yangshao village includes a range of different cultures and time periods. There are four periods present: Yangshao culture similar to the the Yangshao stratum at Miaodigou (Reprensented by painted pottery, pointed-bottom bottles, and stone spades) (see reference 10, Pls. 24; 36: 1, 6; 41; 42; 43: 1-12; 44; 59: 1); the Miaodigou II Culture (Represented by painted pottery with lozenge band pattern, small cups with a red slip, pointed-bottom bottles with basket patterns, *dou* pedestals with reticulated holes, basins, *zeng* steamers, wide-mouthed jars and *ding* tripods) (see reference 10, Pls. 2: 3-6; 9: 4; 10: 2-4; 15: 4-5; 20; 22; 28; 43: 17-19); the "Henan Longshan culture" (Represented by *li* tripods, single-handled cups and jars) (see reference 10, Pls. 1: 2-4; 11; 19: 5, 6) and the Eastern Zhou period (represented by small conical vessels and the *li* tripods) (see reference 10, Pls. 2: 2; 27). They summarized the contents of the Miaodigou site (I, II) and the Sanliqiao site (II, III). These two sites are not more than fifty kilometers apart and they contain similar remains. Thus, there were definitely no local differences between them. The main problem with the Yangshao village was the confusion in stratigraphy caused by Andersson's haphazard excavations, so that the interpretation of the Yangshao culture was in disorder for many years. The excavations of Miaodigou and Sanliqiao produce a strong disproof.

5 *CONCLUSION*

In the course of building the Sanmen Gorge Reservoir in Shan county, the sites of Miaodigou and Sanliqiao were excavated. They were both Neolithic sites that were geographically close to each other, bearing many cultural similarities. As a result of the large scale excavations and abundant finds, we have been able to not only solve some past problems, but also to establish a foundation for systematic research. The many important features are worth a special mention.

I. Miaodigou

The major archaeological finds at Miaodigou were from the Yangshao Neolithic culture. Also found were small quantities of Longshan deposits and a smaller amount of Eastern Zhou material. There were also a few Han and Tang tombs.

The two houses in the Yangshao stratum belong to the common building style of the Yangshao culture. However, the stone post foundations beneath each of the four stone posts are special to this area, and their discovery has pushed back the date of the first use of stone post foundations. We have also found that the red fired-earth in the dwelling floor was not the result of firing, but rather was due to the mixing of red-fired dust. The large number of ash pits found has constructed evidence for determining the shapes of Yangshao pits.

The more than 690 reconstructed pottery vessels, an unprecedented discovery for a Neolithic site in Western Henan, have given us a more complete understanding of Yangshao Pottery. Both the pottery forms and decorations have obvious characteristics; this is especially seen in the many wares with complex patterns, implying not only local influences but probably time differences. The stone tools were mainly chipped, but quite a few ground stone spades were also found. There were very few bone artifacts, and the domesticated animals were few in number and variety. These characteristics represented the primitive aspects of the site, and perhaps are indicative of an earlier period of the Yangshao culture.

The Longshan stratum is an important discovery in our work. For the first time, it enabled us to define its cultural characteristics. For the time being, we will call it Miaodigou II Culture. It may very well be an early Longshan culture, or a transitional culture between the Yangshao and Longshan. Although only one house was found, we have managed to define its structure. Other features such as neat ash pits and a well-planned kiln site indicate greater development. The discovery of marks left by the wooden *lei* shovel not only shows that they had already existed in the Longshan period, but also signifies the use of improved tools for production.

The burials not only give us an insight into the burial customs of the time, but the large quantity of human remains will be valuable to anthropological studies.

Pottery vessels from the Miaodigou II Culture were still hand made and not yet wheel made. In addition to a rich amount of grey ware, there were also small amounts of fine red ware and some painted vessels. The shapes and decorations of these vessels show that while they retained Yangshao influences, they also forecast elements of Longshan vessels. The transitional quality of this period is quite apparent. A reduction in the number of chipped stone tools, an increase in bone vessels, and the first appearance of the shell artifacts all indicate further progress. Advances in agricultural techniques can be seen in the improved productive tools. The increase in the quantity and diversity of domesticated animals show a continuous accumulation of wealth; the great increase in productivity created social developments.

The Eastern Zhou stratum was only found within Area T1, with more of its road earth disturbing the Longshan tombs. The ash layer here was unclear, with only a few excavated remains such as small amounts of potsherds and a few bronze arrowheads. These appear to belong to the Warring States period.

There were only two kinds of coffins for children among the Western Han tombs: Tile and jar coffins. The only Tang tomb contained a wealth of burial objects, probably dating from the mid-Tang period or later.

II. Sanliqiao

The site of Sanliqiao also contains remains from the Yangshao, Longshan, and Eastern Zhou. However, both the Yangshao and Longshan cultural characteristics were different from those at Miaodigou.

The Yangshao stratum had a very well preserved, primitive pottery kiln. The artifact yield of the site was small. The curve-bellied bowls and basins, commonly seen at Miaodigou, were not found here. Instead, a round-bottomed *bo* bowl, not found at Miaodigou, was found here. The decoration on the painted wares was simple, while their number greatly reduced, indicating a slight regression of painted pottery. No stone spade was found; it might have been replaced by wooden tools. The Yangshao stratum here may be later in time than the one at Miaodigou.

The Longshan stratum at Sanliqiao is typical of the "Henan Longshan culture". The kilns we found were larger and better constructed than the Miaodigou Longshan kiln. Similar traces left by the wooden *lei* shovel were found on the kiln walls. There was more wheel-made pottery than in the Yangshao layer. The typical Longshan black pottery was also found, but there were no painted wares. Pottery *li* tripods and other typical vessels of the Longshan culture began to appear, indicating that this culture could have been developed after the Miaodigou II Culture.

Very few artifacts from the Eastern Zhou were found. The excavated materials include pottery and bronze arrowheads from the Warring States period. A piece of "*Anyi Erjin*" coin from the Wei state was found, giving further evidence of the date.

III. Some Observations

The excavations of the two sites of Miaodigou and Sanliqiao not only clarified the characteristics and chronology of the Yangshao and Longshan cultures, but most importantly, it defined their relationship. A major achievement of this excavation was the definition of the Miaodigou II Culture. We not only defined its cultural characteristics, but have laid a foundation for future research. The Miaodigou II culture was a transitional culture following elements of the Yangshao culture, and a predecessor of the "Henan-Longshan culture". Thus the following explanation can be drawn: The Miaodigou II Culture in Henan and Shaanxi was developed from the Yangshao culture while the "Henan Longshan culture" and the "Shaanxi Longshan culture" succeeded the Miaodigou II Culture. The appearance of pottery vessels typical of the Shandong area in the "Henan Longshan culture" might have been influenced by the Shandong Longshan culture. If this was the case, the Shandong Longshan culture probably had other sources of origin. However, this problem requires further study.

Defining the transition from the Yangshao to the Longshan is equivalent to solving the problem of the origin of ancient Chinese civilization. Our ancestors from ancient times, through the Yangshao and Longshan cultures, up until the Yin-Zhou period, were continuously developing a highly complex civilization along the Yellow River. Therefore, this excavation is extremely important in demonstrating the continuity of the development of ancient Chinese civilization.

References

[1] 黄河水库考古工作队：《黄河三门峡水库考古调查简报》，《考古通讯》1956 年 5 期，第 1–11 页。

[2] 黄河水库考古工作队：《一九五六年河南陕县汉唐墓葬发掘简报》，《考古通讯》1957 年 4 期，第 9–19 页。

[3] 黄河水库考古工作队：《一九五六年秋季河南陕县发掘简报》，《考古通讯》1957 年 4 期，第 1–9 页。

[4] 黄河水库考古工作队：《一九五七年河南陕县发掘简报》，《考古通讯》1958 年 11 期，第 67–79 页。

[5] 安志敏、王伯洪：《河南陕县灵宝考古调查记》，《科学通报》1954 年 7 期，第 79–80 页。

[6] 鹰部屋福平：《北方圈の冢》，第 23 页，图 10，1943 年。

[7] 关野克：《日本住宅小史》，图 7–9，1942 年。

[8] М. Г. Левина, Л. П. Потапова Народы Сибири, Стр. 585, 1956.

[9] 安志敏：《古代的糙面陶具》，《考古学报》1957 年 4 期，第 76 页。

[10] J. G. Andersson, The Prehistoric Sites in Honan, *BMFEA* No. 19, Pl. 27, 1947.

[11] 尹达：《中国新石器时代》，三联书店，第 98–108 页，1955 年。

[12] G. D. Wu, *Prehistoric Pottery in China*, p. 50, 1938.

[13] J. G. Andersson, *Researches* into the Prehistory of the Chinese, *BMFEA* No. 15, p.72, 1943.

[14] 夏鼐：《河南渑池的史前遗址》，《科学通报》2 卷 9 期，第 937 页，1951 年。

[15] 黄河水库考古队华县队：《陕西华县柳子镇考古发掘简报》，《考古》1959 年 2 期，第 71 页。

[16] 安特生：《中华远古之文化》，《地质汇报》第 5 号 1 册，第 14 页，1923 年。

[17] 龙非了：《穴居杂考》，《中国营造学社汇刊》5 卷 1 期，第 57–68 页，1934 年。

[18] Anna O. Shepard, *Ceramics for the Archaeologist,* p. 107, 1957.

[19] 阿尔纳：《河南石器时代之着色陶器》，第 8 页，1925 年。

[20] 苏秉琦等：《洛阳中州路》，第 42 页，图版贰贰：1，1959 年。

[21] 夏鼐：《河南成皋广武地区考古纪略》，《科学通报》2 卷 7 期，第 726 页，图 8，1951 年。

[22] 安志敏：《中国新石器时代的物质文化》，《文物参考资料》1956 年 8 期，第 44 页。

[23] 李济：《西阴村史前的遗存》，1927 年。

[24] 董光忠：《山西万泉石器时代遗址发掘之经过》，《师大月刊》3 期，图版四、五，1935 年。

[25] 张德光：《永济县金盛庄与石庄的新石器时代遗址》，《文物参考资料》1958 年 5 期，图一。

[26] 石兴邦：《陕西渭水流域新石器时代的仰韶文化》，《人文杂志》2 期，图版一、四，3–5；图版五，1，1957 年。

[27] 梁思永：《小屯龙山与仰韶》，《庆祝蔡元培先生六十五岁纪念论文集》，下册，第 563–564 页，1935 年。

[28] 考古研究所西安工作队：《新石器时代村落遗址的发现 —— 西安半坡》，《考古通讯》1955 年 3 期，第 15 页。

[29] 安志敏：《中国古代的石刀》，《考古学报》第 10 册，第 42 页，1955 年。

[30] 安志敏：《中国史前时期之农业》，《燕京社会科学》2，第 48–49 页，1949 年。

[31] 梁思永：《龙山文化——中国文明史前期之一》，《考古学报》第 7 册，第 10–11 页，1954 年。

[32] 卫聚贤：《中国考古小史》，第 59 页，1933 年。

[33] 河南省文化局文物工作队第一队：《郑州西郊仰韶文化遗址发掘简报》，《考古通讯》1958 年 2 期，第 1–2 页。

[34] 考古研究所西安半坡工作队：《西安半坡遗址第二次发掘的主要收获》，《考古通讯》1956 年 2 期，第 29 页，图版贰：2，3。

[35] 森本六尔：《日本农耕文化の起源》，图 13，1941 年。

[36] 河南文物工作队第二队：《洛阳涧西孙旗屯古遗址》，《文物参考资料》1955 年 9 期，第 60–61 页。

[37] 恩格斯：《家庭、私有制和国家的起源》，第 155 页，1954 年，人民出版社本。

[38] 刘敦愿：《日照两城镇龙山文化遗址调查》，《考古学报》1958 年 1 期，图版陆，3。

[39] 金关丈夫等：《羊头洼》，第 97–99 页，图 9，1942 年。

Afterword

Miaodigou and Sanliqiao was one of the first few published archaeological reports by the Institute of Archaeology, Chinese Academy of Sciences (Reorganized under the Chinese Academy of Social Sciences in 1977) after the foundation of the People's Republic of China. Shortly after its publication in 1959, the report caught the attention of international scholarly circles. The reason is that the discovery of the Miaodigou Phase II gave proof to a continuous prehistory of the Central Plains, and challenged the dual origin theory of "Yangshao in the west, Longshan in the east", established in the 1930s and 1940s.

What also happened shortly after the publication of the report was the Cultural Revolution. The progress of Chinese archaeology became slow and difficult, and disconnected with the outside world. *Miaodigou and Sanliqiao* was probably made aware to western readers in Professor K.C. Chang's *The Archaeology of Ancient China* (Yale University Press, 1963, 1968 and 1977). From the remaining letters of communication, we can gather the start of this translation process was at least as early as 1980. On July 2, 1980, Professor Gregory L. Possehl of the University of Pennsylvania Department of Anthropology sent a letter to Professor Xia Nai, saying he has translated *Miaodigou and Sanliqiao* jointly with Dr. Walter Fariservis and has contacted the Carolina Academic Press in Durham, North Carolina regarding its publication, who already responded with interest in publishing the work. September 13th of the same year, Xia Nai wrote in the reply, "Your letter has arrived. I am very happy to learn that Dr. Fairservis has already translated the book *Miaodigou and Sanliqiao*. This will have great advantages for introducing the results of New China's archaeology and promoting the mutual understanding of Chinese and American archaeologists. Therefore we and the author of this work enthusiastically accept your proposal to publish this work in the United States." He added, "In order to facilitate publication, we can supply the illustrations and photographs for the work, we hope that after their plates have been made you will return the photographs to us. If you agree to this suggestion, please communicate directly with Professor An Zhimin in order to facilitate mailing." On January 21, 1981, Professor Possehl wrote to An

Zhimin for the illustrations, and forwarded the letter to Xia Nai; finally, he sent his new book, *Ancient Cities of the Indus* to the Institute of Archaeology. On February 19th of the same year, Professor An Zhimin replied, "Your letter to Director Xia Nai and myself has been received and we are much indebted to you for sending us the large work, *Ancient Cities of the Indus River*. Thank you very much. All of the plates and photographs (Pls. I - XCII) of the work, *Miaodigou and Sanliqiao* have already been sent by sea-mail. Please be on the lookout for them. Since these plates and photographs are all held by the Institute of Archaeology, please return them to me as soon as you are finished. We do not think it is necessary for us to see the final manuscript of the translation, since we believe you can translate it very well, but we wish to express our thanks for your thoughtful consideration." In the previous letter from Professor Possehl, we know that he was preparing the final draft of the translation of *Miaodigou and Sanliqiao*, and had told Professor An Zhimin that if An wanted to, the draft would be sent to him for proofreading.

Why was this report being translated? How come it took so much time and effort only to not become published in the U.S.? We cannot answer these questions thoroughly from the records. In a letter sent on December 22nd, 1980 from Professor Possehl to Professor Albert E. Dien of Stanford University, some explanation was given. He said that he was editing a new book series tentatively titled "Library of Early Civilizations", which will deal with ancient archaeological sites. He intended to publish short book (40,000-50,000 words) of some of the great, or interesting archaeological sites of the world. He revealed that he has been associated with a translation of a monograph describing the excavations of Miaodigou and Sanliqiao for many years. This was done under the direction of Walter Fairservis and involved native Chinese speakers at the University of Washington in Seattle. This manuscript sits with him at the moment and was about one draft away from a publishable document. He mentioned that the work was supported by Professor Xia Nai and Professor An Zhimin, and that they agreed to send the original photographs to assist the publication. In the letter he called Professor K.C. Chang his friend, and that Chang had agreed to contribute some kind of a book on Anyang in the not too distant future. The main reason of Possehl's letter was not to seek funding, but in regard to the knowledge that Professor Albert E. Dien's plan to compile lengthy abstracts of the more articles in *Kaogu* and *Wenwu* between 1972 and 1981 (See Professor Albert E. Dien's postor for translation assistance for the publication of *Abstracts of*

Chinese Archaeological Publications on October 15th, 1980). He had hoped that Dien's plan would not conflict with the translation of *Miaodigou and Sanliqiao*.

Professor Possehl was a specialist in South Asian archaeology, very knowledgeable of the Indus Valley Civilization, but was not familiar with Chinese archaeology. The director of translation, Professor Walter Fairservis has served in World War II, and had become an archaeologist after returning to the U.S. from Japan. His field work was mainly in Pakistan. He was also an archaeologist on the Indus Valley Civilization. His interests were broad, and his published works included popular topics such as early human cave paintings, ancient Egypt and the Mongolian Plateau. We do not know for sure how he became interested in *Miaodigou and Sanliqiao* --- perhaps an invitation from Professor Possehl to help edit "Library of Early Civilizations"; We deduce Possehl had first found the report from Professor K.C. Chang.

On January 22, 1981, Professor Possehl contacted Professor Chang, and attached not only his letter to An Zhimin, to let him know the permission given by the Institute of Archaeology to publish the work in the U.S., but also asked Chang to write a preface to the English edition, to let western readers have a bit more background information. On January 27th, Chang replied and accepted the request for a preface, and asked to know more about the reason for translating the work, as well as the translation process and the details of the translators. The reply from Possehl came three days later, and said that the first draft of the translation was done by a group of Chinese students in Seattle under the direction of Professor Fairservis. He added that the draft was pretty "stiff", and so he would work with Cheng Mei Chang to get it into better shape over the summer. On June 2nd, Possehl pressed again for the preface, and told Professor Chang that he had been correcting the draft with a woman called June Li, and hoped to make an end of this project by the coming fall.

The preface from Professor Chang arrived in the hands of Possehl on July 13th, 1981. The article included Chang's own short analysis of the findings of Miaodigou and Sanliqiao, as well as other new findings of the past 20 years, and could be considered a significant piece of reviews in Chinese archaeology. Since the writing of the preface, another 30 years has passed. The last typed copy of the draft was done in 1987. The typist told Possehl that California Science Press should pay her 96 hours of typewriting fees. It seemed the manuscript was at least given to the California Science Press. As for why it was never printed, we may never know.

Dr. Ma Xiaolin of the Henan Institute of Cultural Relics and Archaeology met

Professor Possehl by chance at the annual meeting of Society for American Archaeology in 2009. The draft of the unpublished translation came up in conversation, and soon after, Professor Possehl mailed all of the drafts, finished and unfinished, the original illustrations, and his letters to Xia, An, Chang, and Dien together in one package to Ma Xiaolin. Ma then passed the unopened package to me. The plan to publish a bilingual version of the book was put into motion.

Miaodigou and Sanliqiao was the second Chinese archaeological report to be translated into English. The first was *Chengziya*, which was published in the U.S. in 1956. *Chengziya* was the first archaeological report written by a group of Chinese scholars, and remains until today the only Chinese excavation report to be translated and re-published in a foreign country. However, due to its low circulation, very few people in China know of its existence.

Many scholars continue to cite *Miaodigou and Sanliqiao* even today. The impact and value of the report in the history of Chinese archaeology is indisputable. Unfortunately, the Chinese edition has long been out of print. We dream of a new edition written in both English and Chinese, for the ease of access by natives of either language, and provide a possible insight for young students of archaeology to practice describing archaeological findings in another language.

In this volume, the preface written by Professor K.C. Chang was translated into Chinese by Chen Xingcan. The manuscript was typed by Ms. Sun Dan and Mr. Fu Yongxu, and the draft corrected by Mr. Qi Chen, with Chen Xingcan overseeing the edits. Due to the language limit of the editors, there may be errors. We hope to receive your feedback for the improvement of the work. The publication of this book was made possible by Professor Possehl, who provided the English translation, Professor Fairservis and other unnamed translators and editors, and Dr. Ma Xiaolin, who took great care in transferring the drafts and illustrations to us. 2010 marked the 60th anniversary of the Institute of Archaeology, and this year, coincidentally, marks the 90th anniversary of the discovery of Yangshao Culture. The book thus both commemorates the history of the Institute of Archaeology, and pays respects to Xia Nai, An Zhimin and other scholars of previous generations. Partial funding of the book was given by the Mianchi Municipal Government. Ms. Gu Yanxue put a great deal of work into the publication of the book. We sincerely thank them.

Chen Xingcan

June 19th, 2011, at the Instiute of Archaeology

线图 *Figures*

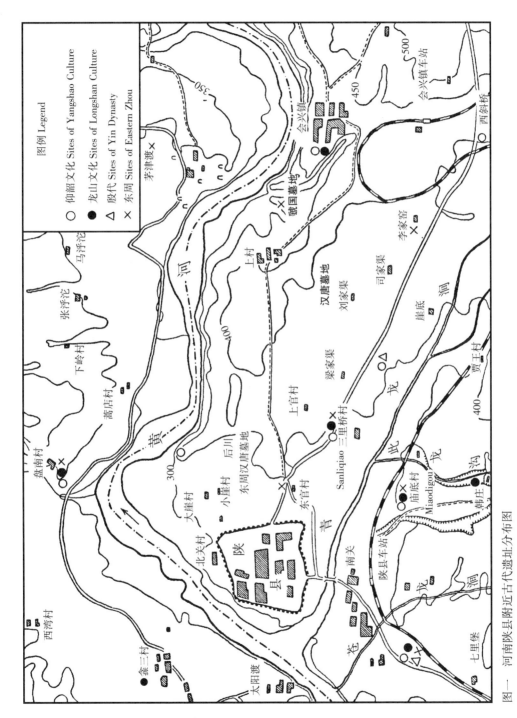

图例 Legend

○ 仰韶文化 Sites of Yangshao Culture
● 龙山文化 Sites of Longshan Culture
△ 殷代 Sites of Yin Dynasty
× 东周 Sites of Eastern Zhou

图一　河南陕县附近古代遗址分布图

Fig. 1　Map showing the distribution of ancient sites in the vicinity of Shan county seat

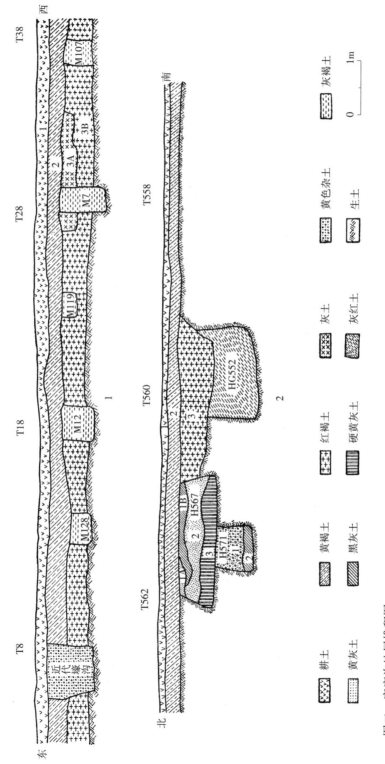

图二　庙底沟地层堆积图

Fig. 2　Stratigraphy of the Miaodigou site

1. T1 区探方 8，18，28，38 南壁剖面（Cross-section of the south wall of pits T8，18，28，and 38 in area T1）

2. T500 区探方 558，560，562 东壁剖面（Cross-section of the east wall of pits T558，560，and 562 in area T500）

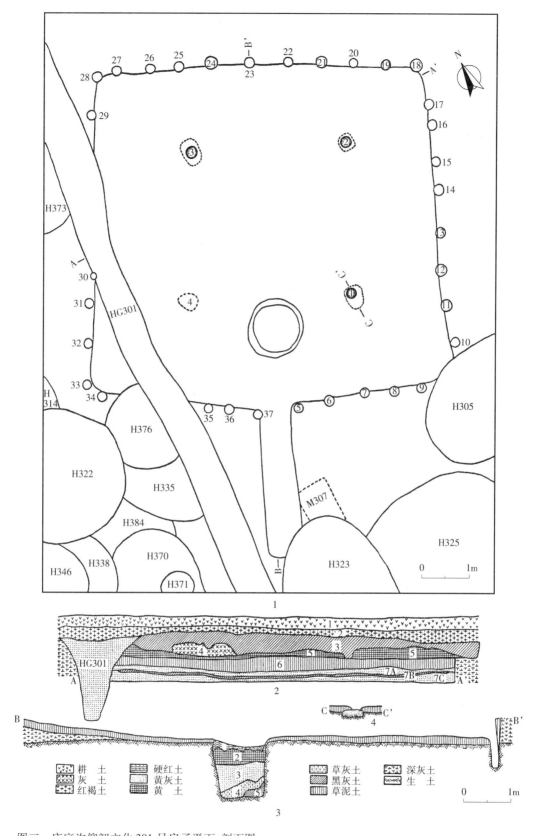

图三　庙底沟仰韶文化 301 号房子平面、剖面图

Fig. 3　Plan and cross-section of house F301 of the Yangshao culture at Miadigou

1. 房子及其与周围遗迹关系平面图（Plan showing the correlation between the house and other features）　2. 房子堆积剖面图（Cross-section of the house deposit）　3. 居住面结构及火塘堆积剖面图（Cross-section of the fireplace deposit and structure of the house floor）　4. 第 1 号柱洞剖面图（Cross-section of No. 1 posthole）

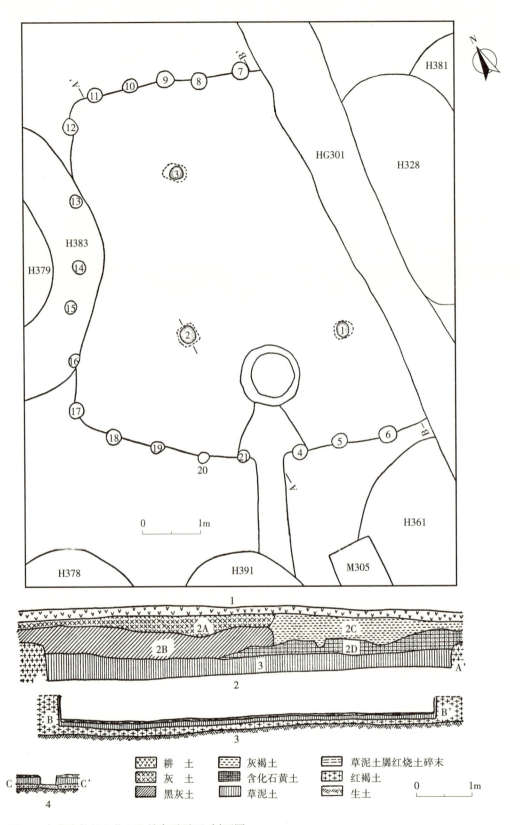

图四 庙底沟仰韶文化 302 号房子平面、剖面图

Fig. 4　Plan and cross-section of house F302 of the Yangshao culture at Miadigou

1. 房子及其与周围遗迹关系平面图（Plan showing the correlation between the house and other features）　2. 房子堆积剖面图（Cross-section of the house deposit）　3. 居住面结构剖面图（Cross-section of structure of the house floor）　4. 第 2 号柱洞剖面图（Cross-section of No. 2 posthole）

图五　庙底沟仰韶文化301号房子复原图

Fig. 5　Artistic reconstruction of house F301 compound of the Yangshao culture at Miaodigou

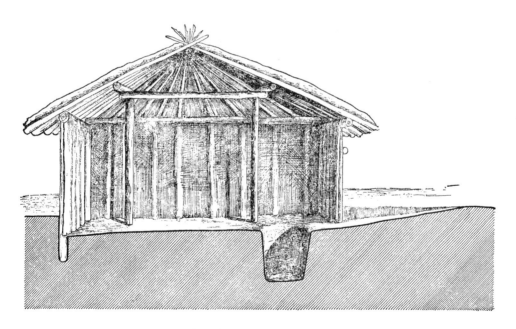

图六　庙底沟仰韶文化301号房子复原半剖图

Fig. 6　Cross-section of artistic reconstruction of house F301 compound of the Yangshao culture at Miaodigou

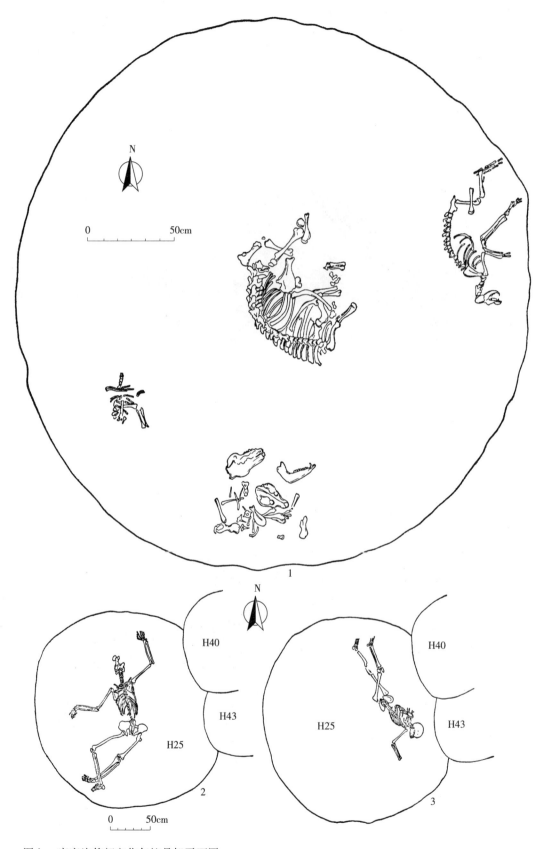

图七　庙底沟仰韶文化灰坑骨架平面图

Fig. 7　Plan of pits with skeletons of the Yangshao culture at Miaodigou.

1. 灰坑22（Ash pit H22）　2、3. 灰坑25（Ash pit H25）

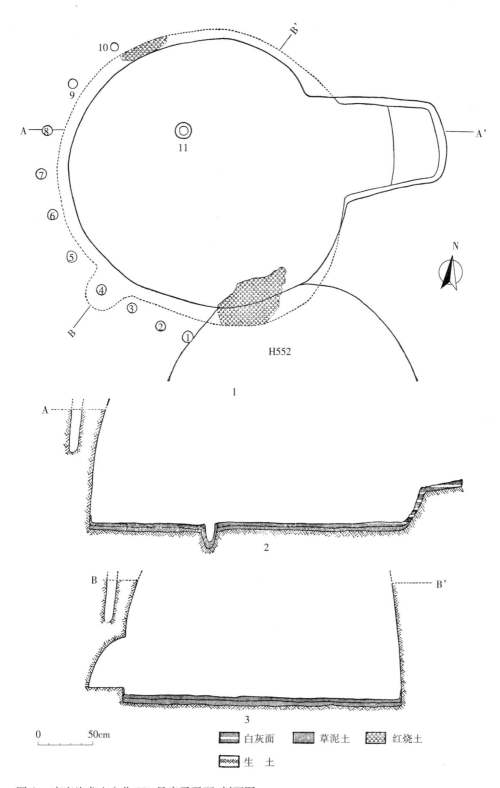

图八　庙底沟龙山文化 551 号房子平面、剖面图

Fig. 8　Plan and cross-section of house F551 of the Longshan culture at Miaodigou

1. 房子及其与周围遗迹关系平面图（Plan showing the correlation between the house and other features）　2、3.
居住面结构及柱洞剖面图（Cross-section of structure of the house floor and the attached postholes）

图例：白灰面　草泥土　红烧土　生　土

图九　庙底沟龙山文化 551 号房子复原图

Fig. 9　Artistic reconstruction of house F551 compound of the Longshan culture at Miaodigou

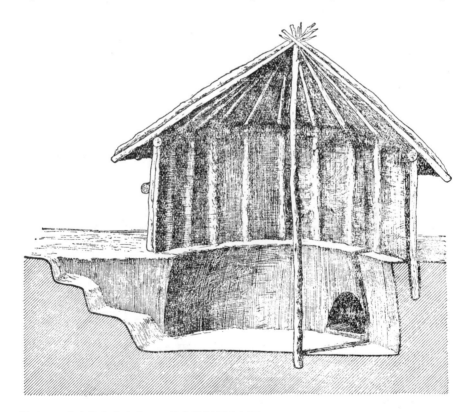

图一〇　庙底沟龙山文化 551 号房子复原半剖图

Fig. 10　Cross-section of artistic reconstruction of house F551 compound of the Longshan culture at Miaodigou

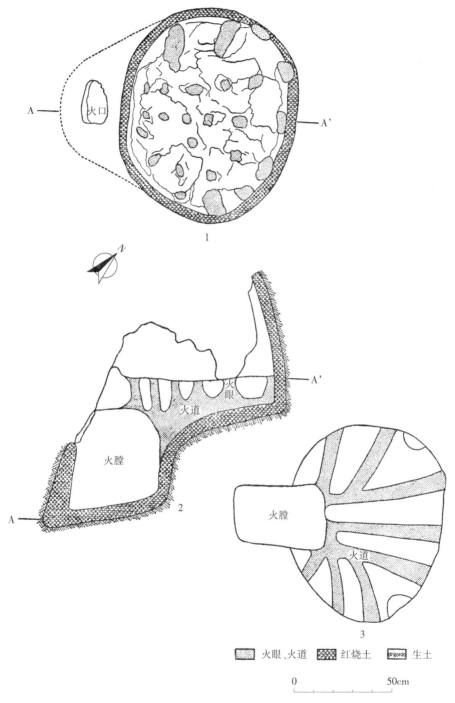

火口

火眼
火道

火膛

火膛
火道

1

2

3

火眼、火道　　红烧土　　生土

0　　　　　　　50cm

图一一　庙底沟龙山文化 1 号窑平面、剖面图

Fig. 11　Plan and cross-section of pottery kiln Y1 of the Longshan culture at Miaodigou

1. 窑箅平面图(Plan of the pottery kiln grid)　2. 窑内结构剖面图(Cross-section of the structure inside
the pottery kiln chamber)　3. 火道平面图(Plan of the firing tunnel)

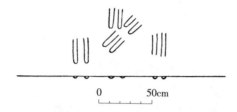

0
50cm

图一二　庙底沟龙山文化灰沟 553 木耒痕迹

Fig. 12　Traces of the wooden *lei* shovel on the north wall of HG553 of the Longshan culture at Miaodigou

N
F301
H323
0
50cm

图一三　庙底沟仰韶文化 307 号墓平面图

Fig. 13　Plan of tomb M307 of the Yangshao culture at Miaodigou

N
0
50cm

图一四　庙底沟龙山文化 99 号墓平面图

Fig. 14　Plan of tomb M99 of the Longshan culture at Miaodigou

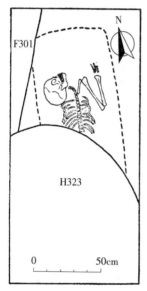

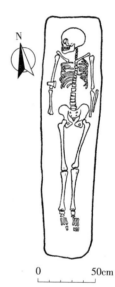

图一五　庙底沟仰韶文化彩陶盆口沿与腹部图案展开图

Fig. 15　Motifs on the main body and along the rim of painted pottery basins of the
　　　　　Yangshao culture from Miaodigou

图一六　庙底沟仰韶文化彩陶盆腹部图案展开图

Fig. 16　Motifs on the main body of painted pottery basins of the Yangshao culture from Miaodigou

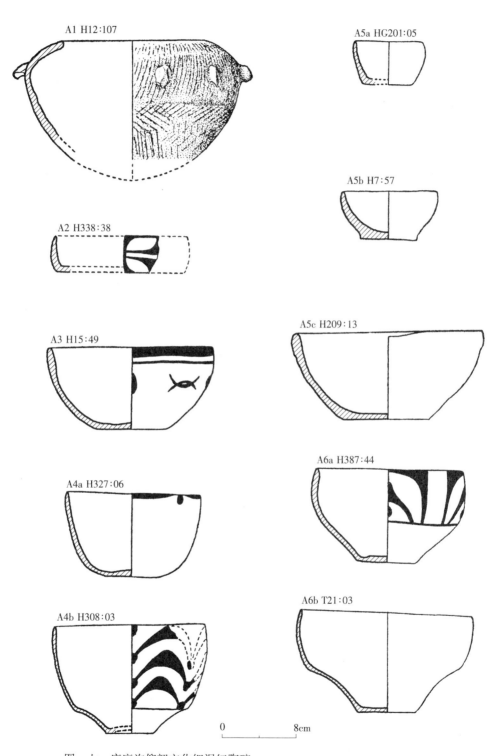

A1 H12:107

A5a HG201:05

A5b H7:57

A2 H338:38

A5c H209:13

A3 H15:49

A6a H387:44

A4a H327:06

A6b T21:03

A4b H308:03

0   8cm

图一七　庙底沟仰韶文化细泥红陶碗

Fig. 17　Fine red bowls of the Yangshao culture from Miaodigou

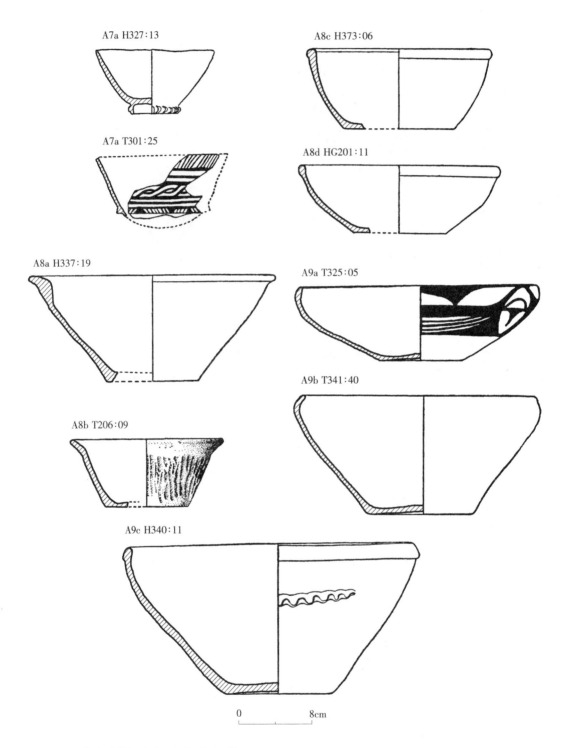

A7a H327:13

A8c H373:06

A7a T301:25

A8d HG201:11

A8a H337:19

A9a T325:05

A9b T341:40

A8b T206:09

A9c H340:11

0　　　　　　8cm

图一八　庙底沟仰韶文化细泥红陶碗、盆

Fig. 18　Fine red bowls and basins of the Yangshao culture from Miaodigou

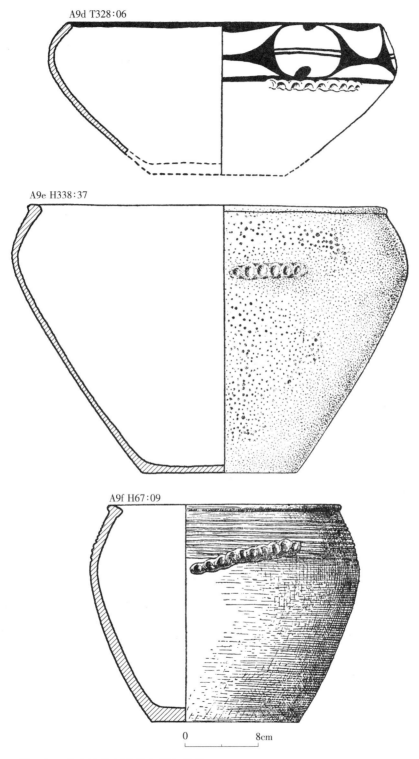

图一九　庙底沟仰韶文化细泥红陶盆

Fig. 19　Fine red basins of the Yangshao culture from Miaodigou

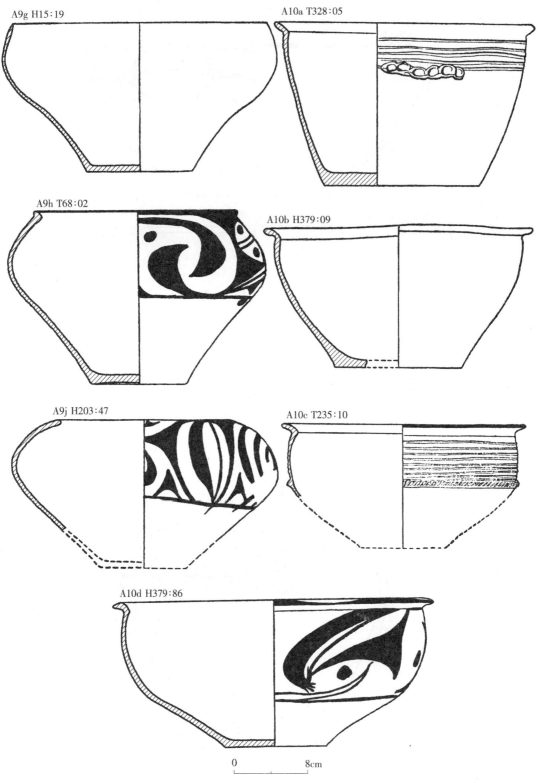

A9g H15:19
A10a T328:05
A9h T68:02
A10b H379:09
A9j H203:47
A10c T235:10
A10d H379:86

0   8cm

图二〇　庙底沟仰韶文化细泥红陶盆

Fig. 20　Fine red basins of the Yangshao culture from Miaodigou

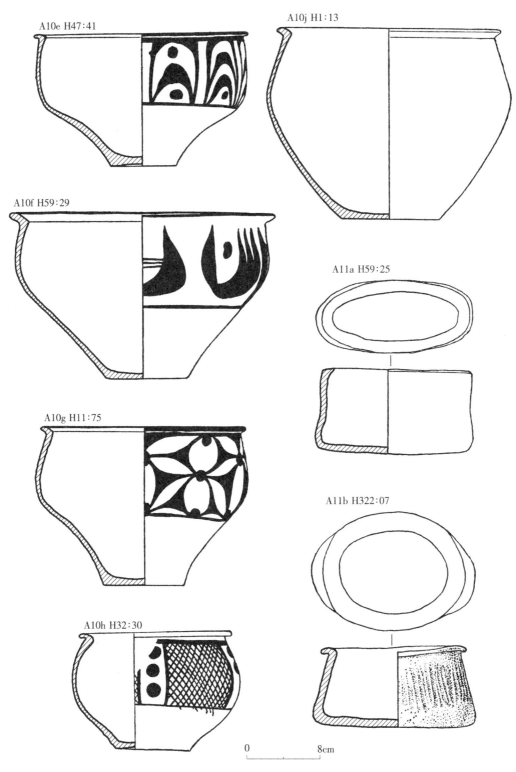

图二一　庙底沟仰韶文化细泥红陶盆

Fig. 21　Fine red basins of the Yangshao culture from Miaodigou

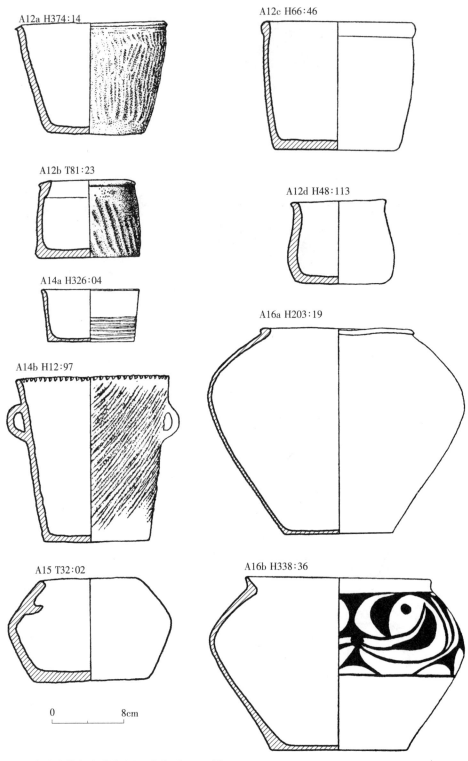

A12a H374:14

A12c H66:46

A12b T81:23

A12d H48:113

A14a H326:04

A16a H203:19

A14b H12:97

A15 T32:02

A16b H338:36

0   8cm

图二二　庙底沟仰韶文化细泥红陶盆、杯、盂、罐

Fig. 22　Fine red basins, cups, *yu* basins, and jars of the Yangshao culture from Miaodigou

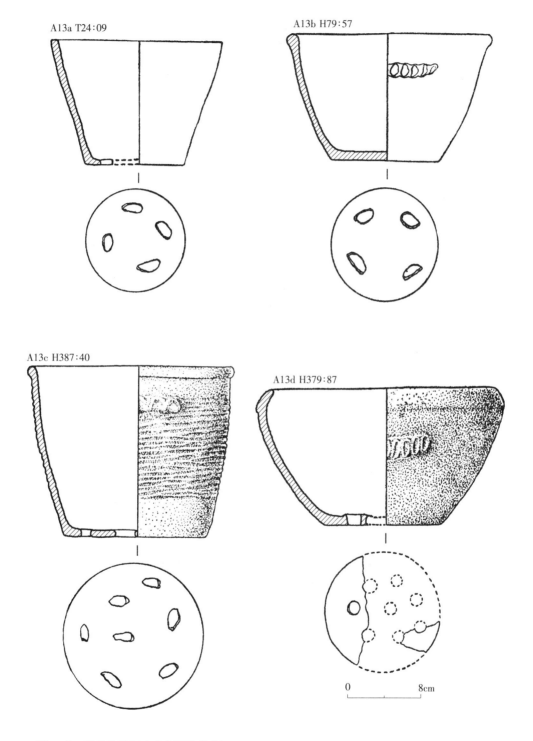

图二三　庙底沟仰韶文化细泥红陶甑

Fig. 23　Fine red *zeng* steamers of the Yangshao culture from Miaodigou

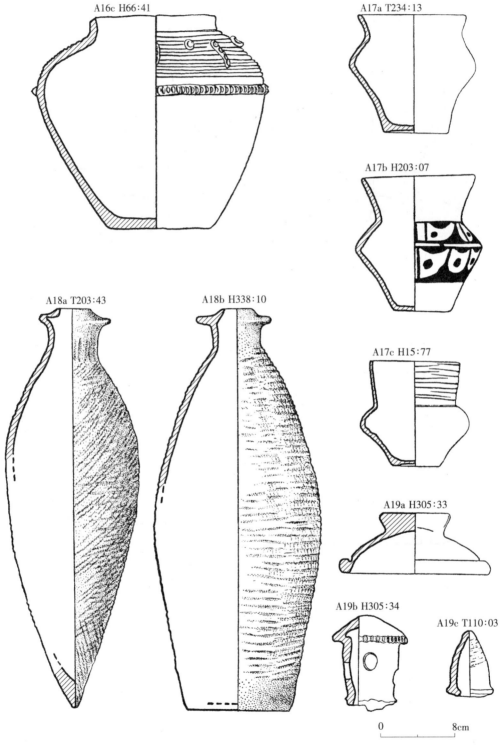

A16c H66:41

A17a T234:13

A17b H203:07

A17c H15:77

A18a T203:43

A18b H338:10

A19a H305:33

A19b H305:34

A19c T110:03

0   8cm

图二四　庙底沟仰韶文化细泥红陶罐、瓶、器盖

Fig. 24　Fine red jars, bottles, and vessel covers of the Yangshao culture from Miaodigou

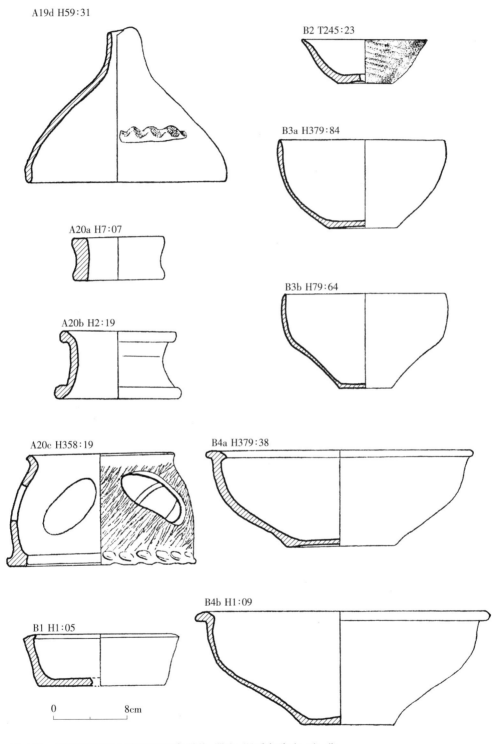

图二五 庙底沟仰韶文化细泥红陶器盖、器座,泥质灰陶盘、碗、盆

Fig. 25 Fine red vessel covers and vessel stands and fine grey plates, bowls, and basins of the Yangshao culture from Miaodigou

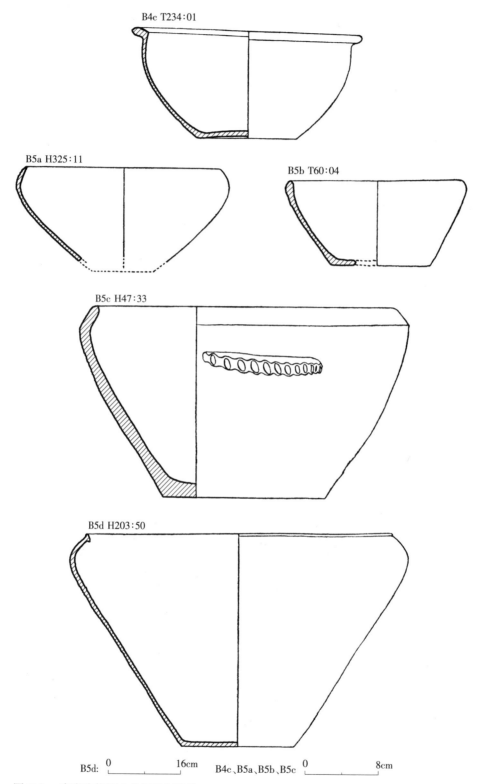

B4c T234：01

B5a H325：11

B5b T60：04

B5c H47：33

B5d H203：50

B5d: 0   16cm   B4c、B5a、B5b、B5c   0   8cm

图二六 庙底沟仰韶文化泥质灰陶盆

Fig. 26 Grey basins of the Yangshao culture from Miaodigou

B6a H52:10

B6b T315:07

B6c T143:06

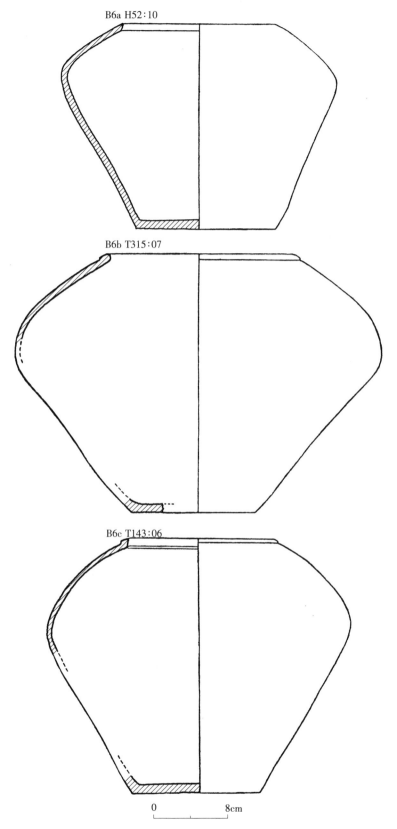

0   8cm

图二七　庙底沟仰韶文化泥质灰陶罐

Fig. 27　Grey jars of the Yangshao culture from Miaodigou

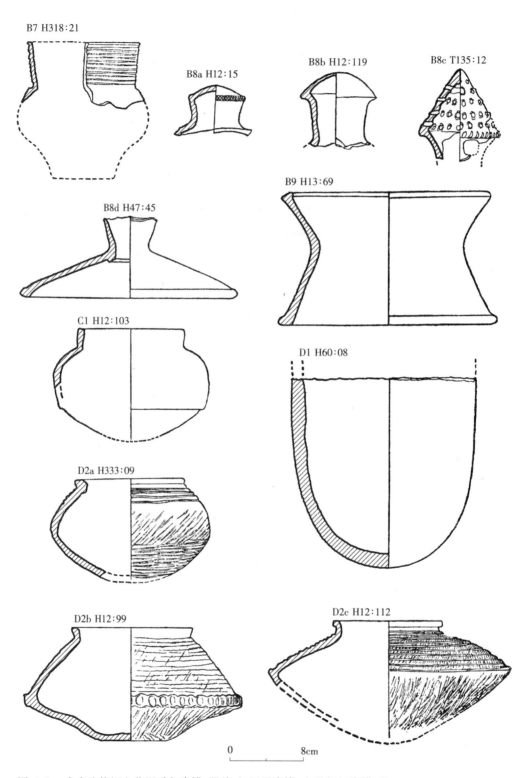

图二八　庙底沟仰韶文化泥质灰陶罐、器盖，细泥黑陶罐，夹砂粗红陶罐、釜

Fig. 28　Grey jar and vessel covers, fine black jars, and coarse, sand-tempered red jars and *fu* cauldrons of the Yangshao culture from Miaodigou

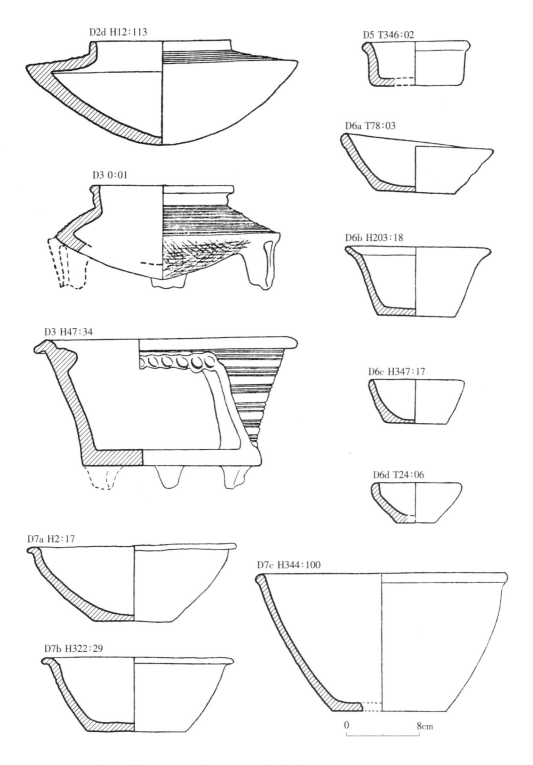

图二九　庙底沟仰韶文化夹砂粗红陶釜、鼎、灶、盘、碗、盆

Fig. 29　Coarse, sand-tempered red *fu* cauldons, *ding* tripod, *zao* stove, plate, bowls, and basins of the Yangshao culture from Miaodigou

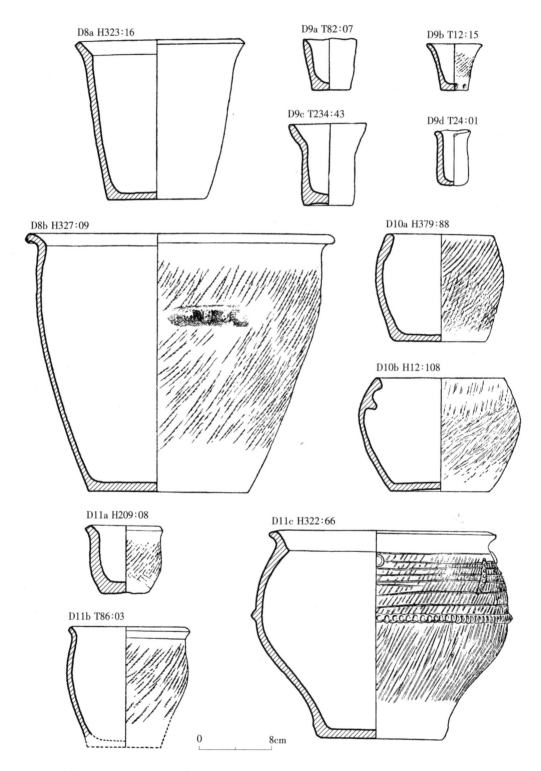

图三〇　庙底沟仰韶文化夹砂粗红陶盆、杯、盂

Fig. 30　Coarse, sand-tempered red basins, cups, and *yu* basins of the Yangshao culture from Miaodigou

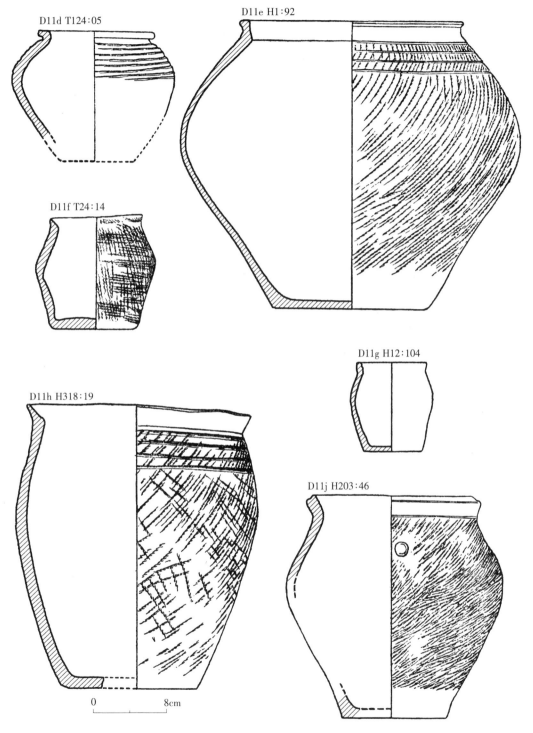

图三一 庙底沟仰韶文化夹砂粗红陶罐

Fig. 31 Coarse, sand-tempered red jars of the Yangshao culture from Miaodigou

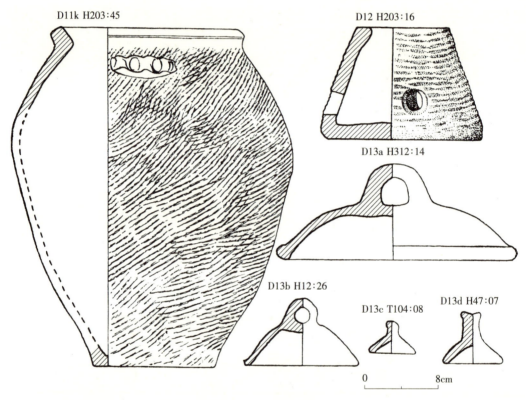

图三二 庙底沟仰韶文化夹砂粗红陶罐、器盖

Fig. 32 Coarse, sand-tempered red jars and vessel covers of the Yangshao culture from Miaodigou

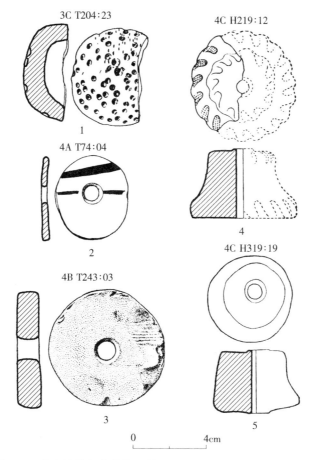

图三三　庙底沟仰韶文化陶工具

Fig. 33　Pottery implements of the Yangshao culture from Miaodigou
　　　　　1. 3C 瓶(Pitted tool)　2 - 5. 纺轮(Spindle whorles)

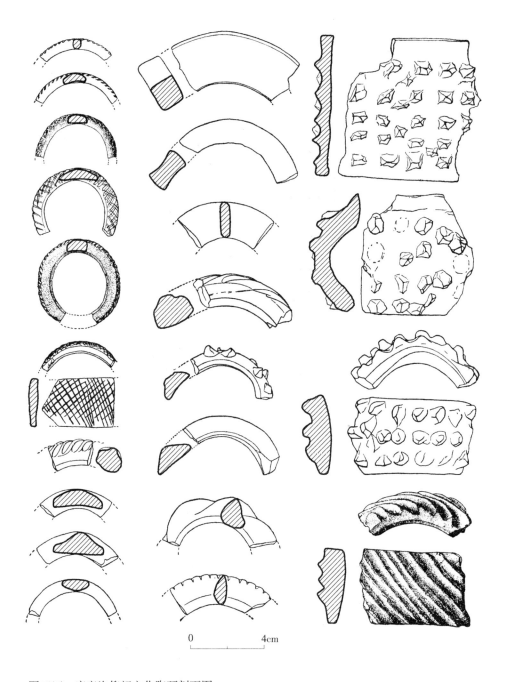

0   4cm

图三四　庙底沟仰韶文化陶环剖面图

Fig. 34　Cross-section of pottery rings of the Yangshao culture from Miaodigou

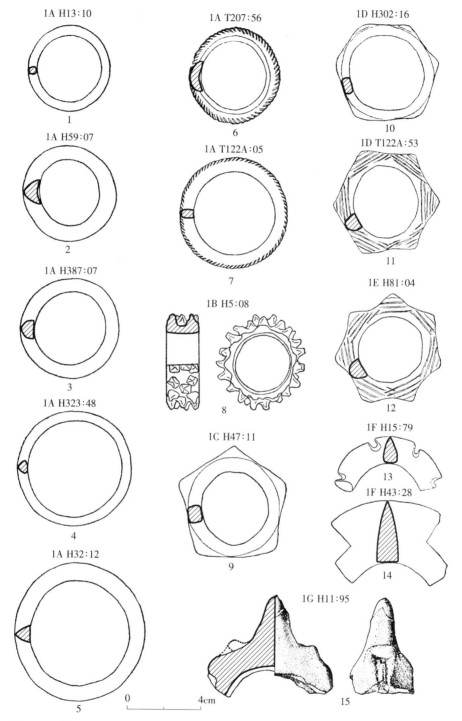

1A H13:10
1
1A H59:07
2
1A H387:07
3
1A H323:48
4
1A H32:12
5
1A T207:56
6
1A T122A:05
7
1B H5:08
8
1C H47:11
9
1D H302:16
10
1D T122A:53
11
1E H81:04
12
1F H15:79
13
1F H43:28
14
1G H11:95
15

0   4cm

图三五 庙底沟仰韶文化陶环

Fig. 35 Pottery rings of the Yangshao culture from Miaodigou

1 – 7. 1A 环(Rings) 8. 1B 环(Ring) 9. 1C 环(Ring) 10、11. 1D 环(Rings) 12. 1E 环（Ring） 13、14. 1F 环(Rings) 15. 1G 环(Ring)

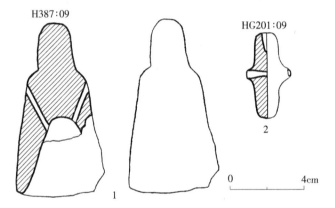

图三六　庙底沟仰韶文化陶玩具

Fig. 36　Pottery toys of the Yangshao culture from Miaodigou

1. 钟(Bell)　2. 坠形器(Pendant)

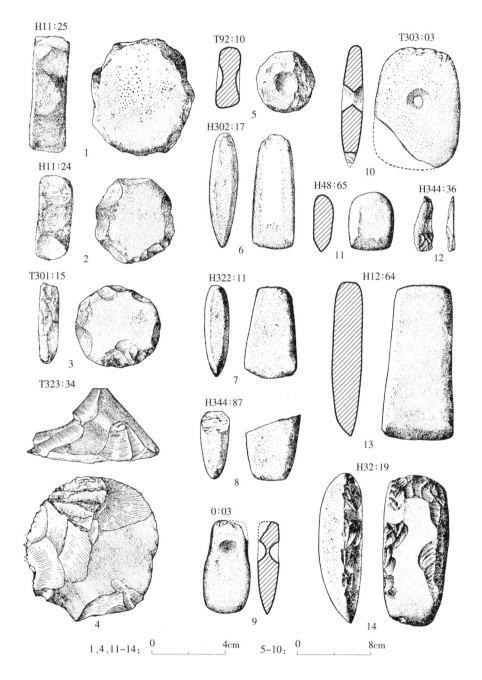

H11:25
T92:10
T303:03
5
H302:17
H11:24
1
H48:65
H344:36
2
11
12
T301:15
H322:11
H12:64
3
7
T323:34
H344:87
13
8
H32:19
0:03
4
9
14

1、4、11-14: 0 _____ 4cm   5-10: 0 _____ 8cm

图三七　庙底沟仰韶文化石器

Fig. 37 Stone implements of the Yangshao culture from Miaodigou

1、5. 1A 盘状器(Disc-shaped tools)　2. 1B 盘状器(Disc-shaped tool)　3. 1C 盘状器(Disc-shaped tool)　4. 1D 盘状器(Disc-shaped tool)　6. 6A 斧(Axe)　7. 6B 斧(Axe)　8. 6C 斧(Axe)　9. 6D 斧(Axe)　10. 6E 斧(Axe)　11. 6F 斧(Axe)　12. 小石片(Stone flake)　13. 7A 锛(Adze)　14. 7B 锛(Adze)

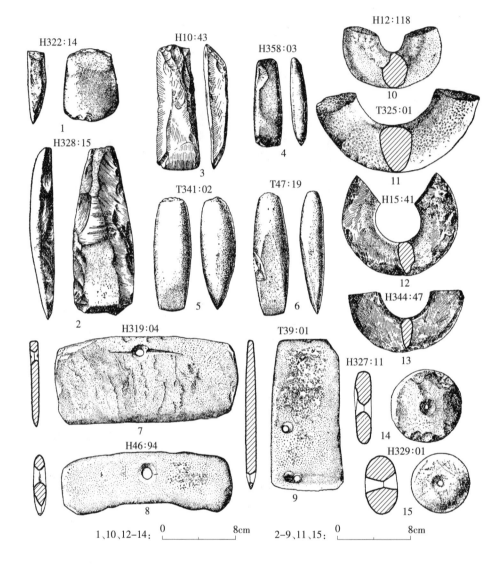

图三八　庙底沟仰韶文化石器

Fig. 38　Stone artifacts of the Yangshao culture from Miaodigou

1. 7C 锛(Adze)　2. 7D 锛(Adze)　3. 8A 凿(Chisel)　4. 8B 凿(Chisel)　5、6. 8C 凿(Chisels)

7. 3C 刀(Knife)　8. 3D 刀(Knife)　9. 3H 刀(Knife)　10. 5A 锤(Hammer)　11. 5B 锤(Hammer)

12. 5C 锤(Hammer)　13. 5D 锤(Hammer)　14. 纺轮(Spindle whorl)　15. 珠(Bead)

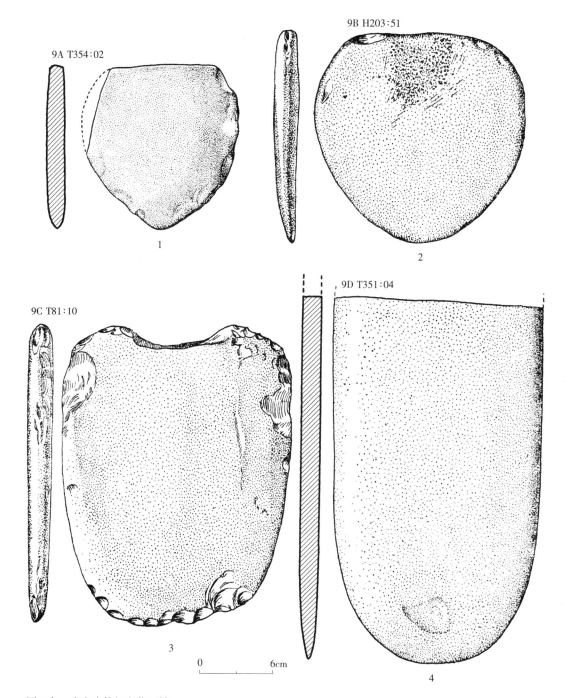

9A T354：02

9B H203：51

9C T81：10

9D T351：04

0   6cm

1

2

3

4

图三九　庙底沟仰韶文化石铲

Fig. 39　Stone spades of the Yangshao culture from Miaodigou

1. 9A 铲（Spade）　2. 9B 铲（Spade）　3. 9C 铲（Spade）　4. 9D 铲（Spade）

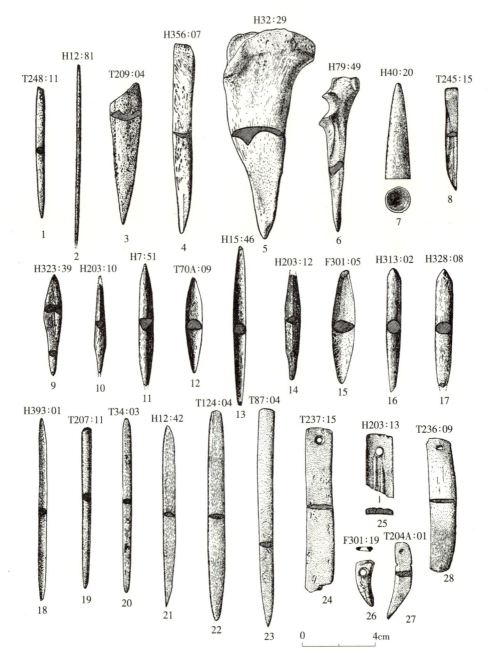

图四〇　庙底沟仰韶文化骨器

Fig. 40　Bone artifacts of the Yangshao culture from Miaodigou

1. 1A 针 (Needle)　2. 1B 针 (Needle)　3、4. 2A 锥 (Awls)　5. 2B 锥 (Awl)　6. 2C 锥 (Awl)　7. 尖状器 (Pointed implement)　8. 凿 (Chisel)　9. 3A 镞 (Arrowhead)　10、11. 3B 镞 (Arrowheads)　12、13. 3C 镞 (Arrowheads)　14、15. 3D 镞 (Arrowheads)　16. 3E 镞 (Arrowhead)　17. 3F 镞 (Arrowhead)　18. 6A 笄 (Hairpin)　19. 6B 笄 (Hairpin)　20. 6C 笄 (Hairpin)　21. 6D 笄 (Hairpin)　22. 6E 笄 (Hairpin)　23. 6F 笄 (Hairpin)　24、25. 7A 弧形饰 (Arc-shaped ornaments)　26、27. 牙形饰 (Tooth-shaped ornaments)　28. 7B 弧形饰 (Arc-shaped ornament)

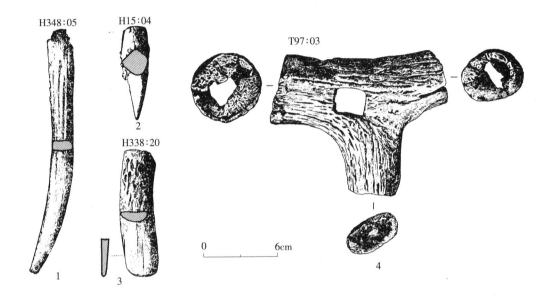

图四一　庙底沟仰韶文化角器

Fig. 41　Antler artifacts of the Yangshao culture from Miaodigou

　　　　1. 1A 锥（Awl）　2. 1B 锥（Awl）　3. 凿（Chisel）　4. 槌（Hammer）

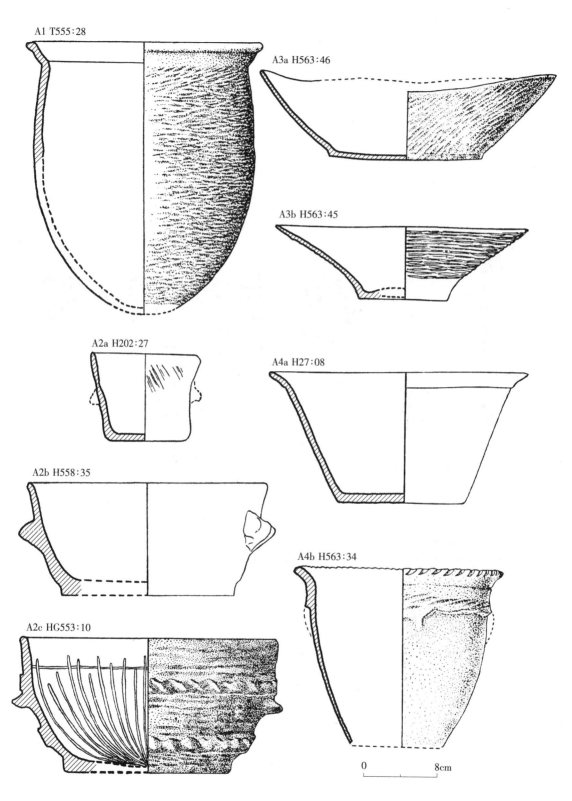

A1 T555：28

A3a H563：46

A3b H563：45

A2a H202：27

A4a H27：08

A2b H558：35

A4b H563：34

A2c HG553：10

0   8cm

图四二　庙底沟龙山文化夹砂粗灰陶罐、盆

Fig. 42　Coarse，sand-tempered grey jars and basins of the Longshan culture from Miaodigou

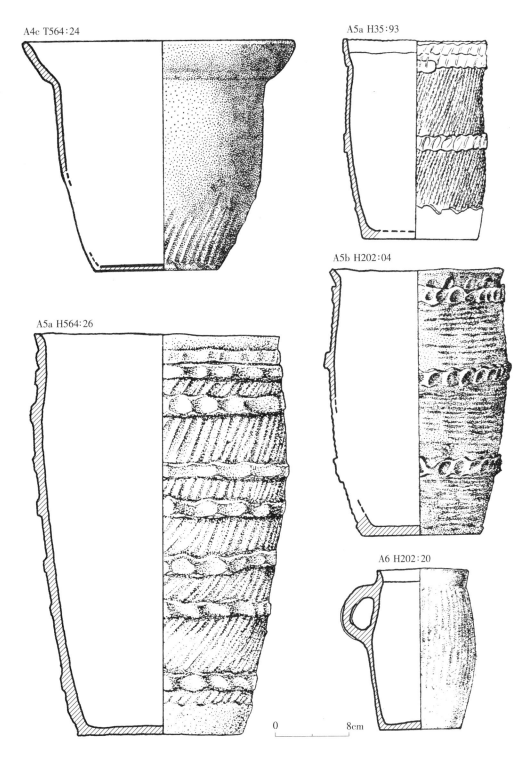

A4c T564:24

A5a H35:93

A5b H202:04

A5a H564:26

A6 H202:20

0   8cm

图四三　庙底沟龙山文化夹砂粗灰陶罐
Fig. 43　Coarse, sand-tempered grey jars of the Longshan culture from Miaodigou

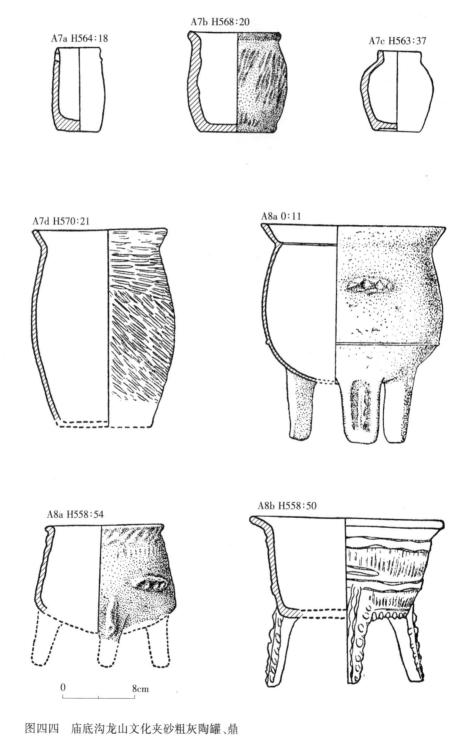

図四四 庙底沟龙山文化夹砂粗灰陶罐、鼎

Fig. 44 Coarse, sand-tempered grey jars and *ding* tripods of the Longshan culture from Miaodigou

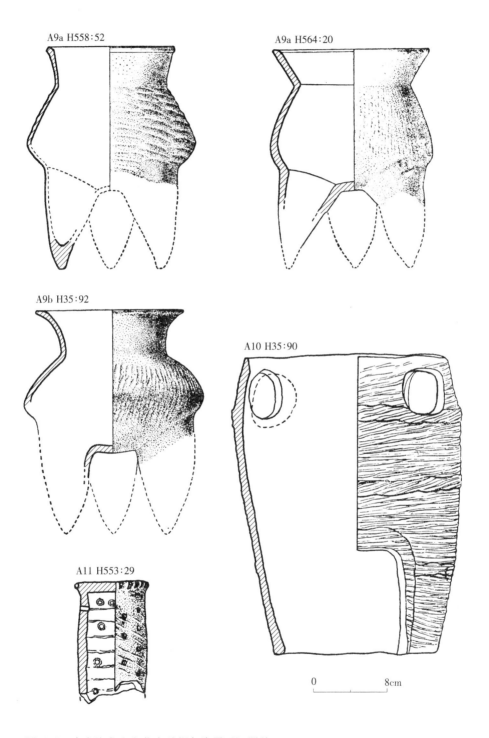

图四五　庙底沟龙山文化夹砂粗灰陶斝、灶、器盖

Fig. 45　Coarse, sand-tempered grey *jia* tripods, *zao* stove, and vessel cover of the Longshan culture from Miaodigou

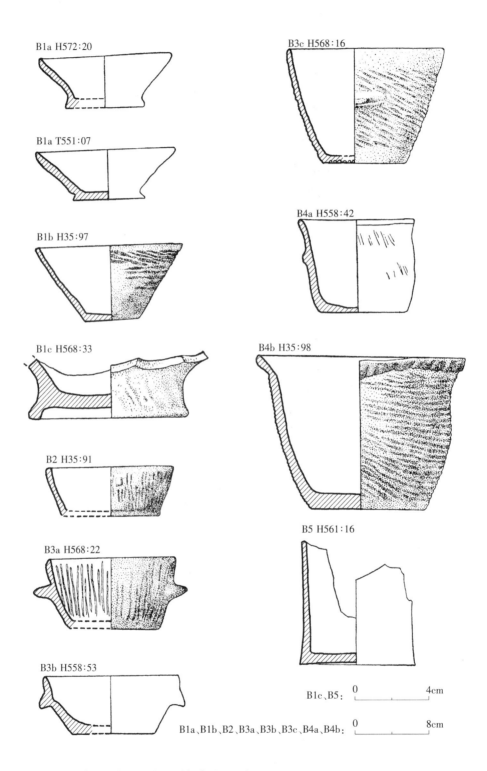

B1a H572:20

B1a T551:07

B1b H35:97

B1c H568:33

B2 H35:91

B3a H568:22

B3b H558:53

B3c H568:16

B4a H558:42

B4b H35:98

B5 H561:16

B1c、B5:　0 ⸺ 4cm

B1a、B1b、B2、B3a、B3b、B3c、B4a、B4b:　0 ⸺ 8cm

图四六　庙底沟龙山文化泥质灰陶碗、盆、杯

Fig. 46　Grey bowls, basins, and cup of the Longshan culture from Miaodigou

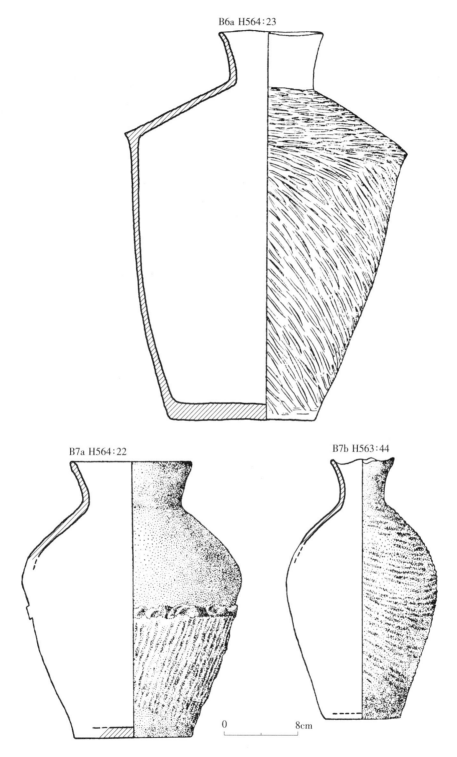

图四七 庙底沟龙山文化泥质灰陶罐

Fig. 47 Grey jars of the Longshan culture from Miaodigou

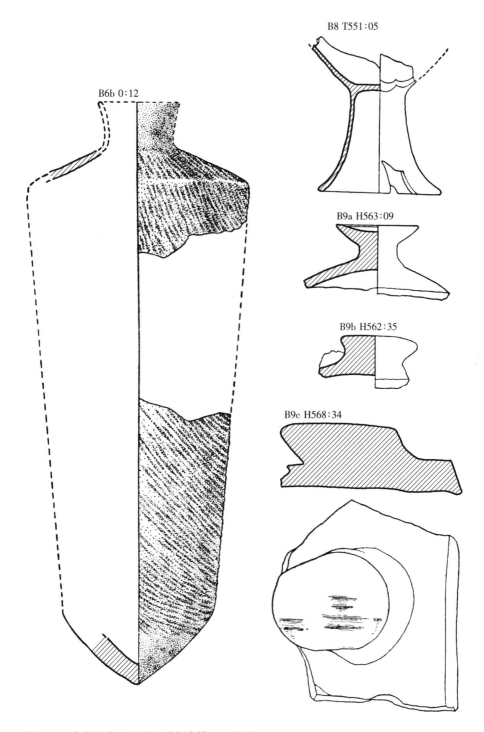

图四八　庙底沟龙山文化泥质灰陶罐、豆、器盖

Fig. 48　Grey jar, *dou* pedestal, and vessel covers of the Longshan culture from Miaodigou

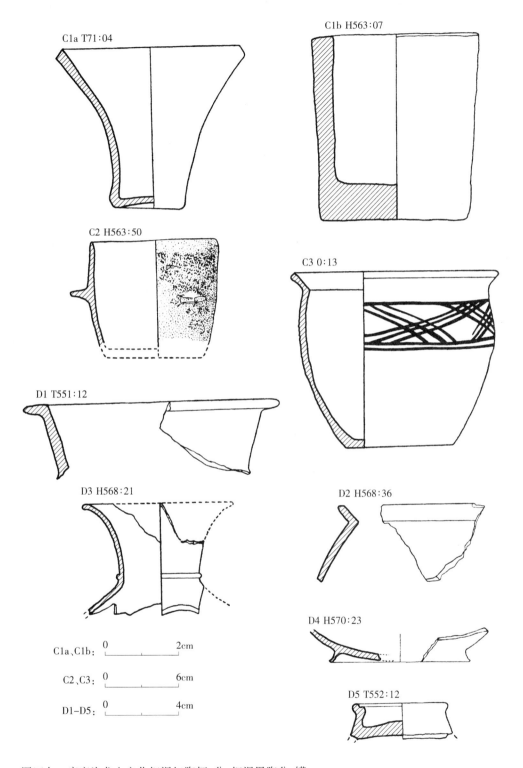

C1a T71:04

C1b H563:07

C2 H563:50

C3 0:13

D1 T551:12

D3 H568:21

D2 H568:36

D4 H570:23

D5 T552:12

C1a、C1b: 0 2cm

C2、C3: 0 6cm

D1–D5: 0 4cm

图四九　庙底沟龙山文化细泥红陶杯、盆，细泥黑陶盆、罐

Fig. 49　Fine red cups and basins and fine black basins and jars of the Longshan culture from Miaodigou

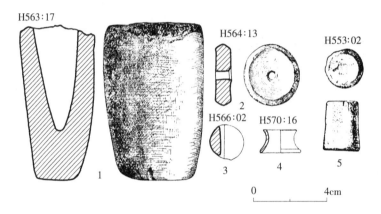

图五〇　庙底沟龙山文化陶器

Fig. 50　Pottery of the Longshan culture from Miaodigou

1. 垫(Anvil)　2. 纺轮(Spindle whorl)　3. 珠(Bead)　4. 管(Tube)

5. 柱状器(Cylindrical object)

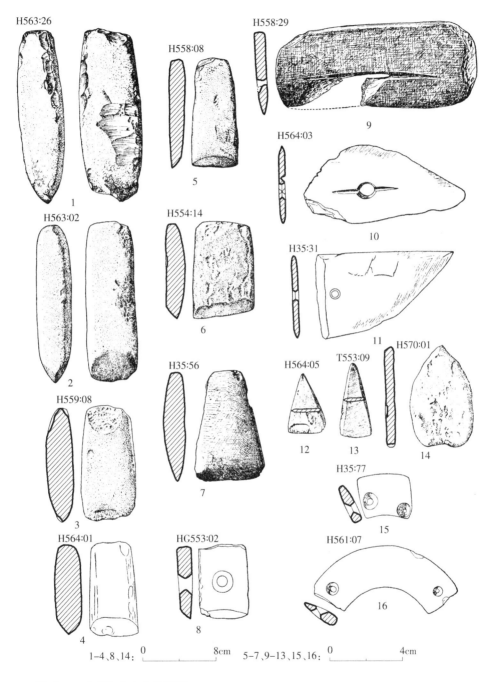

图五一　庙底沟龙山文化石器

Fig. 51　Stone artifacts of the Longshan culture from Miaodigou

1. 1A 斧（Axe）　2. 1B 斧（Axe）　3. 1C 斧（Axe）　4. 1D 斧（Axe）　5. 2A 锛（Adze）
6. 2B 锛（Adze）　7. 2C 锛（Adze）　8. 2D 锛（Adze）　9. 3B 刀（Knife）　10、11. 3C 刀
（Knife）　12、13. 镞（Arrowheads）　14. 叶状石片（Leaf-shaped stone object）　15、16. 石
璜（*Huang* pendants）

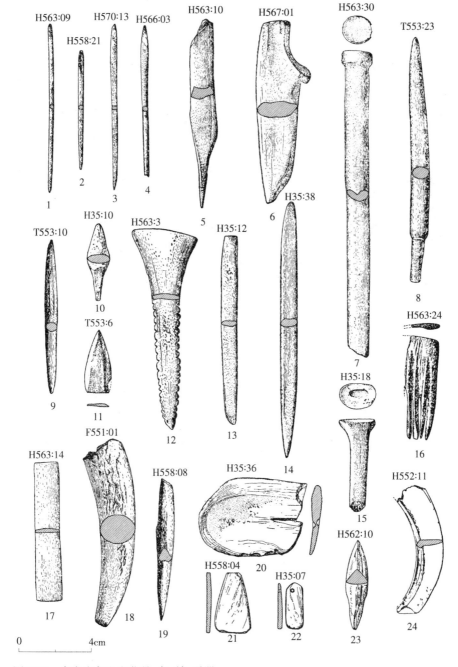

图五二　庙底沟龙山文化骨、角、蚌、牙器

Fig. 52　Bone, antler, shell, and tooth artifacts of the Longshan culture from Miaodigou

1. 1A 骨针（Bone needle）　2. 1B 骨针（Bone needle）　3. 1C 骨针（Bone needle）　4. 1D 骨针（Bone needle）　5. 2A 骨锥（Bone awl）　6. 2B 骨锥（Bone awl）　7. 2C 骨锥（Bone awl）　8. 3D 骨镞（Bone arrowhead）　9. 3A 骨镞（Bone arrowhead）　10. 3B 骨镞（Bone arrowhead）　11. 3C 骨镞（Bone arrowhead）　12. 带锯齿的骨片（Bone artifact with sawteeth）　13. 5A 骨笄（Bone hairpin）　14. 5B 骨笄（Bone hairpin）　15. 5C 骨笄（Bone hairpin）　16. 骨梳（Bone comb）　17. 骨匕（Bone rectangular plate）　18. 角凿（Antler chisel）　19. 角锥（Antler awl）　20. 蚌刀（Shell knife）　21. 蚌镞（Shell arrowhead）　22. 蚌坠（Shell pendant）　23. 牙镞（Tooth arrowhead）　24. 牙片（Treated tooth fragment）

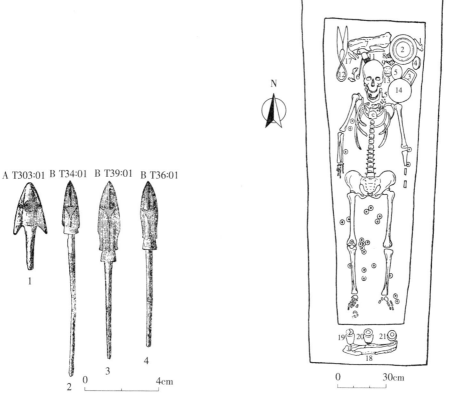

A T303:01   B T34:01   B T39:01   B T36:01

1
2   0   4cm
        3
        4

图五三　庙底沟东周铜镞
Fig. 53　Bronze arrowheads of the
Eastern Zhou from Mi-
aodigou

N

0   30cm

图五四　庙底沟100号唐墓平面图
Fig. 54　Plan of Tang dynasty tomb M100 from Miaodigou
1. 铅人(Lead figurine)　2. 陶罐(Pottery jar)　3.
砚台(Ink slab)　4、5. 瓷碟(Porcelain plates)　6.
铜钗(Bronze hairpin)　7. 漆盒(Lacquered box)
8. 菱形花朵(Hair ornament with mother-of-pearl inlay)　9. 螺钿花钗(Hair ornament with mother-of-
pearl inlay)　10. 银钗(Silver hairpin)　11. 骨梳
(Bone comb)　12. 铁剪(Iron scissors)　13. 玉饰
(Jade ornament)　14. 漆盒(Lacquered box)　15.
项链(Necklace)　16. 鸳鸯形玉饰(Jade mandarin
duck)　17. 铁条(Iron tool)　18. 铁锅(Iron pot)
19、20、21. 陶罐(Pottery jars)

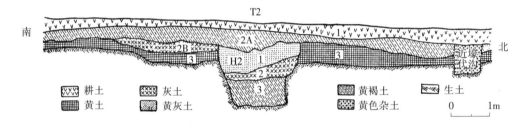

图五五 三里桥探沟 2 西壁剖面图

Fig. 55 Cross-section of the west wall of excavation pit T2 at Sanliqiao

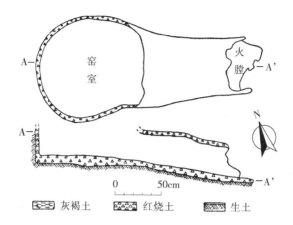

图五六 三里桥仰韶文化301号窑平面、剖面图

Fig. 56 Plan and cross-section of pottery kiln Y301 of the Yangshao culture at Sanliqiao

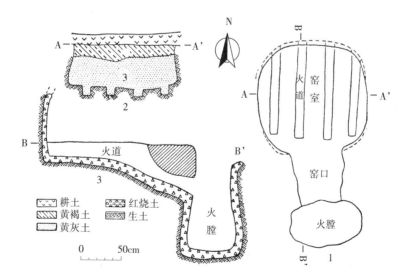

图五七 三里桥龙山文化4号窑平面、剖面图

Fig. 57 Plan and cross-section of pottery kiln Y4 of the Longshan culture
at Sanliqiao

1、3. 窑内结构平面及剖面图(Plan and cross-section of structure of the kiln)

2. 窑内堆积剖面图(Cross-section of deposit in the kiln)

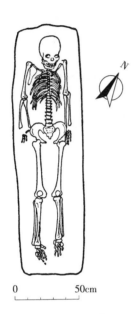

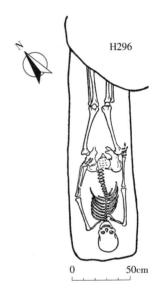

图五八 三里桥仰韶文化 107
号墓平面图

Fig. 58 Plan of tomb M107 of
the Yangshao culture at
Sanliqiao

图五九 三里桥龙山文化 108
号墓平面图

Fig. 59 Plan of tomb M108 of
the Longshan culture at
Sanliqiao

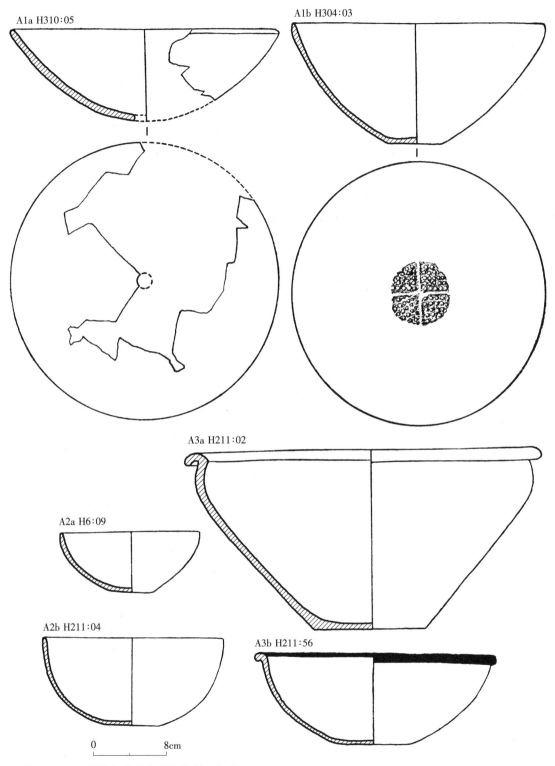

A1a H310:05

A1b H304:03

A3a H211:02

A2a H6:09

A2b H211:04

A3b H211:56

0　　　　8cm

图六〇　三里桥仰韶文化细泥红陶钵、碗、盆

Fig. 60　Fine red *bo* bowls, bowls, and basins of the Yangshao culture from Sanliqiao

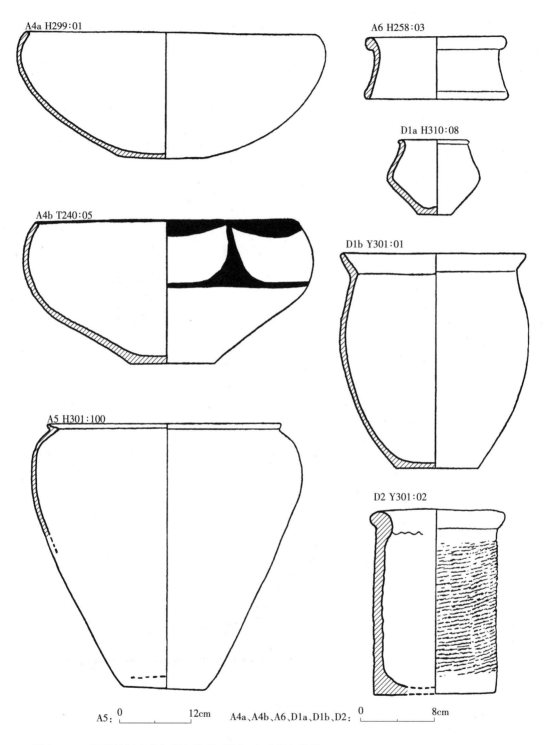

A4a H299：01

A6 H258：03

D1a H310：08

A4b T240：05

D1b Y301：01

A5 H301：100

D2 Y301：02

A5： 0 ⊢——————————⊣ 12cm　　A4a、A4b、A6、D1a、D1b、D2： 0 ⊢——————————⊣ 8cm

图六一　三里桥仰韶文化细泥红陶盆、器座，夹砂粗红陶罐

Fig. 61　Fine red basins and vessel stand and coarse, sand-tempered red jars of the Yangshao culture from Sanliqiao

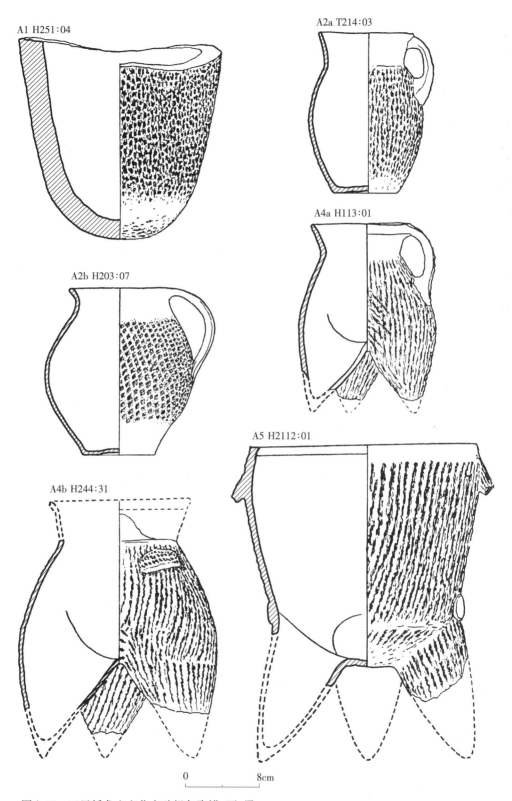

A1 H251:04

A2a T214:03

A2b H203:07

A4a H113:01

A4b H244:31

A5 H2112:01

0   8cm

图六二 三里桥龙山文化夹砂粗灰陶罐、鬲、斝

Fig. 62　Coarse, sand-tempered grey jar, *li* tripods, and *jia* tripod of the Longshan culture from Sanliqiao

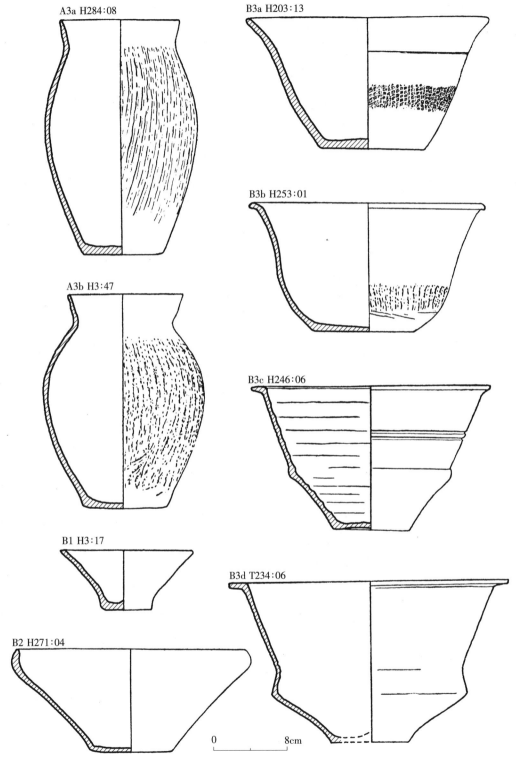

图六三　三里桥龙山文化夹砂粗灰陶罐,泥质灰陶碗、盆

Fig. 63　Coarse, sand-tempered grey jars and grey bowls and basins of the Longshan culture from Sanliqiao

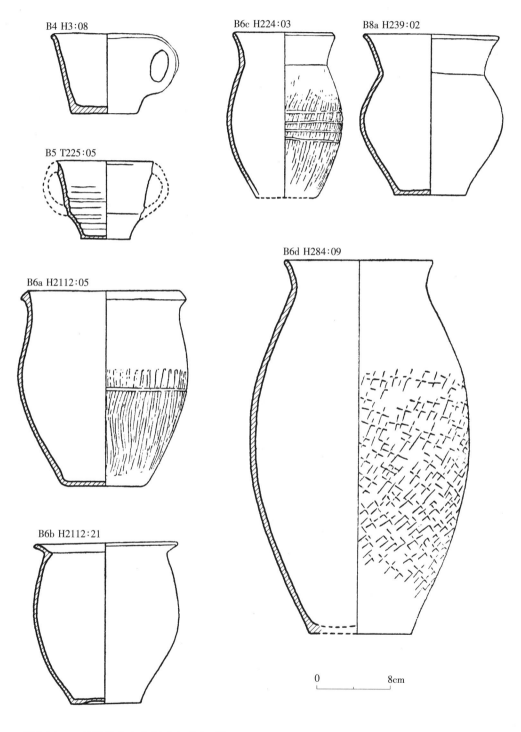

图六四　三里桥龙山文化泥质灰陶杯、罐

Fig. 64　Grey cups and jars of the Longshan culture from Sanliqiao

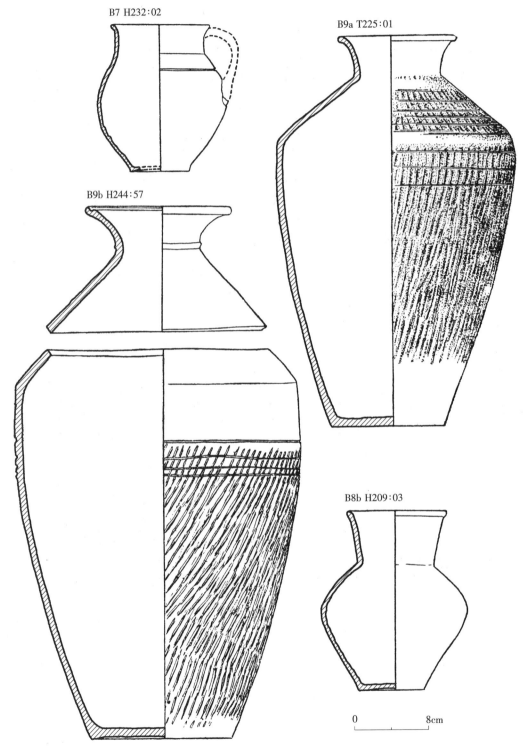

图六五　三里桥龙山文化泥质灰陶罐

Fig. 65　Grey jars of the Longshan culture from Sanliqiao

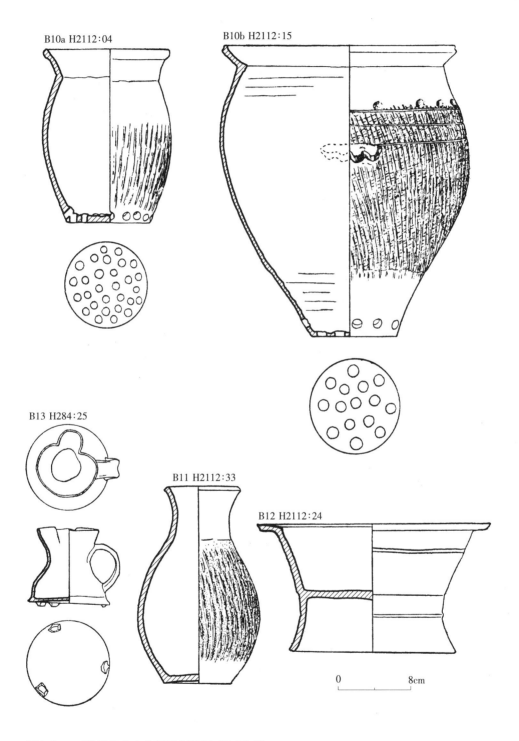

图六六　三里桥龙山文化泥质灰陶甑、瓶、豆、鬹

Fig. 66　Grey *zeng* steamers, vase, *dou* pedestal, and *gui* vessel of the Longshan culture from Sanliqiao

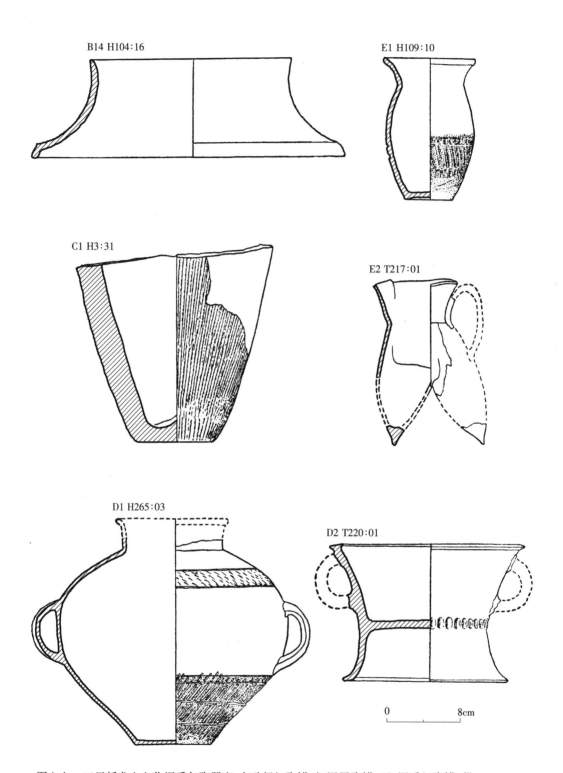

图六七　三里桥龙山文化泥质灰陶器座, 夹砂粗红陶罐, 细泥黑陶罐、豆, 泥质红陶罐、鬶

Fig. 67　Grey vessel stand, coarse, sand-tempered red jar, fine black jar and *dou* pedestal, and red jar and *gui* tripod of the Longshan culture from Sanliqiao

T236:06

图六八 "安邑二鈝"拓片
Fig. 68 Rubbing of bronze
coin "*Anyi Erjin*"

图版 Plates

1. 庙底沟 T1 区工作情况(Work at area T1 of Miaodigou)

2. 庙底沟 T1 区龙山墓葬分布情况(Burial distribution of the Longshan culture at area T1 of Miaodigou)

庙底沟 T1 区工作情况及龙山墓葬的分布
Work at area T1 and burial distribution of the Longshan culture at Miaodigou

1. 庙底沟仰韶文化 301 号房子（House F301 of the Yangshao culture at Miaodigou）

2. 庙底沟仰韶文化 302 号房子（House F302 of the Yangshao culture at Miaodigou）

庙底沟仰韶文化房子
Houses of the Yangshao culture at Miaodigou

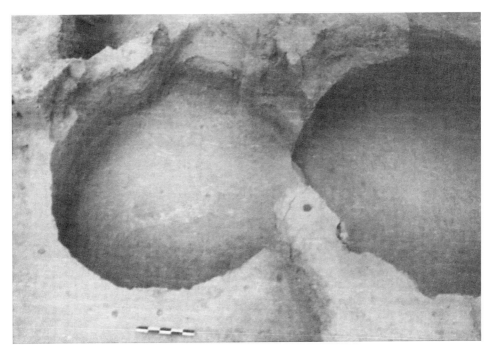

1. 庙底沟龙山文化 551 号房子(House F551 of the Longshan culture at Miaodigou)

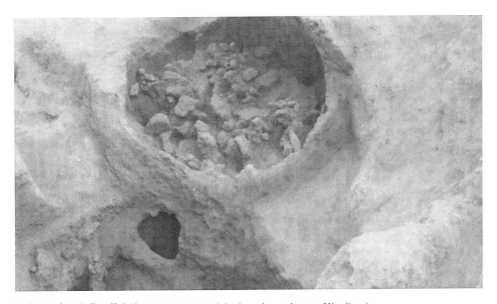

2. 庙底沟龙山文化 1 号窑址(Pottery kiln Y1 of the Longshan culture at Miaodigou)

庙底沟龙山文化房子及窑址
House and pottery kiln of the Longshan culture at Miaodigou

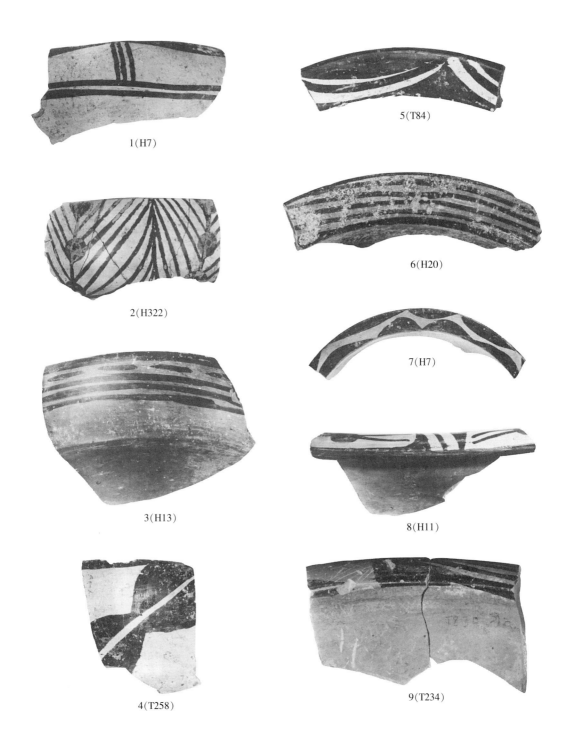

1（H7）

5（T84）

2（H322）

6（H20）

7（H7）

3（H13）

8（H11）

4（T258）

9（T234）

庙底沟仰韶文化彩陶片

Painted potsherds of the Yangshao culture from Miaodigou

1-4. 曲腹碗（Curved-bellied bowls）　5-9. 浅腹盆（Shallow-bellied basins）（1. 2/3 ,2-9. 1/2）

图版伍（Plate V）

1（H72）

6（H481）

2（H346）

7（H48）

3（H72）

8（T70）

4（T244）

9（H322）

5（H48）

10（H318）

庙底沟仰韶文化彩陶片

Painted potsherds of the Yangshao culture from Miaodigou

1-8. 敛口盆（Basins with inward-curved rim）　9、10. 敛口罐（Jars with inward-curved rim）（1、2、8-10. 1/2，3-7. 1/3）

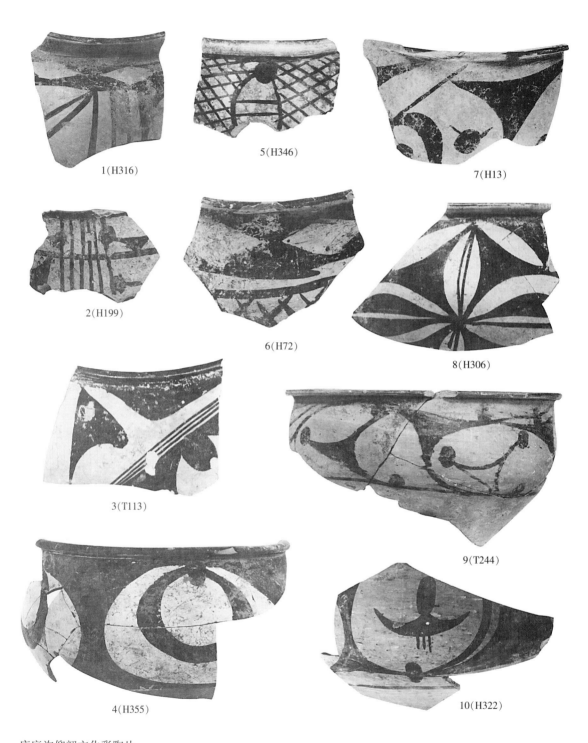

1(H316)

5(H346)

7(H13)

2(H199)

6(H72)

8(H306)

3(T113)

9(T244)

4(H355)

10(H322)

庙底沟仰韶文化彩陶片

Painted potsherds of the Yangshao culture from Miaodigou

1-3. 敛口罐(Jars with inward-curved rim)　4-10. 深腹盆(4 带白衣)(Deep-bellied basins. 4 with white slip)(1、2、5、6. 1/2、3. 1/3、4、7-10. 1/4)

1(H322)

6(T234)

2(H40)

7(H11)

8(H332)

3(H13)

9(T234)

10(H335)

4(H12)

5(H364)

11(T210)

12(H355)

庙底沟仰韶文化彩陶片

Painted potsherds of the Yangshao culture from Miaodigou

1-5. 深腹盆（Deep-bellied basins） 6-8. 敛口罐（Jars with inward-curved rim） 9、11. 小口瓶（带白衣）（Narrow-mouthed bottle (with white slip)） 10、12. 筒形罐（Tubular jars）(1-3. 1/4,4-12. 1/3)

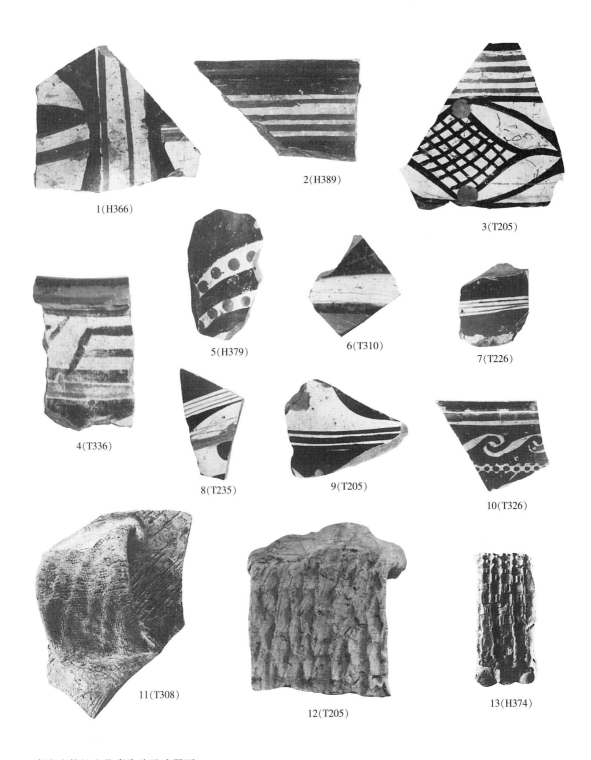

1(H366)

2(H389)

3(T205)

5(H379)

6(T310)

7(T226)

4(T336)

8(T235)

9(T205)

10(T326)

11(T308)

12(T205)

13(H374)

庙底沟仰韶文化彩陶片及残器耳

Painted potsherds and vessel handles of the Yanghshao culture from Miaodigou

1-10. 带白衣彩陶片（红黑彩并用）(Painted potsherds with white slip, contained both red and black patterns)　11-13. 小口瓶器耳（前一种布纹，后二种席纹）(Handles of narrow-mouthed bottle, the first one is woven cloth patterns and the latter two are woven mat patterns) (1、2、4、11、13. 1/2，3. 1/3，5-10、12. 1/1)

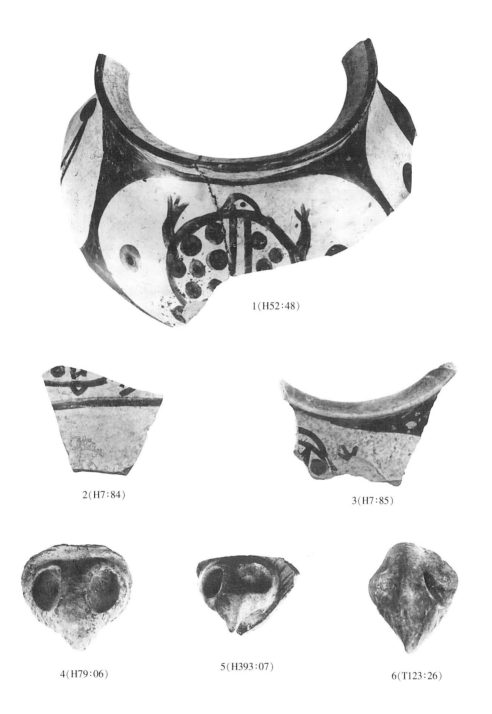

1（H52：48）

2（H7：84）

3（H7：85）

4（H79：06）

5（H393：07）

6（T123：26）

庙底沟仰韶文化彩陶片及残器耳

Painted potsherds and vessel handles of the Yangshao culture from Miaodigou

1-3. 蛙形纹彩陶片（Frog motif on potsherds） 4-6. 鸟头形器耳（Vessel handles in the shape of a bird head）（1. 2/3，4、5. 1/2，2、3、6. 1/1）

1（H12：107）

4（H15：49）

2（H338：38）

5（H59：26）

3（H15：02）

6（H12：100）

7（T235：07）

庙底沟仰韶文化细泥红陶罐、盘、碗
Fine red jar, plate, and bowls of the Yangshao culture from Miaodigou
1. A1 罐（Jar） 2. A2 盘（Plate） 3-7. A3 碗（Bowls）（1、4-7. 1/3、2、3. 1/2）

1(H12:95)

4(T122:20)

2(H371:01)

5(H79:63)

3(H327:06)

6(H308:03)

庙底沟仰韶文化细泥红陶碗

Fine red bowls of the Yangshao culture from Miaodigou

1、2. A3 碗(Bowls) 3-5. A4a 碗(Bowls) 6. A4b 碗(Bowl)(1-3. 1/2,4-6. 1/3)

1（HG201：05）

5（T123：24）

2（T328：08）

3（H11：56）

6（H10：128）

4（T24：16）

7（H10：135）

庙底沟仰韶文化细泥红陶碗

Fine red bowls of the Yangshao culture from Miaodigou

1. A5a 碗（Bowl）　2-7. A3 碗（Bowls）（1-7. 1/2）

1(H206：09)

5(T324：01)

2(H7：57)

6(H59：30)

3(H346：37)

4(H209：13)

7(H305：17)

庙底沟仰韶文化细泥红陶碗

Fine red bowls of the Yangshao culture from Miaodigou

1. A8b 碗（Bowl）　2. A5b 碗（Bowl）　3、4. A5c 碗（Bowls）　5-7. A6a 碗（Bowls）（1、4. 1/3，2、3、5-7. 1/2）

1(T24:12)

5(H7:68)

2(H387:44)

6(H43:47)

3(H43:37)

4(H44:14)

7(H327:05)

庙底沟仰韶文化细泥红陶碗

Fine red bowls of the Yangshao culture from Miaodigou

1-7. A6a 碗（Bowls）（1、4、5、7. 1/2，2、3、6. 1/3）

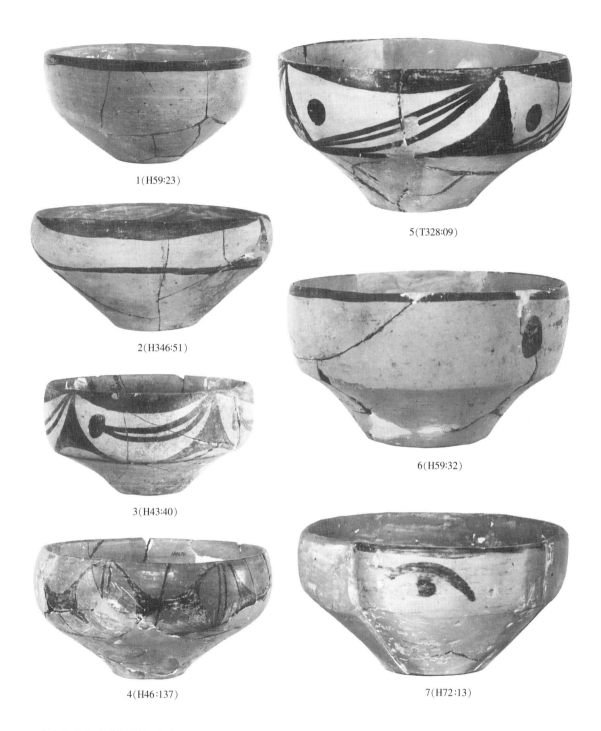

1(H59:23)

5(T328:09)

2(H346:51)

3(H43:40)

6(H59:32)

4(H46:137)

7(H72:13)

庙底沟仰韶文化细泥红陶碗
Fine red bowls of the Yangshao culture from Miaodigou
1、2. A6a 碗(Bowls)　3-7. A6b 碗(Bowls)(1-4. 1/3,5-7. 1/2)

1（H30：07）

5（T122：19）

2（H46：124）

6（H46：127）

3（H10：149）

4（H42：08）

7（H387：48）

庙底沟仰韶文化细泥红陶碗
Fine red bowls of the Yangshao cutlure from Miaodigou
1-7. A6b 碗（Bowls）（1、5.1/3，2-4、6、7.1/2）

1(H10:118)

5(H370:04)

2(H46:133)

3(H79:59)

6(T143:01)

4(H322:07)

7(T315:09)

庙底沟仰韶文化细泥红陶碗
Fine red bowls of the Yangshao culture from Miaodigou
1-7. A6b 碗(Bowls)(1、2、4-6. 1/2、3、7. 1/3)

1（H379：83）

4（T301：25）

2（T21：03）

5（H337：19）

3（H327：13）

6（H66：40）

庙底沟仰韶文化细泥红陶碗、盆

Fine red bowls and basins of the Yangshao culture from Miaodigou

1、2. A6b 碗（Bowls）　3. A7a 碗（Bowl）　4. A7b 碗（Bowl）　5. A8a 盆（Basin）　6. A10d 盆（Basin）（1、2、5. 1/3、3、4. 1/2、6. 1/4）

1(H373:06)

2(HG 201:11)

3(T325:05)

4(H375:08)

5(H10:125)

6(H203:17)

庙底沟仰韶文化细泥红陶盆

Fine red basins of the Yangshao culture from Miaodigou

1. A8c 盆（Basin）　2. A8d（Basin）　3、4. A9a 盆（Basins）　5、6. A9b 盆（Basins）（1-4、6. 1/3、5. 1/4）

1(T341:40)

2(H324:28)

3(T328:06)

4(H340:11)

庙底沟仰韶文化细泥红陶盆

Fine red basins of the Yangshao culture from Miaodigou

1. A9b 盆（Basin）　2、3. A9d 盆（Basins）　4. A9c 盆（Basin）（1、2. 1/3，3、4. 1/4）

1(H338:37)

2(H67:09)

3(H15:19)

4(T68:02)

庙底沟仰韶文化细泥红陶盆

Fine red basins of the Yangshao culture from Miaodigou

1. A9e 盆(Basin)　2. A9f 盆(Basin)　3. A9g 盆(Basin)　4. A9h 盆(Basin)(1. 1/6,2、3. 1/4,4. 1/3)

1（H203：47）

2（T328：05）

3（H379：09）

4（T235：10）

5（H322：18）

庙底沟仰韶文化细泥红陶盆

Fine red basins of the Yangshao culture from Miaodigou

1. A9j 盆（Basin）　2. A10a 盆（Basin）　3. A10b 盆（Basin）　4. A10c 盆（Basin）　5. A10d 盆（Basin）　（1、4、5. 1/3，2、3. 1/4）

1(T235:07)

4(H203:05)

2(H59:28)

5(H47:41)

3(H379:86)

庙底沟仰韶文化细泥红陶盆
Fine red basins of the Yangshao culture from Miaodigou
1-3. A10d 盆(Basins)　4、5. A10e 盆(Basins)(1-3. 1/4, 4、5. 1/3)

1(H338:30)

4(H375:07)

2(H48:107)

5(H46:139)

3(H59:29)

6(H46:125)

庙底沟仰韶文化细泥红陶盆

Fine red basins of the Yangshao culture from Miaodigou

1-4. A10f 盆(Basins)　5、6. A10g 盆(Basins)(1-3. 1/4,4-6. 1/3)

1(H15:51)

4(H47:42)

2(H51:53)

5(H47:41)

3(H11:75)

庙底沟仰韶文化细泥红陶盆
Fine red basins of the Yangshao culture from Miaodigou
1-5. A10g 盆(Basins)(1,3-5.1/3,2.1/4)

1(H46∶129)

2(H322∶84)

庙底沟仰韶文化细泥红陶盆
Fine red basins of the Yangshao culture from Miaodigou
1、2. A10g 盆(Basins)(1、2. 1/4)

1(H10:131)

2(H32:30)

3(H1:13)

4(H59:25)

5(H322:67)

庙底沟仰韶文化细泥红陶盆

Fine red basins of the Yangshao culture at Miaodigou

1. A10g 盆(Basin)　2. A10h 盆(Basin)　3. A10j 盆(Basin)　4. A11a 盆(Basin)　5. A11b 盆(Basin)（1、3.1/4,2、4、5.1/3）

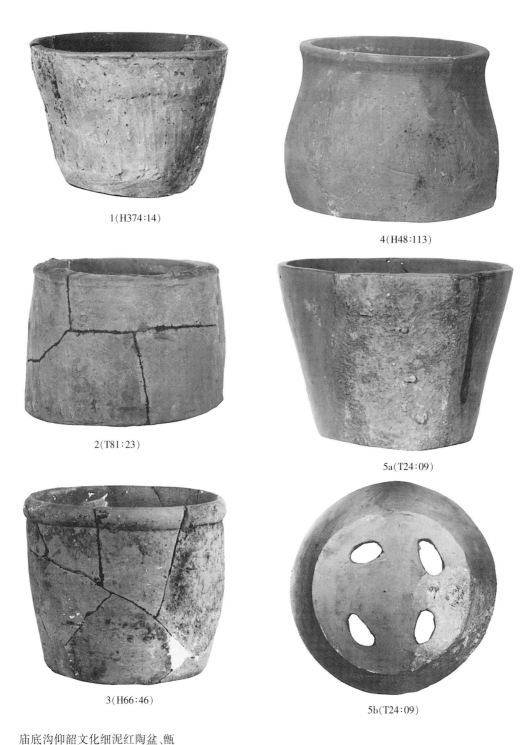

1（H374∶14）

4（H48∶113）

2（T81∶23）

5a（T24∶09）

3（H66∶46）

5b（T24∶09）

庙底沟仰韶文化细泥红陶盆、甑

Fine red basins and *zeng* steamer of the Yangshao culture from Miaodigou

1. A12a 盆（Basin）　2. A12b 盆（Basin）　3. A12c 盆（Basin）　4. A12d 盆（Basin）　5a、b. A13a 甑（*Zeng* steamer）
（1、3、5. 1/3，2、4. 1/2）

1a(H79:57)

1b(H79:57)

2a(H387:40)

2b(H387:40)

庙底沟仰韶文化细泥红陶甑

Fine red *zeng* steamers of the Yangshao culture from Miaodigou

1a、b. A13b 甑（*Zeng* steamer） 2a、b. A13c 甑（*Zeng* steamer）（1、2. 1/3）

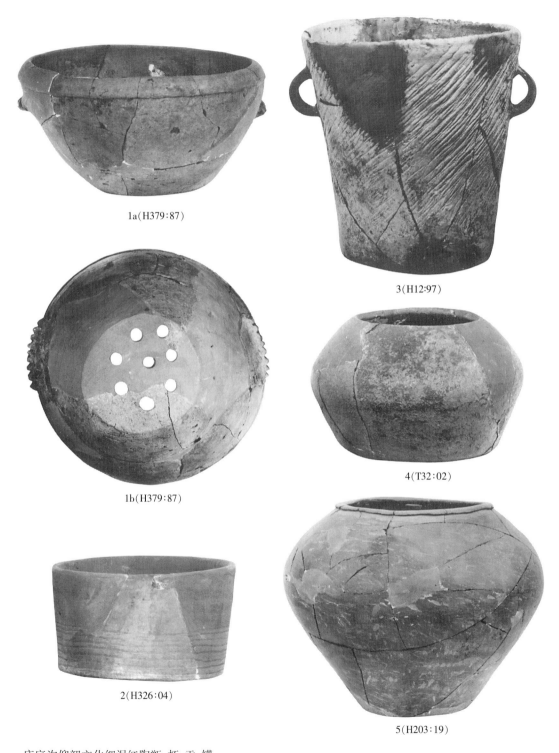

1a(H379：87)

1b(H379：87)

2(H326：04)

3(H12：97)

4(T32：02)

5(H203：19)

庙底沟仰韶文化细泥红陶甑、杯、盂、罐

Fine red *zeng* steamer, cups, *yu* basin, and jar of the Yangshao culture from Miaodigou

1a、b. A13d 甑（*Zeng* steamer） 2. A14a 杯（Cup） 3. A14b 杯（Cup） 4. A15 盂（*Yu* basin） 5. A16a 罐（Jar）（1、3、4. 1/3，2. 1/2，5. 1/4）

1(H338:36)

2(H66:41)

3(H322:105)

4(T234:43)

庙底沟仰韶文化细泥红陶罐
Fine red jars of the Yangshao culture from Miaodigou
1. A16b 罐(Jar)　2、3. A16c 罐(Jars)　4. A17a 罐(jar)(1. 1/3,2. 1/4,3. 1/5,4. 1/2)

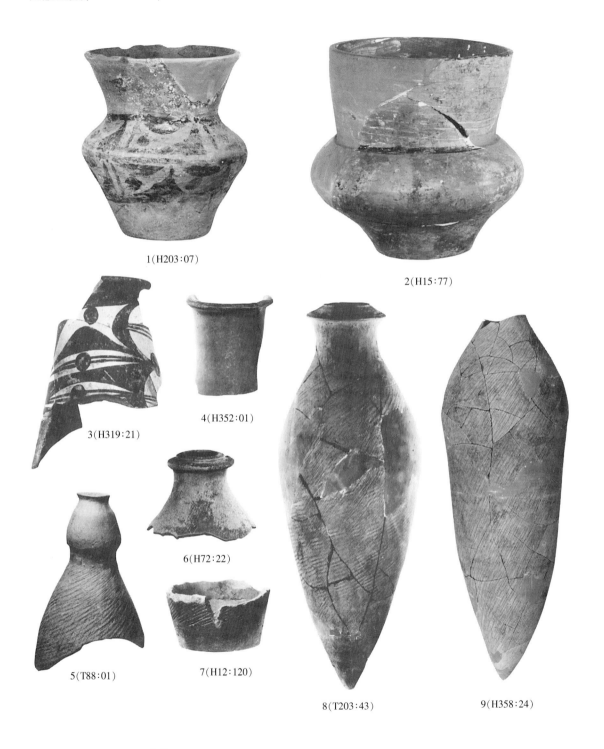

1（H203:07） 2（H15:77） 3（H319:21） 4（H352:01） 5（T88:01） 6（H72:22） 7（H12:120） 8（T203:43） 9（H358:24）

庙底沟仰韶文化细泥红陶罐、瓶
Fine red jars and bottles of the Yangshao culture from Miaodigou
1. A17b 罐（Jar） 2. A17c 罐（Jar） 3-6. 瓶口部（Mouth of bottles） 7. 瓶底部（Bottom of bottle） 8、9. A18a 瓶（Bottles）（1、3、
4. 1/3，2. 1/2，5-8. 1/4，9. 1/8）

1(T338:10)

2(H72:10)

4(H305:34)

5(T110:03)

6(H59:31)

3(H305:33)

7(H7:07)

庙底沟仰韶文化细泥红陶瓶、器盖、器座
Fine red bottles, vessel covers, and vessel stand of the Yangshao culture from Miaodigou
1、2. A18b 瓶(Bottles) 3. A19a 器盖(Vessel cover) 4. A19b 器盖(Vessel cover) 5. A19c 器盖(Vessel cover) 6. A19d 器盖
(Vessel cover) 7. A20a 器座(Vessel stand)(1. 1/5,2. 1/4,3、7. 1/2,4-6. 1/3)

1(H2:19)

4(T245:23)

2(H358:19)

5(H379:84)

6(H79:64)

3(H1:05)

7(H379:38)

庙底沟仰韶文化细泥红陶器座,泥质灰陶盘、碗、盆
Fine red vessel stands and grey plate, bowls, and basin of the Yangshao culture from Miaodigou
1. A20b 器座(Vessel stand) 2. A20c 器座(Vessel stand) 3. B1 盘(Plate) 4. B2 碗(Bowl) 5. B3a 碗(Bowl) 6. B3b 碗
(Bowl) 7. B4a 盆(Basin)(1、4. 1/2、2、5、6. 1/3、3、7. 1/4)

1(H1:09)

2(T234:01)

3(H325:11)

5(H47:33)

4(T60:04)

庙底沟仰韶文化泥质灰陶盆
Grey basins of the Yangshao culture from Miaodigou
1. B4b 盆(Basin)　2. B4c 盆(Basin)　3. B5a 盆(Basin)　4. B5b 盆(Basin)　5. B5c 盆(Basin)(1、5. 1/4,2-4. 1/3)

1(H203:50)

3(T315:07)

2(H52:10)

4(T143:06)

庙底沟仰韶文化泥质灰陶盆、罐
Grey basin and jars of the Yangshao culture from Miaodigou
1. B5d 盆(Basin) 2. B6a 罐(Jar) 3. B6b 罐(Jar) 4. B6c 罐(Jar)(1. 1/8,2. 1/4,3、4. 1/5)

1(H318:21)

2(H12:15)

3(H12:119)

4(T135:12)

5(H47:45)

6(H13:69)

7(H12:103)

8(H60:08)

9(H333:09)

庙底沟仰韶文化泥质灰陶器盖,细泥黑陶罐,夹砂粗红陶罐、釜

Grey vessel covers, fine black jars, and coarse, sand-tempered red jars and *fu* cauldron of the Yangshao Culture from Miaodigou

1. B7 罐(Jar)　2. B8a 器盖(Vessel cover)　3. B8b 器盖(Vessel cover)　4. B8c 器盖(Vessel cover)　5. B8d 器盖(Vessel cover)　6. B9 器盖(Vessel cover)　7. C1 罐(Jar)　8. D1 罐(Jar)　9. D2a 釜(*Fu* cauldron)(1. 1/2,6. 1/4,2-5、7-9. 1/3)

1(H20∶36)

2(T234∶16)

3(T234∶17)

庙底沟仰韶文化壁虎塑像残陶片
Potsherds with molded geckos of the Yangshao culture from Miaodigou
1. 细泥黑陶(Fine black pottery) 2、3. 夹砂粗红陶(Coarse, sand-tempered red pottery)
(1. 2/3,2、3. 1/2)

1(H12:99)

2(H12:112)

3(H12:113)

4(0:01)

5(H47:34)

6(H12:113、H47:34)

7(T346:02)

庙底沟仰韶文化夹砂粗红陶釜、灶、鼎、盘
Coarse, sand-tempered red *fu* cauldrons, *zao* stoves, *ding* tripod, and plate of the Yangshao culture from Miaodigou
1. D2b 釜（*Fu* cauldron） 2. D2c 釜（*Fu* cauldron） 3. D2d 釜（*Fu* cauldron） 4. D3 鼎（*Ding* tripod） 5. D4 灶（*Zao* stove） 6.
釜与灶（*Fu* cauldron（3）and *zao* stove（5）） 7. D5 盘（Plate）(1-6. 1/4,7. 1/2)

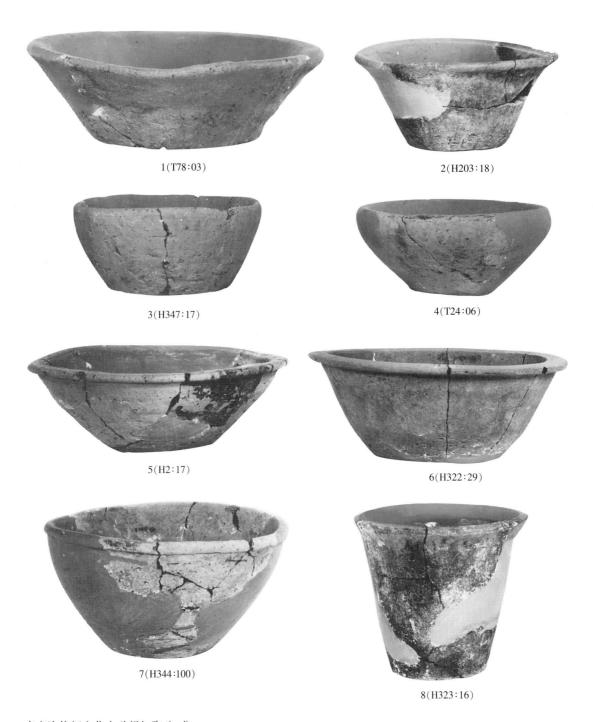

1(T78:03) 2(H203:18)

3(H347:17) 4(T24:06)

5(H2:17) 6(H322:29)

7(H344:100)

8(H323:16)

庙底沟仰韶文化夹砂粗红陶碗、盆
Coarse, sand-tempered red bowls and basins of the Yangshao culture from Miaodigou
1. D6a 碗（Bowl） 2. D6b 碗（Bowl） 3. D6c 碗（Bowl） 4. D6d 碗（Bowl） 5. D7a 盆（Basin） 6. D7b 盆（Basin） 7. D7c 盆
（Basin） 8. D8a 盆（Basin）（1-4. 1/2,5、6. 1/3,7、8. 1/4）

1(H327:09)

2(T82:07)　　　3(T95:04)

4(H12:15)　　5(H59:08)　　6(T234:43)　　7(T24:01)

8(H379:88)　　9(H12:108)

庙底沟仰韶文化夹砂粗红陶盆、杯、盂
Coarse, sand-tempered red basin, cups, and *yu* basins of the Yangshao culture from Miaodigou
1. D8b 盆(Basin)　2. D9a 杯(Cup)　3、4. D9b 杯(Cup)　5、6. D9c 杯(Cup)　7. D9d 杯(Cup)　8. D10a 盂(*Yu* basin)
9. D10b 盂(*Yu* basin)(1. 1/6,2-7. 1/2,8、9. 1/3)

1(H209:08)

4(T214:05)

2(T86:03)

5(H1:92)

3(H322:66)

6(T24:14)

庙底沟仰韶文化夹砂粗红陶罐

Coarse, sand-tempered red jars of the Yangshao culture from Miaodigou

1. D11a 罐（Jar） 2. D11b 罐（Jar） 3. D11c 罐（Jar） 4. D11d 罐（Jar） 5. D11e 罐（Jar） 6. D11f 罐（Jar）（1. 1/2,2、4、6. 1/3,3. 1/4,5. 1/6）

1(H12:104)

3(H318:19)

2(H323:63)

4(H203:46)

庙底沟仰韶文化夹砂粗红陶罐

Coarse, sand-tempered red jars of the Yangshao culture from Miaodigou

1. D11g 罐(Jar)　2、3. D11h 罐(Jars)　4. D11j 罐(Jar)(1,1/2,2、4. 1/4,3. 1/6)

1(H1:11)

2(H1:08)

3(H203:45)

4(H203:16)

庙底沟仰韶文化夹砂粗红陶罐

Coarse, sand-tempered red jars of the Yangshao culture from Miaodigou

1、2. D11j 罐(Jars)　3. D11k 罐(Jar)　4. D12 罐(Jar)(1、2. 1/4,3. 1/6,4. 1/3)

1(H312:15)

2(H12:26)

3(T104:08)

4(H47:07)

5(T87:11)

6(H203:07)

7(T341:43)

8(H12:50)

9(H13:10)

10(T78:08)

11(T204:03)

12(H2:27)

13(H328:21)

14(T237:15)

庙底沟仰韶文化夹砂粗红陶器盖及陶刀

Coarse, sand-tempered red vessel covers and pottery knives of the Yangshao culture from Miaodigou

1. D13a 器盖(Vessel cover) 2. D13b 器盖(Vessel cover) 3. D13c 器盖(Vessel cover) 4. D13d 器盖(Vessel cover)

5-8. 1A 刀(Knives) 9、10. 1B 刀(Knives) 11-14. 1C 刀(Knives)(1. 1/3,2-14. 1/2)

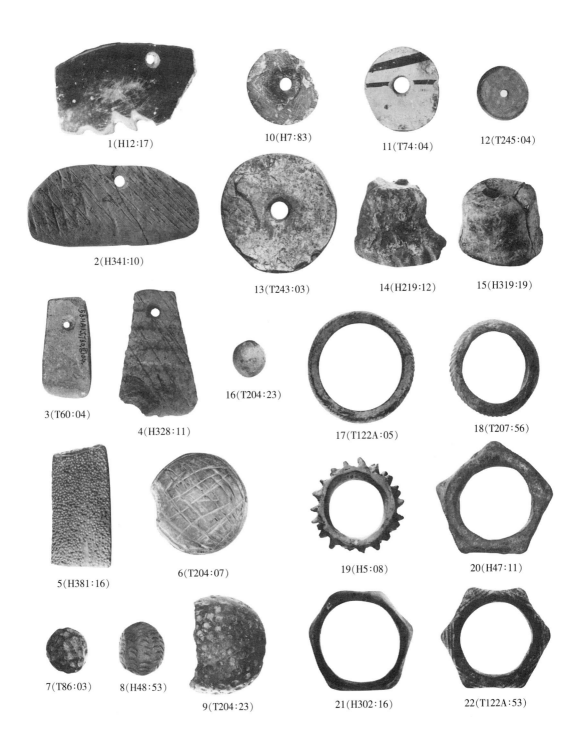

1（H12:17） 10（H7:83） 11（T74:04） 12（T245:04）
2（H341:10） 13（T243:03） 14（H219:12） 15（H319:19）
3（T60:04） 4（H328:11） 16（T204:23） 17（T122A:05） 18（T207:56）
5（H381:16） 6（T204:07） 19（H5:08） 20（H47:11）
7（T86:03） 8（H48:53） 9（T204:23） 21（H302:16） 22（T122A:53）

庙底沟仰韶文化陶制工具及装饰品

Pottery implements and ornaments of the Yangshao culture from Miaodigou

1、2. 1D 刀（Knives） 3. 2A 锛（Adze） 4. 2B 锛（Adze） 5. 3A 瓶（Pitted tool） 6-8. 3B 瓶（Pitted tools） 9. 3C 瓶（Pitted tool） 10、11. 4A 纺轮（Spindle whorls） 12、13. 4B 纺轮（Spindle whorls） 14、15. 4C 纺轮（Spindle whorls） 16. 弹丸（Pellet） 17、18. 1A 环（Rings） 19. 1B 环（Ring） 20. 1C 环（Ring） 21、22. 1D 环（Rings）（1-22. 1/2）

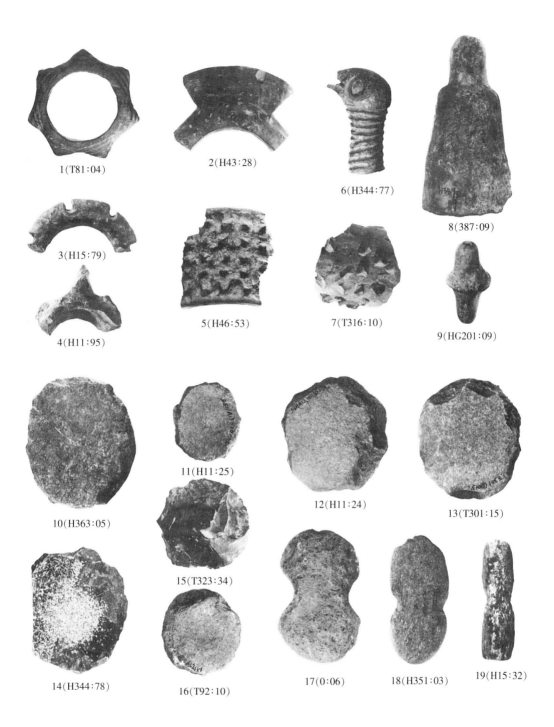

1(T81:04)　　2(H43:28)　　6(H344:77)

3(H15:79)　　5(H46:53)　　7(T316:10)　　8(387:09)

4(H11:95)　　9(HG201:09)

10(H363:05)　　11(H11:25)　　12(H11:24)　　13(T301:15)

14(H344:78)　　15(T323:34)　　16(T92:10)　　17(0:06)　　18(H351:03)　　19(H15:32)

庙底沟仰韶文化陶、石器

Pottery and stone artifacts of the Yangshao culture from Miaodigou

1. 1E 环(Ring)　2、3. 1F 环(Rings)　4. 1G 环(Ring)　5、7. 1B 环(Rings)　6. 鸟头(Bird head)　8. 钟(Bell)　9. 坠形器(Pendant)　10、11. 1A 盘状器(Disc-shaped tools)　12. 1B 盘状器(Disc-shaped tool)　13、14. 1C 盘状器(Disc-shaped tools)　15. 1D 盘状器(Disc-shaped tool)　16. 1A 盘状器(Disc-shaped tool)　17、18. 2A 网坠(Net sinkers)　19. 2B 网坠(Net sinker)(1-9. 陶器,10-19. 石器)(1-9. Pottery artifacts,10-19. Stone implements)(1-3、6、8、9、17-19. 1/2,4、5、7、10-16. 1/3)

1(H323:71)

2(T24:13)

5(H344:63)

3(T226:20)

4(H374:05)

6(T124:01)

7(H302:17)

8(H322:11)

9(0:05)

10(H344:87)

11(0:03)

12(T303:03)

13(H10:13)

14(T81:16)

15(H48:65)

16(T217:01)

17(T235:01)

庙底沟仰韶文化石器

Stone implements of the Yangshao culture from Miaodigou

1-3. 4A 刀（Knives）　4. 4B 刀（Knife）　5. 小石片（Stone flake）　6. 石斧坯（Semi-finished axe）　7. 6A 斧（Axe）
8、9. 6B 斧（Axes）　10. 6C 斧（Axe）　11. 6D 斧（Axe）　12. 6E 斧（Axe）　13-15. 6F 斧（Axes）　16、17. 6G 斧（Axes）（1-4、7-17. 1/2，5. 1/1，6. 1/4）

1（H12:64）　2（H32:19）　3（H322:14）　4（H328:15）

5（H10:43）　6（H358:03）　7（T341:02）　8（H47:19）　15（T303:02）

9（H345:03）　12（H46:94）　16（T341A:03）

10（H344:82）　13（H327:06）　17（H38:04）

11（H319:04）　14（T33:01）　18（T39:01）

庙底沟仰韶文化石器

Stone implements of the Yangshao culture from Miaodigou

1. 7A 锛（Adze）　2. 7B 锛（Adze）　3. 7C 锛（Adze）　4. 7D 锛（Adze）　5. 8A 凿（Chisel）　6. 8B 凿（Chisel）　7、8. 8C 凿（Chisels）　9-11. 3C 刀（Knives）　12. 3D 刀（Knives）　13. 3E 刀（Knives）　14. 3F 刀（Knife）　15、16. 3G 刀（Knives）　17、18. 3H 刀（Knives）（1-18. 1/2）

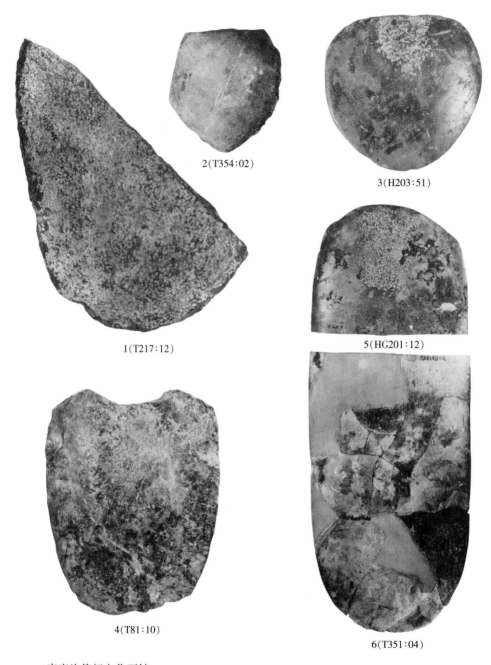

2(T354∶02)

3(H203∶51)

1(T217∶12)

5(HG201∶12)

4(T81∶10)

6(T351∶04)

庙底沟仰韶文化石铲

Stone spades of the Yangshao culture from Miaodigou

1. 石铲坯（Spade blank）　2.9A 铲（Spade）　3.9B 铲（Spade）　4.9C 铲（Spade）　5.9D 铲顶部

（Spade）　6.9D 铲（Spade）（1. 1/3，2-6. 1/4）

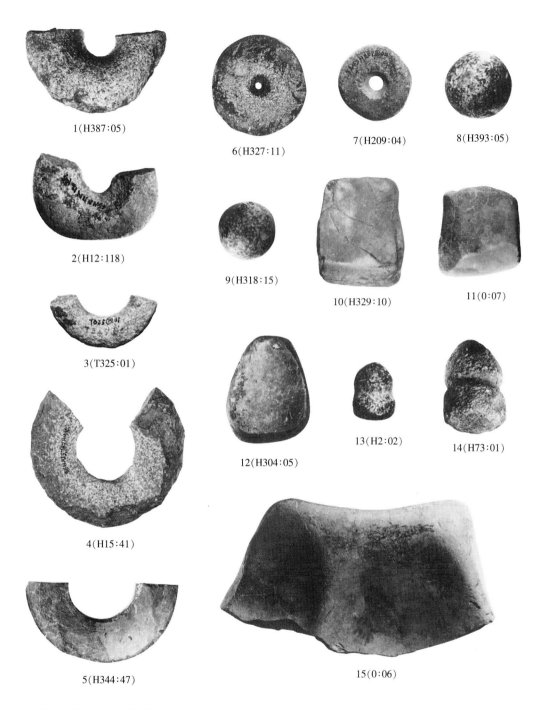

1(H387:05)

6(H327:11)

7(H209:04)

8(H393:05)

2(H12:118)

9(H318:15)

10(H329:10)

11(0:07)

3(T325:01)

12(H304:05)

13(H2:02)

14(H73:01)

4(H15:41)

5(H344:47)

15(0:06)

庙底沟仰韶文化石锤等

Stone hammers and so forth of the Yangshao culture from Miaodigou

1、2. 5A 锤(Hammers)   3. 5B 锤(Hammer)   4. 5C 锤(Hammer)   5. 5D 锤(Hammer)   6、7. 纺轮(Spindle whorls)   8、9. 球(Balls)   10-12. 12A 磨杵(Pestles)   13、14. 12B 磨杵(Pestles)   15. 磨盘(Mortar)(1-8、13、14. 1/3、9. 1/2、10-12、15. 1/4)

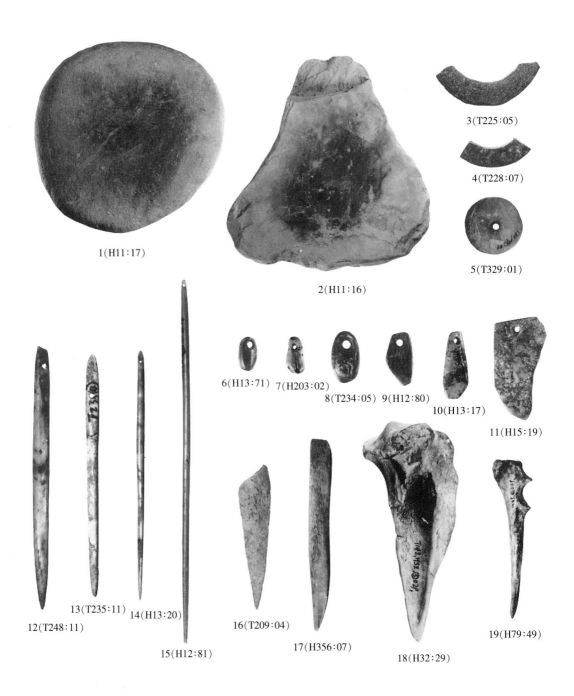

1(H11:17)

2(H11:16)

3(T225:05)

4(T228:07)

5(T329:01)

6(H13:71) 7(H203:02)

8(T234:05) 9(H12:80)

10(H13:17)

11(H15:19)

12(T248:11)

13(T235:11) 14(H13:20)

15(H12:81)

16(T209:04)

17(H356:07)

18(H32:29)

19(H79:49)

庙底沟仰韶文化石、骨器

Stone and bone artifacts of the Yangshao culture from Miaodigou

1、2. 磨盘（Mortars） 3、4. 环（Rings） 5. 珠（Bead） 6-8. 3A 坠（Pendants） 9、10. 3B 坠（Pendants） 11. 3C 坠（Pendant） 12、13. 1A 针（Needles） 14、15. 1B 针（Needles） 16、17. 2A 锥（Awls） 18. 2B 锥（Awl） 19. 2C 锥（Awl）（1-11. 石器，12-19. 骨器）（1-11. Stone artifacts, 12-19. Bone artifacts）（1、2. 1/4，3-5、16、18、19. 1/2，6-15、17. 1/1）

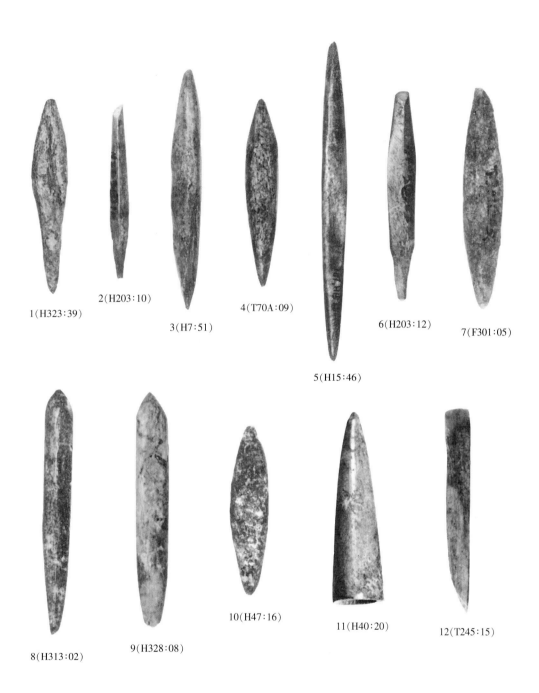

1(H323∶39)

2(H203∶10)

3(H7∶51)

4(T70A∶09)

5(H15∶46)

6(H203∶12)

7(F301∶05)

8(H313∶02)

9(H328∶08)

10(H47∶16)

11(H40∶20)

12(T245∶15)

庙底沟仰韶文化骨镞等

Bone arrowheads and so forth of the Yangshao culture from Miaodigou

1. 3A 镞(Arrowhead)　2、3. 3B 镞(Arrowheads)　4、5. 3C 镞(Arrowheads)　6、7. 3D 镞(Arrowheads)　8. 3E 镞(Arrowhead)

9、10. 3F 镞(Arrowheads)　11. 尖状器(Pointed implement)　12. 凿(Chisel)(1-12. 1/1)

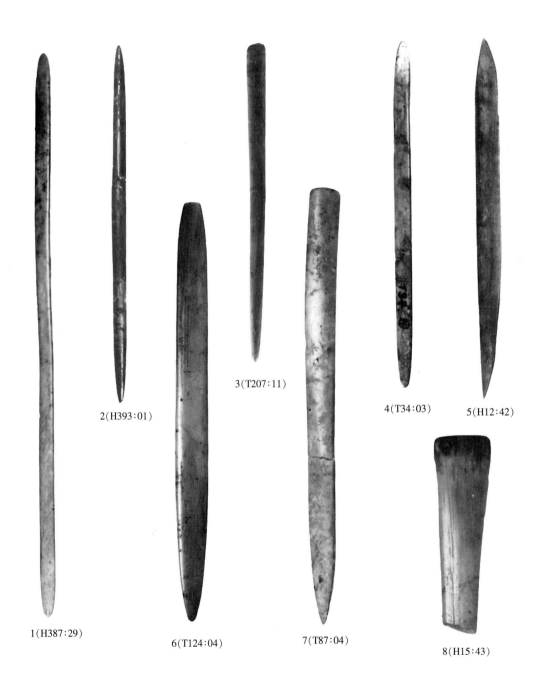

2(H393:01)

3(T207:11)

4(T34:03)　　5(H12:42)

1(H387:29)

6(T124:04)　　7(T87:04)

8(H15:43)

庙底沟仰韶文化骨笄
Bone hairpins of the Yangshao culture from Miaodigou
1、2.6A 笄(Hairpins)　3.6B 笄(Hairpin)　4.6C 笄(Hairpin)　5.6D 笄(Hairpin)　6.6E 笄(Hairpin)
7、8.6F 笄(Hairpins)(1-8.1/1)

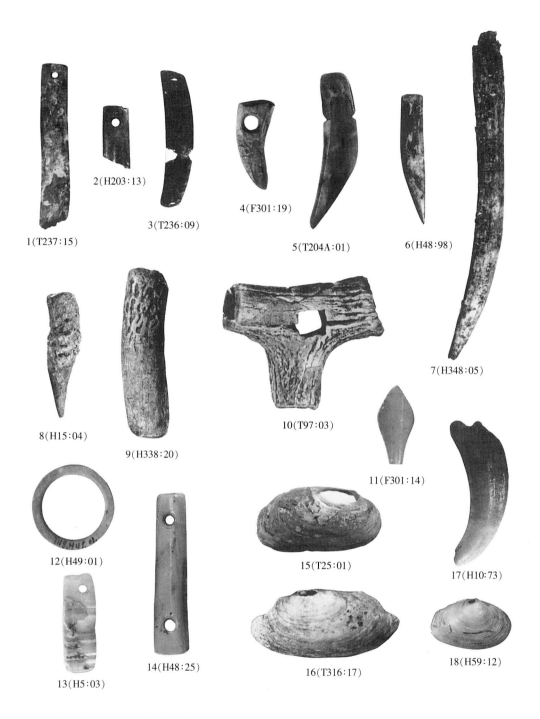

1(T237:15)　2(H203:13)　3(T236:09)　4(F301:19)　5(T204A:01)　6(H48:98)　7(H348:05)　8(H15:04)　9(H338:20)　10(T97:03)　11(F301:14)　12(H49:01)　13(H5:03)　14(H48:25)　15(T25:01)　16(T316:17)　17(H10:73)　18(H59:12)

庙底沟仰韶文化骨、角、蚌、牙器

Bone, antler, shell, and tooth artifacts of the Yanghao culture from Miaodigou

1、2.7A 弧形饰(Arc-shaped ornaments)　3.7B 弧形饰(Arc-shaped ornament)　4、5. 牙形饰(Tooth-shaped ornaments)　6、7.1A 锥(Awls)　8.1B 锥(Awl)　9. 凿(Chisel)　10. 槌(Hammer)　11. 笄?(Hairpin?)12. 指环(Ring)　13.3A 坠(Pendant)　14.3B 坠(Pendant)　15、16.4A 穿孔蚌壳(Perforated shells)　17. 穿孔牙饰(Perforated tooth artifact)　18.4B 穿孔蛤壳(Perforated shell)(1-5. 骨器,6-10. 角器,11-16、18. 蚌器, 17. 牙器)(1-5. Bone artifacts, 6-10. Antler artifacts, 11-16,18 Shell artifacts, 17 Tooth artifacts)(1-3、6-9. 1/2, 10. 1/3,4、5、11-18. 1/1)

1(T553:28)

2(H202:22)

3(H558:35)

4(HG553:10)

5(H563:46)

6(H563:45)

庙底沟龙山文化夹砂粗灰陶罐、盆
Coarse, sand-tempered grey jar and basins of the Longshan culture from Miaodigou
1. A1 罐(Jar)　2. A2a 盆(Basin)　3. A2b 盆(Basin)　4. A2c 盆(Basin)　5. A3a 盆(Basin)　6. A3b 盆(Basin)(1.1/5,2、5.1/ 3,3、4、6.1/4)

1（H27∶08）

2（H563∶34）

3（H564∶24）

4（H568∶30）

5（H564∶26）

庙底沟龙山文化夹砂粗灰陶罐

Coarse, sand-tempered grey jars of the Longshan culture from Miaodigou

1. A4a 盆（Basin）　2、4. A4b 盆（Basins）　3. A4c 盆（Basin）　5. A5a 罐（Jar）（1-4. 1/4，5. 1/5）

1（H35：93）

2（H202：04）

3（H564：27）

4（H568：29）

庙底沟龙山文化夹砂粗灰陶罐

Coarse，sand-tempered grey jars of the Longshan culture from Miaodigou

1. A5a 罐（Jar） 2-4. A5b 罐（Jars）（1、2. 1/4，3、4. 1/5）

1(H202：20)

2(H564：18)

3(H568：20)

4(HG553：1)

5(H563：37)

6(H570：21)

7(0：11)

8(H558：54)

庙底沟龙山文化夹砂粗灰陶罐、鼎

Coarse, sand-tempered grey jars and *ding* tripods of the Longshan culture from Miaodigou

1. A6 罐（Jar）　2. A7a 罐（Jar）　3. A7b 罐（Jar）　4、5. A7c 罐（Jars）　6. A7d 罐（Jar）　7、8. A8a 鼎（*Ding* tripods）

（1-3、8. 1/3，4. 1/2，5-7. 1/4）

1(H569：19)

2(H564：25)

3(H558：50)

4(H35：99)

庙底沟龙山文化夹砂粗灰陶鼎

Coarse, sand-tempered grey *ding* tripods of the Longshan culture from Miaodigou

1、2. A8a 鼎（*Ding* tripods） 3、4. A8b 鼎（*Ding* tripods）（1、4. 1/5 ,2、3. 1/4）

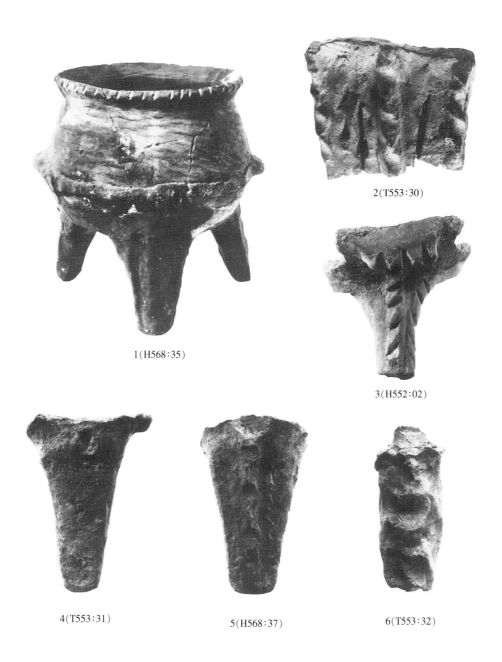

1(H568:35)

2(T553:30)

3(H552:02)

4(T553:31)

5(H568:37)

6(T553:32)

庙底沟龙山文化夹砂粗灰陶鼎

Coarse, sand-tempered grey *ding* tripods of the Longshan culture from Miaodigou

1. A8b 鼎(*Ding* tripod)　2-6. 鼎足(Feet of *ding* tripods)(1. 1/3,2-6. 1/2)

1(H558:52) 2(H564:20)

3(H35:92) 4(H569:03)

庙底沟龙山文化夹砂粗灰陶斝

Coarse, sand-tempered grey *jia* tripods of the Longshan culture from Miaodigou

1、2. A9a 斝(*Jia* tripods) 3、4. A9b 斝(*Jia* tripods)(1-3. 1/4,4. 1/5)

1(H35∶90)

2(H35∶94)

3(T553∶29)

4(H564∶28)

庙底沟龙山文化夹砂粗灰陶灶、器盖

Coarse, sand-tempered grey *zao* stoves and vessel covers of the Longshan culture from Miaodigou

1、2. A10 灶(*Zao* stoves) 3、4. A11 器盖(Vessel covers)(1、2. 1/5,3. 1/3,4. 1/2)

1(H572:20)

5(H35:91)

2(T551:07)

6(H568:22)

3(H35:97)

7(H558:53)

4(H568:33)

8(H568:16)

庙底沟龙山文化泥质灰陶碗、盆

Grey bowls and basins of the Longshan culture from Miaodigou

1、2. B1a 碗（Bowls）　3. B1b 碗（Bowl）　4. B1c 碗（Bowl）　5. B2 盆（Basin）　6. B3a 盆（Basin）

7. B3b 盆（Basin）　8. B3c 盆（Basin）（1-3、5-8. 1/3，4. 1/2）

1(H558:42)

4(H561:16)

2(H35:98)

5(H564:21)

3(H35:96)

6(H564:22)

庙底沟龙山文化夹砂粗灰陶盆、罐,泥质灰陶盆、杯、罐

Coarse, sand-tempered grey basins and jar and grey basin, cup, and jars of the Longshan culture from Miaodigou

1. B4a 盆(Basin)　2. B4b 盆(Basin)　3. A4c 盆(Basin)　4. B5 杯(Cup)　5. A6 罐(Jar)　6. B7a 罐(Jar)(1、2. 1/3,3-6. 1/4)

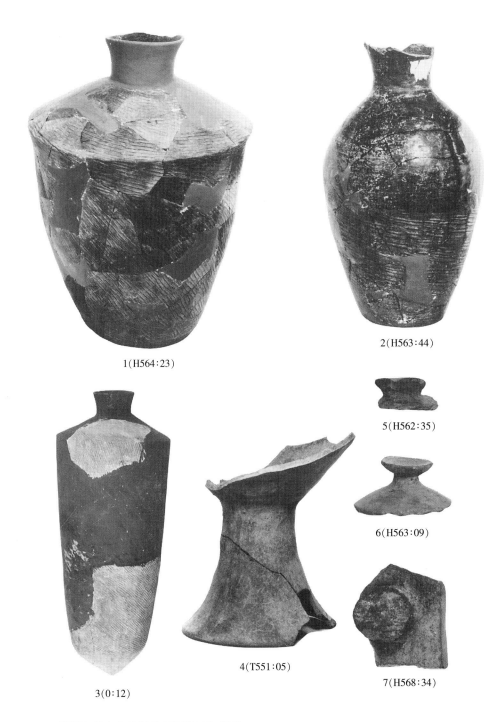

1(H564:23)

2(H563:44)

3(0:12)

4(T551:05)

5(H562:35)

6(H563:09)

7(H568:34)

庙底沟龙山文化泥质灰陶罐、豆、器盖
Grey jars, *dou* pedestal, and vessel covers of the Longshan culture from Miaodigou
1. B6a 罐(Jar) 2. B7b 罐(Jar) 3. B6b 罐(Jar) 4. B8 豆(*Dou* pedestal) 5. B9b 盖(Vessel cover) 6. B9a 盖(Vessel cover) 7. B9c 盖(Vessel cover)(1. 1/5,2. 1/4,3. 1/9,4-6. 1/3,7. 1/2)

1(M99:2) 2(T71:04) 3(M72:1) 4(H563:07)

5a(H563:50)

6(O:13)

5b(H563:50)

7(T551:12)

庙底沟龙山文化细泥红陶杯、盆,细泥黑陶盆

Fine red cups, basins, and fine black basins of the Longshan culture from Miaodigou

1-3. C1a 杯(Cups) 4. C1b 杯(Cup) 5a、b. C2 盆(Basin) 6. C3 盆(Basin) 7. D1 盆(Basin)(1-4. 1/2,5、6. 1/3,7. 1/1)

1(H568:21)　6(H558:46)　15(H563:02)

2(H568:36)　7(H563:17)　14(H563:26)

3(H570:23)　8(H564:13)　9(H564:7)　17(H564:01)

4(T552:12)　10(H561:1)　11(H566:02)　16(H559:08)

5(H568:4)　12(H570:16)　13(T553:02)　18(H558:08)　19(H551:03)　20(H554:14)

庙底沟龙山文化陶、石器

Pottery and stone artifacts of the Longshan culture from Miaodigou

1. D3 罐（Jar）　2. D2 罐（Jar）　3. D4 碗（Bowl）　4. D5 器盖（Vessel cover）　5. 1B 刀（Pottery knife）　6. 1A 刀（Pottery knife）　7. 垫（Pottery anvil）　8、9. 纺轮（Spindle whorls）　10. 弹丸（Pottery pellet）　11. 珠（Pottery bead）　12. 管（Pottery tube）　13. 柱状陶器（Pottery cylindrical object）　14-17. 1A-D 斧（Stone axes）　18、19. 2A 锛（Stone adze）　20. 2B 锛（Adze）（1-13. 陶器，14-20. 石器）（1-13. Pottery artifacts, 14-20. Stone Artifacts）（1-6、8-13、16-20. 1/2，7，14、15. 1/3）

1(H202:5)

2(H570:10)

3(H35:56)

4(HG553:02)

5(H563:40)

6(H558:32)

7(T553:13)

8(H564:14)

9(H563:42)

10(H568:11)

11(T553:12)

12(H558:29)

13(H35:58)

14(H568:9)

15(H563:04)

16(H35:31)

17(H564:03)

庙底沟龙山文化石锛、刀

Stone adzes and knives of the Longshan culture from Miaodigou

1、2. 2B 锛(Adzes)　3. 2C 锛(Adze)　4. 2D 锛(Adze)　5-10. 3A 刀(Knives)　11-15. 3B 刀(Knives)　16、17. 3C 刀(Knives)(1-4、10-16. 1/2 ,5-9、17. 1/3)

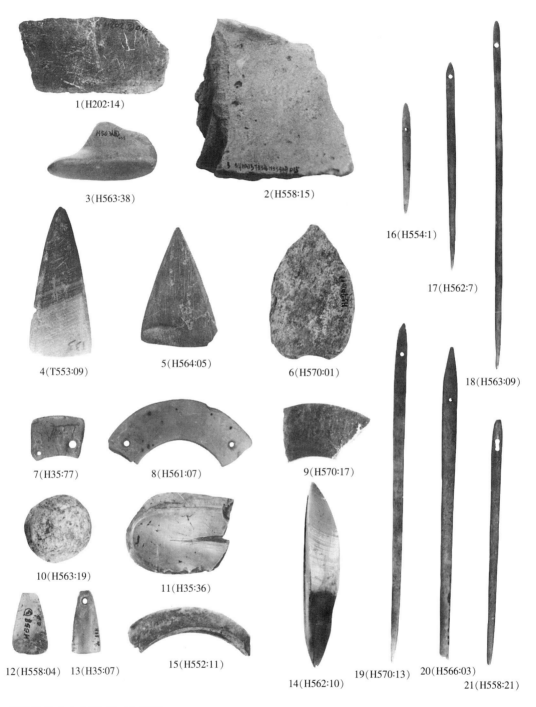

1(H202:14)

3(H563:38)

2(H558:15)

16(H554:1)

4(T553:09)

5(H564:05)

6(H570:01)

17(H562:7)

18(H563:09)

7(H35:77)

8(H561:07)

9(H570:17)

10(H563:19)

11(H35:36)

12(H558:04)　13(H35:07)

15(H552:11)

14(H562:10)

19(H570:13)　20(H566:03)

21(H558:21)

庙底沟龙山文化石、骨、蚌、牙器

Stone, bone, shell, and tooth artifacts of the Longshan culture from Miaodigou

1. 石镰(Stone sickle)　2. 石磨盘(Stone mortar)　3. 石杵(Stone pestle)　4、5. 石镞(Stone arrowheads)　6. 叶形器
(Leaf-shaped stone object)　7、8. 石璜(Stone *huang* pendants)　9. 石环(Stone ring)　10. 石弹丸(Stone pellet)11. 蚌
刀(Shell knife)　12. 蚌镞(Shell arrowhead)　13. 蚌坠(Shell pendanter)　14. 牙镞(Tooth arrowhead)　15. 牙片
(Treated tooth fragment)　16-18. 1A 骨针(Bone needles)　19. 1C 骨针(Bone needle)　20. 1D 骨针(Bone needle)
21. 1B 骨针(Bone needle)(1、7、11-13、15. 1/2,2. 1/5,3、6、10. 1/3,4、5、8、9、14、16-21. 1/1)

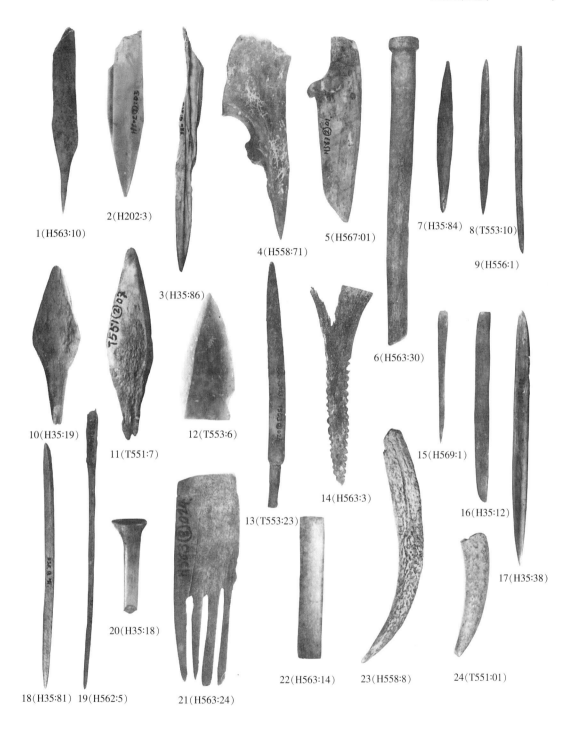

1(H563:10)　　2(H202:3)　　3(H35:86)　　4(H558:71)　　5(H567:01)　　6(H563:30)　　7(H35:84)　　8(T553:10)　　9(H556:1)　　10(H35:19)　　11(T551:7)　　12(T553:6)　　13(T553:23)　　14(H563:3)　　15(H569:1)　　16(H35:12)　　17(H35:38)　　18(H35:81)　　19(H562:5)　　20(H35:18)　　21(H563:24)　　22(H563:14)　　23(H558:8)　　24(T551:01)

庙底沟龙山文化骨锥等

Bone awls and so forth of the Longshan culture from Miaodigou

1-3. 2A 锥(Awls)　 4、5. 2B 锥(Awls)　 6. 2C 锥(Awl)　 7-9. 3A 镞(Arrowheads)　 10、11. 3B 镞(Arrowheads)　 12. 3C 镞 (Arrowhead)　 13. 3D 镞(Arrowhead)　 14. 锯(Saw)　 15、16. 5A 笄(Hairpins)　 17-19. 5B 笄(Hairpins)　 20. 5C 笄(Hair-pin)　 21. 梳(Comb)　 22. 匕(Rectangular plate)　 23. 鹿角(Antler awl)　 24. 角凿(Antler chisel)(1-7. 1/2 , 8-22. 1/1 ,23、24. 1/3)

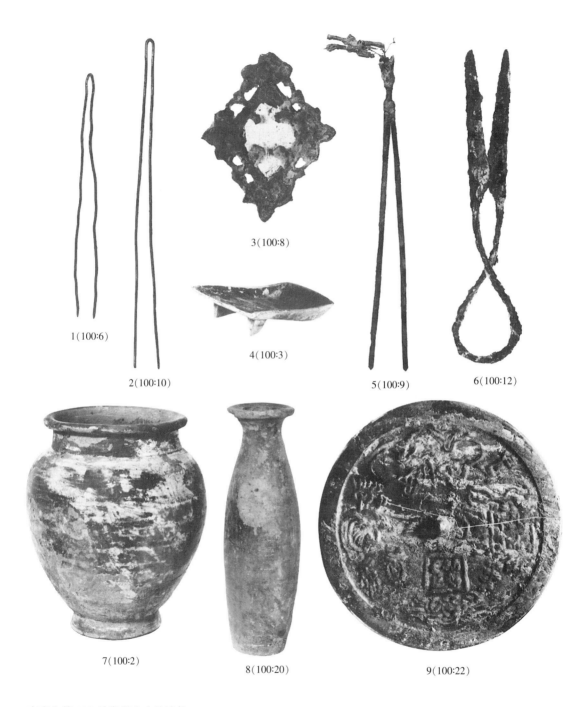

1（100:6） 2（100:10） 3（100:8） 4（100:3） 5（100:9） 6（100:12） 7（100:2） 8（100:20） 9（100:22）

庙底沟第 100 号唐墓出土的遗物

Artifacts from Tang dynasty tomb M100 at Miaodigou

1. 铜钗（Bronze hairpin） 2. 银钗（Silver hairpin） 3. 菱形花朵（Hair ornament with mother-of-pearl inlay） 4. 砚台（Ink slab） 5. 螺钿花钗（Hair ornament with mother-of-pearl inlay） 6. 铁剪（Iron scissors） 7. 陶罐（Pottery jar） 8. 陶罐（Pottery jar） 9. 铜镜（Bronze mirror）（1、2、5、9. 1/2、3. 1/1、4、7、8. 1/3、6. 1/4）

1(100:11)

2(100:13)

4(100:16)   5(100:16)

6(100:23)

3(100:1)

7(100:5)

庙底沟第 100 号唐墓出土的遗物
Artifacts from Tang dynasty tomb M100 at Miaodigou
1. 骨梳（Bone comb） 2. 玉饰（Jade ornament） 3. 铅人（Lead figurine） 4、5. 鸳鸯形玉饰（Jade mandarin ducks） 6. 瓷粉盒（Porcelain powder box） 7. 瓷碟（Porcelain plate）（1-6. 1/1，7. 1/2）

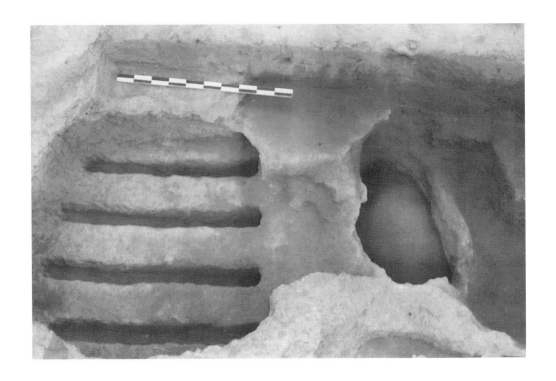

三里桥龙山文化 4 号窑址

Pottery kiln Y4 of the Longshan culture at Sanliqiao

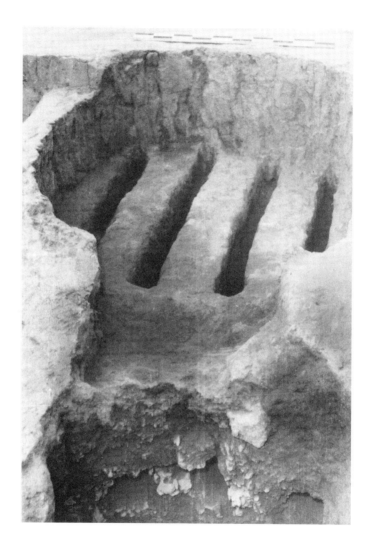

三里桥龙山文化 4 号窑址
Pottery kiln Y4 of the Longshan culture at Sanliqiao

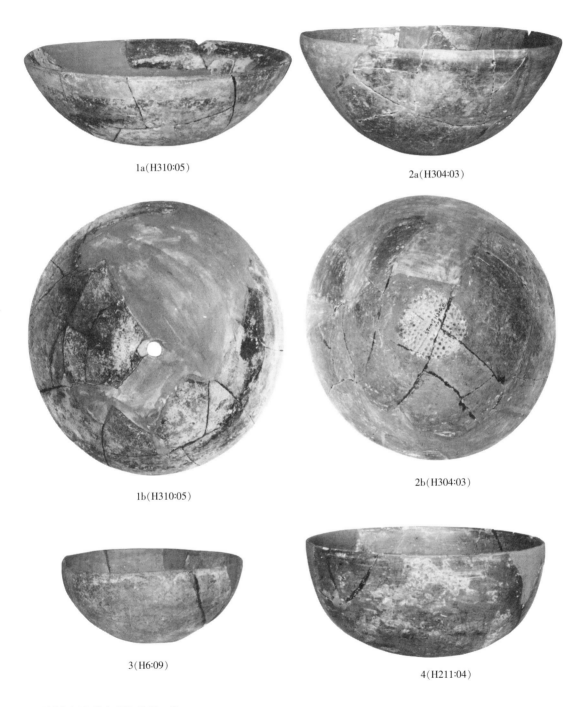

1a(H310:05)

2a(H304:03)

1b(H310:05)

2b(H304:03)

3(H6:09)

4(H211:04)

三里桥仰韶文化细泥红陶钵、碗

Fine red *bo* bowls and bowls of the Yanghshao culture form Sanliqiao

1a、b. A1a 钵(*Bo* bowl)　2a、b. A1b 钵(*Bo* bowl) 3. A2a 碗(Bowl)　4. A2b 碗(Bowl)(1、2. 1/4、3. 1/2、4. 1/3)

1（H211:02）

4（T240:05）

2（H211:56）

5（H301:99）

3（H299:01）

6（H301:100）

三里桥仰韶文化细泥红陶盆、罐

Fine red basins and jar of the Yangshao culture from Sanliqiao

1. A3a 盆（Basin）　2. A3b 盆（Basin）　3. A4a 盆（Basin）　4、5. A4b 盆（Basin）　6. A5 罐（Jar）（1. 1/5,2-4. 1/4,5. 1/3,6. 1/7）

1(H258:03)

2(H310:08)

3(Y301:01)

4(Y301:02)

三里桥仰韶文化细泥红陶器座,夹砂粗红陶罐

Fine red vessel stand and coarse, sand-tempered red jars of the Yangshao culture from Sanliqiao

1. A6 器座(Vessel stand)　2. D1a 罐(Jar)　3. D1b 罐(Jar)　4. D2 罐(Jar)(1,3. 1/3,2. 1/2,4. 1/4)

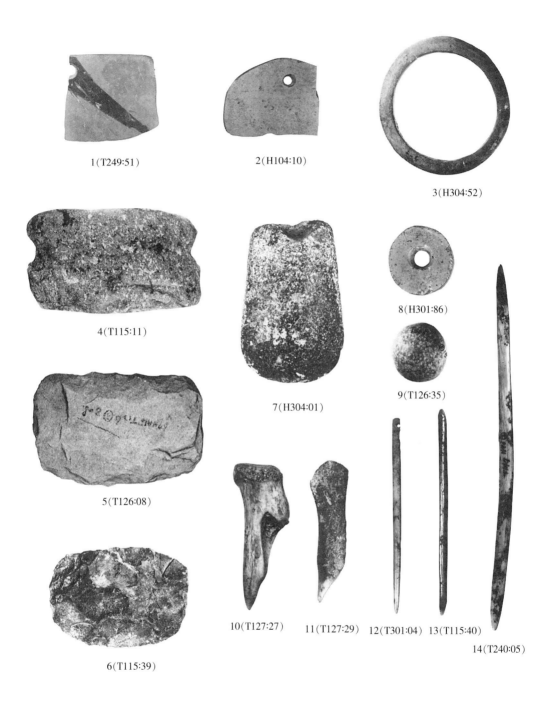

1（T249:51） 2（H104:10） 3（H304:52）

4（T115:11） 7（H304:01） 8（H301:86） 9（T126:35）

5（T126:08）

6（T115:39） 10（T127:27） 11（T127:29） 12（T301:04） 13（T115:40） 14（T240:05）

三里桥仰韶文化陶、石、骨器

Pottery, stone, and bone artifacts of the Yangshao culture from Sanliqiao

1. 1B 陶刀（Pottery knife） 2. 1C 陶刀（Pottery knife） 3. 陶环（Pottery ring） 4. 1A 石刀（Stone knife） 5、
6. 1B 石刀（Stone Knives） 7. 石斧（Stone axe） 8. 石纺轮（Stone spindle whorl） 9. 石球（Stone ball） 10、
11. 骨锥（Bone awl） 12. 骨针（Bone needle） 13、14. 骨笄（Stone hairpins）（1-11、13、14. 1/2，12. 1/1）

1(H251:04)

2(T214:03)

3(H203:10)

4(H203:07)

三里桥龙山文化夹砂粗灰陶罐

Coarse, sand-tempered grey jars of the Longshan culture from Sanliqiao

1. A1 罐(Jar) 2、3. A2a 罐(Jars) 4. A2b 罐(Jar)(1. 1/4,2、4. 1/3,3. 1/2)

1（T126:07）

3（H244:31）

2（H113:01）

4（H2112:01）

三里桥龙山文化夹砂粗灰陶鬲、斝

Coarse, sand-tempered grey *li* tripods and *jia* tripod of the Longshan culture from Sanliqiao

1、2. A4a 鬲（*Li* tripods)   3. A4b 鬲（*Li* tripod)   4. A5 斝（*Jia* tripod)（1、2. 1/3，3. 1/4，4. 1/5）

1（H284:08）

2（H3:47）

3（T220:01）

5（H271:04）

4（H3:17）

三里桥龙山文化夹砂粗灰陶罐，泥质灰陶碗、盆

Coarse，sand-tempered grey jars and grey bowls and basin of the Longshan culture from Sanliqiao

1. A3a 罐（Jar）　2. A3b 罐（Jar）　3、4. B1 碗（Bowls）　5. B2 盆（Basin）（1. 1/4，2、3、5. 1/3，4. 1/2）

1（H203:13）

2（H253:03）

3（H246:06）

4（T234:06）

5（H3:08）

6（T225:05）

三里桥龙山文化泥质灰陶盆、杯

Grey basins and cups of the Longshan culture from Sanliqiao

1. B3a 盆（Basin）　2. B3b 盆（Basin）　3. B3c 盆（Basin）　4. B3d 盆（Basin）　5. B4 杯（Cup）　6. B5 杯（Cup）（1、3、4. 1/4，2.
1/3，5、6. 1/2）

1（H2112:05）

2（H284:03）

3（H2112:21）

4（H224:03）

三里桥龙山文化泥质灰陶罐
Grey jars of the Longshan culture from Sanliqiao
1. B6a 罐（Jar） 2、3. B6b 罐（Jars） 4. B6c 罐（Jar）（1、3、4. 1/3，2. 1/4）

1（H265:01）

2（H239:02）

3（H284:09）

4（H232:02）

三里桥龙山文化泥质灰陶罐

Grey jars of the Longshan culture from Sanliqiao

1. B6c 罐（Jar）　2. B8a 罐（Jar）　3. B6d 罐（Jar）　4. B7 罐（Jar）（1、2、4.1/3，3.1/6）

1(H320:02)

3(T234:01)

2(H209:03)

4(H244:57)

三里桥龙山文化泥质灰陶罐
Grey jars of the Longshan culture from Sanliqiao
1、2. B8b 罐(Jars)　3. B9a 罐(Jar)　4. B9b 罐(Jar)(1、3. 1/4, 2. 1/3, 4. 1/7)

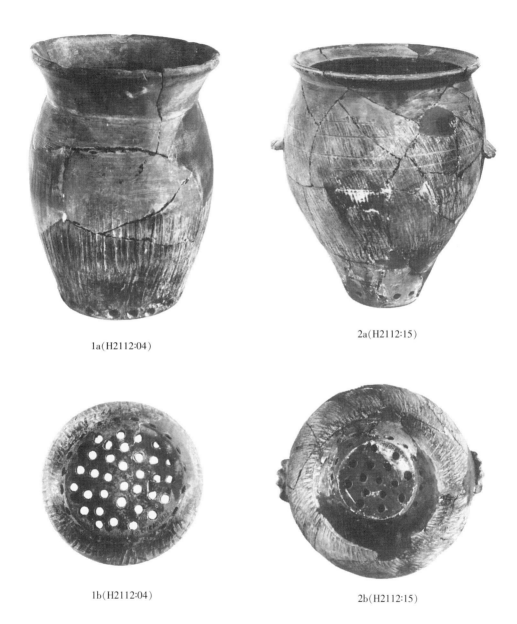

1a(H2112:04)

2a(H2112:15)

1b(H2112:04)

2b(H2112:15)

三里桥龙山文化泥质灰陶甑
Grey *zeng* steamers of the Longshan culture from Sanliqiao
1a、b. B10a 甑(*Zeng* steamer)　2a、b. B10b 甑(*Zeng* steamer)(1. 1/3,2. 1/5)

1(H2112:33)

4a(H284:25)

4b(H284:25)

2(H203:22)

5(H104:16)

3(H2112:24)

6(H3:31)

三里桥龙山文化泥质灰陶瓶、豆、鬶、器座,夹砂粗红陶罐

Grey vase, *dou* pedestal, *gui* vessel, vessel stand and coarse, sand-tempered red jar of the Longshan culture from Sanliqiao

1. B11 瓶(Vase)　2、3. B12 豆(*Dou* pedestals)　4a、b. B13 鬶(*Gui* vessel)　5. B14 器座(Vessel stand)　6. C1 罐(Jar)

(1、2、4. 1/3,3、6. 1/4,5. 1/5)

1(H265:03)

3(H109:10)

2(H220:01)

4(T217:01)

三里桥龙山文化细泥黑陶罐、豆,泥质红陶罐、鬶

Fine black jar and *dou* pedestal and red jar and *gui* tripod of the Longshan culture from San-liqiao

1. D1 罐(Jar)   2. B2 豆(*Dou* pedestal)   3. E1 罐(Jar)   4. E2 鬶(*Gui* tripod)(1、2. 1/4 ,3 ,4. 1/3)

1（H263:13）

2（H2112:23）

5（H2112:138）

6（T103:98）

7（H2112:44）

3（H2112:37）

4（H122:13）

8（H203:04）

9（H284:11）

10（H284:19）

11（H3:32）

三里桥龙山文化陶、石、骨器

Pottery, stone, and bone artifacts of the Longshan culture from Sanliqiao

1. 陶垫（Pottery anvil） 2、3. 石刀（Stone knives） 4. 石锛（Stone adze） 5. 骨锥（Bone awl） 6、7. 骨铲（Bone spades） 8. 石斧（Stone axe） 9. 骨镞（Bone arrowhead） 10. 骨针（Bone needle） 11. 骨笄（Bone hairpin）

（1-4、6-8. 1/2，5，9-11. 1/1）

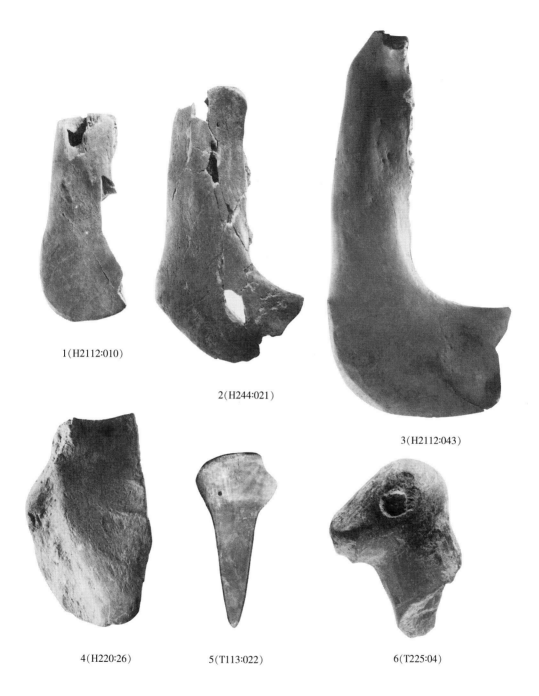

1(H2112:010)

2(H244:021)

3(H2112:043)

4(H220:26)　　5(T113:022)　　6(T225:04)

三里桥龙山文化陶、骨、蚌器

Pottery, bone, and shell artifacts of the Longshan culture from Sanliqiao

1-4. 骨铲(Bone spades)　5. 蚌笄(Shell hairpin)　6. 陶鸟头(Molded figures of a bird head)(1-4. 1/2,5 ,6. 1/1)

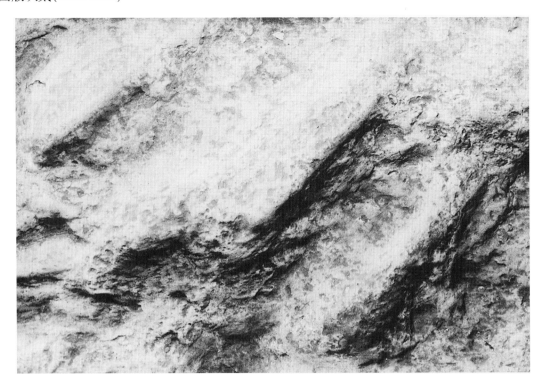

庙底沟龙山文化木耒痕迹

Traces of the wooden *lei* shovel of the Longshan culture at Miaodigou

（据原痕迹翻出的石膏模型，约1/3 弱）（Plaster cast of the original，about 1/3 actual size）

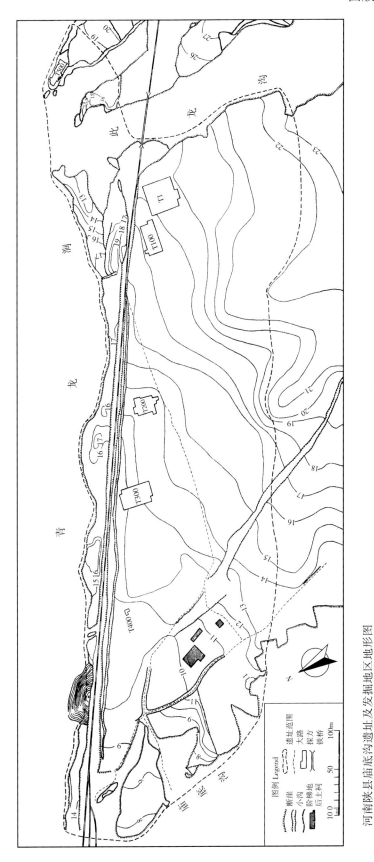

河南陕县庙底沟遗址及发掘地区地形图

Map showing the location of the site and excavation areas at Miaodigou, Shan county, Henan province

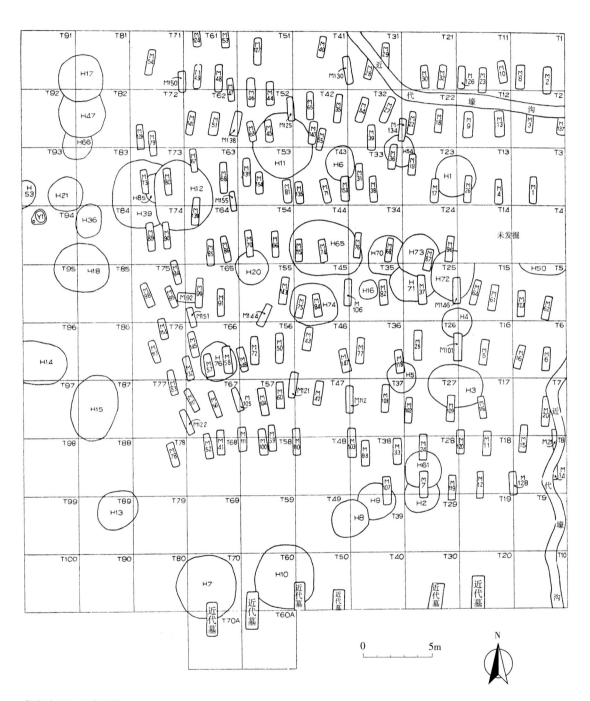

庙底沟 T1 区平面图
Plan of area T1 at Miaodigou

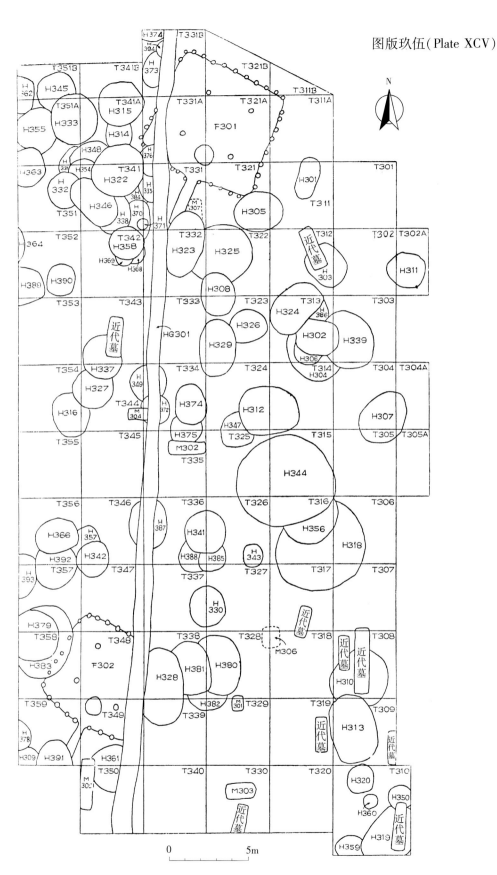

庙底沟 T300 区平面图

Plan of area T300 at Miaodigou

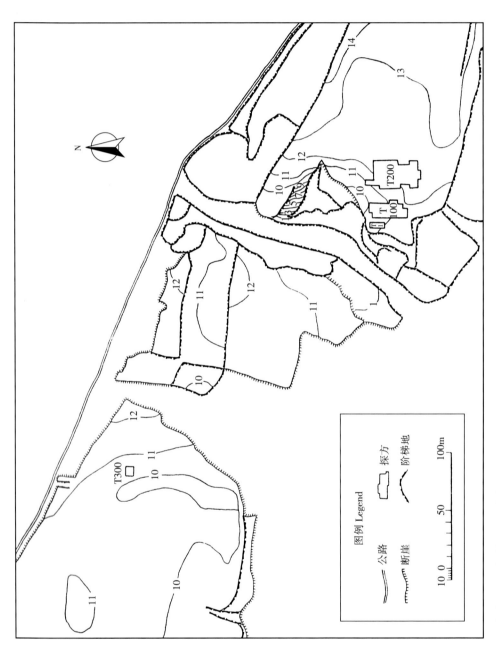

河南陕县三里桥村遗址及发掘地区地形图

Map showing the location of the site and excavation areas at Sanliqiao, Shan county, Henan province